SOCIAL ORGANIZATION

Essays Presented to Raymond Firth

Raymond Firth.

SOCIAL ORGANIZATION;

Essays Presented to Raymond Firth.

Edited by
MAURICE FREEDMAN, *1902 –*

ALDINE PUBLISHING COMPANY
Chicago

First published 1967 by

Aldine Publishing Company
320 West Adams Street
Chicago, Illinois 60606

Frank Cass & Co. Ltd., London

Library of Congress Catalog Card Number 67-25816

Printed in Great Britain

Contents

Preface

THESE essays have been written to honour the man who taught their writers. They are about different problems within the general field of 'social organization'; they have been composed in many styles; and they deal ethnographically with a heterogeneous collection of peoples and countries. By their variety they may serve to illustrate an important aspect of Professor Raymond Firth's influence as a teacher: the range of his interests and his success in promoting social anthropological research on the broadest front. He came from Polynesia and won his first reputation by his Polynesian studies; but he has never sought to marshal his pupils to form a cohort of Oceanists. He came from economics, and made economic anthropology his own; yet he has given the least economics-minded of his pupils their head.

The breadth and the variety in the work of his students taken as a whole are a reflection of his own catholicity. From economics he moved on to reach into every corner of the field covered by social anthropology, and many of the emphases in his interests can be traced in this sample of essays. Four are on themes in kinship and marriage (by Barić, Benedict, Kaberry, and Leach). Three are on religious subjects (by Freedman, Morris, and Stanner). Two are on the study of modern social change (by Little and Mayer). One is on art (by Forge). It is altogether fitting that three essays should be devoted to subjects in economic anthropology (by Belshaw, Swift, and Ward). On all these topics Raymond Firth has himself written extensively and taught untiringly.

The Polynesian expert remains. (While this book is in press he is making his third field trip to Tikopia and other parts of the Solomons.) But he is a regional expert with a lively sense of the need for contrast; and the man who could have rested on his Tikopian laurels went on to become the foremost student of Malay society and the founder of anthropological studies of 'modern' kinship in the country where he made his home. It is a thousand pities that no Polynesian society is dealt with in this book, for that compliment was certainly due. But at least Malaya makes its appearance (in the paper by Swift); New Guinea is represented in the essays by Forge and Kaberry, for that too, of course, is a country where Raymond Firth has worked; while Little's contribution on West Africa and Morris's on Sarawak may serve to remind us that while Raymond Firth was associated with the Colonial Social Science Research Council he made a short tour of Gambia, Sierra Leone, the Gold Coast, and Nigeria, and a visit to Sarawak. For the rest, the societies discussed in the book are scattered over a large part of the world. It is appropriate that they should be so when they are being used to demonstrate the influence of a teacher who has urged his pupils to range widely and to consider the relevance of social anthropology for the study of society in all its forms.

Raymond Firth came to the London School of Economics as a postgraduate student in 1924. He had already written his first monograph (on the kauri-gum industry) as an economist trained in New Zealand, and he arrived in Houghton Street strongly inclined to pursue his studies in economics and, as he himself puts it, 'do anthropology as a hobby'. It will come as a surprise to the anthropological world that he planned to write his doctoral thesis on the frozen meat industry in New Zealand; and our imagination may be agreeably exercised in speculating on what his career might have been if he had not so soon taken to anthropology and anthropology to him. He had already read Malinowski on the Trobriands, was delighted to be told that the anthropologist was at the L.S.E., and within six months was on the road that led him, via the primitive economics of the New Zealand Maori, to Tikopia.

In the forty-two years that have gone by he has absented himself from the L.S.E. only during the time he has been in the field, during the three years he taught in Sydney University (1930–32), when he visited Australia (1951–52) and the United States (in 1955 and 1958–59), and in the years (1941–44) of his war service as a 'geographer' in Naval Intelligence. He began teaching at the L.S.E. in 1933, and in a third of a century has trained and brought to maturity several generations of anthropologists. There can be few departments of anthropology in the universities of the British Commonwealth which do not number scholars who learnt at his feet; outside the Commonwealth, scholars he has taught are to be found in nearly every place where social anthropology has taken root. Of his many pupils the contributors to this volume are a sample.

They are, of course, a very small sample. I must explain how it came to be constructed. To have invited as contributors everybody who owed Raymond Firth an intellectual debt would have been impossible—apart from anything else, I should not have known how to set about compiling a list of them. Professor I. Schapera suggested to me that I limit the invitation to those who both worked for higher degrees under Raymond Firth's supervision and now teach social anthropology in the universities. In this way a manageable number of potential contributors was defined. Happily, nearly all of them were able to accept the invitation. In approaching them I gave contributors a free hand in choosing their subjects, asking them only that they write on themes close to Raymond Firth's interests. I think we have succeeded at least in illustrating the breadth of those interests.

Raymond Firth's importance in the history of British social anthropology lies in the fact that, coming into the profession when it was small and unformed, when it existed only in the tiny groups of people around Malinowski and Radcliffe-Brown, he urged it on, by intellectual leadership, by careful organization, and by devoted service, to the comparative prosperity of the 1960s. He was one of a small band of scholars; he created a large school. He inherited an esoteric seminar from Malinowski; he turned it into a great class where, over the years, hundreds of students have marvelled at his skill and learned their craft as analysts and field workers as they listened to his formulation of problems, his critique of methods, and his courteous but unrelenting dissection of arguments. And from their observation of his virtuoso performances as a seminar-leader many of these students have learnt their job as teachers, even though none can live up to the standard set by their exemplar.

Raymond Firth has been one of the chief creators of a subject which has never ceased from being re-created. At every stage of its development he has welcomed new ideas, encouraged pioneers, and promoted innovations in research. We greet him as a senior in whom the years have not dimmed enthusiasm, as a teacher who still strides ahead of his pupils, as a leader who builds for tomorrow.

These essays we present in respect and friendship.

M. F.

London School of Economics and Political Science
September, 1966

Levels of Change in Yugoslav Kinship

LORRAINE BARIĆ

1. *Conflict of meaning in studies of changing kinship*

In the various phases of its development, social anthropology has had different characteristic problems. One anthropological generation's favourite problems cease to excite the next generation, but not always because these problems have been solved. Anthropological theory rather progresses, or at least continues, partly by cannibalizing odd bits of previous approaches, but, more characteristically, by simply disregarding the unresolved problems of the past and going on to new and, it is hoped, more promising lines of enquiry. The battle of new analogies and new approaches thus ranges over the field, but theories left for dead years ago have a way of springing up again. They have been by-passed, not dealt a fatal blow; in other words, they have not been set up in terms of precise hypotheses which are amenable to testing and thus to disproof.

One recurrent theory, which forms the subject of this paper, concerns changes in the structure of family and kin ties, and associates them with changes in the economic aspects of a society.

Nineteenth-century evolutionary theories, which linked together family and kinship structure with type of economy in terms of stages, were theories of social change in kinship. Unilinear evolutionary schemes of kinship change in early societies (for example, the sequence of promiscuity, group marriage, matrilineal systems, patrilineal systems) represent dead theories, not so much because they have been disproved, but largely because the evidence is lacking.

Other large-scale generalizations specifically concerned with change in kinship are, however, still alive, and one at least seems very generally accepted. Goode (1964, p. 108) writes: 'Family research in the post World War II period has documented one gross empirical regularity whose processes are not yet clearly understood—that in all parts of the world and for the first time in world history all social systems are moving fast or slowly towards some form of the conjugal family system and also toward industrialization.' This is a wide generalization, but also cautious, in that Goode merely asso-

1

ciates industrialization and kinship change. He wisely emphasizes the fact that the processes are not fully understood, since it is certainly the case that the more one goes into the question, the more complex it appears, and its superficial obviousness or even apparent triviality melts away. Much recent research has aimed at attacking it; but the results are inconclusive, largely, I believe, because of the imprecision of concepts involved.

The situation is epitomized in a controversy on the topic involving an anthropologist and sociologist: Professor Raymond Firth and Professor Peter Townsend. I emphasize their professional orientation, since it has some significance in the outcome of their discussion.

In 1947, a series of empirical studies under Firth's direction began in London, concerned among other things with the question of the isolation of the conjugal family. Results led to a number of modifications of the commonly accepted idea of the isolated unit, at least in parts of London. It was found that households were frequently at the centre of an extensive network of kin and that a kinship principle in social relations was widely recognized (Firth, 1956). So here was one of the most industrialized countries in the world—in which one would expect the generalization to hold—but where the isolated conjugal family was not a universal type.

It was some time before this research appeared in print (and in fact the research in new phases still continues), but the ideas involved had spread widely so that many subsequent pieces of research followed similar lines and were influenced by the data and concepts which emerged from this early study. They included work by Young and Willmott (1957, 1960), Bott (1957), Marris (1958), Townsend (1957), more recently, Rosser and Harris (1965), and others. All these pieces of research questioned through empirical study the stereotype of the disappearance of kin ties outside the elementary family.

In this recent disputation, Townsend said: 'This [the existence of recognized kin, forming a cohesive organization, outside the elementary family] is no longer a wayward belief of a few eccentric sociologists and anthropologists working in areas which are supposed to contain quaint cultural survivals. It is a fact. Despite the danger of making such emphatic statements like this before an academic audience without the space to develop all the necessary qualifications, I feel it is right to do so to discourage so many of our colleagues from going on using the tired hypotheses of the turn of the century' (1964, p. 92).

On this point Firth and Townsend would seem to agree. But differences appear. Townsend objects to Firth's referring to 'the extended family giving way to some variety of the nuclear family' (Townsend, 1964, p. 90, with reference to Firth, 1964a, p. 74). This is an unexpected objection, considering Firth's part in drawing attention to the pervasiveness of kin relations in our society, and considering too that he explicitly stated that he did *not* think extra-familial kin ties are likely to decrease in modern Western society (Firth, 1964a, p. 83).

One might suspect cross-purposes in argument here. In fact, I believe that their differences arise from differences in their standpoints— one as an anthropologist, the other as a sociologist. When we speak of extra-familial kin and their importance, we sometimes have in mind a clearly defined jural entity of the type of the lineage or joint family corporation. On the other hand, we may have in mind a much less clearly defined sector of social relationships which has been variously referred to as a kin group, a network, a kin set, or even, loosely, an extended family. If Firth, as an anthropologist, is evaluating change in kinship in terms of the kin corporation familiar from the study of small-scale and technologically primitive societies, then there is quite a good case to be made out for the generalization that with the growth of non-agrarian occupations, mainly in industry, this type of group tends to change in character or to disappear entirely.

On the other hand, if Townsend has in mind a kindred or bilateral set of kin ties familiar in English-speaking societies and Western Europe, it may be the case that this set of ties does not necessarily change, qualitatively, with industrialization. Thus, at this point of the argument it becomes clear that Firth may be commenting on social change in terms of one sort of grouping of kin (i.e. corporate, local unit) and Townsend commenting on another sort of grouping, in terms of personal kindred involving both consanguineal and affinal relationships.

One need not see a contradiction here, but assume that both generalizations may be right within their own terms of reference, and one should be prepared to explore the matter further. In my attempts to examine the problem, with special reference to kinship in Yugoslavia, I was forced to the conclusion that precise and refined concepts for studying change in kinship are lacking. Subtle terminologies, typologies, and analyses of kinship processes which are essentially synchronic exist in abundance, as Leach (1961) has pointed out; but with respect to a framework in which to study progressive change as distinct from cyclical changes, social anthropology has only fairly crude criteria. I wish to suggest in the rest of this discussion that one clarifying concept worth adopting involves thinking of change in family and kinship in terms of levels, and that with respect to one of these levels the idea of family and kinship can be dissolved into simpler, sometimes unfamiliar, elements. The use I have made of this notion suggests that in practice it facilitates the study of change.

The question cannot be discussed in the abstract; so I turn now to the relevant aspect of social change in Yugoslavia.

II. *The levels of kinship in Yugoslavia*

I believe that one can distinguish at least two levels in Yugoslav kinship and that one can examine them in a temporal sequence. In terms of a visual analogy, there is the substratum level of the recognized set of kin outside the nuclear family which exists in every society to a greater or lesser extent. In addition, there is the grouping of certain categories of kin into structured corporate units. One may take this as a second level superimposed on the first. Visual analogies are useful but dangerous, since one cannot control their exact meaning for a reader. Here the analogy emphasizes the fact that the second level may or may not be there, but that it never exists without the sub-structure of the web of kin on the first level. Thus, in the course of time, the superimposed second level may disappear while the substratum level still remains. This provides a framework in which to examine different *types* of structural change over time. The approach also provides a framework in which interpersonal dyadic relations can be explored and changes in kin roles examined. Such an exploration and examination of Yugoslav kinship before the Second World War has been made by Erlich (1964) in a study of excellent ethnographic detail but lacking a theoretical framework such as this—congruent with modern kinship models—which would permit comparative study of change.

In Yugoslavia, the level of the corporate unit once existed but has now disappeared. In order to trace the characteristics of change it is necessary to go back in time and follow the transformations of the unit in the nineteenth and early twentieth centuries. Such a study must of necessity draw on material other than the data of traditional small-scale anthropological fieldwork.[1]

1. I collected field and documentary material during the years 1960-63. A good deal of it is relevant to Yugoslavia as a whole, but the needs of field work have meant that I confined detailed study to one part of the country, Croatia, particularly in the north-west. Specific references, unless noted to be otherwise, are to Croatia. I am indebted to the Ford Foundation for a grant to cover field expenses.

(a) The zadruga level

The main features of the traditional kinship system of old Yugoslavia are fairly well-known to Western sociologists. The *zadruga* system, as it is usually called, is founded on the group with the patrilineal kin-core which formed the basis of agricultural collectives. It is necessary to stress the collective aspect of the zadrugas since, in the nineteenth century, it was legally possible for a person not related through kinship or affinity to any existing member to join a zadruga as a full member (Tončić, 1902). Nevertheless, the core of membership was the kin-core; the rights and duties of the members of the zadruga were to a large extent those of kin relationships; this was the moral basis of behaviour. The head of the zadruga, the *starešina* or *domaćin*, was usually in a position of kin authority as well as being the effective director of economic activities. Marriage was exogamous and virilocal, so that wives were the strangers in the community. The size of the zadruga could vary considerably. There is a fairly widespread notion, even in Yugoslavia, that the zadruga was regularly everywhere very large, but this is not so. For example, the average size in Croatia and Slavonia in 1890 was approximately ten persons (Meyer, 1910), and the proportion of zadrugas with over a hundred members was quite small. There is no doubt that the zadruga was an effective corporation in Maine's sense, and from the jural point of view could continue indefinitely through the generations. Land holding was in the hands of the zadruga, and zadruga land was worked as a whole, not divided up into plots worked by individual elementary families. The legal existence of the zadruga was recognized; in nineteenth-century Croatia it was in fact registered with the State.

The precise, clearly delimited, and formal nature of this kin grouping is evident. It was characteristic of Yugoslavia but by no means universal: in some parts—particularly the Dinaric coastlands—the major land-holding and domestic unit was a joint family sometimes called a *velika kuća*. This was not a collective which could be joined by contract, but a segment of a patrilineage, jurally exogamous and under the patriarchal authority of the senior kinsman. In this part, unlike the zadruga areas, a feud could be prosecuted on behalf of a lineage member. Sometimes the distinction between these two types of unit is denied (Halpern, 1958) or overlooked (Dedijer, 1961, p. 39), so I shall not make too much of it in the present context and confine what I have to say to the zadruga.

We have comparatively complete historical information on the way in which the zadruga family collective disintegrated, at first

slowly, then, from the middle of the nineteenth century on, more
swiftly. The change followed a process of denudation and division.
Division did not resemble the segmentation familiar to anthropologists from the study of lineages, in which division or fission leaves
the resulting segments still in relationship with one another as sub-
units within a wider whole, and still potentially capable of uniting in
some particular context. On the contrary, the division of the zadruga
was a complete separation of all property and all joint economic
activity, although, of course, friendly personal relations might
continue to exist among former members, who also could give economic and ritual support on an interpersonal basis. The advantage of
looking at this process in the Yugoslav context is that it was not a
wholly organizational rearrangement but rather a definite legal act
which either resulted in the formation of two or more smaller zadrugas from the large one—completely separate in all property-owning
and administrative spheres—or in the emergence of elementary families, which did not then consider themselves to be either zadrugas or
parts of zadrugas and were not registered as such with the administration.

The elementary family which hived off from the whole is sometimes referred to as the *inokosna familija* or the elementary family.
In cities this was a common form of family grouping from quite an
early period, even before the nineteenth and twentieth centuries. In
addition to the nuclear or elementary family, a household might
bring together as members other lineal and collateral relatives
and thus be, in general sociological parlance, an extended family
(cf. Young and Willmott, 1957, p. 32). Nevertheless, it cannot be considered a joint family of the zadruga type even though it might hold
certain property in common: for instance, an apartment, house,
furniture, or other goods.

The immediate cause of the division of zadrugas lay in the wishes
of individuals. Behind their decisions to divide, however, lay a number of factors which are amenable to sociological analysis. It appears,
for example, that divisions of zadrugas nearly always took place
along elementary family lines. The potential separateness of elementary families of procreation was recognized in a number of pro-
verbs: for example, '*Gdje je braće, tu je i dijela*: where there are
brothers, that's where the division is.' This aspect of division was
often a question of pressure on resources, particularly in those parts
of Yugoslavia such as Croatia where land was restricted and where
zadrugas increased in size without being able correspondingly to increase their land for cultivation. Then the discrepancy was such that

division, with its connotations of new and more efficient management, might seem a welcome alternative even though in fact it would achieve nothing in terms of practical improvement, or even worsen the situation through fragmentation of land.

The differential contribution to communal labour of different elementary families was another factor associated with division, especially where members of the zadruga were hard pressed to subsist on their land. Where a number of elementary families contained children who were too young to contribute greatly to production, then it could be the case that the parents in the elementary family with fewer children might object to working for the good of the whole and thus, in effect, to supporting children of other elementary families within the zadruga (see Rayner, 1957).

The need for division was frequently put down to the supposed inability of women in the zadruga to get along together. As I have mentioned, the women were for the most part outsiders. Each newcomer had to accept the dominance of all men and of the older established wives. This could lead to problems of authority and demarcation of fields of activity. Where there was a large number of young children in the zadruga, a great deal of the increased work in the house fell upon women rather than upon men, so that often it was the women who expressed most forcibly the dissatisfaction inherent in the situation.

These features are sometimes taken to be enough to explain the immediate causes of the division and disappearance of the zadruga. There is, however, an even more important element of the situation which is often overlooked. When women married into the zadruga they brought with them a dowry, referred to in some parts as *osobina*. It was not amalgamated with the zadruga property but belonged to the woman herself, and, through her, to her elementary family of procreation. Cattle which might form part of this personal property were not kept with the other zadruga cattle but separately, and any increase to them augmented the size of the osobina and not the zadruga property. This personal property could grow quite rapidly since all the basic necessities for members of an elementary family were supplied by the zadruga. In the course of time, all sorts of items could be quietly absorbed into this private sector; hemp and flax fields could be worked by women on their own account when there happened to be no regular work necessary on zadruga land or the house. In this sense the work of the women tended to become more and more individualistic and a conflict could arise between demands on their time for zadruga work and for 'private' work.

B

Women put great energy into working on their property in order to raise the levels of consumption of their family of procreation. This was associated with a change in the egalitarian patterns of behaviour and of values in the zadruga, together with the general disruption of the former similarity of consumption not only as between one elementary family and another, but also as between individuals performing similar social roles. Vukosavljević (1936, reprinted 1962), writing some thirty years ago when zadrugas were already ethnographic curiosities, although still vividly remembered, has described the development of this heterogeneity. He has emphasized that differentiation of need preceded attempts within the zadruga by members, wives and mothers in particular, to meet this need.

In all these processes of change the idea of individualism enters, although as a simple explanatory concept 'individualism' is more or less meaningless. It belongs to the sphere of 'psychological' explanations of the actual antecedent causes of change as distinct from the form in which processes of change are expressed; however, individualism cannot be made the basis of a full explanation except through the assumption that in zadrugas which divided the members were in some way more 'individualistic' than in other zadrugas—an untestable and probably circular proposition.

'Economic change' as a simple explanatory concept also presents certain problems. It is too broad and too imprecise; it stands at several removes from the antecedents of immediate individual choices which in aggregate add up to the patterns of change in the overall system of the traditional corporate grouping; but without the economic opportunities of working outside the zadruga in other jobs provided by the growing industrialization and urbanization of the country, the peasants would have had no alternative but to maintain their solidarity as members of agricultural collectives based on the ownership of their land and property. In this sense economic change is basic but not immediate in effect.

Political change comes into the picture in the same way, as providing a new framework, particularly a new legal framework, in which new choices could be made. For example, in Croatia up until the middle of the nineteenth century, the feudal system—still powerful—restricted the division of zadrugas since feudal lords who held urbarial (feudal) rights over peasant families found the zadruga system a good way of ensuring that duties would be fulfilled. But after feudal rights were abolished and the land given to the peasants, then the way was open to permit division.

In 1870 a law allowing zadruga members to request division or separation was passed. Previous discontent was revealed when division spread like an epidemic. Two years later another law had to be passed to try to damp down the effects, and this was shortly followed by two more laws with the same aim. Many zadrugas at that time were divided *de facto*, but preserved a legal fiction of unity. When, by the first quarter of the twentieth century, political pressure to maintain the zadruga as a conservative factor in the economy became weakened, division and denudation had become regular. Thus it might be said that in this sense political and legal changes were of basic importance in the changes in the corporate kin group, but only at one remove. Political and economic changes provided the opportunity for altering the internal structure of the zadruga if the members wished it, but the other aspects I have mentioned must be put in the forefront of an explanation of processes of change.

Now that the level of the corporate zadruga grouping of kin has disappeared completely, the substratum of the web of kin which comprises formally patrilineal ties as well as matrilateral and affinal links, has emerged as the most significant systematic feature of kinship. The zadruga was distinguished by the fact that it operated as a contractual corporation rather than by its large size; nevertheless, it was regularly larger than one elementary family, and the disappearance of the zadruga household is reflected in the relatively small size of present-day households. In 1961, the average size of households in the whole of Yugoslavia (see Census for 1961: *Statistički Godišnjak F.N.R.J.*, 1962, p. 308) was 3·98 persons. For the different states of Yugoslavia, the averages were as follows: Slovenia 3·43, Croatia 3·57, Serbia 3·95, Montenegro 4·39, Bosnia and Hertzegovina 4·63, and Macedonia 5·01. Only a relatively very small proportion of households in any state contain ten members and upwards. In the past ten years the tendency throughout the country has been for households to decrease further in size. Decline in birth rates forms one of the factors responsible for decline in household size, but another factor has been the division of constituent elementary families and their separation from one another, analogous to what we have seen in the case of the former traditional kin zadruga.

Even though three-generation families in households are a well-recognized norm and may be called extended families, they are not, as I have noted, joint families legally owning corporate property; furthermore, the lineal relationship providing the core of the extension in the three-generation household is sometimes traced through males and sometimes through females, thus revealing no clear picture of jural rules governing the formation of corporate groups.

To sum up, it may be said that the level of the corporate jural kin grouping in Yugoslavia has disappeared, but that in its place the previously recessive but now dominant level of the web or network containing ego-centred sets of cognatic or affinal kin provides the channel for activities governed by kinship rights and obligations. Not only is extra-familial kinship still important, but it has taken on new significance in a number of spheres in which it was not operative in the time of the corporate group.

(b) The substratum of kin relationships in Yugoslavia

In discussing the substratum of kin relations in Yugoslavia I must make it clear that when I use the concept of network, I am using it in the most general possible way, and I should like to avoid images (such as spring readily to mind) of closeknit or looseknit networks or of shrinking or expansion of the network, since I believe that such analogies can be misleading (Lancaster, 1961). In the present context, I merely wish to describe the empirical data which suggest variables involved in relevant changes in the network and sets of kin.

It is easiest to begin with the most visible indices of change: those already codified by customary usage and in some cases written into law, that is, the rights, obligations, and institutionalized forms of behaviour within a kindred. Yugoslavia is a society in which the rights and duties of kinship as set down in laws are much more far-reaching than in, for example, Britain. The Basic Law on Relations between parents and children (Section 32, paragraph 2; see Bakić, 1962) specifies the material support which it is the duty of everyone to supply to all lineal ascendants and descendants in need, as well as to brothers and sisters. Kin can apply for support from relatives when they can prove they are incapable of working through old age, illness, or accident and when any income they may have is insufficient for their support (Section 36). The needy person applies for aid to his close kinsmen as defined by law, and then to those more and more distant. The law is clear about the binding nature of these claims and the fact that the source of the claims is degree of kinship alone. The claims are irrevocable and permanent, and cannot be waived or mortgaged. The force of the claims of kinship demonstrates from one angle the continuing importance of kin roles; but some change in kin roles has also occurred, which, in turn, is a basis for change in links between persons associated in a network of kin, and also affects the extent of ego-centred kin sets in a numerical sense.

One useful index is provided by changes in terminological usage.

On the whole, there is much greater precision in kin terminology in Yugoslavia than in Britain. For example, the language distinguishes between uncle as father's brother and uncle as mother's brother. The first is referred to as *stric* and the second as *ujak*. One may commonly hear nowadays in the area in which I carried out research the term *stric* used as a general term, in the way in which 'uncle' is in English, to cover that kinsman on either side of the family. The word may also be used to give a quasi-kin status to a friend or neighbour who is not in fact connected to the speaker. I was discussing the growth of *stric* (FB) as a general term with a sophisticated informant in Zagreb (not a student of society or having any familiarity with sociological writings) who provided for me a 'Leachian' analysis of the question (cf. Leach, 1958) in maintaining that since in the former zadruga or *velika familija* household the father's brother was the uncle likely to be associated with ego as a fellow member, the words *stric* basically implied 'closer uncle' or 'uncle of our group'. On the other hand, *ujak* implied 'uncle of another group', thus effectively dividing the categories. It was therefore more friendly to use *stric* than *ujak*. Father's sister and mother's sister, both theoretically in the old system members of other groups, could be referred to by the same term, *tetka*, and this is still a general term for aunt. Thus, geographical dispersal and the localization of groups are consistent with the usage.

In the course of change over time, however, the terminology of kinship has become less precise, particularly in urban areas. There are many instances of a single term being used to cover several categories which strictly speaking have their own terms of reference and address. This is an important sign of the way in which cumulative change in individual recognition of relationship and obligation becomes sanctioned by custom, and is an important clue to the preserving of relationships in action. Other clues of importance concern the formal or informal modes of address which may be used. The Serbo-Croat language, like many European languages, distinguishes between the informal and the formal (plural) second person pronoun. The usage of *ti* (informal) and *vi* (formal) is quite strictly regulated on the basis of mutual expectations, friendship and kinship being treated alike in this context. This is a significant point which I shall take up again later.

Spatial mobility, which is one of the most important factors in changing the structure of networks, largely takes the form of movement from village to town. Migration can mean separation; the degree of rural-urban migration in Yugoslavia is such as to have reached the proportions of a problem. Its economic aspects have been well studied, although the effect on family relations is less precisely known. (But see Halpern, 1965, for an enlightening description of results in individual cases.) Several situations may arise from migration, each of which provides a different variable in the analysis.

On the one hand, because of much recent migration, there are many urban dwellers who have kin in the country; the migrants tend to keep up their relationship with those kinsmen who are farmers and landholders. This is partly because of the obligations and duties of kinship, which they accept, but also because landed property (in the country) is the focus of family unity, and any kinsman with a claim on the use of the property will preserve his right in it—even though he may not expect to inherit. This has all sorts of practical implications; it offers a possibility of safely maintaining and even extending a family property in a society in which private capital investment in industry is not feasible; there is a prospect which concerns the household economy and which includes tasks such as fattening pigs and providing other produce for the urban household (as domestic preserving of food is still a very important contribution to subsistence in many Yugoslav households); and it provides a place in the country for rest and recreation for town dwellers and their children.

When rural dwellers come to town, on the other hand, they usually attempt to follow up the channels of kin communication in order to obtain lodging and moral and/or material support while in the cities. Communications make it possible to keep in touch by mail or by telephone, although it must be said that posting a letter or making a telephone call in the country is not the easy task that it is in Britain. Much more communication is by personal message in Yugoslavia than by either of these remoter forms. Contact is maintained with friends too on the same basis, but it appears that where possible people expect to rely on kin rather than friends to provide this linkage within mobility. An illustrative instance occurred in a town household: it involved a young man who arrived unexpectedly from England in order to work on the roads in the communal student enterprise. After an elaborate sorting out of genealogies it was established that he was a child of a British branch of the family, to wit, a sister's son's son to the head of the household in Yugoslavia; and although he was a complete stranger to everyone in the household, he was accepted as a relative without any confusion as to the role he fulfilled, and was immediately incorporated into the household as a member. Thus, migration would seem at first sight to lead immediately to attenuation of kin links; nevertheless, there are many factors operating against this result which serve to emphasize the value of kin duties and obligations in a situation of rapid social change.

Another type of variable involved in the recognition which makes a kin network is that of joint economic enterprise. It is not possible in Yugoslavia for a number of people to band together privately and create a business enterprise. It is, however, still possible for people to retain two jobs provided one job is in agriculture, so that it very often happens that a man will have a factory job and also be helping to maintain a family farm. A great deal has been written about the deleterious effects of this in Yugoslavia, again largely from an economic point of view, but also from the point of view of the effect it may have on family relations (cf. Bičanić, 1956). Where a member of a household holds two jobs, it may create a certain amount of conflict since differential incomes could lead to different levels of consumption within the household unit, and the factory worker may feel he has a right to special services and comforts and a higher standard in, for example, clothing and entertainment. On the other hand, unless enough members of the household acquiesce and co-operate, this type of division of a man's working day between labour on the land and work in the factory or in other similar enterprise is not possible. Consequently, it is an important factor in unification. It enters into two situations in particular: the one in which the worker-peasant commutes to the city every day (and this is a point at which official disapproval is directed since it overburdens the transport services quite severely); and the other that occurs where factories are being built in the countryside in order to tap labour reserves there. In the second case the possibility of combining two roles becomes less of a strain and it may be expected to continue unless officially forbidden.

As a society becomes more urbanized so the importance of certain additional variables in the study of changing kinship tends to increase. This is the case in Yugoslavia with respect to the shortage of urban housing. Accommodation is not very difficult to find in the countryside, and of course it is always possible for a man to build his own house or get one built for him if he owns any land; but in the city the cost of housing is extremely high, and although government housing projects are extensive and building is going ahead very rapidly, nevertheless it is hard for a new elementary family to find the ideal accommodation. This has all sorts of repercussions. On the one hand, as one might expect, despite the ideal of neolocality after marriage, many young people continue to live with their parents.

There is no commonly accepted or customary rule that a newly married urban couple should take up residence with the husband's parents, although in the country this is still the more likely pattern. In the town a newly married couple is quite likely to live with the wife's parents, and no stigma is attached to this practice. (I should mention that even today there are rude country terms in Zagorje which apply to a man who takes up residence with his wife's kin. This represents the injunction of virilocality.) A number of case studies suggest that in urban areas of Croatia the newly married couple is most likely to live with the parents who have resources available in terms of rooms or wealth, so that if a husband marries up in terms of access to such resources then he will possibly live with his wife and his wife's parents. If a woman marries up then she will tend to join her husband and her busband's parents. I should point out that this is only a very simple and non-quantified picture of what is in practice a very complex set of variables.

Another aspect of the operation of kin relations lies in the fact that it is largely through kin links (although here links of friendship cannot be excluded) that it is possible to obtain the all-important housing. In this sphere one can see the operation in a network of what are largely channels of communication.

In the diagram below the links involved in obtaining housing in one instance are set out.

Diagram 1

HOUSEHOLDS

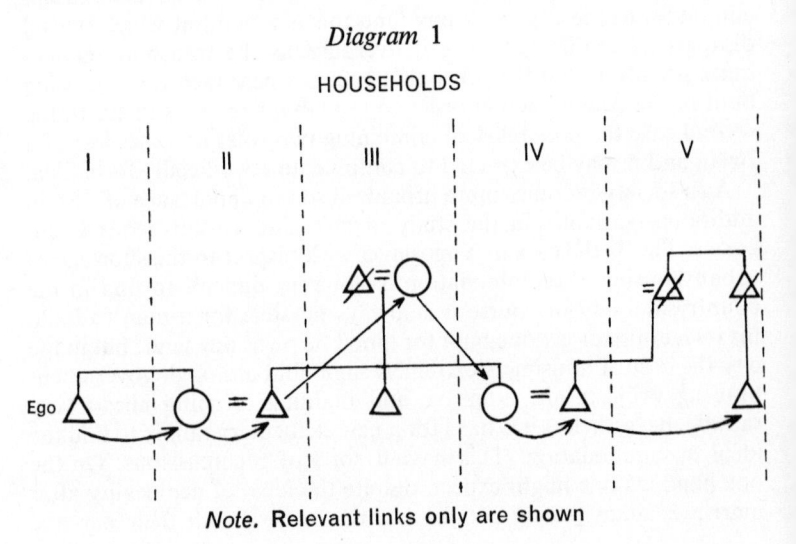

Note. Relevant links only are shown

The actual procedure in obtaining an apartment was that Ego asked his sister who, after mentally searching through her (and Ego's) own kindred, asked her husband, who went to ask his mother (living elsewhere) who knew a further network of relations which could be operated in order to use this channel of information, and provided the kin contact by inviting to her house the principals involved. There is thus a two-way process between shortage of housing in an urban environment and the validation of the network of relations. On one side, shortage may lead to propinquity and thus to constant reinforcement of links, and, on the other, even distant links may be used as channels of information and influence in order to obtain the needed housing, which very often will lead in turn to propinquity and thus to further reinforcement of kin links within the network.

In every society which is becoming more industrialized and which has had until recent times a framework of kin ties as one of its most important features in many spheres of action, there is a problem in reconciling the need for objectivity in large-scale organization with the still-existing recognized rights and duties of kinship. In extreme cases, in the political and administrative sphere, one might speak of 'nepotism', but the term has a moral and from some points of view ethnocentric connotation which is sometimes inappropriate. The point goes beyond the question of the Weberian concepts of rationality and specificity in bureaucratic organizations. In the present context all I wish to point out is that kin rights and duties frequently override political and economic considerations (although no doubt examples of the opposite situation can also be found). Within one family one may find members of varying shades of political opinion and varying positions of security within the economic framework. Nevertheless, kin ties and inter-familial relations will be maintained. The diagram below of one case shows how the principle can work.

Diagram 2

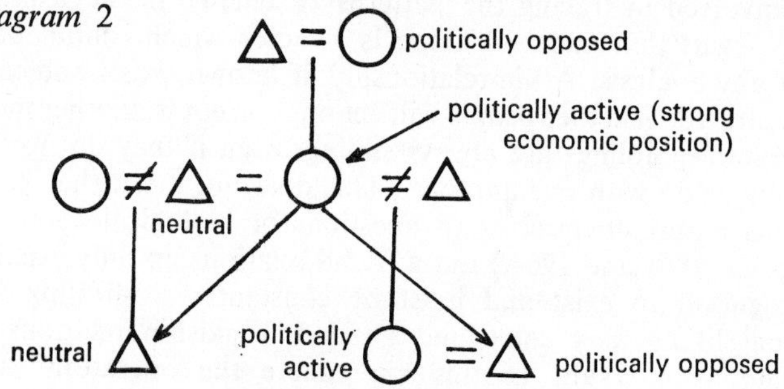

In this case support was given by the politically active woman, who was also in a strong economic position, to kinsfolk who were not linked to her along any economic or political lines but only on the basis of affinal relationship. (Incidentally, in the context of the social network with which I am dealing there is no point in making a strict and rigid distinction between kin and affines in the bilateral system. As I have already pointed out—Lancaster, 1958—certain affines in one generation must be considered blood relations—consanguines— in the next.)

One might argue that in a planned social, political, administrative, and economic system, where the legal provisions may weigh heavily on those who by accident or design find themselves in some officially unacceptable position, kinship relations are an absolute necessity. The rights and duties of relations through birth and marriage are constantly being invoked as a buffer against misfortune. Another variable emerges as being particularly important in those areas of the kindred in which the kin relationship is most attenuated. This variable may be referred to as status. One may use 'status' with a variety of referents; I use it here to cover not only position in the hierarchy of prestige or wealth but also in the ordinary sociological sense of a social position implying a role such as that of 'mother' or 'fellow-worker'. Status similarities, as a basis for preservation of ties, appear to be most important when genealogical distance is greatest. It is here that similarities of income, of interests, of stage in life cycle, of age, of shared values, and of style of life (all characteristics which may also influence the maintenance of friend relationships), become extremely significant. Cousins who differ in all these features may find it harder to maintain close personal relationships with one another than cousins who could easily have become friends quite apart from their kin ties.

Finally, although I do not believe that this exhausts all the variables involved in tracing the patterns of change in Yugoslav kin sets, it seems that personal liking is a factor which cannot be left out of any analysis. A kin relationship, if known, exists and can be demonstrated. Whether people will act on it or not is another matter. For example, siblings are always siblings even if they do not have anything to do with one another. (This does not mean that kinship relations reduce themselves to questions of biological connexion; cf. Barnes, 1961 and 1964.) But a friend relationship only exists if it is recognized to exist and must be constantly reaffirming itself. Personal liking may come and go and friendship relations may fluctuate as a result. In this kin sphere the operation of the principle can best be seen in case studies such as the one set out below.

Diagram 3

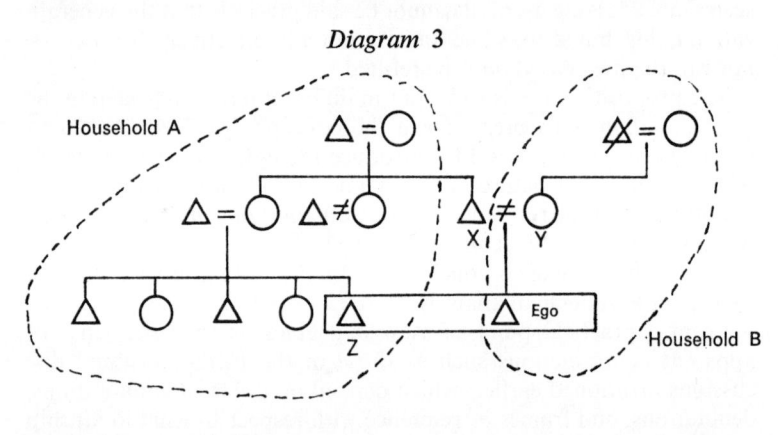

The explanation of this complicated relationship is as follows. Households A and B were in close contact until the divorce of X and Y and the movement of X away from the city. Formerly, he had lived in household B. Ego, a child, had previously been the close associate of the child Z, his cousin of the same age. With the disappearance of X, relationships were broken completely between these two households for about two years. There was no reason why Ego and Z should meet and their paths did not cross. Then the children Ego and Z, voluntarily and unbeknownst to the members of each household, began again to associate as friends, and in the course of time this relationship was openly accepted by both households, although other members of the households were not in any contact. These two children were attached to each other and, following their own personal liking, were able to establish a contact in which the kin component had been severely undermined.

III. *Theoretical implications of the ethnographic data*

At the outset of the present discussion, I emphasized the fact that in social anthropology there are many generalizations and many theories which are not quite dead and not quite alive. This is the case with some of the broad generalizations concerning family and kinship systems in rapidly changing societies. Some years ago, for example, it seemed to some commentators fairly clear, and to others quite obvious that, broadly speaking, increasing industrialization and economic growth would lead to the emergence of a universal form of isolated conjugal or elementary family. Now the situation seems much less clear-cut: it cannot be said precisely that the generalization holds, but at the same time it cannot be effectively disposed of, nor can theories based on it be refuted.

The proposition needs to be put in different terms; one step in the right direction is to break down the concepts involved. As a first procedure it seemed useful to introduce the notion of the two levels of change in the structure of family and kin relationships.

I then set out the relevant Yugoslav ethnography analysed in terms of change on these two conceptual levels.

Now I should like to conclude by briefly outlining what I think we can gain by such an analysis.

From a practical point of view it enables us to make sense of apparent contradictions such as those of the Firth-Townsend discussions mentioned earlier, which depend on different connotations, denotations, and frames of reference with respect to what in kinship is changing or can be expected to disappear.

I would, however, consider that the greatest significance in stressing different levels emerges with the understanding that, since they *are* different levels, they may show quite different patterns of change. It is even possible to discover, as in the case of Yugoslavia, that kinship which ceases to provide a basis for action on one level in fact becomes more important in new spheres which arise through economic and political changes.

In order to put the argument in more abstract terms we may call the substratum level Level 1 and the corporate level Level 2. Now it is possible to have a society in which the characteristic system only exists on Level 1. Long-term change here may reduce the number of kin recognized by individual egos while the system as a whole preserves the same form. As an empirical example of this, one may take English commoner society, where there has been no phase in which legally or jurally recognized unilineal corporate kin groups were the characteristic form. The kinship system under the Anglo-Saxons was similar in many respects to the kinship system we have today (Lancaster, 1958), although quantatitively we recognize fewer kin; overall, and looking at the situation broadly, one cannot trace a structural alteration, only an organizational change. On the other hand, where both levels exist and there is an interaction between them—that is, extra-familial kin groups, unilineally based are, as it were, selected out from the frame of recognized kin ties—change over time, involving the disintegration of Level 2, will change the overall structure.

This is a qualitative change as distinct from quantitative and primarily organizational change.

The question of the isolation of the conjugal family may be analysed on either level. On Level 1, the level of the substratum, isolation is a function both of the loss of recognized kin roles and of quantitative reduction in actual persons in kin sets. On Level 2, it is associated with progressive division and subdivision within corporate groups and, in a nonsegmentary society such as Yugoslavia, their eventual disappearance.

At present, great interest lies in the study of Level 1. For anyone concerned with customary forms of behaviour in peasant societies that are rapidly becoming more industrialized and urbanized, an accepted framework for the study of change and kinship on this level is extremely valuable.

Throughout the discussion, I have taken the concept of web or network as given. I believe that my interpretation of it, with special reference to kinship, is in line with some recent explorations of the concept of network and set, but in the present context I do not need to go into all possible meanings since they are not relevant to the task of locating variables in change. It seems to me that enough work has been done to show that this is a valuable conceptual tool in carrying out an analysis and that, although there are logical objections to its being loosely used in a kinship context (see Lancaster, 1961; Mayer, 1965), it has become established as a way of analysing relationships. Since also we may find a place for topological and other mathematical concepts in studying relationships and patterns of sets, we should not argue against this framework of analysis but attempt to refine it as a tool. For my purposes, the most important refinement would be one that would enable us, using this analytical framework, to speak of change in the substratum level. In order to do so we may examine networks formed by the recognition of kinship as a special case of a more general principle of the recognition of social relationships. Although at first sight it might seem harder to study a general case than a specific case, nevertheless I think that in operation this turns out not to be so. (Compare Polya, 1957, p. 109.) Consequently, we may consider kin relationships as essentially similar in many respects to relationships of friendship. There is nothing strange in considering kin as friends: in fact in 1958 I mentioned the correspondence of kin and friends in Anglo-Saxon kinship (Lancaster, 1958) and subsequently (1961, pp. 324–5) pointed to the difference between 'achieved' friends and friends 'ascribed' by kinship as a field of investigation which would repay research. Eric Wolf (1966,

p. 10) has recently arrived at a rather similar type of approach and terminology, and has examined various aspects of the kin, friend, and client tie. We are, however, so inclined to make a clear distinction between kin relationships and other relationships in society that it is difficult to amalgamate them in this way. Nevertheless, if we do take the general problem of changes in friend relationships over time, then we shall find that some suggestive analysis has been done in this field which is immediately applicable to the study of kin networks and sets of kin. In this context we may consider kin as 'ascribed' friends and ordinary friends and associates as 'achieved' friends, using ascribed and achieved in a similar way to that in which the adjectives were employed by Linton to describe status and role (Linton, 1936, ch. 8, *passim*); or, more accurately, one might consider that kin recognition implies a component of ascription plus a component of achievement in relationship. The less the dominance of the component of ascription, the more important the component of achievement may be. For instance, if kin are distantly related then one can consider the component of ascription to be a very small one; whereas if kin are closely related, say within one or two degrees of kinship, then ascription would be so dominant that it would take a considerable number of factors working against kin recognition for a relationship not to be kept up. The notion of amalgamating kinship and friendship for the purpose of exploration of concepts is most applicable to the level of network and becomes more important the more complex the society one is investigating. A number of consequences flow from looking at the situation in this manner. For example, one can assume that kin friends come in clusters. That is to say, where one member of a nuclear family is recognized as a kinsman, other members of the nuclear family are likely similarly to be recognized. Friends who are not kin can, however, belong to a network either individually or together with their nuclear familes as the case may be. Naturally, clusters of friends can arise as well—in that case there exist series of linkages to kin clusters, which begin by being attached at one point to the network and subsequently develop a number of subsidiary ties.

Under certain circumstances, one might be able to measure the strength of the kin component as against the friendship (associational or achievement) component in a relationship. For instance, quasi-experimental research such as that done by Young (1954) and by others into the use of kin relationships in times of crisis point up the balance of one component as against the other. Other things being equal, people often feel that they can demand—as a consequence of kin expectations, rights, and obligations—services which they could not demand from friends unless they were very close. The advantage of this sort of analysis, combined with the concept of levels, is that it provides a basis for evaluating, in a time scale, variables in a situation. One can see, for instance, how certain variables in the maintenance of the relationship may have at one point of time a positive weighting and at other points of time negative or zero weighting. Thus one can imagine, for instance, that geographical separation may be a negative factor in maintaining kin links within the network at one point of technological development in the society, whereas at another point, with increasing ease of communication, this factor could become more or less neutral. Another example is the relative importance of extending economic help. In some countries, at some points in economic development, aid of this kind is very important; in other countries, at other points in economic development, it is of far less importance in maintaining kin links than personal liking or shared interests.

It is not difficult to conceptualize this substratum of kin relations about which I have been talking. It is much more difficult, however, to make this concept operational. There is a considerable problem in evolving the easiest methods for examining the dynamics of the primary relations in kin sets, even allowing for the fact that we may gain many clues from the study of primary relations in other fields such as friendship. First of all, it appears that when relationships on this level have been institutionalized by custom, then regular terms of address and reference can be valuable as role indices. I have mentioned this point in an historical context earlier. In the short run one can chart the progress of friendship by familiarity in terms of address. This is particularly useful in those societies in which there are a familiar and a formal mode of address in personal pronouns. English-speaking societies are excluded from some aspects of this form of enquiry, but Beidelman (1963) has examined this approach to social relationships to some effect. These indicators permit investigation on a wider scale than that of the traditional micro-sociological unit of village or small community.

A second line of enquiry is through investigating people's own assessment of the significance of kin relations, friend relations, and the links between the two. For example, Francis and Stone (1956) examined a random sample of people in a government agency to examine their ideas about obligations, in ideal form. 100 per cent of the sample put obligations to 'family' (immediate family) above obligations to friends. 87·7 per cent put obligations to closest relatives, as defined by the authors, above obligations to friends; but only 17·7 per cent put obligations to distant relatives above obligations to friends. This shows that the weighting of the importance of kinship obligations varies directly with genealogical distance. But the usefulness of this approach for comparative analysis depends on the precision of indicating which 'friends' and which 'relatives' are involved and under what circumstances.

A third and probably most promising means of examining relationships is through exploration of features shown already to have possible significance in the maintenance of interpersonal ties in general and kinship in particular. Propinquity is one of the most important of these, although it is not in itself a simple variable and has to be taken together with the opportunities for maintaining comunications at a distance. A number of studies have examined friend relationships in housing estates and discovered the way in which propinquity influences social ties. 'Centrality', to use Whyte's term (1956), emerges as extremely important; it has its part to play also in maintaining kin ties where certain members within a set happen to be living in a more central position or along a line of communication important for some other purpose, such as shopping or reaching transport. Economic support is another important dimension to examine. Traditionally accepted availability for ritual meetings is also significant. The decision about who is to be invited to christenings, weddings, and funerals is a balance sheet of kinship and friendship and reveals the existence of the sets for individuals for certain points of time, and may bring out latent links not otherwise operative.

Similarity of status in a hierarchy of wealth or prestige is another variable which has to be examined. It appears that similarity of status, as measured in various dimensions, can be positively correlated with the wish of two persons to maintain social relationship, even kin relationship. Here there is a complicating factor in that a part of one's status may in any case be ascribed by kin links, so that in a comparatively non-mobile society one's kin largely locate and limit one's potential statuses. But with greater mobility there may be quite distinct discrepancies among kin in terms of status and prestige, and this is likely to affect interaction.

Consensus on values is another factor of importance. It may be associated with the more general concept which Lazarsfeld and Merton (1954) have described under the general term of 'homophily'. By this they mean a tendency for friendships to form between those who are alike in some designated respect. This is a useful notion since it permits one also to cover such characteristics as stage in life cycle (mentioned previously), presence or absence of young children, and even sharing of similar interests in recreation and entertainment. The values which bring people together through homophily do not necessarily have to be particularly fundamental. If relationships are established on some basis satisfactory to both parties, then it is possible that some care may be exercised in not revealing potential differences in values which could disturb the relationship.

IV. *Conclusion*

In this paper I have examined change in kinship in Yugoslavia as an example of a society rapidly becoming more industrialized, and attempted to show that simple generalizations about disintegration may be inappropriate. I have suggested that two levels of kin relations—that of corporate units and that of network—should be distinguished, subject to different regularities in change, and that, according to level, one may discriminate between structural (qualitative) and organizational (quantitative) change. Where the substratum of the web of kin becomes relatively more important than that of corporate unit, a new approach to kin relations imposes itself: that of considering kinship as a special case of expressive relations such as friendship. Under certain circumstances it reveals the same patterns of recognition and validation. I have shown the way in which this approach applies to Yugoslav kinship, where factors led to disintegration on one level but ties on another level of relations are still powerful. It cannot be said that kinship is, in absolute terms, less important than it was in the days of the operating corporate kin group. It is different, certainly, but the extent of communication through kin links brings a wider variety of bilateral kin and affines into day-to-day contact than in the days when kin group, work group, and local community largely coincided.

Industrialization, urbanization, and economic growth as factors of change are mediated through the provision of new ranges of possibilities from which individuals may make choices that establish a pattern. Greater permissiveness leads to features which, on the level of network, can be analysed by considering kinship in Yugoslavia in a new light as a basis of or, rather, component in, the diffuse relationship of friendship.

The approach I have put forward grew out of the analysis of field data and documentary material relevant to kinship in Yugoslavia. Nevertheless, since this country shows very clearly the effects of rapid urbanization and industrialization, such an analysis may

C

have validity for meaningful explanations of the disappearance of kinship from one level of action and behaviour and its reaffirmation, in a different form, at another level, in similarly developing and industrializing societies.

Theoretical Problems in Economic Anthropology

CYRIL S. BELSHAW

WHILE *Argonauts of the Western Pacific* and the early articles of Malinowski (1921) opened up the possibility of a serious approach to economic anthropology, it was Raymond Firth's monographs (1929, 1939, 1946) which first raised issues and provided data of equal value to anthropology and economics. To secure the acceptance of his position in the body of anthropological thought, Firth directed himself to a series of problems. He incisively and systematically attacked the older typologies and evolutionary assertions; he analysed field data to show the bearing of all institutions upon economic questions; he examined the universality, the limitations, and the utility of economic concepts and applied them in a context of anthropological analysis; and he emphasized, in all his anthropological thought, the primacy of choice and organization in the explanation of working societies (Firth, 1951). It might even be argued that Firth's theory of anthropology is an economic one (though certainly not in a materialistic or technological sense), and that this is its unique contribution, even when such matters as religion are under review.

Not many British anthropologists have taken up the challenges that emerge from these beginnings. Among the reasons for this are the increasing preoccupation with kinship studies, a growing difficulty of communication between economics and anthropology as the former has emphasized a mathematical orientation, and a belief that economic anthropology, because of its association with economic development, has 'applied' characteristics which somehow render it scientifically impure. In addition there seems to be an opinion that most of the interesting issues have been settled, and that all that is left is to perform a number of mechanical counting operations in a variety of societies, leading to the compilation of more and more tables which are not theoretically exciting.

In the United States in the meantime, events have taken a somewhat different turn. The pioneers of economic anthropology tended to be theoretically limited (Herskovits, 1952) or to concentrate on descriptive studies in peasant societies (Tax, 1953). The contemporary development of economic anthropology is looser and more diversified, and tends to cluster around two approaches. One seeks a constructive link between anthropology, sociology, economics, and other social sciences for the analysis of functioning societies in a manner quite close to that of Firth (here we have Nash, 1958, Mintz, 1964, Geertz, 1963, and Salisbury, 1962). The other makes use of such notions as multilinear evolution, human ecology, and cultural energy, with many analogies drawn from the biological sciences (here we have Steward, 1955, Sahlins and Service, 1960, and White, 1959). The issues are lively and in a constant state of flux.

My purpose in this paper is to consider some problems in economic anthropology which arise out of Firth's point of view, not in order to provide the answers, but to demonstrate that further intensive work in this field is of strategic significance in the further development of the main body of anthropological thought. I have left out of consideration the issues raised by the attention now being given in the United States to ecological and evolutionary systems, issues which require complex critical treatment.

UNIT ACTION

The figure of Robinson Crusoe has, perhaps unfortunately, almost disappeared from scholarly literature. Crusoe was a pedagogical device which dramatized, personified, and to some extent reified a model which contained all the elements of action in individual isolation. Crusoe was clearly the product of a culture, in that he had tools, concepts, and values, but the operation of culture in forming him was not examined, and values at least were handled in speculative and general terms which ought to have applied in any culture. Having established this model and examined its implications, economists were in a position to introduce variables, and particularly those of exchange, which placed action in a social context.

The two central assumptions of the model were that action maximized goal-achievement, and that choice was based on rational calculation of advantage and disadvantage (or cost). The model worked well for Man, the abstract actor, and all that seemed to be needed to give it reality was to feed into it a schedule of wants, weighted according to value, and another of costs, based upon a given pattern of resources and technology. But as the model was placed in social context, it naturally took on features characteristic of Western capitalist society, and its universality was compromised. Maximization came to be thought of in terms of monetary profit and accumulation of material wealth, and goals which did not meet these criteria were dismissed as irrational, outside the economic orbit.

Anthropologists found this to be a serious limitation to the potential universality of economics. For if irrationality, when we mean by this the adoption of a wider set of goals than those relevant to economists' discussions, was present in our own society, how much more so was it a factor in others.

There are several ways of attempting to overcome this difficulty. One is that followed by Karl Polanyi (1957) and his group, which states that institutions are based on an economic model in some societies but not in others. This is unsatisfactory, since problems of classification become enormous (when is there money? a market? profit? and is it possible to have some but not all of these?), and since, if carried to a logical conclusion, it tends to remove institutional analysis from a single concept of the unit act. Another method is to state that certain institutions are economic and others are not. Peasant marketing is consistent with the model, religious worship is not. This view is widespread among both economists and anthropologists, and has some utility. But the utility may be more apparent than real, since the alternative formulation has not been adequately explored. Scott Cook (1966) has drawn attention to the pitfalls of these two approaches.

The third method is to adopt a model which is useful not only as an economic unit act but also as a social unit act; that is, a concept of action useful to both economics and sociology and, presumably, cultural anthropology. In searching for such a model we are endeavouring to do in a formal and abstract way what the lay commentator does when he speaks of 'human nature' and then uses his concept of human nature to explain or deny interpretations of social behaviour and institutions. Some minimal concept of the unit act is an integral part of any explanation of social processes.

Ultimately, the model of the unit act should be integrated with psychological theory, forming a bridge between the psychological and the socio-cultural dimensions of enquiry, for those who wish to pass from one to another. But from the point of view of anthropology, the only *necessary* requirement is that the model be drawn from our own materials of observation, and that it should not contradict psychological statements unnecessarily.

Raymond Firth's approach to the problem has been to introduce emotion and irrationality into the model. This is now a common solution, but I do not think it is the most useful way of elucidating the socio-cultural dimension. For one thing, to put emotion and irrationality into some kind of orderly system requires the whole arsenal of psychological and psychiatric ideas. For another, it misinterprets the use of the word 'rational' in the economic model and in much of philosophy (Spiro, 1964). In the socio-economic model of the unit act we are not, I think, concerned with the emotions, and we assume that thought is normal in the sense that it is not disorganized. Where the actor identifies an end, a want, or a goal, and where he makes choices based upon some spectrum of ideas, knowledge, and values, and where, through choice, he relates resources to his goals, we speak of rationality; and the emotive and subconscious processes which lead him to his decision are external to the model.

It can be seen that the model is very close to Talcott Parsons's 'unit act' (Parsons, 1937). According to Parsons, the unit act has four elements, namely the actor, the situation, the end, and the normative orientation. But to have predictive or explanatory value, the elements need to be filled out with relevant variables. Parsons has attempted to do this, for example, with normative or value orientations, but the result is by no means wholly satisfactory. Thus a central dichotomy in the scheme of orientations is the contrast between ascription and achievement as affecting the nature of social roles. But ascription cannot readily be placed in the schema of a unit act. Achievement can, but it is fraught with ambiguity. For if achievement is used within a universal model, it becomes achievement *of any goal* (the only valid cross-cultural statement). Yet Parsons contrasts it to ascription, and those who have followed him tend to argue that some societies are achievement motivated and others not. The universality breaks down, and the unit act disappears.

What then are the elements in a socially-placed unit act of relevance to economic anthropology? The following categories are by no means complete or logically pure. They are, however, a reflection of current approaches and indicate the need for further conceptualization and elaboration.

(*a*) The availability of resources to the actor. Resources include not only material objects, but [also time, knowledge, symbolic systems, and organization, and are affected by property institutions.

(*b*) The actor. This includes his skills in so far as they affect choice, his value emphases (or personal culture), and his perception of advantage and cost.

(*c*) A schedule of wants, and the selection of a goal or goals which are prepotent, that is, which govern action. This implies the simultaneous existence of goals which are rejected and others which are potential.

(d) The actor's social relations within a structure of social roles. It is this characteristic which identifies the actor as a member of a society (or of an economy). It places social interaction and exchange transactions on the same plane of analysis.

(e) Normative orientations, or principles of choice. These are linked very closely to value emphases in (b) above, but whereas value emphases relate to particular preferences in particular cultures, normative orientations are universal themes which describe choice regularities.

Maximization of value satisfaction is one such orientation which can be accepted, provided one does not predetermine specific values, and provided that in empirical verification it is borne in mind that choices take into account costs as well as positive values. It may be objected to this principle that it is tautological, in that it will be presumed that for any act in any society satisfactions and costs will have been judged. This objection is formally correct. However, many of the judgments are not self-evident, and the attempt to reveal the bases of judgment in terms of maximization and cost frequently leads to the revelation of new data and relationships. Nevertheless, it is a task of economic anthropology to set out other normative orientations, or to refine the maximization principle in such a way that it can become predictive, either by reference to economic theory or by departing from it. Little work has yet been done to construct, for example, a formal theory of Melanesian economics based upon the fundamental propositions of economics applied in a Melanesian cultural framework.

But there is ample evidence to show that the maximization principle cannot apply in its purity unless we expand the variable goals very much beyond the normal range of material wants and basic services. This can be done, formally, by introducing such notions as the preference for leisure, or the demand for religious satisfaction. Again, anthropology has not done very much with this except in loose descriptive terms, and has not yet decided whether this is the best way of proceeding towards a useful abstract model, and if so what the most crucial variable goals should be.

In attempting to do this we may find that it is most satisfactory to retain the maximization principle when we are dealing with those goals for which resources and time must be used directly, but to introduce modifying principles to describe limitations on maximization which may be traced to other considerations. For example, in a study I have completed of various types of exchange and market systems (Belshaw, 1965) it became apparent that in all systems there is a dominant search for regularity and security in socio-economic relations which seriously modifies the operation of competition between individuals. Perhaps, then, we could introduce into the model the variable 'maximization of continuity' so that continuity, a form of security, is seen to be judged alongside other competitive goals. But this would be clumsy since, although the achievement of continuity may be calculated to have an opportunity cost, the amount of continuity achieved cannot be assessed in terms of time and resources spent on it as would be the case with a preference for leisure or for ceremonial goods. We thus need to introduce a principle of continuity alongside the principle of maximization, the one modifying the other: and if this is the case we need to search for other principles of a similar kind which, taken together, give the model greater validity.

SOCIAL TRANSACTIONS

As social anthropologists we are interested in the map of relations between social roles. There are many ways of examining the quality of relations, for example jurally or affectively, and there is some disagreement (based mainly on the training, taste, and preference of the anthropologist) as to which of these is most satisfying. But there is one approach which is of particular significance to economic anthropology, since it offers the possibility of placing economic propositions in the same nexus as propositions which have usually been held to describe different or supplementary aspects of relations. This is the analysis of social transactions.

The idea of social transactions is not of course a novelty, and whether explicitly stated or not underlies most analyses of social interaction. In sociological theory the term is frequently applied to interactions between institutions, or, in Parsonian terms, inputs and outputs across the boundaries of social sub-systems (Parsons and Smelser, 1956). George Homans (1960) endeavoured to make the idea of exchange a basis for examining interpersonal relations. In anthropology, Marcel Mauss's *Essai sur le don* (1923–4) and the work following it, and the whole history of the idea of reciprocity, reflect a concern for transactions as a foundation of social relations. Yet despite this interest the theoretical implications of such an approach have not been made nearly explicitly or precisely enough to command satisfaction.[1]

1. Since writing this section I have become aware of the penetrating study by

To take an example, transactions, and particularly though not solely exchange, involve a division of labour. It is a commonplace in sociology that division of labour is a special case of role differentiation. In one sense, this provides the Marxist link between technology, which demands a certain kind of division of labour, and the structure of society. Many contemporary sociologists follow Parsons, who sees economic institutions as producing goods and services to satisfy the wants of society, and Marion Levy (1952), who states that the division of labour is role differentiation based upon production. But to link this notion with general and economic usage Levy is forced to talk of 'the production of allocation', which is a very clumsy way of allowing for the different roles of management on the one hand and distribution on the other. Apart from such modest discussions, there is little attempt to bring role theory and division of labour theory together, or to test the propositions of economists which refer to the division of labour.

In anthropology, most of our approaches to role differentiation are based initially upon symbolic data or statements about ideal norms or patterns. We may then limit ourselves to the examination of these phenomena at a cultural level. Some social anthropologists do precisely this when they study systems of kinship terminology. Or we may attempt to relate the symbolic or normative data to other behavioural regularities, thus leading to the abstraction of social roles which contain transactional dimensions.

The obvious alternative, from the point of view of economic anthropology, is to begin with the transactions themselves, and by observing their flow and their implications, arrive at a functioning model of a social system. There have been attempts in this direction. For example, Raymond Firth has successfully introduced ritual roles into the production-distribution complex, and has shown what is given and what is received by the ritualist. Numerous accounts of ceremonial transactions have stressed the significance of give and take, helping to define roles in terms of duty, obligation, and self-interest.

But in this we are, I think, inhibited by the assumption that division of labour is only part of role differentiation, when it could be argued that it is the whole of it; by the idea that division of labour is

---

Peter M. Blau (1964). Although I should prefer a change in certain emphases (for example, by avoiding the distinction 'economic exchange—non-economic exchange', and by widening the notion of power so that it would include both influence and the exercise of wealth), this to me is the most elegant and satisfying elaboration of the problem to date.

economic, and belongs in that part of the social system concerned with the production and distribution of material goods and some special services; and by a materialistic approach to economics. If we were to abandon these points of view, what would happen?

We should first be forced to give theoretical status to the everyday anthropological observation that social relationships comprise unit acts which taken together constitute transactions involving an admixture of material and non-material considerations. Even the simplest of social structures would be seen to be cemented by transactional regularities. Social roles would be observed, and hence defined, by the regularity of transactions.

In this system, husband and wife are roles identified by the transactions between them. The passage of material goods between husband and wife is particular to the relationship; so is the giving and receiving of non-material services. But husband is also father, and wife mother, and children siblings. The flow of transactions, if regular, creates the family structure. Simplistic teleological formulations such as 'the family exists to provide sexual fulfilment, procreation, and socialization' become unnecessary and the lack of explanatory value clear. None of these things *prevents* the family from splitting.

The forces holding the family together are more immediate and tangible. They are based upon day-to-day decisions taken in the framework of the unit act. The normative orientations of such actions are not yet adequately formulated, but the principle of maximization coupled with the principle of continuity provides for an interplay of self-interest and regularity. It may be argued that the roles involved derive from the search for continuity, and are given reality by the pursuit of complex but specific objectives. These, varying from culture to culture, lead to differing structures. Here, it seems, is a fruitful field for theoretical elaboration upon the foundations of Mauss, Homans, Firth, and now Blau, and upon ideas about the economy of social relations.

CORPORATE INSTITUTIONS

Social transactions, carrying with them continuities and reciprocal (though sometimes indirect) implications, thus delineate the network of roles and can be used to map social relations. But the moment transactions involve two or more persons, questions of dominance and the major direction of flow arise. Power becomes the ability to influence the decisions of others; authority, the ability to make choices which dictate the decisions, or the limits of decision-making, of others.

A corporate institution, or organization, is sometimes described as a continuous association of roles organized to achieve common purposes. While most such institutions have charters, or charters can be deduced for them, it is nevertheless true that the nature of the common purposes is often ambiguous, contradictory, and changing. The fact of the matter is that organizations have wants rather like individual wants, and although they are often much more restricted in range, they are based on the same kinds of appraisal as are the choices of individuals. The unit act schema for decision-taking should therefore hold good.

In so far as a corporate institution contains differentiated social roles, it encompasses transactions between them in the same manner as any other set of roles in the society. It is true that the transactions may be more deliberate, and more subordinated to a corporate purpose, than is the case with many other sets of roles, but this cannot be taken for granted and is not inherent in organizations. The kinship system can contain highly deliberate and purposive transactions, and periodic ritual or ceremonial without a church framework can involve the subordination of individual decisions to the goals of an over-all matrix. Furthermore, it cannot be assumed *a priori* that transactions within an organization are in fact or of necessity deliberately subordinated to a common purpose.

The distinction here between overt and latent purpose may be misleading. For example, in a club there may be the overt purpose of providing recreation, with a latent purpose of providing social contacts which can be of use to individuals in their business dealings, the first being embodied in the charter, the second not. It would be more appropriate to regard these, and other objectives, as being competitive or complementary ends affecting the individuals concerned, and hence transactions between persons embodying such roles as member, guest, director, manager, and employee. In other words, the unit action schema provides for a schedule of wants which compete in various ways for prepotency, and which can be complex in themselves, thus removing or modifying the necessity to distinguish overt and latent goals. (But it does not remove the distinction between effective and potential wants or goals.)

The corporate institution differs from other sets of roles in that within defined social situations its authority pattern is self-contained, and this authority may extend to the administration of joint property. It is necessary to state 'within defined social situations', since strictly speaking no corporate institution, or any other set of roles, can be entirely autonomous or independent of external authority in the contemporary world. It is also probably necessary to a corporate institution that there be a mechanism for expressing decisions on behalf of the total role set, and that this supreme authority be specifically located.

This approach to corporate institutions by no means removes all ambiguities, and in some respects increases the number of questions that arise for answering. In particular, it should bring back into anthropology some questions which have been raised in economics, but which have not been examined comparatively in economic anthropology.

It should be apparent that corporate institutions, or organizations, represent merely one set of themes according to which men organize or co-operate. The question was early posed in economics as to why a division of labour should exist at all, and certain general answers, based upon advantages and effectiveness, were provided. The question was then extended to an enquiry into the structure of firms, and a general theory was formulated to explain why some industries and firms integrated their sources of supply and their marketing arrangements within one authority-complex, and some did not; and why, in some instances, integration was horizontal rather than vertical. There are also questions of the existence or non-existence of monopolies, cartels, partnerships, and co-operating consortia. Sometimes a broadly conceived contract between two firms can have the effect of integrating their decisions and policies.

Despite the existence of such a general theory in economics, there is no parallel theory in sociology. Yet one would have thought this to be a critical set of problems in social organization, social structure, and role theory. This is particularly the case since firms are a special class of organization more generally conceived, and other organizations have similar problems, and because the dividing line between a formal corporate institution and a non-corporate but effective set of roles is at best fuzzy. In other words, the economic theory of the structure of the firm should be a special case of a more general theory of social organization, and we have not yet made it so.

Furthermore, precisely the same kinds of problem exist within non-literate and peasant societies, albeit on a different scale. A simple example to use is that of house production. In tropical communities, a house of reeds and thatch can sometimes be built by a single individual, who can gather all materials himself, often from his own property, or by minimal arrangements with others who administer lands on which materials can be found. Usually, however, the help of at least one or two others is required for heavy labour (the raising of posts, for example), and it is frequently obtained from the immediate family circle or close kin. Under such conditions, the entrepreneur is both consumer and producer, and is controlling all stages of production under his own immediate authority to the maximum extent permitted by social practice governing the owner-ship of resources, including labour.

But clearly, there are many other ways in which this could be or-ganized. The consumer may step out of the production role, engaging an entrepreneur to carry out the task, as is frequently done in Fiji. The entrepreneur in turn may engage skilled specialists, for thatching, ritual, post laying, and the like. He may set his labour team to gather all the raw materials and process them to the stage at which they can be used in building (for example, stripping and preparing sennit). Or he may order or purchase these from other production units, interesting himself only in the supply of the finished product. He must decide, in other words, to what extent he should integrate production in one unit, or depend upon supply from independent units. In so far as he integrates production into one unit, he must decide upon the nature and extent of the transactions within the unit, including rewards and punishments.

This hypothetical example can be duplicated in every field of pro-ductive endeavour and is merely an extension of the decision as to whether or not an individual should be self-supplying and self-sufficient, or whether one of the myriad alternatives should be adopted. In economic anthropology we have tended to content our-selves with describing and analysing the system in operation in the culture under examination, and have tended to argue that the social structure determines the flow of transactions, and hence the relational patterns which govern decisions about integration and exchange.

But this is not good enough, because these are merely aspects of the same phenomena. Relational patterns are abstracted from the flow of transactions; social structure is abstracted from relational patterns; they do not explain each other. We need in economic anthropology a general theory, either similar to or a replacement of that in economics, which will explain why it is that it is sometimes advantageous, desirable, or customary to integrate or to distribute productive tasks in particular ways. This is no mean challenge, since if we can do this, and if we are right in intimately relating social structure to transactional patterns, we shall then be well on the way to providing a general theory of social organization.

SOCIAL COMPLEXES

It was pointed out earlier that the distinction between corporate institutions and other constellations of social roles was by no means sharp. In addition, attempts to separate economic and non-economic institutions from each other are bound to fail, since all action involves choices about the combination of resources to achieve selected objectives, and hence all action is economic.

These points taken together imply that if economic anthropology contains general propositions and theories, the ideas should be applicable to social complexes which are not normally conceived of as corporate institutions and which are frequently put into some sort of non-economic box. Two examples which come to mind are political arrangements in a society without centrally located authority and religious activity where there is no church. In each case, of course, there may be interaction between corporate groups such as lineages. But even if the interaction is between individuals without corporate reference, the transactions are of the same order as those we have been discussing above. It makes no difference to the scheme of the analysis if the goal that is to be achieved is the establishment of order through the expenditure of labour, or religious security through the manipulation of ritual paraphernalia. In other words, politics and religion contain a dimension which can be regarded as the economy of social relations. Economic anthropologists have not yet attacked this question and examined its implications, although it is inherent in much of their work.

FUNCTIONAL RELATIONS

The next questions I wish to consider are those which build up toward a model of a functioning society or economy (from the point of view of economic anthropology, the two should be co-terminous). In this connexion, one may consider the systematic effects of institutionalized social complexes, and changes which may occur in them. As an example, one may analyse the effects of ceremonial.

Ceremonial is a pre-eminently anthropological topic. The preoccupation has been with symbolic and emotive meanings and with psychosociological interpretations of function. In so far as ceremonies have been classified cross-culturally, it has been in terms of their position in a total social and cultural scheme, broadly conceived. Thus, we have the *rites de passage*, and theories as to their significance.

Ceremonies and rituals are inescapably transaction complexes, and hence it has been inevitable that transactions have, on the whole, been better reported than is the case with other institutions. What have not been reported quite so well have been transactions which feed into and support the ceremonial complex and those which flow out of it, although even here Mauss, Malinowski, and Firth pioneered, and some other writers have followed their lead. How are ceremonial goods and services produced, at what cost, and with what choice flexibilities? Under what circumstances do the goods circulate after the ceremonial?

These questions are in themselves unimportant, but the data which produce answers provide information which can be used to analyse the effects of ceremonial upon the economic system. Does the demand for ceremonial goods and services call forth production of different kinds or in excess of that which would be required if domestic consumption continued without the intervention of ceremony? Are the goods consumed immediately, merely replacing domestic consumption? Are they durables, retained in stock for further consumption later, or for further circulation, so that ceremony has the effect of increasing supply for future use, and is therefore a capital investment? Is consumption diverted to non-capital, non-durable items, thus decreasing instead of increasing the stock of resources? Do the transactions involved imply a network of social relations along which future transactions flow, so that the complex, rather than being isolated, is part of a much more widely balanced system? What is the elasticity of demand for ceremonial values? In other words, if resources increase, to what extent will this fact be reflected in an increased diversion of resources to ceremonial purposes?

Not all ceremonies in all cultures have the same relations with the total economy. There is sufficient knowledge available now for us to be quite certain that in many cultures ceremonial has a positive role to play in supporting an economic dynamic, and is not the destructive and wasteful institution so often described. But the variations have not been explored systematically and abstractly. And what has been done for ceremonial has not been done on as large a scale for other phenomena such as the family, social stratification, or (in primitive societies) land use.

The analysis of such effects and transactions opens significant possibilities for elucidating dynamic relations. If there is increase in wealth, is there ceremonial inflation, and what effects has this on the social network? How do alterations in ceremony affect the demand for land? If ceremony is linked with agricultural production and land comes to be short in supply, does this mean that some social obligations cannot be honoured and that the social structure is then affected? If this is accompanied by an increase in communications, is it then likely that the search for viable social relations will be spread more widely into new categories of partnerships?

Answers to questions such as these now abound. They are almost entirely provided in studies of social change, for such interconnexions are best revealed in a diachronic context. Dissatisfactions with the status of propositions of this order in anthropology are connected mainly with their scattered nature, for they tend to be empirically and opportunistically based. They have not been integrated into coherent theories: when this is eventually accomplished, diachronic theory will be more productive than the static functional theory which is now necessary.

A Re-view of Complex Economy

In what I have written above I have implied from time to time that theoretical issues and formulations in economics might be examined through the comparative data of anthropology and introduced, with amendments, into the body of social theory. It should be apparent, however, that if transactions are to be used as a basis of analysis, traditional economic theory will be insufficient to handle problems that arise in describing and accounting for the total social nexus.

Indeed, the question can be turned to lead in another direction. If social relations and transactions are essentially the same phenomena, then market relations and the behaviour of the firm are social relations, and propositions about social relations should apply to these fields. It is at least possible in this connexion that sociologists and anthropologists have allowed themselves to be too readily convinced that market behaviour and institutions are different in character from those which exist in other parts of society.

This over-persuasion is reflected in theoretical categories. Not only do we have the dichotomy between achievement (applicable to capitalist based societies) and ascription (applicable elsewhere), and other similar polarities, but we tend to accept the impersonality of market relations and the cold-blooded pursuit of maximal profit as the primary goal of market activity.

It is more than time that anthropologists began to challenge these assumptions, and support alternative formulations based upon empirical data. I have already drawn attention to the variety of business associations and combinations. Much more objective information is needed about the processes which lead to the creation of contracts, and the transformation of persistent contractual arrangements into partnerships and associations. Does this combine maximizing competition with the realization that maximal advantage sometimes accrues when contractual continuity is assured? If so, does it have characteristics similar to the Haitian market place with its institution of *pratik*? What role do informal social relations play in creating the knowledge and confidence upon which business arrangements are founded, and in channelling market transactions?

We could go very much further. Research on ceremonial in Western economies has not been undertaken, but could start from points of view derived from the more recent analyses of ceremony in anthropology. This is not unimportant, even to the economist. Casual reflection would indicate that in the United States and Canada it is probably true to say that Christmas, Easter, Thanksgiving, and other festivals, together with marriage, birth, and death ceremonies, are becoming much more complex and are inflating with the increase in wealth (Blau, 1964; Belshaw, 1965). It may well be that such ceremonies in their totality account for upwards of 10 per cent of total family consumption expenditure. Along the same lines, some forms of credit (for example, department store credit) in Western society carry with them obligations which are close in character to prestation. (The difference between prestation and contract is by no means the sharp polarity that Mauss described.)

Such considerations do not lead us as yet to write on the matter with assurance, but it is at least possible that an adequate socio-economic theory of transactions in Western society would bring about a substantial modification of our views about economic processes. As a by-product, this might well have the effect of removing some of the moral judgments which are concealed in theories of economic development (for example, those concerned with individualism or ceremony).

The Socio-Economic System

In the modern world, it is probably true to say that there is, empirically, no such thing as an entirely autonomous self-contained socio-economic system. Nevertheless, we talk of social, economic, and cultural systems by arbitrarily abstracting out of consideration those variables which we do not wish to handle in the enquiry of the moment. The choice of system under examination is not a matter of caprice, but is determined ideally by whether it contains within it variables sufficient to explain the phenomena or answer the problems that have been initially posed. Thus a nuclear family in a particular culture, nuclear families in general, kinship systems, corporate organizations, or the relations contained in a cultural area, can be

D

considered as systems for specific purposes. A social, economic, or cultural system is an abstraction, as is any system based upon combining social, economic, or cultural modes of analysis, and is not to be *observed* in the same way that a biological organism can be observed. It is this characteristic which distinguishes the social sciences from the biological or natural sciences, and which suggests that a classification of social systems is a logical exercise rather than a method of natural history. (It also follows from this that much can be learned by the logical examination and manipulation of imaginary systems, as is indeed the case in economics.)

Nevertheless, there is one kind of social system of considerable practical significance today, and which is commonly, though not exclusively, referred to as 'society'. This is the contemporary organized state. Strictly speaking, this should be referred to as polity rather than society, since its identifying mark is over-all political authority. The boundaries of polity are, for various purposes, regarded as boundaries of economy, and the social relations contained in them are often thought of as bounded also, and of a special character.

In economics, the questions are frequently asked, how do economic systems, thus politically identified, work? What are the deficiencies in their operation? And what is the standard of their performance?

In anthropology we have very good accounts of the working of many politically autonomous groups. The attempts of sociologists to provide analyses of specific complex societies, or to develop a frame of reference for their comparison, have been fraught with difficulty because of the burden of massive data and the problem of bringing under control the multifarious processes which, for example, make up the society of the United States. Thus the analogous first question, how do societies work? has received a great deal of attention, but the answer, or even the most appropriate manner of formulating the answer, is by no means clear.

It is I think quite possible for economic anthropology to develop along lines which would enable it to make a contribution to these questions, asked of a politically identified society. Such a society will operate through transactions between roles and between role-playing corporate institutions. The formation of a model of social structure can thus be carried out in a manner consistent with the kind of transactional analysis which has been referred to earlier. Furthermore, the social model can be built up through the identification of roles, which should place heavy emphasis upon the roles played by corporate institutions. Rather than beginning with an *a priori* functional sub-system, as does Talcott Parsons, it would be possible to ask what roles are in fact played by corporate institutions in given societies, and what transactions lie between them. This might well be closer to empirical reality, yet not prevent abstract argument and reasoning, and would at the same time be closer to anthropological methodology.

The necessity for abstract argument and reasoning is particularly apparent when we address ourselves to the second question: what are the deficiencies of operating societies? We already know from the work of economists, and from the incorporation of such concepts as dysfunction and eufunction in sociology, that functioning models are ideal constructs rather than reflections of absolute empirical truth. Economists use models of functioning economies to test the adequacy of the reality; they are prepared to admit that the performance of economic systems can be improved by alterations in the system. The diagnosis of imperfection is helped by comparing the reality with an ideal model.

The same issues are with us in anthropology; we are inhibited in dealing with them because we cannot avoid their difficulty, as the economist does, by pretending that the objectives of differing societies are similar.

Nevertheless, politically organized societies do make decisions which reflect choices, and, quite apart from central decision-taking, exhibit directions of movement which are the resultant of the transactional processes which occur within them. Their institutions react upon one another in ways which justify the use of the term 'system' to describe the totality.

If this is the case, the structural arrangement of corporate institutions should be the central feature of the socio-economic model, and the workings of the system should be revealed by the analysis of transactions. Anthropology is more at home in this kind of analysis for simpler societies than is sociology for complex ones; perhaps this can suggest an anthropological contribution to the study of sociology.

Further, if methods are successfully devised for the analysis of total social systems, in this sense, it should be possible, and even desirable, to compare reality with the models, and to ask, of particular societies, are the institutions contributing with maximal effectiveness to social goals? Do we, as anthropologists, always have to take societies for granted as we find them? Can we not sometimes ask what would be the consequences of an altered institution, and learn from the asking? This, it seems to me, is a legitimate scientific query, particularly in the absence of experimental conditions, and one which is inherent in the nature of economic anthropology.

The Equality of the Sexes in the Seychelles

BURTON BENEDICT

> In this community [the Line Islands], too, whereas a woman who uses her body for commercial purposes incurs no special reproach, one who uses it for pleasure and does not obtain any economic reward is contemned. This relation of chastity to material wealth is probably to be correlated with the unequal position of women in that community as compared with men, and the different structure of family life (Firth, 1936a, p. 520n.).

Professor Firth is discussing the evaluation of virginity in Tikopia in the chapter in which this note appears. It compares with the comment of a woman in the Seychelles who described a 'bad' woman (*'une dame qui faire vice'*) as one who cohabited with a man who she knew would not help her. The purpose of this essay is to examine the relations between the sexes in the Seychelles,[1] with particular attention to the relative status of the partners in the domestic group and the forces keeping them together and pulling them apart. It will attempt to test Firth's hypothesis by examining the relationship of chastity to material wealth and by seeing if this is correlated in any way with equality or inequality of the sexes, and the structure of family life. Chastity I shall define as the absence of sexual relations before marriage. In the Seychelles, as in most other societies, it is a concept which applies to women rather than men and this, of course, already implies inequality. Equality I shall take to mean an equivalence of rights and duties. As applied to a man and woman living together, it includes control over property, jural rights over children, rights over income and expenditure to maintain the household, wage earning, division of labour in the domestic economy, and the ease with which one or other of the partners may leave the household. What I shall be examining is the balance of rights and duties between

1. I carried out fieldwork in the Seychelles between 17 March and 15 September 1960 under a grant from Colonial Development and Welfare funds for which I express my deep appreciation. All opinions expressed in this article are those of the author and not of any government authority. My work was chiefly among low income groups and my information for them must be regarded as more complete and authoritative than for middle and high income groups.

43

the male and female partners in domestic groups to see whether one
of the partners has a preponderance of rights which puts the other
partner in a position of dependence, and in what ways this distribution of rights is related to types of family structure found in the Seychelles.

The Seychelles is an archipelago of some ninety-two islands in the
western Indian Ocean. It consists of a fairly compact group of
granitic islands and a widely scattered group of coral islands. The
population in 1961 was estimated at 42,936 (Seychelles Report
1961–62, p. 4) and is concentrated on the granitic islands. The largest
of these is Mahé with an area of 57 square miles and over 80 per cent
of the Colony's population. There were no indigenous inhabitants
of the Seychelles. The islands were discovered by the Portuguese
early in the sixteenth century, probably by Vasco da Gama during his
second voyage, 1502–3 (Scott, 1961, p. 34). The Portuguese made no
attempt to colonize the islands, and they remained uninhabited for
more than two and a half centuries except as an occasional refuge for
pirates.

During the second half of the eighteenth century the islands were
colonized by French settlers and their slaves from the Île de France
(now Mauritius) and Bourbon (now Réunion). They established a
plantation economy raising rice and maize which were sold pro-
fitably to passing ships. Later sugar, cotton, coffee, and cloves were
planted. During the Napoleonic wars the Seychelles repeatedly capi-
tulated to British squadrons, and in 1814 the islands, as dependencies
of Mauritius, were ceded to Britain under the Treaty of Paris. They
continued to be administered from Mauritius until 1903 when they
became a separate colony.

After the abolition of slavery in 1835 large numbers of liberated
Africans were brought to the Seychelles by ships of the British navy
which had captured slavers operating from Zanzibar and East
Africa. Between 1861 and 1872, 2,409 Africans were 'liberated'
in the Seychelles (Webb, *Population Census*, p. 29). Many were
indentured to planters under conditions not unlike slavery. Little
is known about early social conditions in the Seychelles,[1] but the
following factors appear important for the purposes of this article.

1. The wide variety of tribes and areas from which slaves came
   and the conditions of slavery itself militated against the preservation of African cultural traits and social organization.

[1]. A somewhat fuller discussion of the social history of the Seychelles will be
found in Benedict, 1966.

2. Europeans and Africans lived in very close contact from the earliest times.
3. There were far fewer women than men in the early settlements and very few European women.
4. Facilities for legal and religious recognition of marriage were lacking for a very long time (the first Roman Catholic mission was not set up until 1853).
5. Unemployment and underemployment became endemic at least from the time of the emancipation of the slaves (1835).
6. The Seychelles became dependent on the import of basic food-stuffs from the middle of the nineteenth century onwards. This dependence has been increasing.
7. The vast majority of the population of the islands has always had a very low material standard of living. On the other hand, it has always been fairly easy to obtain bare subsistence until quite recent times.

Economy

The economy of the Seychelles is based on the production of copra and to a lesser extent on cinnamon and vanilla. Fifty-six proprietors hold two-thirds of the commercial agricultural land of the Colony (Webb, *Agricultural Census*, p. 25). They draw on a labour force much larger than they require. Wages are low. Payment for extra work and odd jobs is meagre. Job security is minimal. In 1960 only 67·7 per cent of the population between the ages of 15 and 64 were economically active (Webb, *Population Census*, p. 111) and only about one-third of these (3,180 males and 2,024 females) were employed as labourers on plantations (*ibid.*, p. 39). Traditionally labourers supplemented their small cash wage with locally grown foodstuffs and fish. This still obtains to some extent in the rural areas, but the Colony is undergoing a rapidly accelerating change in the direction of a more complete dependence on cash. Prices are rising; the quantity of foodstuffs available free or in return for labour is diminishing. In general wages are not keeping pace with this change, and this is causing considerable economic distress in the poorer sections of the population, particularly in Victoria, the town and port, where the need for cash is greater than in the country districts.

After the plantations the next largest employer in the Seychelles is Government with about 3,000 employees. Over half of these are temporarily engaged by the Public Works Department under Colonial Development and Welfare grants. When these come to an end, it is feared the unemployment rate will rise to about 14 per cent (Seychelles Report 1961–62, p. 26). Other major occupations pursued by between 300 and 1,000 each are domestic service, fishing, and crafts, notably carpentry. In all of these supply far exceeds demand. Retail trade is largely in the hands of Indian and Chinese shopkeepers. Economically the vast majority of Seychellois depend on a very few employers and enjoy minimal job security. Opportunities for economic advancement are few and depend chiefly on networks of personal influence.

The Seychelles is a Crown Colony administered by a Governor with the advice of a legislative and an executive council both with official majorities. Political control is basically in the hands of a small number of appointed officers most of whom are non-Seychellois on limited periods of service in the Colony. Programmes of economic development have tended to enlarge the sphere of government. Local government is poorly developed. There are no village councils or similar bodies. Several district councils have been formed, but they are chiefly channels for passing orders and funds from the central government downwards rather than funnelling information or the desires of the inhabitants upwards (see Benedict, 1963).

Culturally, except for the small numbers of Indians, Chinese, and Britons, the Seychelles is homogeneous. The inhabitants speak Creole, a French patois, though many also know French and English; 90·7 per cent of the population is Roman Catholic (Webb, *Population Census*, p. 117), and in general they share the same values and customs. This contrasts strongly with the neighbouring island of Mauritius, which is a plural society with each section having its own language, customs, religion, and values (see Benedict, 1961).

The Domestic Group

A domestic group consists of the inhabitants of a household. They share a common roof and common domestic arrangements including the provision and consumption of food and a system of division of labour (cf. Fortes, 1962, p. 8). The members of the domestic group are usually related to each other by consanguineal or affinal ties, but friends, servants, or boarders may be members. The term 'domestic group' is preferred to 'family' because members of a domestic group may or may not constitute a family. In a household census which I took in the Seychelles only 18 per cent of urban domestic groups and 29 per cent of rural domestic groups consisted of nuclear families. In 26·1 per cent of urban domestic groups and

30·4 per cent of rural domestic groups there were no cohabiting partners (Benedict, 1966, p. 27).

The relationships which obtain among most members of the domestic group are highly particularistic. The standards for judging the performance of their roles by domestic group members depend on who they are more than on what they do.

Such ties are important in considering the various factors relating to the equality of the sexes. Analytically we must separate out the various strands or components of roles between domestic group members. Thus we may examine the economic aspects of the roles of husband and wife or their respective rights over children, but in fact these are embedded in a matrix of other relationships constituting the roles of husband and wife. These roles are not functionally specific, though analysing their economic or socializing aspects may make them seem so.

The ideal domestic group in the Seychelles is composed of a nuclear family. The spouses have been married in church. The husband is the breadwinner. He owns the house. The wife stays at home looking after the children and running the household. This ideal of marriage, family, and household in the Seychelles is sanctioned by custom, religion, and the law, but it is by no means the universal pattern. In 1959, 43 per cent of children born in the Seychelles were illegitimate and only 68·9 per cent of women had ever been married by the end of their reproductive period, i.e. 45 to 49. *De facto* unions which have neither legal nor religious sanctions are known in the Seychelles as living *en ménage*. It is clear that there is considerable deviation from the ideal. What forms do these deviations take? How do they affect the rights that husbands, wives, and children have in one another? To answer these questions at least three sets of factors are involved: class, status, and factors having to do with the developmental cycle of the domestic group itself.

Class

In its economic sense there are two major classes in the Seychelles: a small proprietor and business class who control most of the economic resources of the islands and a very large labouring class living at a low economic level. Between them is emerging a small and as yet ill-defined class of white collar workers, civil servants, and small proprietors. The landowners and upper civil servants exhibit some class consciousness. They tend to associate only with one another or with British civil servants from overseas, and exhibit the characteristics of what Weber (1946, pp. 186–8) terms a status group.

The planters and proprietors are endogamous as to class. Men may take mistresses or have casual sexual relations with lower class women, but they do not marry them. Though party politics were not well developed in the Seychelles in 1960, many of this class supported a property-owners' party. Among white collar workers and labourers there was little class consciousness in 1960, but a nationalist labourers' party claiming nearly 2,000 members has been formed since (*Time*, 10 September 1965, p. 31). The Seychelles is not striking for class consciousness but for the acute consciousness of the relative status of individuals.

Status

Status is measured on two scales of prestige, an ascribed scale of skin colour and family pedigree and an achieved scale of material possessions, behaviour, occupation, and public expenditure.

A light skin is prestigeful. In some contexts it can be an economic advantage. A light skinned person is more apt to be engaged in a managerial capacity than a dark skinned person. A light skinned person has opportunities for emigration (e.g. to Australia) which are denied to a dark skinned person. A light skinned man will not marry a girl darker than him except in very exceptional circumstances (e.g. if the girl is wealthy or has a high prestige occupation such as teacher), though light skinned men will have sexual relations with dark skinned girls and may even set up *en ménage* with them. Light skin is recognized as evidence of social superiority. In one settlement there was a very light skinned man who was notorious as a drunkard, scoundrel, and wifebeater. He was penniless and usually unemployed, yet he was able to get a series of darker skinned women to live with him. Neighbours made such comments as 'She wouldn't put up with such treatment if he were a black man. She stays with him because he is white.' Dark skinned men who are relatively wealthy or have high status jobs often attempt to marry light skinned girls. In the matter of equality between the sexes, the partner with the lighter skin is considered to have some claims to innate superiority and will incur less blame in the public eye for leaving a dark skinned partner.

Pedigree is closely allied to colour. The ability to trace one's ancestry back to France or failing this to French colonists from Mauritius or Réunion gives a certain amount of social prestige, though it can hardly override a very dark skin. African ancestry is never mentioned. Light skinned people deny common ancestry with dark skinned people bearing the same surname, often claiming that an estate owner may have permitted his slaves to use his name or that the slaves, lacking knowledge of their own names, appropriated the name of their master. Illegitimate children of white fathers, though they bear their mother's surname, may proudly claim descent from their genitor's family. A dark skinned person who cannot claim to be white can at least claim descent from European ancestors. Ancestry can be used by a man or woman to claim superior prestige over his partner, but it is not as strong an argument as colour.

Occupation is an important index of status. Women school-teachers from poor families often remain unmarried because they cannot find a spouse of high enough status. On the other hand, men with clerical, managerial, or professional jobs can easily find a wife. At the lowest levels there is not much distinction in prestige between estate labourer, fisherman, artisan, or government labourer, though the latter job is preferred because the pay is higher. Women can also be labourers though they are paid at a lower rate. In households in which both partners are working there is a good deal of equality.

Where the woman has a higher occupational status, or is earning more money than her spouse, she is in a strong position. In one case the unemployed husband of a teacher was suspected by her of flirting with another woman. In the row that ensued she was able to bring him back into line. He was dependent on her not only for the usual domestic offices performed by a wife, but for cash income and social standing. To have a teacher as a wife is prestigeful and the man would lose prestige if he ran off with another woman. In higher income groups women do not work and are much more dependent on their husband's wage. Thus occupation is important in determining the relative statuses of a couple living together. In general the higher the occupational status of the man the more dependent is the woman.

The ownership of land confers prestige though in fact it may yield very little wealth. It shows that an individual has risen above the common herd of the landless and so has symbolic importance. Of the 3,077 holdings of land in the Seychelles 1,934 or 62.9 per cent were under two acres, the average size of these small holdings being 0.35 acre (Webb, *Agricultural Census*, p. 25). Many property owners are women. In a sociological census taken in an urban area and a rural settlement I found that overall there were an equal number of male and female proprietors of small properties, there being two males and one female in the urban area and twelve males and thirteen females in the rural settlement.

Women usually acquire land through inheritance. French community property laws were dissolved in 1948 (Lane, 1953, Title XV,

Cap. 102) and married women may hold, acquire, and dispose of property as though they were single. Disputes as to ownership of property between husband and wife are decided by the Chief Justice in a summary way. A surviving spouse is entitled to maintenance from the estate of the deceased spouse and this claim takes precedence over the claims of heirs. Legitimate children inherit equal shares of their parents' property. Acknowledged natural children are entitled to the whole of the succession of their deceased mother provided she has left no legitimate descendants or ascendants. In a similar way, acknowledged natural children are entitled to the whole of their father's property, if there are no legitimate descendants, ascendants, brothers, sisters, or legitimate descendants of such brothers or sisters (Lane, 1953, Title XV, Cap. 103, paras. 3, 4, 8). A father is liable to maintain an acknowledged natural child (*ibid.*, Cap. 104) and in 1964 an ordinance (No. 10 of 1964) was passed providing for the maintenance of unacknowledged illegitimate children, provided a woman can prove to the satisfaction of the court that a given man was the father of her child.

Some women have purchased property with money earned in domestic service in Kenya or Bahrein. Occasionally an employer will deed or will land to a female employee of long standing, particularly if she has had children by him. A woman with land may take a husband or ménager, but does not usually give him control of her property. She is in a strong position, particularly if she has grown children or siblings to aid her and can force an unwanted mate to leave. Small holdings are usually managed by women even when they do not hold the title. The man of the domestic group must go out to work. He usually cannot earn enough from his land to maintain himself, but a woman can earn small sums raising vegetables, pigs, or chickens or by selling palm toddy. Regardless of title, people refer to land as belonging to Madame So-and-so, indicating the pivotal position of women in the domestic sphere. Without a woman to assist him a man cannot manage a small property. He cannot afford to hire labour and the property does not yield enough for him to make his living from it. The land can only be made productive through the use of unpaid family labour. Women managing small properties have considerable rights in their products, making them less dependent on the man in the domestic group.

The currency of prestige

For most domestic groups in the Seychelles, the adult men provide the money and it is through spending money and giving money that men acquire prestige. The demands on a man for money are many. He should support the woman with whom he lives. Indeed, if he does not she is very likely to leave him. When my wife asked a woman whether her husband was faithful to her, she replied, 'I think he gives me all his money, but I can't be sure.' A man should give money to his mother. He should give money to other women by whom he has had children. He should stand his companions drinks and lend them money. If he does not do this, he may find himself unable to borrow in time of need. Lavish and generous spending wins high prestige. At a public auction of livestock prices paid were consistently higher than the buyers could hope to realize from their purchases. The prestige of public spending outweighed the question of profit and loss. At a local fish sale in a rural settlement men shouted loudly that they would buy whole fish when they could only afford and in fact only did buy small pieces (see Benedict, 1966, pp. 57f.). Men often boast about how much money they give to their wives or former mistresses. They give money or food to friends and relatives with elaborate carelessness. Often men in the lowest income groups fail to live up to the many expectations on them to provide money. Their meagre earnings are spent on drink. As men get older and lose their earning power, they become dependent on wives or daughters or may eke out a precarious existence making baskets and living alone in a hovel.

For women the material objects of prestige are clothes and furniture. Women will make great sacrifices, cutting down on food, in order to have fine clean clothes to wear on public occasions. The chief occasions for fine dress are Church festivals, Sunday mass, weddings, and funerals. Men too like to be well dressed on such occasions. To be poorly or slovenly dressed on any public occasion is very shaming. Women refuse to send their children to school if they cannot afford to dress them properly. In households where women are earning they buy their own clothes and those of the children from their own wages, depending on the husband or ménager for food. In households where the women do not work they depend on their men for money for clothes. A length of dress material is a very acceptable present for a man to give his mistress.

Furniture is not only an item of prestige but may be looked on as a kind of investment which may be given or left to children. Women usually acquire furniture from men. Carpentry and cabinet-making are among the most widely practised skills in the Seychelles. A man will often present his wife, ménagère, or mother with a piece of furniture to demonstrate his generosity and show that he is pleased with her. The most usual items presented are chairs, which are relatively inexpensive, and one sometimes finds a house so crammed with chairs that there is hardly room to sit down. Women are proud of the amount and quality of their furniture and the best pieces will be kept in a salon (if there is one) which is rarely used. On marriage the bridegroom and his family often give furniture as their main contribution to the new household. A woman setting up en ménage is less apt to receive gifts of furniture, but if the union persists her ménager and mother may give her some pieces. As a woman gets older she is apt to acquire more furniture. If she has her own house she fills it with furniture. If she leaves her man she takes her furniture with her. A woman is proud of the status her furniture gives her. It is a symbol of her achievement. She can use it to help her children, particularly her daughters. Before she dies, even if she makes no will, she indicates exactly who is to get each piece.

In determining the degree of equality between the sexes in any domestic group these status symbols play a part. Where skin colour and pedigree differ markedly between partners, the advantage lies with the partner with the lighter skin and the more distinguished ancestors, but these considerations do not override all others. Occupation is important. A man with a high status occupation is more likely to have a non-working wife who is consequently more dependent upon him, both for material necessities and for her social standing. She gains her status as the wife of a teacher or a planter or a government clerk. Where both partners work at similar occupations, such as agricultural labour, occupation in itself does not differentiate them in a significant manner. Economically a man's chief function is to provide cash for the domestic group. The more successfully he does this the more likely the woman is to be dependent on him and the more prestige he wins from other members of the community. In so far as the woman provides cash, it lessens her dependence on her partner. If she owns the land on which they live this gives her greater independence. A man's prestige depends on his earnings and the generosity with which he dispenses them. A woman's prestige depends on being well dressed on public occasions and on having a stock of furniture. There is more apt to be an equality of rights and duties in domestic groups of the lowest economic class than among those of higher income groups. But equality of the partners in a domestic group is not entirely a matter of economic considerations, status symbol, and prestige; it also depends on the nature and cycle of the domestic group itself.

Courtship

Ideally a girl should be a virgin when she marries. At all levels of Seychelles society there is a good deal of talk about a girl's reputation and this invariably means her reputation for chastity. In the middle and upper economic classes girls are very carefully chaperoned. At dances boys and girls are seated or cluster on opposite sides of the room. A boy formally asks a girl for a dance at the end of which he returns her to the group of girls. Boys and girls leave separately at the end of the dance.

This pattern persists among the poorer classes not only on such formal occasions as wedding receptions, but also at the dances or 'bals' which are held in rural settlements. Behaviour at the bal is circumspect. The sexes arrive separately and remain apart when not actually dancing. Men do not dance with the same partners throughout the evening, nor do partners dance in close embrace. Drink is carefully rationed: only a single glass to each male dancer between sets of music. Girls receive only lemonade, though at midnight they may be given a single glass of bacca (fermented sugar cane juice). Inexpensive snacks such as bread and peanuts are served. Though dancing becomes more spirited as the evening progresses, it becomes more individualistic. Men who become obstreperous through drink are ejected by the organizers. The dances are French country-style (camptolet) dancing, the schottische, polka, waltz, and foxtrot.

The segregation of the sexes and their formal behaviour towards each other which is so marked a feature of public occasions, such as the dance, is backed up by the church and by sexual segregation in the schools which are largely run by the church.

Parents of all social and economic levels in the Seychelles are eager to preserve the reputation of their daughters. In the wealthier domestic groups daughters can be carefully supervised and efforts are made to ensure that they do not associate, unsupervised, with boys. Girls try to evade parental control, but they are aware that they must keep a reputation for chastity and propriety if they are to marry well. Among the clerical and professional classes, girls sometimes have to work as teachers, nurses, or secretaries. The schools are very strict about the morals of their teachers. A girl who gets a reputation for promiscuity loses her job. In the course of their work girls of this class meet men, but they should not go out with them unaccompanied.

In the poorest domestic groups there is still the effort to preserve a girl's reputation, but a number of difficulties stand in the way. Many girls have to work as domestics or labourers where they are

subject to the advances of employers or managers. To refuse is to
risk losing the job. To accept may mean additional benefits in the
form of gifts of goods or money or possibly being set up as a mistress.
Furthermore, it is difficult for poor girls to marry. Weddings are
expensive, and the families of such girls often cannot afford to
finance a wedding even if a suitable husband can be found. Among
the poorest domestic groups parents, however much they would like
to, cannot afford to keep a girl at home chaperoned. They have less
time to arrange a marriage and, of course, scarcer means. Girls
themselves appreciate this situation. Girls of this class are much more
apt to lose their reputation.

Engagement

Engagements are long in the Seychelles. Ideally they are formal
arrangements between the families of the intending spouses. Sometimes a boy may write directly to the mother of a girl asking for her
hand, but the proper procedure is, after the boy and girl have
reached an understanding, for the boy's parents to approach the
girl's parents and formally request her hand. After both sets of
parents have agreed the engagement is announced. Weddings are a
major occasion for the accumulation of prestige. They are very expensive. The two sets of parents usually share expenses and this is a
rich source of disputes. Engagements may last from six months to
three years, while all the financial and social details are being worked
out. During this period the betrothed couple may go out together,
but ideally they should still be under some supervision. Poorer
domestic groups tend to have longer engagements, as time is needed to
amass sufficient resources, and this means that the chances of the
engagement being broken off, or the couple setting up en ménage,
are greater.

Wedding

Weddings are elaborate in the Seychelles. The number and quality
of the guests and the quantity and quality of the food, drink, and
entertainment offered to them are important indices of the status
of the two families. In upper and middle income domestic groups the
expenses of the reception may be largely borne by the bride's family.
The groom's family provide gifts, often including the house where
the newly-weds will live. In low income domestic groups the expenses
of the reception are shared. Negotiations as to how much each side
will contribute and how many guests each will invite are protracted

and laden with disputes which may even lead to the cancellation of the wedding.

Weddings are often held after vespers in the hope that people attending the service will be attracted to the wedding as spectators. Church weddings are chiefly women's affairs. The reception is arranged by men. The relative importance of the two functions can be judged by the fact that siblings of the bride and groom and sometimes even the father of the groom do not attend the church service, being too busy preparing the reception. In addition to friends and relatives, both bride and groom attempt to get their employers or patrons to attend. Cars, taxis, and sometimes even a bus are hired to convey guests to the reception. A troop of musicians meets the wedding party in the road and accompanies them to the reception which is held in the grandest house that the contracting families can borrow or hire. At the reception formal speeches are made by the guests. These are usually set pieces memorized from books and are in French rather than Creole, the *lingua franca* which all speak normally. Guests sing songs and after each speech or song the performer says '*Hip, hip, hip*'. The guests respond, '*Hooray à sa santé.*' Prestigeful foods such as *palmiste* made from the hearts of palm trees, chicken, pork, and curry are served. There is a large wedding cake and imported wines, apéritifs, spirits, and liqueurs are served in preference to the cheaper and more readily available palm toddy (*calou*) and fermented sugar cane juice (*bacca*). Guests drink and dance until the early hours of the morning. A wedding and reception of even modest proportions cost about one year's wages for the average labourer.

Weddings and, to a lesser extent, funerals are the most important public occasions for gaining prestige. The financial outlay and public display are essential features. Without these elements a wedding has virtually no social meaning. A quiet wedding is almost a contradiction in terms. Weddings are primarily affirmations of status and prestige of the parents and only secondarily social recognition of a bond between intending spouses. Social recognition of a union without marriage is very common in the Seychelles.

Marriage and ménage

In the social relations leading up to marriage, the potential bride and groom have fairly equal rights to decide whether the marriage shall take place. Marriages are not arranged in the Seychelles as they are in many African and Asian societies, yet parental pressures operate. The desire of wealthy families to make suitable alliances with families similarly placed, and the importance and prestige of

E

the wedding itself in low income domestic groups, exert pressures on marriageable children which may force them into or out of alliances.

These factors are far less important in setting up unions which have neither religious nor legal sanctions supporting them. In the two settlements in which I worked the figures for conjugal unions were as follows:

Occupation and Type of Union among Males in two Settlements

Occupation	Urban			Rural		
	Married	en ménage	Unknown	Married	en ménage	Unknown
Managerial	4	1	0	11	1	0
White collar	15	5	0	5	0	0
Artisan	35	16	1	22	10	0
Labourer	35	35	0	59	26	0
Fisherman	5	9	0	4	2	0
Domestic	9	0	0	7	0	0
Pensioner	3	3	0	8	0	0
None	3	3	0	4	1	1
Unknown	2	0	0	0	0	0
	111	72	1	120	40	1

Occupation and Type of Union among Females in Two Settlements

Occupation	Urban			Rural		
	Married	en ménage	Unknown	Married	en ménage	Unknown
Managerial	0	0	0	0	0	0
White collar	5	1	0	2	0	0
Artisan	1	0	0	0	0	0
Labourer	14	18	0	38	18	0
Domestic	6	10	1	2	0	0
Washing and Sewing	13	8	0	14	4	1
Pensioner	2	2	0	2	0	0
None	69	32	0	62	18	0
Prostitute	0	1	0	0	0	0
Unknown	1	0	0	0	0	0
	111	72	1	120	40	1

The tables show that couples living en ménage are to be found at all economic levels, but that their incidence increases at the lower economic levels. In both rural and urban populations taken together, only about 17 per cent of males in managerial and white collar occupations are living en ménage. Among artisans about 21 per cent of males are living en ménage, but among labourers, fishermen, and domestics the percentage rises to 38 per cent. Among females there is a similar pattern. 13 per cent in the white collar occupations are living en ménage, 29 per cent of those engaged in washing and sewing on their own account, and 28 per cent of those without paid occupations; but among labourers and domestics 43 per cent of women are living en ménage.

Setting up en ménage is a characteristic of lower income groups. They are less able to accumulate funds for a marriage and the pressures operating to set up a household are harder to resist. These pressures are partly economic and partly cultural. They differ for boys and girls. A young man from a low income household must seek a job as soon as he is able, but jobs are scarce and wages are low. To marry is clearly out of the question, but he often lacks sufficient money to set up en ménage. In such a situation a boy who has formed an attachment to a girl may continue to live in his maternal household. He may give the girl gifts of money, food, or clothing and acknowledge any children she may bear, but they still live apart. There are also certain cultural patterns operating against the setting up of an early ménage. A young man is expected by his peer group to have many affairs. It is a mark of his manhood. The rather formal *bals* which have been described often end by young men having sexual relations with girls or older women after they have left the dance. It is also common for young men to have affairs with older women who may have been abandoned by their husbands or ménagers. Men are not eager to take on family responsibilities in their early youth, but there are certain social pressures which lead them to it.

As a man begins to earn more steadily he may begin to resent the contributions which he is expected to make to his mother's household. Relations with his mother's husband or ménager, particularly if the man is not his genitor, become strained. If he has been keeping steady company with a girl, it is likely that his mother will resent the relationship, not only because the boy begins to assume some financial responsibility for the girl, thus diminishing the contributions he can make to her, but because of his divided loyalties. The boy's subordinate status in the household becomes an increasing source of friction and this, coupled with the pressures brought to bear on him by the girl, particularly if she has a child, force him to attempt to set up a household of his own. A man should provide for a woman by whom he has had children and this is a value of a man's peer group as well as of the girl and her parents. Yet, even without entanglements with a girl, the pressures driving a man out of his mother's house are considerable. If he cannot find a job locally he may move to another settlement or more likely to town. Here it is difficult for him to manage on his own and he may set up en ménage with an older woman who has been deserted by her husband or ménager. In the rural settlement in which I worked the woman was older than the man in 12·5 per cent of couples living en ménage, but in the town the figure was 40·5 per cent.

The pressures on a girl from a low income domestic group to set up en ménage are also considerable. She must often go out to work as a domestic or a labourer at an early age. She has many opportunities of meeting men unchaperoned. The advances of an employer are sometimes difficult to resist. The period during which a low income domestic group can afford to keep a girl at home under supervision to ensure her good reputation is very limited. If the girl becomes pregnant she has very little chance of contracting a marriage. Having a baby in her mother's house does not give a girl fully adult status. An indication of this is that such a child will often call his mother's mother 'maman' and his mother by her Christian name.[1] A girl in such a position has strong incentives to move out of her mother's house and will try to get the father of the child or another man to set up en ménage with her.

A marriage involves large numbers of people. As we have seen, it is a large public display. Both the boy's and the girl's kin are involved. Setting up en ménage, however, only involves the contracting parties.[2] This often means that the couple setting up en ménage cannot rely on the support of their kinsmen. The relationship is a delicately balanced one which depends on the continuing agreement of the two parties to remain together. If they break up there are unlikely to be pressures from kinsmen attempting to bring them back together, nor are there any legal sanctions supporting the union. Do they then have equal rights in the union? Again this depends on their stage in the developmental cycle and on economic factors. A couple recently set up en ménage with no children and both working are very evenly balanced as to rights. One or the other may leave with impunity. A woman with small children, however, is in a much more dependent

1. A similar phenomenon has been reported by Smith (1956, p. 143) in British Guiana.
2. This point was recognized by van Gennep: '. . . except in the case of a "common-law marriage" there are always groups of various kinds and sizes which are interested in the union of two individuals' (1960, p. 118).

position. She cannot easily go out to work unless she can get her mother or a relative or neighbour to look after her children. She cannot go off with another man unless he is willing to take her children. It is during these early childbearing years that a woman is most dependent on her husband or ménager to provide for her. It is also when she is youngest and most sexually attractive. As the children grow a woman's potentiality for independence increases. An older sibling may look after young children while she works. Later the children themselves begin to earn and contribute to the household expenses, and the woman becomes more independent of her husband or ménager.

There is often a delicate balance of expectations between couples living en ménage. The woman dominates the domestic sphere. She must prepare the food, make the clothes, and do the housework for all members of the domestic group. In this she may be assisted by children, especially girls. The man provides the money. With his daily earnings he may buy the food and bring it home, but we have seen there are other demands on his wage. He may give it to his mother, a comrade, or another woman or he may spend it on drink for himself. If he returns home late and without food, his ménagère may not make a fuss, hoping for improvement on the morrow. On the other hand, she may fight with him. This may lessen the chances of his returning the next day. He may begin to take up with another woman or return to his mother's household. A woman fighting with a man can be clearly heard by the neighbours. It is shaming for the man. She may refuse to cook for him, which is very shaming. She may begin to seek the favours of another man. In so far as they wish to preserve the union, couples living en ménage must treat each other carefully. Marriage often changes these expectations. The man feels the woman must remain bound to him no matter what his behaviour. The woman feels she need not be pleasant, that her husband is bound to support her in any case. Thus what may have been a successful ménage for many years breaks up on marriage. Marriage carries with it the implication of a much more dependent status of the woman. A ménage carries with it the implication that either party is much more free to leave the domestic group.

Conclusions

Let us now return to the two questions raised by Professor Firth's footnote. What is the relationship of female chastity to material wealth? How is this relationship correlated with the relative status of men and women and the structure of family life?

We have found in the Seychelles that pre-marital chastity among women is an ideal throughout the society, but that it is in fact related to economic class. The higher the income group the more likely it is that pre-marital chastity will be observed. The attitude of the Line islanders would certainly not apply to upper income groups in the Seychelles. In the lower income groups the situation differs. Here marriage itself is rarer. Pre-marital chastity, though still an ideal, is not expected. A woman may grant sexual favours in the expectation of material rewards in the form of support or gifts. A woman who grants such favours without receiving any reward is considered at best foolish and at worst licentious. In the Seychelles pre-marital chastity clearly has a value, but it is a value the lower income groups usually cannot afford. If we change our focus slightly from pre-marital chastity to post-marital fidelity among women, a similar pattern prevails. The ideal throughout Seychelles society is that a woman should remain faithful to her man. In upper income domestic groups there should be no suspicion of an adulterous affair by a woman. If affairs do occur, they must be clandestine. Among lower income domestic groups, women should also remain faithful. A persistent open affair with another man is a way of dissolving one union and beginning another. This course of action is not open to upper income women. The church does not permit divorce and the state makes it extremely difficult and costly. Women from lower income domestic groups would be considered foolish to leave one man to live with another if there were not some economic and social advantages in doing so. The Line islanders' attitude prevails.

These attitudes to female chastity and fidelity are linked with equality of the sexes. Taking upper and lower income domestic groups as polar types, we can examine various sets of rights and duties and statuses:-

(1) *Sexual rights.* In upper income groups a man is considered to have exclusive sexual rights in his wife. Transgressions are serious moral and social offences, the blame attaching entirely to the adulterous woman. Ideally a woman should also have exclusive sexual rights in her husband, but this is not really expected. Men from upper income groups often have casual affairs or maintain mistresses from the lower income groups. The fact is generally known and widely accepted. It also seems to be common in ex-slave societies in the Caribbean (cf. Smith, 1963, p. 37). Thus in the higher income domestic groups there is considerable inequality between men and wo-

men in sexual rights. The same ideals prevail in lower income groups, but the actualities differ considerably. A man is considered to have exclusive sexual rights in the woman with whom he is living. If she begins to have an open affair with another man, her husband or ménager can throw her out. He has been wronged in the public eye, yet if he is known to have treated his woman cruelly or stingily, little blame will attach to her leaving, especially if her new lover is willing to support her and her children. If the couple are living en ménage rather than in legal wedlock, even less blame is attached to the breakup of the union. The degree of infidelity which a woman will tolerate in her man depends largely on his performance in supporting her. If he continues to support her, she may overlook his affairs with other women, or even his taking another mistress. If he does not, she will leave him or, if she owns the house, force him to leave. Thus in lower income groups there is a good deal more equality in sexual rights than in upper income groups. Lower class women have more socially accepted alternatives than do upper class women.

(2) *Rights in immovable property.* Control of land is an important right. Among upper income planters it is the most important economic resource. Normally the land is controlled by the man, but a woman who has inherited considerable land often arranges in her marriage contract to retain control of it. Such women are in a strong position in their domestic groups. Some manage their own properties or hire a manager to do it for them. In other domestic groups the husband will manage the property. Where the woman controls the land it gives her economic equality or even superiority over her spouse. As we are talking about domestic group role relationships which are functionally diffuse, superiority or inferiority in one set of rights carries over into others. A woman who controls the land can make more demands upon her husband's conduct than one who does not. In lower income groups the situation is similar. Where the woman owns the land she has power over her man. He lives on it by her sufferance. In higher income groups labour can be hired to work the land. In lower income groups, however, the land can rarely provide subsistence. In order to operate it at all a man must have unpaid labour, and this is nearly always the labour of a wife or ménagère and her children. Thus rights in land constitute a variable in reckoning the degree of equality between the sexes in any domestic group. In

higher income groups where women own land it gives them power over their husbands. In lower income groups land requires female labour no matter who owns it, but a female owner acquires power and prestige by virtue of her rights in land.

(3) *Rights in movable property*. Most movable property is acquired by women through inheritance or as gifts from men. In upper income groups movable property is not an important part of the economic resources of the domestic group. A woman's jewels are her own. She may own china or furniture, but these possessions are not significant in calculating her rights vis-à-vis her husband except that, in so far as she receives them from him, they are symbolic of her dependence on him. By accepting them she accepts obligations to her husband. These considerations hold too in lower income groups, but here possessions are a more significant part of the total economic resources. In all groups possessions are an index of prestige. In lower income groups, possessions, notably furniture, are important assets for women. Yet, because they are less valuable, rights in movable property are not as significant in differentiating rights between a man and woman in a domestic group as are rights in land and income.

(4) *Rights in income*. I have stressed that a man's chief duty is to provide a cash income for the domestic group or groups of which he is a member. (He may be a member of more than one, e.g. his wife's, his mistress's, his mother's.) The women and children of these groups have the right to expect maintenance. This right is backed by law. In so far as a man successfully fulfils this role, he controls expenditure and has considerable rights over his wife, mistress, or ménagère. In so far as a woman has her own income, however, the power position between her and her man is much more equal. If there is no legal marriage, it is relatively easy for the domestic group to break up. If a man cannot fulfil his obligations to maintain his wife or ménagère or mistress, he has very few rights over her.

(5) *Rights to domestic labour*. A man has rights to the domestic labour of his wife or ménagère. She must cook the meals, make the clothes, clean and maintain the house (except for major repairs like re-roofing which are a man's job), care for the children, and work the property if there is one. A woman who fails in these duties has few rights over her man. An accepted way of precipitating a domestic crisis is the refusal by a

woman to cook her man's meals. Another is to act the role of '*domineur*'.[1] This means she yells at and even strikes her man. She attempts to run him. This behaviour is generally condemned by both men and women, but failure of a man to fulfil his obligations, particularly in providing food, will lead a woman to act this role. It is very shaming for a man, attracting public attention to his failure. It calls his very masculinity into question.

(6) *Obligations to children.* A man has a duty to maintain his children. He should help maintain even those children he has had by women outside his own domestic group. Often he is unable to do this. A wealthy man can, of course, meet these obligations more easily. Later on he may help such children get jobs. Children nearly always remain with their mother when a domestic group breaks up. In lower income groups the main *de facto* responsibility for the children lies with their mother. It is recognized that a woman and her children should not be separated. When a man takes a mistress or ménagère, he must take her small children with her. '*Si ou aste boeuf, bizin aste avec les cornes*' (if you buy a cow, you must buy it with its horns) is a Creole expression meaning if you take a woman you must take her children with her. In socializing children men take far less responsibility than women. Children of unmarried parents usually take their mother's surname and are closer to their matrilateral than to their patrilateral relatives. If a woman cannot care for a child, it is to her mother or her sister that the child is usually sent. Financially too it is a woman's first duty to support her children rather than her spouse. Thus lower income group women have more obligations to children than men.

(7) *The relative status of the sexes and the structure of family life.* We have seen that there is a difference in the relative status of men and women in upper and lower income domestic groups. Are we justified in saying that there are two different structures of family life in the Seychelles? If we define structure in terms of roles played by individuals and if we define roles in terms of expectations, rights, and duties, I think there is some justification for postulating two types of family structure. They are, of course, polar types or models and the relationships in many actual domestic groups in the Seychelles

1. The masculine form is used in Creole, perhaps indicating the woman is playing a masculine role.

will be seen to fall between them or to take some features from each type. Nevertheless the distinction would appear to be analytically useful. In the low income type there is a good deal of equality between the sexes. The economic responsibilities are fairly evenly matched (though they vary in the course of the developmental cycle of the group) and there is a balanced commitment to the union which either party may break. In the upper income group the relationship is much less equal. Here the woman is dependent on the man both economically and for her social position. The woman cannot easily leave her husband.

Perhaps the difference in family structure is best shown by those couples living en ménage who later are persuaded to marry (usually by the local priest). Once married their expectations of each other's roles change. The more or less egalitarian balance which maintained the ménage relationship may be destroyed at a stroke. The wife believes she has a right to maintenance. Each believes the other does not have the right to leave. Where these radical changes in expectations occur the union usually breaks up. I do not wish to place too much emphasis on the ménage relationship. Married couples in the low income group also develop a similar kind of egalitarian relationship and are also apt to break up if one or the other partner attempts to assert rights which will not be granted by the other, but the ménage relationship is a useful model for distinguishing this type of family structure from that which exists in upper income groups.

The Abelam Artist

ANTHONY FORGE

ONE of Raymond Firth's earliest articles, 'The Maori Carver', published in 1925, testifies to the early formation of that interest in art which has remained with him ever since. It is an enthusiastic piece, establishing the right of the Maori artist to be judged by his own standards and not merely as a primitive whose attempts to reach the style and vision of the Greek artist are vitiated by his dull and brutish nature. That such arguments do not have to be repeated today is due to the change in attitude which Raymond Firth has had a part in shaping. Although he would hardly have called himself a social anthropologist in those days, his approach to the problem of the artist in society was basically sociological, and that it was also ahead of its time is amply demonstrated by the several officious and carping footnotes inserted by the editors of *The Journal of the Polynesian Society*. A quotation shows his approach well and might be taken as a text for the present essay in his honour. 'It is important to know what kind of a person the carver was, what position he and his work occupied in the social scheme, and the seriousness with which both he and his labour were regarded.' This attitude, which was elaborated and refined in his later publications (Firth, 1936a, and 'The social framework of primitive art' in Firth, 1951), has always distinguished him from his contemporaries and immediate successors in social anthropology. He has always made it clear that to him art is not only a fit subject of study by social anthropologists but also a field of human activity which they ignore at their peril. Always opposed as he has been to any narrowing of the field of social anthropology, this attitude stems both from his interest in and appreciation of art, and from his view that it is in such highly regarded and deeply felt activities as art that human societies and their members express their values.

This essay is rather heavily ethnographic. I wish it could be more analytical, but despite Firth's advocacy we have still not developed the necessary concepts to be able to handle the relation of art and its creators to their society at anything above the descriptive level. How-

65

ever, it is at least now realized that such concepts are necessary, not only for plastic art, but for music, dance, architecture, and poetry as well as ritual and myth.

The truism of art history, that art reflects the society that produced it, is usually expounded with reference to some period of history in which known artists expressed their view of their culture and times in terms of the acceptance or rejection, and subsequent modification, of the art of the period immediately before their own. The artist is envisaged, as is the poet or musician, as expressing himself and his times in two main ways: first, by developing and perfecting forms and techniques used by his predecessors; second, by expressing in his art different conceptions and values, either by modification of the available styles and forms, or by the introduction of new ones. In short, the artist is seen as an individual receptive to his social environment and capable of mirroring his view of it in his art. The artist also codifies change; he starts with the conception of beauty common to the society of his childhood, and if he is great, he leaves the society with a modified conception of beauty, with new standards —a changed aesthetic. This view of the artist in his social setting presupposes change both in the society and the art; not just actual change, but also a conception of change, frequently, but not always, of progress. What the artist really expresses is not the values of his culture in any direct way, but the change in those values. A study of the art can therefore tell us nothing about the artist or even his values unless we also know something of the society and culture in which he operated, as the reflections of aestheticians on prehistoric and ethnographic art have frequently demonstrated. Just as it is impossible to have history without some concept of change, so art history and its techniques, being concerned primarily with change, cannot be used in any simple way on the sort of material presented by New Guinea societies. These societies have no concept of history or indeed of change, although since the advent of various European administrations they have become aware of the effects of change. In the view of members of these societies, they had always been the same since they came into existence and should ideally remain the same for ever. Similarly, the art of these societies had magico-religious value for them precisely because it re-created the art of the ancestors; its whole social function consisted in being unchanging. What then becomes of the artist as the super-sensitive receiver and distiller of the essence of his culture and times? Does he become merely a craftsman skilfully reproducing traditional objects in the traditional style to satisfy social demands whose springs are in concepts of magico-religious efficiency rather than any ideal of beauty? Someone must have created the art, and to judge from the favour many, though by no means all, of the highly prized objects have found with European artists and critics, the creator or creators were artists rather that craftsmen.

I shall not be able to give final answers to the problems outlined above, but hope at least to clarify some of them. In this essay I shall be examining the artist in his society with reference to the Abelam tribe of New Guinea.[1] The Abelam number about 30,000 and live in the southern foothills of the Prince Alexander mountains to the north of the Sepik River. They live in large villages from 300 to 800 in population, and have a vigorous art. They also distinguished for a cult of long yams; single yams of up to twelve feet long have been recorded.

The context of Abelam art

As in most New Guinea societies, all art among the Abelam is basically cult art and can only be displayed in the context of the ceremonials of the tambaran cult.[2] Decorative art, of course, exists, but its *motifs* are entirely drawn from the art of the tambaran cult; and it carries with it overtones of status from that cult. Half coconut shells, polished black and beautifully engraved with designs filled with white, are among the finest small objects produced by the Abelam; they are used for drinking soup, but may be carried only by big-men or men fully initiated in the tambaran cult and successful in the yam cult; young men can and do inherit them but cannot use them until they have the full ceremonial status of organizers of ceremonies. Similarly the engraved pottery bowls, holding anything from one to four gallons of white soup, made by women but decorated by men, can be used for serving soup only when ceremonial exchanges are taking place. Such examples could be multiplied to cover the whole field of decorative art, showing that not only is it stylistically derived from the cult art, but that the use and display of decorated objects are limited, by virtue of their decoration, to prescribed contexts and statuses also stemming from the cult. There are therefore

1. I am grateful to the Emslie Horniman Scholarship Fund of the Royal Anthropological Institute and to the Bollingen Foundation, New York, for financing two trips to the Abelam, in 1958–9 and 1962–3 respectively. For a general description of Abelam society see Kaberry, 1941 and 1966.
2. The Pidgin English (Neo-Melanesian) words tambaran and big-man have become part of anthropological terminology, so I use them here without italics. Tambaran corresponds to the Abelam word *maira*, while *nemandu* is exactly translated as big-man.

no artists who produce decorated objects who are not also cult artists, and it is in the context of the cult that they acquire and perfect their skills. There is one exception to this statement: the women who make netted string bags (*wut*) using red, yellow, white, and a sort of dark purple string, in various excellent designs. The use of the bags by the men is determined by their ceremonial status, one design being reserved for fully initiated men, another for those who have only one ceremony to go, and so on. The small bags used by young men gradually increase in size with the age and status of their users. The production of the bags, however, is regarded simply as a skill which a woman learns from her mother or mother's or father's sister, and the ability to produce any design, although highly prized, is no indicator of status.

The tambaran cult shares its basic features with such cults throughout New Guinea. In essence it is a series of ceremonies at each of which the initiates are shown art objects of one sort or another and are told that these are the sacred spirits, tambaran. At the next ceremony they are told that the last one was just pretence but that this time they are going to see the real tambaran, and so on until the last of the ceremonies when they are in fact shown the most sacred objects; and as fully initiated men they may go through the cycle again, this time as stagers of the ceremonies and themselves initiators. Each ceremony is performed by one half of a dual organization, called *ara*, who initiate the sons of their exchange partners in the other *ara*; the initiators are fed by their partners while they prepare the ceremony, and after the initiation are presented with pigs. *Ara* perform ceremonies alternately: one will perform ceremonies 1, 3, 5, and 7, the other 2, 4, 6, and 8, going on then to 1, 3, 5, and 7, so that two full cycles have to be performed before an individual has been initiated into all the eight ceremonies.

All ceremonial activity is regarded as balanced exchange between *ara* and the individual partners who compose them. There is three-way reciprocity with increasing exactness of return at each level. First the food and the live pig are regarded as a return for ceremonial services in preparing the ceremony, acting as initiators, and providing decorations for the initiate (the son of the donor). A man will reproach his partner if the decorations are not up to standard, asking whether he has been eating all the food provided just to produce this. Second, the next ceremony of the cycle will be performed by the other *ara* and the donor will now be recipient. Rough equivalence is expected in size of pig between each pair of ceremonies, 1 and 2, 3 and 4, etc.; the scale increases until 7 and 8, which may require three months each to prepare, a very large drain on the resources of the *ara* responsible for feeding the initiators, and demanding the most enormous pigs for presentation at the end. The third and final form of reciprocity, at which exact equivalence in the girth of the pig presented is essential, comes with the next cycle, when the *ara* who initiated at ceremony 1 last time are now paying for their sons to be initiated into the same ceremony. The lapse of time involved in the completion of a cycle can never have been less than ten years, and is nowadays, and probably always was, considerably longer. Although this is not the place for an analysis of the social structure, it is worth noting that these inescapable reciprocal obligations, stretching over the decades covered by two full cycles, are a potent factor in maintaining the stability of the component groups of the ceremonial organization, since to default imperils the ceremony and exposes the culprit to sanctions from the whole village and not just from his own clan or ceremonial partner.

The preparation of tambaran ceremonies provides the context in which all Abelam artists work, and the ceremonies themselves the only opportunity for them to display their work to any large group of people. It is also during the preparations that the training, if it can be called that, of future artists takes place. All the ceremonies have as central features the display of some series of objects which stand for the *nggwalndu*, that is, the major clan spirits. The earliest of the sequence are said to be very simple, but I have never seen either of the first two in any part of the Abelam area, and it would seem that they have been dropped from the repertoire, at least since the war. To go by the descriptions of older informants, the tambaran consisted of patterns on the floor of the ceremonial house made with the four earth paints (red, yellow, white, and black) with the addition of flowers, particularly the scarlet single hibiscus, and certain leaves, those with a silvery grey back being present in all tambaran ceremonies. While these patterns are the focus of the initiation and the representation of the *nggwalndu*, and give little scope for artistic expression, they are surrounded by painted panels of sago spathe which line and provide the ceiling for the initiation chamber constructed inside the ceremonial house—the painting and arrangement of which provide ample opportunity for the artists to display their skill, and which are the basis on which visitors from other villages evaluate the success of the ceremony. These paintings on the flat are sacred in that they are associated with the *nggwalndu* and the ceremonial house, whose façade is decorated with similar paintings, but the designs are not tambarans, being open and visible on the façade to women and uninitiated males. When used inside the house the designs and the panels on which they are painted are called *wut*, and referred to as the beautiful string bags of the *nggwalndu*. *Wut* has, however, many other meanings and is one of the most emotionally loaded words in Abelam. In this instance the most obvious symbolic referent is *nyan wut*—womb (*nyan* meaning child)—the initiation chamber being a small dark room built inside the large female house with its low entrance through which the initiates crawl when entering and leaving. The women are not supposed to know that *wut* is used for the painted panels which they, of course, never see in place, and I have heard artists, as they paint, laughing at the women's illusion that only they can make beautiful *wut*.[1]

Wut panels are to be found at all eight stages of initiation into the tambaran cult, but in later ceremonies the tambaran itself has a larger and more elaborate structure. There is a great deal of variation within the Abelam area in what is displayed at each stage, although there is far less variation in the names of the ceremonies, the same name being used for very different displays in different parts of the area. Much more is involved than simple wood-carving and painting on the flat in all parts of the area. For example, there is the setting up of 50 ft. poles with great masses of dry and thorny yam vines, and leaves of the spiny lawyer cane fastened on them to represent *nggwalndu* (see Plate III, Forge, 1966); bamboo roots are made into bird heads; and larger than life-size seated figures with extended arms and legs, covered with brightly painted patterned matting and stuffed with fibre, have to be constructed on armatures of wood and palm, themselves difficult to construct, with only split cane lashings to fasten the pieces together. Of such a figure all that is saved after the break-up of the display is the carved wooden head. The fact that much of the work of the artist for such ceremonies is ephemeral does not mean that the demands of the public are less, or that a high degree of both technical skill and aesthetic sense is not essential in the artist.

Each ceremony of the tambaran cycle has as its core a specified tambaran with a definite name and a prescribed form. The form is traditional and highly valued because it is believed to be that used by the ancestors and therefore the most powerful in a supernatural sense. Abelam tambaran ceremonies appear to the casual attender

1. In view of the anomalous position of *wut* as an artistic production of both sexes, it is worth noting that for a man to use the words *nyan wut* in the presence of a woman is a formidable insult, certain to result in a quarrel, and possibly leading to a hostile exchange relationship with her protector, or even to a complex village-wide ceremony of cross-sex hostility.

to be secular occasions; the emphasis is all on the magnificence of the decorations, both of the objects and of the initiators, and the desire to create an impression on the visitors. The fathers of the initiates are watchful that all should be correct, but when they do complain it is on the grounds of value for the food and pigs they are providing rather than out of concern for the proper instruction of their children. In general, the initiates, the ostensible purpose of the ceremony, get scant attention, the parts of the ceremony that concern them are often rushed, and they are hustled off and told to wait until wanted again. In most ceremonies a few initiates get lost at some stage, either because they have run away or have simply wandered off; their fathers may protest, but the rituals continue without them and they are considered fully initiated, whether they were there or not, as long as the father has fulfilled his exchange obligations. Nor is there any sort of instruction of the initiates; they are told what to do but never why to do it. There are puberty initiations which involve seclusion and a certain amount of instruction of youths, but these are usually separate from the tambaran ceremonies and the instruction is not about these ceremonies.

The initiates have to observe some minor food taboos and a period of sexual abstinence before and after the ceremony, but it is on the initiators that the burden of the ritual restrictions falls. It is only during the preparations for a ceremony that the observer becomes aware of the magico-religious elements of the whole: elements that are represented during the ceremony by a brief invocation almost drowned by the noise of the audience, or the fumbling of the bewildered initiates as they try to perform some ritual actions of which they understand nothing. The supernatural benefit of the ceremony to the community, the other communities that assist, and the individuals concerned, accrues during the long and careful preparations, and the observance of a whole series of taboos and ritual performances by the initiators, some continuing for three months before and six months after the ceremony. All the artistic and other work of preparation is performed in the name of the *nggwalndu*, and their benevolence is assured, first by the performance of ritual and the observance of taboos, and second by the skill of the artists in creating the objects to which the *nggwalndu* names are given, and the magnificence of the ancillary *wut* and other decorations both of humans and objects. The magico-religious benefits of the ceremony may be released during the noisy and crowded public climax, but they are created by artists and organizers working in small groups during the preceding months behind sago palm frond fences which

F

may not be passed by women, uninitiated men, or even initiated men of the other *ara*.

There is a clear necessity for artists in Abelam society. Every ritual group has to be able to draw on artists with the varied skills necessary to produce displays adequate to please the *nggwalndu* and other spirits, maintain the prestige of the group vis-à-vis other ritual groups and villages, and keep up the ceremonial exchange system within the group. The *ara* dual organization and the exchanges between partners which provide the social framework for ceremony also act to restrict the availability of artists from within the group. Each ceremony is prepared by one *ara* for the other, and members of the initiates' *ara*, whether fully initiated or not, may not take any part in the preparations, or even see the raw materials used, until all is ready and displayed at the ceremony itself. Thus any artist, no matter how skilled, may only work on alternate ceremonies within his own ritual group. It is very rare for one *ara* of any ritual group to be able to supply all the necessary talent from its own ranks, and recruitment from outside is the rule.

Peace is anyhow necessary for the performance of a ceremony, but neutrality is not enough; active co-operation is necessary between enemy villages for any of the more elaborate ceremonies. Peace ceremonies involve the exchange of men of equal age and social status between villages; each pair so exchanged become *waunindu* and call each other brother, and it is through these relationships that help is mobilized. Usually the work is sub-contracted, that is, so many painted panels of specified sizes and so much patterned matting are prepared in the enemy village and ceremonially carried in when the whole job has been done. The party bringing such contributions appears as a war party in full war paint, preceded by a screen of spearmen. They cut down young trees and lop branches off bigger ones, destroy banana plants, and generally leave a trail of licensed destruction in their wake. As they approach the ceremonial ground the spearmen advance and throw spears at warriors from the recipient group. These warriors are especially selected for their ability to dodge; no reciprocation is allowed and casualties are said to occur —certainly on the occasions when I have been present, great skill in dodging was very necessary. The rest of the party throw armfuls of rubbish and the remains of the ruined breadfruit and banana trees into the doorways of the dwelling houses. The demands of hostility are then superseded by the demands of hospitality, and the visitors are stuffed with the finest soup and yams, and laden with yams and pork to take away with them; but uneasiness prevails on both sides until the visitors are safely on the way home, having promised to attend the final ceremony and a further and major food distribution after it.

Aid from friendly and allied villages is obtained in more informal ways, but again only by the activation of specific pre-existing interpersonal relationships. Help, whether for general labour or from a specific artist, can only be solicited through established relationships, and for a big ceremony every possible link, through kinship, clanship, and the various forms of quasi-brotherhood and exchange relationship, is utilized. From the point of view of the artist, the *ara* system means that although he may be debarred from half the ceremonies of his own ritual group, if he has any sort of reputation he will be in demand for the ceremonies of others, and his rewards are not only in the immediate return for his work in food, honour, and prestige, but in the activation of remote and otherwise dormant ties with men in other villages. Wide-spreading ties are of benefit to him in everyday life and enhance his prestige within his group. In short, a successful artist is sought after both within his ritual group and outside it, and if he can speak well in debate and grow reasonably long yams for presentation to his partner, he is assured of high prestige. An artist of considerable experience will often be called a big-man, but very rarely are artists big-men in the aggressive entrepreneurial sense —they are not leaders in secular affairs and manipulators of public opinion as are the real big-men. Although I am neither competent nor possessed of adequate systematic material to make any generalizations about the temperament of Abelam artists and big-men, my entirely subjective impression from acquaintance or friendship with several dozens of each is that the artists are nearly always comparatively modest men (no Abelam could be called modest *tout court*!), not given to violent expressions of emotion; their debating style tends to be quiet and authoritative but not excessively controversial, and they can usually expect a respectful and attentive hearing; the practice of their skills gives them general prestige and particularly a reputation for understanding and knowledge of the supernatural which invests their opinions with something of wisdom. These differences have some social concomitants; successful carving and painting are believed to be incompatible with the practice of sorcery, whereas the entrepreneur big-man is usually believed to be an adept at sorcery. Furthermore, the artist's reputation may be expected to grow until he is literally too weak to hold an adze or a paint brush, while the big-man is in constant danger of being displaced by more energetic rivals from the moment he achieves his position, and is virtually certain to have lost his position by late middle age. Whether it is due to an increased sense of security or a manifestation of the artistic genius, artists, in my experience, claim fewer homicides, their adulteries are more discreet, and they quarrel less flamboyantly with their wives and clansmen. In fact, the Abelam expect their artists to be good men (*yigen ndu*), and by and large the artists conform to those expectations.

The materials and techniques of Abelam art

Although the tambaran cult demands the use of many materials for its ceremonies, an artist's reputation is based primarily on his ability as a wood-carver and painter; skill in engraving on coconut shell, bone, and pottery is also highly valued, but is considered to go with ability as a carver, while the making of basketry masks, and shell decorated mannikins from string by a sort of crochet technique, are important, but much more widely distributed, skills. The traditional equipment for carving was thoroughly neolithic: polished stone adzes, pig, dog, and flying fox teeth mounted as awls, gravers, and chisels, certain lizard skins and even a rough-surfaced leaf for smoothing. Fire was used for hollowing out drums or the backs of large figures. Softwoods were used green and the splits that tended to occur were deplored but disregarded unless they seriously distorted the figure. Current tools, although vastly improved by the use of steel, have hardly changed; the steel plane blades are mounted in exactly the same way, with the same angle between blade and handle as before. Indeed, some of the handles, beautifully carved, were originally made for stone blades and have been inherited from the preceding generation of artists. Cheap trade knives or large nails replace the teeth, but the method of mounting and use is traditional; sides of tins full of nail holes make a sort of rasp, but finishing work, now less necessary because of the superior edge of steel tools, is often done with the old materials. European adzes may be used for roughing out, but never for carving. The adze is always used with short rapid strokes towards the carver, removing only very small amounts of wood at each stroke. Modern carvers using four or five graded adzes often carve so finely that no further smoothing is needed. The backs of figures and masks are usually left rough, or hollowed out to reduce the weight, but in the case of pierced plaques and wood headdresses both sides are carved and engraved with equal care.

All Abelam carvings are painted in polychrome and engraving is often added round the eyes, penis, and navel so that the effect of the paint is enhanced by low relief.

Paint itself is highly valued by the Abelam, and almost all magic involves some form of coloured mineral substance that is classified as paint; a form of paint is also the active principle of sorcery and long yam magic. The paint used for tambaran ceremonies is not, unlike the other types, inherently powerful; it is obtained locally or in open trade, and large quantities are assembled, whereas the powerful paints are always obtained in small quantities in secrecy from distant villages. Red and yellow ochres and white and black are the only colours used, the first three being stored in the form of powders; the black, however, has to be made as required by chewing scrapings from the bottoms of cooking pots, sap from a species of shrub, and leaves from a tree, and spitting the result into a paintpot as needed. This rather unpleasant task is delegated to young assistants, and forms a part of the apprenticeship of the would-be artist.[1]

Although the paint itself is not intrinsically powerful, painting is a sacred activity, and after the paint has been used on tambaran carvings, or *wut*, or on the initiators themselves, it becomes the principal vehicle by which the benefit of the ceremony is transmitted to the participants. Carving, although carried on in seclusion either in the bush or in an enclosure near the ceremonial house, is hardly a ritual activity; some artists have their own spells to stop the unseasoned wood splitting, but carving has no communal ritual connected with it. It is only when the artist has finished the carving and put in the eyes and pubic hair with a piece of charcoal that the figure becomes an object of concern to the whole ritual group. If the charcoaling is done in the village, the log gongs are beaten to announce the arrival of the tambaran. This call also serves to warn everybody that the final phase of preparations is about to begin. Stocks of paint are checked and augmented, and the final food distribution before the ceremony takes place. The work of painting is carried out under taboos similar to and almost as stringent as those of the long yam cult; men who are going to participate in the painting bleed their penes and must abstain from all sexual contact until after the ceremony; meat and certain vegetable foods are forbidden, but they can and do eat large quantities of the yam soup and finest steamed yams provided by their exchange partners. Painting is done at great speed —usually all the workers sleep within the ceremonial enclosure and work from dawn till dusk with frequent but short breaks for food and betel nut. To begin with, any old figures that are being re-used have to be washed, and this is done in running water, the standard

1. For a fuller discussion of the manufacture and use of paints and their magical character, see Forge, 1962.

Abelam way of disposing of potentially dangerous material. Then both wood and the sago spathe *wut* have to be coated with the mud base on which the painting is done. A good deal of technical expertise is needed to get just the right sort of mud mixed to the right consistency, so that it will provide a smooth absorbent surface and adhere to the material. Sago spathe, which has a very shiny surface, is particularly difficult and is usually rubbed down before the mud is applied with stinging nettles and the bulb of a species of wild ginger (?), both substances which, in the Abelam view, bite and therefore improve the adhesion. The mud base used is black throughout the southern and eastern Abelam but grey in the north. On the grey mud, black has to be applied as a separate colour, but with the black mud those portions of the design calling for black are usually left unpainted, simply being glazed with tree sap when the painting is finished.

Abelam painting technique is extraordinary because it combines great speed with firm control by the artist. All the preparers of the ceremony join in the painting and all are found employment regardless of their lack of talent. The artist outlines the design to be painted in thin white lines. He may use lengths of split cane to help him work out the proportions of the design relative to the panel, or cane tied in rings to give him a guide for a smooth curve or circle; but he usually just starts from one edge and builds up the design as a series of elements as he works across the panel. With carved figures, artists usually start with the head, which is the most intricate part; the proportions are of course given by the form of the carving, but otherwise the techniques for figures and panels are identical. As soon as the artist has painted a few white lines for one part of the design, he instructs an assistant to paint a red or yellow line just beside it. Abelam art rarely uses a single line—multiple lines of varied colour, often further emphasized by white dots on one of the colours, are the rule. The artist now moves on to the next part of the design but keeps an eye on his first assistant. When the white lines have been satisfactorily doubled or trebled by the assistant or assistants, a second grade of assistant is employed to fill in solid areas of a single colour: subordinate grades of assistant are employed to put on the lines of white dots and glaze the black mud with tree sap or chew up black paint if the painting is on grey. Other men will be employed powdering and mixing paints and coating objects and panels with mud. An artist at work on painting usually keeps from eight to ten men more or less busy while still maintaining complete control over the design and its execution.

The paints are mixed with water in which certain very bitter species of wild lime have been steeped; again the idea of bite is produced as an explanation. The containers are usually half coconut shells, but they must be lined with a portion of wild taro leaf; wild taro is an important plant in all Abelam ceremonial—intimately connected with the ancestors, it is also a symbol of the *ara* and their rivalry, and is much used in tambaran ceremonies. Brushes are made from fibres tied to the end of a splinter of wood; small feathers or the chewed end of a fibrous twig are similarly used. For the drawing of white lines a long narrow single chicken feather, made pliable by bending, is drawn along with about two inches of the feather flat on the surface. This technique, which properly used produces a narrow line but manages to keep a reasonable charge of paint on the brush, is employed with great boldness by experienced artists and enables them to draw the sweeping curves characteristic of Abelam design with speed and accuracy.[1]

Although supplies of mud base are kept handy in case of mistakes, artists rarely need it; they refer to no model or sketch and appear to lay out the whole design in their heads. When several artists are painting together, as happens during the painting of a ceremonial house façade, they share out the available width between them and each paints his own section of the bands of identical motifs that stretch across the façade. In such a case they agree in advance on the proportions and number each is going to paint; while working they watch one another's progress to ensure that the styles are reasonably matched and that the meeting of their respective zones will be harmonious, but there is nothing like copying involved; no artist who is not known to be capable of producing the required designs in isolation would be employed on a façade.

At the conclusion of the painting stage, when the display has been

1. In the Wosera area, S.W. Abelam, a further type of brush is used, made of a single short feather, found between the tail plumes of the lesser bird of paradise, mounted in a grass stem. This will produce exceptionally fine lines, which are used mainly in polychrome cross-hatching. Bands of such cross-hatching are typically used to replace the polychrome multiple lines of the northern Abelam, and as an embellishment to certain other patterns otherwise common to both styles. The technique is laborious but aesthetically effective. Painting with these brushes cannot be delegated to the less skilled, and the number and size of the *wut* panels so painted were a sure index of prestige. Although painting with the fine line technique was visible on the façades of Wosera ceremonial houses, the means by which these results were produced was secret, the brushes themselves being regarded as a tambaran and very carefully concealed; they were called *vi* (spear) and were integrated into the spear/penis symbolic complex. Brushes elsewhere in the Abelam area are not specially regarded and are abandoned without concern.

completed, the log gongs are beaten to announce the fact to the entire area, and the artists are honoured by having the log gong calls of their totems beaten immediately after the announcement. The initiation chamber is now sealed and final arrangements are made about facepaint, feathers, head-dresses, and other decorations by the initiators, and about pigs by their exchange partners. The ceremony follows in three or four days.

The artist in society

Every initiated Abelam man aspires to be an artist in some way or other. All, in the context of the tambaran ceremonies, have a place in the process of artistic production. The amount of time they spend helping with the actual painting and carving, as opposed to the many other activities necessary in the preparation of ceremony, is largely a matter of choice. A rebuff to a middle-aged man for bad work from one of the directing artists can be expected to disillusion him with artistic activity for the rest of that ceremony, but younger men are less conscious of their dignity and stay and learn.[1] The training and selection of artists are completely informal. A youth who shows aptitude will be encouraged and allowed to perform increasingly difficult tasks under supervision until he is allowed to try the painting of a minor figure and later a small *wut* panel for himself. The artist will correct and guide him, taking over now and then when difficulties occur. A young man will have to do all stages of the painting himself, unless a friend will help him, since the various grades of assistant are attracted only to artists of established prestige. A young man with interest in becoming an artist is not restricted to his own village for tuition, nor does he attach himself to one artist as an apprentice; he can of course attend all the ceremonial preparations in his own village for which he is qualified as an initiator, and assist and learn from all the artists who are at work there. He can also, through ties of kinship or clanship, help in ceremonies at allied villages or with contracted-out work which his own or allied villages are performing for enemy villages, always provided he has been initiated into the ceremony concerned. In this way a young man may well be able to work every year on some preparations or other, and come into contact with artists from villages five or more miles apart. Since considerable variation in style and type of production is to be found

1. Since the only two essential qualifications for initiation into a ceremony are that the initiate be alive and that the father or guardian be prepared to pay, babies are frequently initiated; it follows that youths of fifteen or so appear among the initiators.

even in such short distances among the densely packed Abelam, a would-be artist will acquire a wider range and understanding of tambarans and their production than would be possible if he were confined to the set traditional to his natal village.

What has been said about training applies to the painting and constructional phases of ceremonial preparation; to obtain instruction in carving is more difficult, while a reputation as a carver is essential if an artist is to have prestige. Every Abelam male claims to be able to paint, and painting is a semi-sacred activity, the responsibility of personnel laid down by the social structure (particularly the system of initiation grades and the dual organization), performed at a prescribed time during the ceremonial preparations, preceded and closed by essential ritual, and governed by a series of taboos which apply to all the initiators whether in fact they paint or not. Carving, on the other hand, is a much more personal activity and not subject to the formal prescriptions of painting. All carving is undertaken either for the clan of the carver or as a commission from another clan or village, and except for the head board that goes across the base of the painted façade of a ceremonial house, a carving is the responsibility of a single artist. 'Commission' does not imply a contract with a stated reward. Carvings are occasionally produced in return for a stipulated payment in shell rings and pigs, but usually only under exceptional circumstances for a major undertaking such as the carving of new *nggwalndu* when the village and its immediate allies lack sufficient talent, or in the introduction of new types of figure or tambaran where what is being bought is not just the carvings but also the right to display them and to reproduce them in the future. In general, however, carvers are recruited with the promise of no more than good food, as much betel and tobacco as they need, and, of course, the prestige that will accrue to them. All the work of preparation is divided up among the initiators according to their clans and sub-clans; each sub-clan owns its own figures and assumes responsibility for them as well as its share of the *wut* panels and other decorations. Large clans have one *nggwalndu* and are split into sub-clans divided between the *ara* so that there is always a group among the initiators to care for the *nggwalndu*; clans too small to have sub-clans have to form pairs, one in each *ara*, and look after two *nggwalndu* at any ceremony. It is the responsibility of the clan to provide the necessary artistic talent, and it is through the social relationships of individual clan members that the artists are recruited. In addition to the panels or figures necessary for the particular ceremony, each clan has minor figures, often unnamed, which it also includes in the display. Their number and beauty reflect the prestige of the clan, although in many cases they are so numerous that they have to be placed on top of one another and sometimes even obscure the tambarans that are the focus of the ceremony. A big-man would usually commission at least one minor figure at an important ceremony as a mark of his prestige. Such a new carving would become the property of his exchange partner at the end of the ceremony and exchanges; the exchange partner of course would provide all the food for the artist, and reciprocation would be expected at the next suitable opportunity.

A carver selects his timber on the land of the commissioning clan, and they cut it and drag it to his studio, also doing the cutting to size and other unskilled tasks. The studio may be on the ceremonial ground. If so, it will be away from other activities; more frequently it is in a secluded patch of bush near the artist's house; it will always be in the shade to minimize the risks of splitting. The artist does not welcome company or conversation, and spends a good deal of time sitting in silence and looking at his work—this is in great contrast to normal Abelam activity, and especially to painting, where speed, movement, and noise are predominant. An assistant is usually present, but some artists carve entirely alone; anyone else, such as the curious ethnographer, is regarded as a pest. Young men who cheerfully help in the painting do not always care to spend days in silence and inactivity doing occasional minor tasks, and it is only the minority who persist and start to acquire carving skills. These gradually undertake more and more skilled parts of the work until they try some small simple object themselves, showing it to the artist at each stage and relying on him to give the finishing touches. When such a piece is accepted for inclusion in a display the apprenticeship phase is coming to an end. It is here, in the carving and the acceptance of their work for display, that the relationship between the artist and his society can be seen most clearly.

From the view of the Abelam as a whole the tambaran cult and the art associated with the long yam cult are means of creating and releasing magico-religious power and benefit; the art is essential for the performance of ceremonial, and the artist is a technician whose chief virtue is his power to reproduce exactly the powerful patterns and designs used by the ancestors. The tambarans and their benefit are traditional; to be effective they must be re-creations of the original tambarans, and, furthermore, the fathers of the initiates are anxious to ensure that the ceremony they are paying for is full and correct. These are both forces opposed to innovation, but at the same time the ceremonies are opportunities for display and the acquisition of prestige by the village, ritual group, *ara*, clan, and individuals concerned; magnificence is consciously sought; magical bundles are fastened to the newly painted figures and carvings, not connected with the ritual but solely so that the eyes of the beholders shall be dazzled by the brightness of the paint and the beauty of the workmanship. Obviously this aspect of the ceremonial allows an element of fashion into the art, but since the benefits of the ceremony extend beyond the village, innovation that has not some good magico-religious justification or precedent will be subject to wide disapproval.

The Abelam artist works within fairly narrow stylistic limits sanctioned by the total society in which he lives; any work he produces cannot be shown outside the tambaran cult, and will only be accepted for that if it satisfies the criteria of magico-religious effectiveness. A young man of Malmba village who had found a growth on a tree that resembled in general shape the human head, had taken it home and carved on it eyes, nose, and mouth and painted it in the traditional style. When he produced it during the preparations for a ceremony at which he was an initiator, the organizers refused to display it or allow it in the ceremonial house; although the painting was in correct style, the shape of the head was nothing like any of the head shapes of tambaran figures. His plea that it was the shape of a human head carried no weight and he was forced to wrap it up and hide it in his hut until he sold it to me in 1959. In 1962, at Yanuko village a mile or so to the south, two artists painting the façade of a new ceremonial house introduced a very narrow band of stylized leaf decoration similar to a traditional form but with important differences. There was some doubt about it, and some of the older men were against it; the two artists and their helpers were adamant—they were both of high reputation and no alternative artists were available; in the event this innovation was much admired in the surrounding villages. The artists were courted by people from other villages who wished to be able to call on them for houses in the future, while the ritual group whose house it was won more prestige than the other ritual group of Yanuko village whose new house, without any innovation, opened at much the same time.

A much more important example of innovation occurred at Wingei village in 1959. While a new house was under construction the organizers and the six artists involved decided to abandon the traditional style of façade-painting in favour of one that was used around Kalabu, a village about ten miles to the west; the reason for the change was the superior length of long yam grown in Kalabu. The experiment was not a great success—the bottom row of huge *nggwalndu* heads, which was the principal innovation, was badly painted, mainly because of the unaccustomed style. That Wingei changed the style of their ceremonial house façade to get longer yams, rather than change the planting season which is three months earlier in Kalabu, indicates the confidence the Abelam have in the power of art, and brings into focus the position of the artist who, if not exactly a mediator between man and the supernatural, is in contact with it and able to influence it through his skill as a carver and painter. The latter point is reinforced by the explanation offered for the bad painting: one of the artists died a week after the painting had been completed; the sorcery that killed him had obviously been working in him and prevented him and his fellows from correctly releasing the supernatural energy inherent in the design. Since this explanation was accepted even among traditional enemies of Wingei it was presumably sincerely believed and representative of Abelam thought on these matters.

The Abelam language has no vocabulary of aesthetics; there are two words of approbation used about art; one means 'good' and can be used about almost anything; the other appears to mean primarily 'correct', that is, traditional, powerful. Neither has any necessary connotations of beauty and I know of no word that has. The social demand for art is concerned with its magico-religious power. This is said to depend on the correct placing of the elements of any design with no prescription of a harmonious relation between them. Criticism of art is always in terms of correctness and effectiveness. Artists, particularly when carving, discuss among themselves such things as the shape and size of a limb and its relation to other parts of the figure, but these things are not appreciated by the non-artist. I have heard carvers reproached for holding up the beginning of the painting by fiddling about, taking a piece off here and there, when the figure already had all the necessary attributes, legs, penis, navel, arms, and head. The artists, although they lack any specific terms, do talk about such things as form and proportion, and derive considerable pleasure from carving and painting things satisfying to their aesthetic sense. They carefully examine and discuss works by other artists and rate one another as more or less talented by criteria that are primarily aesthetic. Although not capable of, or not interested in, discussing art in the same terms, most non-artists asked to rate a group of figures or paintings in order of effectiveness, both in ritual power and secular prestige, rank them in the same order as do the artists and the ethnographer. Since, with Raymond Firth, I believe in a universal human aesthetic, this is not surprising; what is important, I think, is that the skilful artist who satisfies his aesthetic sense and produces beauty is rewarded not for the beauty itself but because the beauty, although not recognized as such, is regarded by the rest as power.

Apart from conscious innovation seen as such by the whole community, there also occurs a gradual change in style which is much more difficult to document. Several villages possess very old *nggwalndu*, and at least two villages have a series of *nggwalndu* obviously made at various dates. How far back these specimens go it is difficult to say, but genealogical information about their carvers suggests that the oldest might be eighty to a hundred years old. These old figures invariably show a different style from that of the present; those in series show a consistent change in style, the development of the recent style from the antecedent one. The differences are much greater than could be attributable to a change from stone tools to steel—there are definitely changes in the way the human form has been conceived over the period. This situation leads to some difficulties, since the present style is the correct style, that is the ancestral style, yet it is different from the style in which the old *nggwalndu* were actually carved by the ancestors. When such *nggwalndu* are washed and repainted, as they are for the final ceremony of each tambaran cycle, the current style of painting does not fit happily on the old style of carving; the surfaces and their relationship to each other are different and the painted designs sit uncomfortably on forms intended for different designs. While the painting is going on such difficulties are recognized. Normally, however, the stylistic difference does not worry anyone; it is simply ignored; only when the impertinent ethnographer holding an artist firmly by the wrist has pointed out all the differences, will he admit their existence; otherwise, the insistence is firm on all sides that the present style is the ancestral style. In discussion with me, artists have speculated on the change in style, wondering whether their style or the old style is the right one, ending by saying that anyhow they know how to carve only in their present style and could not re-create the old style if they wanted to. It is interesting to note in passing that the older figures invariably have much more definite sculptural form—the features are boldly carved and in general they do not seem to be merely pleasant surfaces for painting as much of the present Abelam carving is. Their forms, though varied, are often more reminiscent of the Iatmül styles of the Middle Sepik to the south. It seems possible that the very high development of polychrome painting so much admired among the Abelam may have resulted in the declining interest in sculptural form evident in the figure sequences. With its conscious desire for ostentation and display it has to be confessed that some Abelam sculpture tends to be rather vulgar by European standards.

This gradual stylistic change makes it obvious that whatever they believe, Abelam artists do not slavishly reproduce the work of their predecessors. It would be surprising if they did since, as already mentioned, they never copy one another or any model. A famous artist of Kalabu, asked by a village across a dialect boundary to produce a type of figure that was used in their ceremonies but not at Kalabu, was given a 2-foot-high carving to work from. This he studied but kept in his house, never taking it to his bush studio until the 10-foot carving was finished, when he satisfied himself that he had done it correctly. As everything an artist produces comes from his picture of what the object required should look like, every artist must to some extent impose his own vision of a 'good' piece on the work in hand.

The artist is free to express himself within the stylistic limits prevailing at the time, and by so doing may marginally change those limits. There is of course a feedback here; the society may impose stylistic limits on what is acceptable for a tambaran ceremony and so control the artist, but the artist creates all the art and therefore forms the society's conceptions of what is acceptable. In such a situation gradual change is probably inevitable. It offers the artist self-expression, and keeps the art vital and capable of expressing the changing values of the society, while at the same time ensuring that it can continue to fulfil its main function of being the traditional and powerful mode of access to the supernatural. I have argued elsewhere (Forge, 1966) that Abelam art is intimately connected with the values of Abelam society, and that it makes statements about Abelam society that are not made by other means. If this is so the artist must be the essential link. Up till now the contact with the Australian administration and the missions has not affected the art in style or content. The war and its aftermath virtually stopped artistic activity, but it has been taken up again, at least in the north, with great vigour. This revival has coincided with, and been a symbol of, a withdrawal from excessive contact with European values and a reaffirmation of traditional values. In fact up to now, the art, far from changing, has been reinforced in its conservatism by taking on the additional value of acting as a symbol of Abelam culture in the face of colonial culture.

Ancestor Worship: Two Facets of the Chinese Case

MAURICE FREEDMAN

The Chinese, for example, keep their clan and lineage interests, and also maintain their moral emphasis on the fate of the soul by operating spirit homes in terms of ancestral temples and spirit kingdoms—but with a multiple soul concept (Firth, 1955, p. 45).

1. *Tablets and graves*

In the Chinese cult of the ancestors the personality of the dead is divided, or better, multiplied in such a way that a man or woman may be worshipped for all time as an ancestor and yet undergo the experience of divine judgment and rebirth. Dead ancestors rely for their perennity on the ritual memory of their descendants. Consequently, their number is constantly being reduced. They are given a place in the community of the living by being located in wooden tablets and tended in shrines which belong to domestic families and to lineages and their segments. At the same time, they are given earthly abodes in their graves, where again they are cared for by their agnatic descendants. In shrine and tomb the ancestors are allotted a continuing role in the lives of their issue. But, like all men and women, ancestors at death are ushered through an underworld from which, once they have accounted for their lives and been helped by the prayers and sacrifices of their kin on earth, they pass on by reincarnation to a world of anonymity. (The exceptionally fortunate are sent to the Western Paradise, the outstandingly miserable to the terrible suffering of an inferno.) The screen of anonymity may be pierced soon after death to allow the living a glimpse of the new identity of their late kinsman, but it is an identity that has no direct connexion with them and in which they will take no continuing interest. In this division of mortal fate we find our first important distinction. The morality of the individual life leads to the rapid extinction of the social personality. A chain of lives connects a man with his past and his future, but his kinsmen in one incarnation quickly lose sight of him as he slides over the horizon to his next. The social personality of the ancestor lives on because it is grounded, not in individual morality, but in the perpetual bond between men and their respected forebears.[1]

To be in the shrine, the grave, and (for a while) in the underworld, and to be treated ritually in all three places, a dead man must have three souls. They are provided in the analysis of the human personality into three *hun* and seven *p'o*. (But it is not necessary that this 'theology' be present in the minds of all worshippers. From their point of view, there are three contexts in which the honoured dead are approached, and it does not follow that the different contexts will be severally associated with defined metaphysical entities.) The *p'o* are *yin*; they emanate from and return to earth. If they form a continuing personality, it is *kuei* ('devil' or 'ghost', as it is usually translated in the Western literature). The *hun* are *yang*, heavenly in their connexions; they form *shên*. So that for his descendants a dead man is *shên* and offers three *hun* for their ritual attention. To people other than his descendants he may be *kuei*; and it is possible for me to speak of other people's ancestors as their *kuei*, but mine are *shên*. The dualism of *yang* and *yin* separates an ancestor as *shên* from a ghost as *kuei*; and an ancestor as he lives on in the shrine is unambiguously *yang*. Yet as he survives in his grave he is at one with earth, and it follows that he partakes of the nature of *yin*. *Yin-yang* makes a primary distinction between ghosts and ancestors; it goes on to discriminate between two aspects of one ancestor: his status in the tomb and his status in the shrine.

Ancestors in their shrines are attached to tablets. (Their *hun* are placed there by the rite of 'dotting' which establishes the relationship between the tablet and the soul for which it stands. As a result, only one domestic tablet can exist for one person. But, as we shall see, independent worship before substitutes can be performed by people no longer members of the house where the tablets of their immediate ancestors are kept.) The ancestors are tended, reverenced, and fed. The living acknowledge them as their superiors, owing them a debt for their lives and the goodness of those lives; for the ancestors not only engendered their offspring but also now endow their descendants with the merit they themselves accumulated. In a very general sense the ancestors collectively embody the dignity and the authority of the groups over which they preside. Their due is gratitude and praise. And in paying them their due, the living are made conscious

1. I have had the great advantage of listening to lectures by Professors Arthur P. Wolf and Robert J. Smith on Chinese and Japanese ancestor worship respectively; and I am in their debt for a number of valuable criticisms and suggestions. I am similarly indebted to Professor Lucy Mair, Dr. B. Benedict, and my wife.

of their membership of the groups within which they worship. The smallest of these groups is the domestic family, the largest, a higher-order lineage (Freedman, 1966, pp. 21 ff.) that may have a population of tens of thousands.[1] In the family the ancestors tended are rarely more than four generations distant from the living head; in a lineage the first ancestor may be forty generations away. In a finely segmented lineage, an individual (although not all individuals equally, given the uneven character of the segmentation—see Freedman, 1958, pp. 49 f., and Freedman, 1966, pp. 37 ff.) may be a member of a rising hierarchy of ancestor-worshipping groups, each with its own rites and sacrifices.

Something of the same sort may be said about the worship of ancestors in their tombs. Here too offerings are made and ancestors preside over groups of agnates worshipping together. But the ambiguity of the buried ancestor (as distinct from the ancestor in his tablet) enters at this point: he is not only a soul, discarnate and awesome, but also a corpse—*yin*. As a set of bones, an ancestor is no longer in command of his descendants; he is at their disposal. They no longer worship him; he serves their purposes. We have arrived at the subject of *fêng-shui*. We shall see that it is, as it were, the reverse of ancestor worship.

Geomancy (for by an unfortunate convention *fêng-shui* is translated so) delivers a man's ancestors into his hands. He may determine his own fortune by siting one or more of his ancestral graves in such a way that the geomantic influences (the 'winds and waters') of the landscape are channelled through the bones of the ancestors to their agnatic descendants. (Cf. Freedman, 1966, pp. 118 ff.) By geomancy a Chinese may seek riches and success for himself in order to outpace his agnates; he can do so by choosing ancestral graves that will give him the smallest number of fellow descendants with whom to share the benefit induced, and by procuring (through a geomancer) that the siting and orienting of the graves favour him among the descendants. It is for this reason that brothers will often wrangle

---

1. On the other hand, domestic ancestor worship is not so unambiguously a form of group worship as is the ancestor worship by lineages and their segments. The ritual focus *par excellence* of a family as a domestic entity is the Kitchen God. Every family has its own hearth, and consequently a separate identity in the worship of that god. In ancestor worship, however, the members of two or more families may worship at the same tablets; units resulting from a recent division of a family may continue to pay their devotions to the ancestors represented in the altar retained by one of them. In domestic ancestor worship the relations between the dead and the living are more personal and individual than in the worship performed in ancestral halls.

G

long among themselves over the siting of their father's or mother's grave, each one seeking to ensure his private success at the expense of the others. Where *fêng-shui* is carried to its highest degree of development (as appears to be the case in south-eastern China), bones may be exhumed and reburied in the pursuit of good fortune. In all this seeking after riches, progeny, and success by the manipulation of their remains, the dead are virtually passive. They transmit the virtues of a site to their descendants, but they cannot initiate the flow of benefits or block it off. They may be dissatisfied with their position and uncomfortable in their graves; and so being ill at ease they may interfere with the process set going by geomantic technique; but, with the necessary readjustments made, they must continue to act as the channels through which their descendants seek to tap the benefits of their burial sites.

By geomancy, then, men use their ancestors as media for the attainment of worldly desires. And in doing so they have ceased to worship them and begun to use them as things. The authority implied in descent is ritualized in the worship of ancestors. In geomancy the tables are turned: descendants strive to force their ancestors to convey good fortune, making puppets of forebears and dominating the dominators. In ancestor worship, the ancestors are revered; in *fêng-shui* they are subordinated. In the former, the ideal ties between the generations are reinforced; in the latter they are denied. In the first, men are brought together to underline their common group membership and solidarity; in the second, they seek to differentiate themselves one from another, each individualizing his fate within the common fate procured by the ancestors as *yang*.

The geomancy of graves is part of a large system of ideas and practices in which topography and man are made to interact. The Chinese have elaborated for all sorts of constructions (houses, government offices, villages, cities, and so on, as well as graves) a theory and set of practices which rest on the idea that men are, so to say, members of the universe. They do not walk the world as intruders. Changes made in the landscape are not (as we should say) simply modifications of nature; they are changes of man-in-the-world. As an important part of Chinese culture, *fêng-shui* has gone where that culture has gone. We find it everywhere in China and in three great independent centres of the sinicized world: Japan, Korea, and Vietnam. Yet the distinction that the Chinese themselves make between the geomancy of *yang* (buildings for the living) and that of *yin* (graves) is at once relevant to the fashion in which *fêng-shui* has spread. For while within the greater 'Chinese' world we can everywhere find the geomancy of buildings, we do not always see that of graves. The geomancy of graves is present in Korea (see Osgood, 1951, pp. 149, 244) and Vietnam (Hickey, 1964, especially p. 40), but not in Japan.[1] It is general in China itself, but not everywhere of equal importance. We may well suspect that the distribution is not accidental. Japan appears to supply the clue.

We might argue at great length about the precise nature of patriliny in Japan, but it is at least clear that we cannot find there the kind of agnatic descent system that we associate with China and which we can see also in Korea and Vietnam (cf. Nakane, 1967). The Japanese kinship system, in which subordinate houses may be linked to main houses, not necessarily through agnatic ties, does not produce a regular hierarchy of agnatic ancestors marking out a hierarchy of nesting segments (cf. Nakane, 1967, pp. 105 ff.). Moreover, within China itself there is, I suggest (this must be stated as a hypothesis, not a fact, because the relevant ethnography has not yet been combed), a relation between the elaborateness of the geomancy of graves and the elaborateness of lineage structure. Deep and complex lineage organization is by no means universal in China, and it is probably no accident that in the south-eastern part of the country (principally the two provinces of Fukien and Kwangtung) both lineages and the *fêng-shui* of the tomb have been carried to extreme forms of development. Where (we may suggest) the authority of the past generations, as represented in the cult of the ancestors, weighs heaviest, there men redress the balance by recourse to the geomancy of the tomb. They take a kind of geomantic revenge, using as things what are otherwise symbols of autonomous virtue. As *yang* the ancestors are

1. Professor Smith told me what to read on geomancy in Japan. It is of course impossible for somebody who must confine himself to the Western literature on that country to get a clear picture of so complex an issue as geomancy; but I think I am right in asserting that the geomancy of graves does not appear in Japan. It is a matter of great interest to me that Plath (1964) in a paper on Japanese domestic ancestor worship says that when misfortune occurs 'the usual first line of appeal is to geomancy: something is suspected to be wrong about the physical structure of the house itself' (p. 310). He then gives an informant's statement which speaks of the geomantic alterations carried out to a house, and adds in a note (note 12, p. 314) that we 'stand in need of a study of the social correlates of geomancy'. May I, as an outsider to Japanese studies, raise the problem (which occurs to me as I read what little is readily available) of why the latrine is so important in Japanese geomancy? See Plath, *loc. cit.*, and Dore, 1958, p. 368. In commenting on this question, Professor Smith suggests that I had better ask 'Why the latrine and the kitchen?', since both are considered 'dirty' and therefore ideal entrances for evil. The kitchen of a Japanese house is its only dirt-floored room.

revered, as *yin* manipulated. Doubtless, in any system of ancestor worship, the ancestors honoured must also be resented. In the Chinese case, men are conscious of deriving benefits both from ancestors in their shrines (through their merits and their blessings) and from ancestors as bones. They are free agents when they seek to use the *fêng-shui* of graves, and can sometimes allow themselves to be cynical about their ancestors as *yang*. A French missionary working in Shuntê, Kwangtung, in the early 1930s, quotes a local saying: 'Que la tombe soit bien orientée, que le vent du bonheur soit favorable. A quoi bon le culte rendu aux morts? Si la tombe est mal orientée, à quoi bon les vénérer?' (Fabre, 1935, p. 132).[1]

2. *Benign ancestors*

Ancestors are worshipped in many different kinds of society, and we shall find the cult wider or more narrowly spread according to the meaning we give to the word 'worship'. And even if we start from the Chinese case, taking the tendance of forebears and their continuing interest in the affairs of their descendants as the basis of a definition, we shall be dealing with a very heterogeneous collection of societies. In some societies the ancestors worshipped serve as foci of determinate units constructed on a principle of unilineal descent. This is in fact the kind of ancestor worship that has traditionally captured the imagination and retained the interest of anthropologists. Radcliffe-Brown's exposition of this form (it will be recalled that he touched on the cases of ancient Greece and Rome—following Fustel de Coulanges—China, the Bakongo, and the Nayar) is the *locus classicus* (Radcliffe-Brown, 1952, pp. 162 ff.). It is important to remember that Radcliffe-Brown defined ancestor worship in such a way as to limit the use of the term to those societies in which 'the cult group . . . consists solely of persons related to one another by descent in one line from the same ancestor or ancestors' (*ibid.*, p. 163). It is therefore unreasonable to object to his argument, as Evans-Pritchard has done (1965, p. 24), that 'there are many societies with ancestor cults without a trace of a lineage system'. By Radcliffe-Brown's definition such a cult would not fall within the range of the discussion.

It is now common ground among anthropologists (*pace* Evans-Pritchard) that there is a 'fit' between a cult of ancestors and a system of unilineal descent groups. Professor Evans-Pritchard's colleague, Dr. Beattie, puts it fairly: 'Societies which attach high value to uni-

1. For a variation see Fabre, 1937, p. 586.

lineal descent . . . often have an ancestral cult' (Beattie, 1964, pp. 225 f.). It does not follow that we should be surprised to find systems of ancestor worship in societies with non-unilineal systems of kinship or that we should be alarmed by not finding them in the kinds of society to which Radcliffe-Brown limited his argument. It may well be that we shall never get to the point of understanding why only some unilineally constituted kinship systems display cults of ancestors. Indeed, it may be pressing functionalist arguments too far to suggest that we ought ideally to be able to account over the globe for the presence of such a cult in some 'suitable' societies and its absence from other such societies. But where the cult is found in a system of descent groups, there is surely no difficulty in seeing the appropriateness of a religion in which, either collectively or individually, as the case may be, ancestors stand at the centre of the attention of the people descended from them. Every agnatically constituted unit in China stands out as a religious congregation worshipping its common forebears. Every lineage has its ancestral hall or shrine; in the most elaborate halls the rows of tablets on the altar and the honour boards hanging from beams and walls are a triumphant and awe-inspiring display of success. Every segment of a lineage has a hall or at least the tomb of a focal ancestor at which rites comparable to those in the main hall are performed. But the point hardly needs stressing; it has been so well treated in the context of other societies (cf. Fortes, 1965, p. 123) that we can afford to pass on to a different aspect of ancestor worship.

Radcliffe-Brown's approach turned attention to ancestors as foci. In recent years (principally as a result of Fortes's work on the Tallensi) anthropologists have been studying the ritual aspect of the relationship between men and their proximate ancestors. In other words, they have been asking questions about the roles of ancestors among the people with whom they were once linked in life. In a first attempt to deal with this matter among the Chinese (Freedman, 1957, pp. 218 ff., and Freedman, 1958, p. 84) I spoke of 'memorialism'; more recently, trying to give a name to the thing that must be distinguished from the cult of descent group ancestors, I have written about the cult of immediate jural superiors (Freedman, 1966, pp. 144 ff.)—certainly an inelegant form of words, but I can think of no other. The two cults do not necessarily go together, since the latter can exist without the former. (In my earlier discussion on the point I instanced the case of the Manus.) But whether in isolation or in conjunction with a cult of descent group ancestors, the cult of immediate jural superiors raises some highly interesting questions about the relationship between domestic authority and the attitudes maintained to recently dead superiors.

The matter on which I think it profitable to concentrate is the general character of the intervention of which the ancestors are considered capable. Reading the general ethnography one may be struck not simply by the harshness of the behaviour of ancestors but, more important, by its capriciousness. In very broad terms, we may say that it seems as though authority, once raised to the plane of the after-life, is loosed of its fetters and may lash out at unfortunate mortals, even when their wrong-doing has been negligible or non-existent.[1] Consider, as an example from the copious African data, the case of the Lovedu, as set out by the Kriges (Krige and Krige, 1954, p. 63): 'Ancestors are capricious: their complaints . . . are usually about being neglected; but they may cause illness to those they most love in order to receive recognition, have their name perpetuated, or their beads worn. They are said to "hold" the woman experiencing difficult labour, to afflict children with sore eyes, and even to prevent the queen from making rain. Their complaints need imply no omission or neglect on the part of the afflicted descendant, but merely some special desire that could not have been anticipated.' Yet not all societies in which ancestors are worshipped credit dead forebears with behaviour of this sort. The Chinese do not. In order to avoid going over ground I have covered before (Freedman, 1958, pp. 88 f., and Freedman, 1966, p. 151), let me summarize what in my view is the characteristic behaviour imputed to Chinese ancestors. While they will certainly punish their descendants if they suffer neglect or are offended by an act or omission which affects them directly

1. On this point I find that what Fortes writes in the paper already cited leaves me somewhat puzzled. He says, at p. 135, that the 'ancestors persecute in the etymological sense of persistently following and harrying their descendants; they do not punish for wickedness or reward for virtues, as these are defined by human standards . . .'. Yet on the next page he says: 'In short, the persecuting ancestor is not a supernatural being capriciously punishing wrong-doing or rewarding virtue. He is rather to be thought of as an ultimate judge and mentor whose vigilance is directed towards restoring order and discipline in compliance with the norms of right and duty, amity and piety, whenever transgressions threaten or occur. When misfortune occurs and is interpreted as a punitive, or to be more exact, corrective intervention by the ancestors, they are believed to have acted rightfully, not wantonly.' In a society where many misfortunes are attributed to ancestral intervention, it must be difficult for men to avoid considering some of the behaviour of their dead forebears as capricious. Doubtless, in a general and theoretical way ancestral conduct as a whole may be thought to be based on some underlying principle, but from an individual's point of view what his ancestor does to him must surely sometimes appear arbitrary.

(chiefly, the failure to secure for them a firm line of descent), they are essentially benign and considerate of their issue. Before taking action against their descendants they need to be provoked; capricious behaviour is certainly alien to their benevolent and protective nature. (It may be worth adding, since I have referred to the Lovedu case, that the ancestors of the latter people also appear to be unconcerned about the general moral conduct of their descendants; but in respect of the personal offences against themselves they are harsh in their reaction, while in general, as we have seen, their behaviour is capricious—Krige and Krige, p. 79.)

Now, it is possible to treat the problem (for such I take it to be) of the benign Chinese ancestor in different ways. From one point of view, and coming back to the question of authority, we may ask whether Chinese ancestors are kindly because, in making them ancestors, their descendants are not conscious of having displaced them from coveted positions of power. The weight of the ethnographic evidence on ancestor worship seems to be in favour of the hypothesis that, by being displaced, a man-become-ancestor is thought at once to resent his successor and to endow that successor with the authority to rule in his place. Everything, then, turns on there being a man with domestic authority who, so to say, has snatched it from the recently dead and who now reigns by virtue of that succession. At first sight it might well appear as though the Chinese case met these conditions. Is not the *chia-chang* (the family-head) a powerful patriarch who yields his office only by dying? But the reality of the nature and the transfer of power in the Chinese family is different.

It is necessary, in the first place, to consider the constitution of the Chinese family and the place of primogeniture in it. An assumption is built into the official Chinese view of society that a family perpetuates itself through all time by means of the succession of the oldest son to the position of the father. There was a period in fact when primogeniture was a fully fledged institution in China: in the Chou dynasty (eleventh to third centuries B.C.). In noble families (we know little about the ordinary people) the oldest son stepped into his father's shoes to hold his property rights and exercise his authority. But when the 'feudal' system of ancient China was superseded by the centralized state, the principle of equal inheritance among sons became established alongside the principle (essentially ritual, as we shall see) that the oldest son was to succeed his father. So that for the last two millennia there has existed in China a family system in which two apparently conflicting principles have been at work. From one point of view, the family can be seen as a corporation which passes down a senior line of descent; the oldest son succeeds his father, taking charge of the domestic stock of ancestor tablets, enjoying a prior right to the main part of the physical house, and, in this connexion, often benefiting from the allocation to him of a share in the family property over and above that which is his due as one among several sons. The special position of this continuer of the main line of descent is ritually underlined by his unique role in the mourning for his parents and for his paternal grandfather if his father is already dead.

From another angle (and this the more realistic), the Chinese family is a property-owning estate which dissolves on the death of each senior generation to reform into successor-estates, none of which can be said to have the identity inhering in its predecessor. As each son is born (or adopted) he is automatically endowed with a potential share in the family estate. That estate is under the control of the *chia-chang*, and no son can realize his share against the opposition of living parents. But as soon as they are dead, the partible estate is divided, the family segmenting into new units which are residentially (they may partition the old dwelling or set up new quarters), economically, and ritually distinct. The new units may continue for some time to maintain a common ancestral shrine (which is in the keeping of the oldest son), but, since each is now endowed with a separate hearth, it is at liberty to establish its own shrine by setting up a board on which are inscribed the names of the ancestors individually represented in the original shrine by the several wooden tablets.

The so-called 'joint' family (cf. Freedman, 1966, p. 49, on the inappropriateness of the term) has a short life. If its head dies leaving a married and an unmarried son, they will continue to form one family until such time as the junior, now married, asserts his separate rights. (A *chia-chang* is privileged to prevent his own son taking out his share, but he cannot exercise a similar right vis-à-vis his brother or brother's sons.) Married brothers rarely continue in one family once the mourning period for their parents is over. The ritual precedence of the oldest son does not confer on him the authority to control his younger brothers, and indeed, the fragility of the fraternal bond in Chinese society is such that domestic harmony is improbable in the absence of the senior generation. Every new marriage inserts into the family a potential point of segmentation; a married son is potentially the head of a new *fang* (a term which, at all levels of the descent system, can be translated as segment), and he is not dissuaded from asserting his status as an independent *chia-chang* merely by reason of the ritually emphasized position of his oldest brother.

It follows that no one son can step effectively into his father's shoes to exercise authority over the same range of people. But there is more to it than that. Even during his life, a father as *chia-chang* may need to shed his authority—and sometimes well in advance of his death. If he fails (because of sickness, senility, or sheer incompetence) to maintain his position as ruler of his household, then he has in a way anticipated his death, and in handing over his authority to his oldest son he is likely to provoke the split which ideally should wait upon his being gathered to his ancestors.

The death of their father (or, more accurately, the end of the mourning period of the second parent to die) is the point at which most sons come fully into their inheritance. But they may, in reality, have advanced to their status as men well before that time. Marriage sets a man up as a mature human being; on his begetting a son he is unambiguously come to the fullness of life. And it is of the greatest significance that every Chinese father tries his best to marry off his sons as early as he possibly can. He does not see his married sons as a threat to his position. They, for their part, do not look upon him as a serious barrier to the attainment of their economic and ritual maturity. There is, in fact, a more gradual transfer of authority and a greater dispersion of it than is suggested by the rule of ritual primogeniture and the law which makes it an offence for men to take out their shares of family property against the wishes of their seniors by generation in the house.

Once installed as an ancestor in his tablet, a father does not in any precise sense support the authority of his sons over their juniors. He is worshipped (by acts of reverence and offerings of incense and food) but cannot be used as a major instrument of domestic discipline. True, he symbolizes ancestral authority and the honour of the family; and wayward juniors can be shamed before him. But there are no terrible ancestral sanctions that a *chia-chang* intent on maintaining his authority can call down on the people under his hand. No son effectively replaces his dead father; that father, now promoted to *shên*, cannot channel his supernatural authority through a true successor.

We have seen that the ritual primogeniture of modern China rests historically on the true primogeniture of a much older phase of Chinese society. It is extremely difficult to see, through the classical sources on this period, what view was taken by the ancients of their ancestors. Confucian orthodoxy (we may assume) has masked for us the nature of dead ancestral beings, for it tends markedly to set aside speculation about the world of the spirits. But consider the contrast between what we know to be the modern state of affairs and the kind of attitude implied in the following statement in a text, supposedly of the first century A.D., which purports to be an official discussion of the Classics. In the section on marriage the *Po Hu T'ung* speaks of the sadness not only of the bride leaving her parental house (which could, of course, be paralleled from modern China) but also of the terrible significance of marriage for the groom's family. According to the *Li* ('rites'), the bride's family brood over their coming separation from their daughter. ' "In the family of the man who takes the wife no music is made during three days: they think [of the fact that the son is going to] succeed his father." They feel sad at [the thought that] the father has grown feeble and old in the course of years and that [the time of his] being replaced [by the son] has arrived. The *Li* says: "The wedding is not [a case] for congratulations; it is [a case of] generations succeeding each other." ' And when the father sends off his son to meet his bride, he tells him to go that 'thou mayst succeed me in the sacrifices to the ancestral temple' (Tjan, 1949, p. 249). To realize the full implication of the text we need to know that the *Li* prescribes thirty as the age of marriage for men (*ibid.*, p. 245); it is the very reverse of the modern situation in which men are to be married young and in joy.

We may well suspect that the aristocratic institutions of ancient China produced an array of stern and disciplinary ancestors. And (while I certainly lack the scholarship to document such an assertion) I think it likely that over the course of Chinese history, the worship of ancestors in their shrines has been gradually overtaken by the attention paid to ancestral graves. This, indeed, appears to be Granet's conclusion in a remarkable passage in which (without mentioning the term) he relates the growth of *fêng-shui* to a decline in the importance of the cult centring on the ancestral tablets. With the rise of imperial China, he writes, the cult of the ancestors assumed a new character: 'ce fut un culte d'ordre moral, tout symbolique, tout abstrait'; whereas among the 'feudal' nobility there had been an intimate and emotionally charged communion with the ancestors. And from the official point of view, at least, the cult became formalized, the ancestors being kept at a distance from their worshippers. Graves and funerals began to be elaborate. 'Plus de vénération se porta sur la tombe, monument public de la piété filiale et moins sur la tablette, centre abstrait d'un culte tout domestique. Le culte des Ancêtres tendit à devenir un culte des tombeaux. Par là, il se rapprocha à nouveau des cultes agraires. Placées dans un paysage favorable, disposées de façon à capter l'influx des forces sacrées de la Nature,

visitées et propitiées au moment du renouveau, les sépultures trans-
mettaient aux vivants les bonnes influences qui venaient se concré-
tiser dans le corps des Ancêtres. Le culte ancestral n'avait qu'une
efficacité symbolique et morale. . . . La vertu des tombes et celle des
ossements furent utilisées par la magie. . . . Ce que la piété demandait
aux tombeaux des Ancêtres, ce ne fut jamais des grâces particulières,
mais une protection étendue à toute la famille. La religion des tombes entretenait des sentiments plus concrets que ne pouvaient faire
les tablettes. . . .' (Granet, 1951, pp. 114 ff. *Fêng-shui*, under that
name, is referred to again at *ibid.*, pp. 167 f.)

There are two further aspects of this evolution. The noble cult of
the ancestors in 'feudal' times was tightly bound up with proximate
forebears; the communion with the dead from whom authority immediately derived was intense. When ancestor worship became generalized in Chinese society, the elaborate hierarchies of tablets in halls
entailed a distancing between the worshipper and the great host of
his ancestors; and their comparative remoteness may perhaps have
influenced domestic worship to make it a less personal and intimate
traffic with the dead. In the second place, I think it could be argued
that, as the domestic cult of the ancestors became popularized, it
tended to be relegated in effect to the women of the house, the men
concentrating their attention on the more recent dead in their tombs
and the remote dead in the halls. When I studied overseas Chinese
in Singapore (many of them of very recent immigration from China)
I was struck by the extent to which domestic worship was left in the
hands of women, the adult men taking very little interest in it
(Freedman, 1957, pp. 45, 220). And in the fascinating paper by
Fabre, to which I have already referred, we read that domestic ancestor worship is carried out by the women of the house, 'en droit par la
mère de famille, la belle-mère, parfois par l'une des brus. Mieux
que les hommes, elles s'entendent à adresser leurs pétitions aux
défunts, à leur exposer les besoins d'un mari, des enfants, de toute la
famille. L'homme se désintéresse: il n'a un rôle actif dans les offrandes
que lors de la fête du génie de l'âtre [the Kitchen God, as he is usually
called in English]. . . . Il se dédommage enfin au temple des ancêtres et
aux tombeaux' (Fabre, 1935, p. 121).[1] Chinese women are trans-
ferred on marriage to the shadow of their husbands' ancestors; so
much do these ancestors become their own that they assume the
main responsibility for their tendance.

But they may do more than that. It is possible to argue that women
are the main (perhaps sometimes the sole) means for bringing into

1. And now cf. Gallin, 1966, pp. 148, 247 on this point.

play such hostile activity as is attributed to ancestors. The benignity of forebears springs from the relations to them of men; it may be that married women, standing in a different relation to these fore-bears, tend to perceive them as potentially hostile. And we may find on closer study that when, as sometimes happens, ancestors are credited with punitive behaviour, the attribution of this behaviour has been made by the women of the house. In Chinese domestic life married women are seen by men to be the ultimate source of trouble (cf. Freedman, 1958, pp. 21 f.; 1966, pp. 46, 55 f.); perhaps these women take their revenge on occasion by converting the kindly ancestors of their husbands into the originators of misfortune.

For modern China, then, we may argue that ancestors are kindly, at least from the point of view of men, because, in the absence of a corporate family, in the turnover of the generations a new head does not effectively displace his predecessor. But lest we imagine that the matter is quite as simple as that, we ought to glance at the compara-tive evidence from Japan. In that country too (and perhaps even more so than in China) the ancestors are benign. And yet in Japanese society the family is ideally a perpetual unit, each head of family be-ing replaced by a single successor. The successor is not necessssarily the oldest son; indeed, he may well be an adopted son (*yōshi*) or an adopted bridegroom (*muko-yōshi*). All sons failing to secure the succession must become members of other corporations or start their own. It might seem as though the situation were well designed to produce disciplinary ancestors. But: 'So strong is the feeling that the household dead are friendly and supportive, that antagonism is not easily verbalized and must be glimpsed obliquely' (Plath, 1964, p. 310).[1] In fact, the key to the benignity of the Japanese ances-tors may lie in the manner in which the succession to family head-ship is effected. Ideally, succession should precede the death of the senior male in the family in order that he may, along with his wife, enjoy a period of retirement before he joins his ancestors (Plath, p. 306, and Dore, 1958, p. 10). One recent writer puts the relevant points very succinctly: 'Succession . . . or retirement . . . [is] ceremoniously observed when a successor's father reaches the age of sixty or when the successor's first son is born, at least in northern Japan, but be-coming a gradual process there as elsewhere without the performance of ritual. The eldest (or chosen) son succeeds to leadership and, tradi-tionally, supreme status in the household . . . , while the former house head attains the status of grandfather . . . or retired person . . .

1. I am greatly in debt to this paper not only for the insight it affords into Japa-nese ancestor worship but also for its discussion of many important problems.

relieved of major responsibility' (Beardsley, 1965, p. 110. And cf. Nakane, 1967, pp. 4, 16 ff.) In other words, as in the Chinese case (but not now because the family is dispersed among a number of heirs), the death of one generation and the coming to majority of the next are not coincident events. There has been a transfer of authority *inter vivos*. One steps into a live man's shoes. I wish it were possible for me to pursue the enquiry within the same contexts as are necessary for the comparative study of geomancy; but I do not have at my command the necessary data on succession and attitudes to ancestors for Vietnam and Korea.

This is one possible approach to the problem posed. Another approach requires a broadening of the sociological framework. Can it be that Chinese and Japanese ancestors are typically benign because their societies are highly differentiated? It seems to be characteristic of small-scale societies (in which individuals are bound together in complex webs of relationships) that evil and misfortune are seen to be embedded in personal ties. The things men fear— sickness, death, and barrenness of land, women, and beasts—tend to be ascribed to the actions or evil impulses of people with whom the sufferers are intimately connected. And it is along such lines that many anthropologists nowadays discuss the significance of witchcraft accusations and sorcery. (Cf. Gluckman, 1965, especially pp. 242 ff., and Mair, 1963, 160 ff.) Of course, it may seem odd to put ancestor worship into the same class as witchcraft and sorcery, since it is the living human being who is thought to practise black arts or project evil, and a dead man who is said to inflict ancestral punishment. But we need to consider by what mechanisms the ancestors are able to affect their living descendants.

An ancestor may take punitive action either because he is invoked or on his own initiative. In the former case, the man who invokes him is calling down an ancestral sanction against the people over whom he himself has control. (And, as we have seen, no man in China derives his power from ancestors in such a fashion.) In the latter case, the punitive action taken by the ancestor is first a misfortune of which the cause is unknown and is then laid at the ancestor's door. Its origin must be divined, and the process of divining again asserts the relevance of relationships between persons closely linked, for the diagnosis must say that the afflicted man has misbehaved or failed in his duty either towards some kinsman or neighbour or towards the punishing ancestor himself. (The ancestor, though dead, is a person with rights and duties.) That witchcraft and ancestor worship can be seen to belong to the same religious universe is brought out vividly in Middleton's data on the Lugbara: here witchcraft is the unjustified calling down of the same evil that lineage elders can summon legitimately by an appeal to the ancestors. Lugbara use the same word for the 'indignation' of the witch and that of the elder. Whether a particular case of misfortune caused by an elder is to be attributed to his witchcraft or to his invocation of the ancestors depends on the relationship to him of the interpreters: if the elder's authority is recognized he has invoked the ancestors; otherwise he is a witch (Middleton, 1960, pp. 34 ff., 153, 225 f.).

Chinese society does not in any marked way predispose its members to seek explanations for their misfortunes in the evil thoughts and mystical malpractices of their kinsmen and neighbours. There are perhaps professional sorcerers, and sorcery is said sometimes to be practised by ordinary people. (Cf. De Groot, 1907, Pt. III.) Accusations are sometimes made that one man or group has harmed another's *fêng-shui*; and certainly brothers may quarrel because each is striving to promote his success by geomancy at the expense of the others. But the dominant mode of explanation is impersonal: misfortune is either the bitter reward for misconduct (in this or a previous incarnation) or the effect of some non-human power or entity undirected by men on earth. Except that the ancestors may in exceptional circumstances hit out at their descendants and in a very vague and general way be responsible for the ups and downs of their fortune, they are not automatically turned to when personal mischance must be explained. One may well divine the ancestors' satisfaction with the sacrifices made to them, but there is otherwise little attempt to make communication flow from them to men. It is instructive, in this connexion, to consider the Chinese use of spirit-mediumship.

In the major form of spirit-mediumship clients bring their troubles to a medium (usually male) who, in a public or semi-public performance, provides advice and cures by speaking with the voice of a deity. It would appear that it is extremely rare for ancestors to be in question in such consultations. (Cf. Elliott, 1955, pp. 160 f.) On the other hand, communication with the dead is the *raison d'être* of the minor form of spirit-mediumship. So far as the evidence on southeastern China goes, at any rate, in strictly private séances female mediums search out the dead in the underworld in order to bring them to speak with their clients. The most significant aspect of these séances, from the point of view of the present enquiry, is that not only are some of the souls raised those of kinsmen who are not ancestors, but all the souls brought to the séance belong to the recently dead. That is to say, if ancestors are contacted then they are conversing with their descendants in the short period between their death and the time when, having passed out of the underworld, they will be accessible to the living only in their tablets and graves.

The relatives who seek in this manner to communicate with their dead are concerned primarily to assure themselves that the dead in this phase of their other-world existence lack for nothing that the living can provide. Yet they may bring problems with them that are elicited in the course of the séance. Elliott's study of the subject is the best observed available, and although it was conducted in Singapore, I think we may safely assume that, in this regard at least, it reproduces what happens in south-eastern China. He writes: 'Some of the more susceptible members ask the ghost about particular problems that are worrying them. Some of these problems may involve personal antagonisms within the family or questions of rights to property. In each case the ghost gives a judgment which must be observed by those who hear it' (*ibid.*, pp. 138 f.). But, more important, there is a poignant passage in Elliott's account in which he tells us how, by gaining admission to a séance of this sort (no mean feat of field work, as I can testify from my own experience),[1] he came to realize why séances are held in the strictest secrecy and seclusion. 'A skilful soul raiser is capable of laying bare many of the skeletons in a family's cupboard and bringing to light some of the personal animosities of which an outsider might well remain ignorant' (*ibid.*, p. 136). A consultation with the recently dead may be allowed to bring out for their advice and adjudication the problems of the families they have left behind, but it is significant that there is no institution for continuing the conversation. Once the dead have gone from the underworld they are no longer capable of being invited to intervene so decisively in the affairs of the living.[2] It is as though Chinese society

1. And cf. Giles, 1879, pp. 244 f., where, referring to 'dark séances', he says that he found it impossible to gain access to one, for, apart from anything else, such séances are almost, if not entirely, confined to women. Giles did not experience a similar difficulty in seeing other kinds of divination practised. His account appears to be about Amoy.
2. Cf. the account of the same institution given by De Groot, 1886, pp. 295–9, and 1910, pp. 1332 ff. It is worth noting that De Groot, 1910, at p. 1333 says that the séances are often held in 'the private female rooms' of the house in order to exclude men. 'Scepticism exercises an obstructive effect in spiritualism, and of scepticism menfolk are the only representatives.' Another reference to this kind of séance in south-eastern China is to be found in Kulp, 1925, p. 288. Osgood, 1963, pp. 316 f., presents some comparable data for Yunnan, but Hsu, 1949, pp. 167 ff., writing of sinicized Min Chia in that province, describes a very different kind of séance, which takes place in a temple. The séance is usually held within the mourning period of the person about whom the enquiry is to be made. It will

protected itself against too great an interference by the dead in the relations between kinsmen. And it would seem that it falls mainly to women to exploit what little opportunity there is to bring the ancestors actively into the lives of their descendants.

3. *Conclusion*

In writing about China one is forced to take the large view. Yet our knowledge of it (as anthropologists) is piecemeal, and every attempt to be systematic about a particular subject involves us in a scramble for bits of data to fit together. But data there are, and they are being rapidly increased by the new work in Taiwan and Hong Kong,[1] so that we are not for ever condemned to the task of trying to extract meaning from facts collected by people with problems in mind very different from those which now drive us on. Yet as our understanding of Chinese society builds up, we shall find that the more consistent a picture we make of it, the less satisfied we shall be. It will become more apparent than it is now that the variations in institutions and beliefs are of greater importance than the consistencies. Well documented, China (or even a section of it) could provide an admirable framework for testing, by a study of variation, the validity of an analysis proposed for one small set of data.

In the second part of this essay I have raised the issue of the possible relationship between ancestor worship on the one side and the distribution of family authority and social differentiation on the other. Between town and country, farmer and merchant, peasant and official, rich and poor, landsman and fisherman (the simplified contrasts could be extended on and on) there must surely be crucial differences in the working out of domestic authority and in the nature of the social ties which bind individuals to those among whom they live out their lives. And these differences ought to be exploited in the effort to understand both the place of ancestor worship in the total system of control of Chinese behaviour and the relation between that worship and the dynamics of family life. But the framework of comparison will not be kept down to that scale, for already it is clear that there are opportunities for fruitful comparative study in the institutions and beliefs of the various countries which share with China a common classical tradition. I have tried in the first part of the essay

be seen from the responses recorded by Hsu at pp. 173 ff. that only the vaguest information is given about the fate of the dead, and the dead are not consulted about the affairs of the living.

1. See, e.g., the impressive analysis of 'Gods, Ghosts, and Ancestors' by Arthur P. Wolf, based on his field study in Taiwan. This important paper is in press.

to show, for example, that it is meaningful to ask why Chinese geomancy differs between Japan on the one hand and China, Korea, and Vietnam on the other. And a systematic comparison between ancestor worship (especially perhaps as it is related to the transmission of domestic authority and the roles of married women) in all these countries would take us a step forward in our understanding of the social correlates of religious practices and ideas.

H

The Plasticity of New Guinea Kinship

PHYLLIS M. KABERRY

In 1936 Professor Firth emphasized the plasticity of Polynesian kinship and pointed out: 'The extent to which recognition of the tie through the mother is incorporated into the scheme of social institutions, particularly into principles of group membership, is to be correlated especially with variations in the economic structure of the community' (1936a, p. 596). The type of residence after marriage, the need for personal labour as a basis for economic support, and, especially, the relation of population to size of territory, are all factors which may determine the rigidity with which the principle of unilineal descent is applied in any particular community (pp. 597–8). Even in Tikopia, however, where succession to office and the transmission of landed property are patrilineal, Firth is able to show that the kin of the mother have an important role to play and that they form 'a necessary part of the social mechanism' (p. 344). In other words, in his analysis of Tikopia social structure Firth does not simply restrict himself to an examination of the patrilineal principle, but shows how its operation is affected by other kinship and also local relations. Fortunately for us, he has also refrained from what Leach has called 'butterfly collecting' or the classification or arrangement of things according to types and sub-types (Leach, 1961, p. 2); that is, he did not produce a battery of terms to denote types and sub-types of patrilineal descent in Polynesia, let alone throughout the world. As I interpret his approach, the ideology of the people concerned is all important, and it is the anthropologist's task to see how far the composition of effective kin groups on the ground is determined by the patrilineal principle; and, if the principle is weak, what then the factors are that tell against it.

Firth did not then and would not now, I think, assume that there is any society with a 'perfect' form of patrilineal descent, let alone that the working of the society can be explained in terms of one principle to the exclusion of others. In fact, it is precisely because of the interplay of a number of principles that patrilineal systems of descent vary from community to community. Moreover, Firth has always stressed the importance of individual choice, of adjustment to circumstances and emergencies; and he would, I think, agree with Leach that 'in all viable systems there must be an area where the individual is free to make choices so as to manipulate the system to his own advantage' (1962, p. 133). He would (and again this is my own interpretation) go much farther and say that not only must the individual on occasion escape from the straitjacket prefabricated for him by the society in which he lives, but that the community as a whole, and its component groups, must adjust to the conditions imposed by the environment, to the availability of natural resources, to decimation of numbers by war or sickness (or both), to differential size of families, and so on.

In the publication of the results of field work since the Second World War, many writers have emphasized the flexibility with which rules of recruitment to kin and local groups are applied in many New Guinea societies. However, data were not lacking for the earlier period, as instanced by Mead's analysis of Arapesh patriclan organization: 'Thus, while there is a concept of a gens hamlet, gens garden land, gens hunting bush, and a gens *marsalai* place, all of these are subject to the tendency towards family line ownership and either temporary or permanent alienation to matrilineal and affinal kin. The emphasis on individual ties rather than upon collective activity makes it possible for all these tendencies to find expression. So a man invites his brother-in-law to garden with him, or to share a house in the hamlet, or to hunt with him. He is not asking his brother-in-law to join his gens; it is a transaction between two individuals, but some dozen such transactions a year serve effectively to break down the residential, gardening, and hunting unity of any of these theoretically gens-owned, territorially based groups' (Mead, 1947, p. 182).

In my own work in 1939–40 among the neighbouring Abelam, who also have patrilineal descent, I found a similar emphasis on ties of amity and co-operation between brothers-in-law and between a man and his matrilateral kin. Moreover, when a man's father or even both his parents die, he may ally himself with the clan of his mother's brother, thereby obtaining rights of inheritance to land, sylvan resources, and property (Kaberry, 1941–2, pp. 88–9). Even if he continues to reside in his deceased father's hamlet for a period, he may subsequently quarrel seriously with an elder brother or father's brother and he then allies himself with a mother's brother or cross-cousin (p. 91). The relationship between a mother's brother and sister's son is a particularly important one in the social structure: it is maintained by sentiment, by constant association, by ritual affiliations, and by a chain of reciprocal services. It thus modifies and indeed balances the patrilineal principle (p. 93).

In a paper read in 1955 to the Association of Social Anthropologists, I gave both a qualitative and a quantitative analysis of effective descent groups and showed that in the Abelam village of Kalabu in 1939–40 only 59·2 per cent of the 125 married males remained effective corporate members of their fathers' clans. In that paper, some of which is incorporated here, I was concerned with the analysis of those factors which favoured active co-operation and co-residence of agnates on the one hand, and of those factors which in certain situations favoured co-residence and co-operation with non-agnatic kin and affines. And I then went on to question the validity of constructing a model of society in terms of *one* principle alone, and also of disregarding quantitative data in the construction of a model. It is clear that if one were to interpret Kalabu social structure in terms of one principle alone, namely that of patrilineal descent, and to view patriclans as providing, as it were, the steel framework of Kalabu society, then it would be found that in practice the people of Kalabu made haywire of their structure.

However, my own view has been that, in constructing a model of a particular society, one must take into account not only the principle of descent and relations between kin groups, but also dyadic relations of various kinds and the underlying ideology of all. Necessarily there will be, in any particular society, some relative weighting of the importance of principles or relationships; and, at times, there may be at the theoretical level considerable consensus among informants. But since individuals in the natural course of events have to cope with the exigencies of life, they can be expected to make, and as human beings do make, choices in which they decide whether or not it is expedient or even morally right to attach more importance to one relationship than to another in a particular situation. Hence what appear to be deviations are, more often than not, indices of the viability of a social system.

Among the northern Abelam agnatic ties were very important, but so also were relations with non-agnatic kin, affines, neighbours, and also ceremonial partners, who were involved in initiation ceremonies and the competitive exchange of long yams and pigs. In favourable conditions, and all things being equal, the rights and obligations involved in these relationships did not necessarily conflict; and there were of course many instances where members of a clan were nearly all linked by actual ties of agnation, and resided and worked together under the leadership of their elders and big-men, while at the same time maintaining close links with uterine kin and affines and fulfilling obligations to ceremonial partners. But things are rarely equal, anyway for all people at the same time. Unequal birthrates, deaths, sickness, quarrels, misfortunes, suspicion of sorcery, temperamental incompatibility, ambition to become a big-man—any one or several of these might operate to create a situation in which the individuals concerned had to make a choice among a number of important relationships.

Now communities of this type in which there is a considerable degree of optation in affiliation are sometimes referred to as 'loosely structured' and, as such, 'unstable'. But in my view the phrase 'loosely structured' is a loose one, and I would agree with Pouwer that it seems to contain a terminological contradiction: 'incoherent coherence' (Pouwer, 1961, p. 3). Moreover, some of the New Guinea societies in which there is a considerable degree of optation have a complex organization. The Northern Abelam are a case in point. Moreover, the degree of optation that exists in regard to clan affiliation does not necessarily result in an unstable political community or parish (as the autonomous political unit is sometimes described by New Guinea ethnographers). It is true that in the village of Kalabu the composition of localized descent groups varied and that a percentage of members did change their affiliation either during adolescence or after marriage. But what gave stability, or perhaps it would be better to say coherence, to the village was the integration of these small localized descent groups into hamlets, each hamlet having institutionalized relationships with other hamlets in the village and particularly with adjacent hamlets. Furthermore, there existed a dual organization into *ara*, in which clans sometimes acted competitively, as in the exchanges of long yams; at times they were mutually dependent on one another for the initiation of males into the various stages of a cult believed to affect success in yam-growing and warfare—the two major interests for all men; and at other times again clans united and co-operated, as in the construction of a 'house tambaran' (men's ceremonial house) or in the defence of the village against attacks made by neighbouring villages who were traditional enemies (*mama*).[1]

In the discussion since the Second World War of the characteristics of descent groups studied in the New Guinea area, and more particularly in the Highlands, there has been considerable controversy about the status of so-called non-unilineal or ambilineal or cognatic

1. A detailed account of political organization among the Northern Abelam is contained in Kaberry, 1966.

descent systems on the one hand, and about the status of patrilineal descent systems in which there is a considerable degree of optation on the other. It was Firth who as early as 1929 drew the attention of anthropologists to what he termed the ambilineal descent groups (the *hapu*) of the Maori. These were corporate descent groups in which membership was obtained ambilaterally, that is, through either parent, according to circumstances. It is the ideology of descent which distinguishes groups of this kind from kindreds (which are ego-based), or from local groups (such as Andamanese or Könkämä Lapp bands) where individuals take up residence on the basis of a cognatic or affinal tie. The ambilineal or cognatic descent group is lineally organized and is an ancestor-based group. The circumstances which determine whether an individual affiliates exclusively or predominantly with one descent group rather than another vary from society to society. In some cases, active membership in a particular group is determined by the residence of a person's parents, as in the *kainga* of the Gilbert Islands (Goodenough, 1955, pp. 74–5); in others by the type of marriage contracted by the parents, as was formerly the case among the Mambila of Northern Cameroons (Rehfisch, 1960); in others, again, by personal choice, subject to the fulfilment of certain obligations. Where the choice is made by the individual, Firth has described the system as *optative*. In some systems of the optative type, an individual may change his membership of groups several times during his life-time and filiation is, to use Firth's term, *reversible*; in others, such as the Iban, once a choice is made it is *irreversible* (Firth, 1957a).

Some anthropologists have denied that ambilineal or cognatic descent systems are *in fact* descent systems. Leach, for example, states that descent refers to the unambiguous permanent and involuntary membership of a sectional grouping within the total society (1962, p. 131); and Fortes would seem to adopt a similar position when he says that he does 'not see how the concept of a "descent group" is applicable in the conditions of "ambilateral affiliation" described by Professor Firth, for the "group" is never closed by a descent criterion' (1959, p. 211). Firth in a subsequent publication deals with some of these points in detail and suggests that to reserve 'descent' for cases of unilineality of group entitlement is an unnecessary restriction (1963, p. 36). The *hapu* in traditional Maori society was a group of kin who traced their relationship to one another by genealogies with an ultimate point of reference in a common ancestor. The *hapu* was named; it commonly had a generation depth of eight to ten generations; and it was a localized group and acted as a group on certain occasions and in regard to certain resouces (pp. 30–32). I am in agreement with Firth, but this is not the place to discuss the matter in much detail. If we are prepared to accept the definition in *Notes and Queries on Anthropology* (1951, p. 71) that 'socially, descent is the recognized connexion between a person and his ancestors', then this does not commit us to the view that descent groups can be only unilineal. What is crucial is that descent is a necessary qualification for membership. This is true for both unilineal and ambilineal descent groups; but in the case of the latter an individual, by virtue of descent from his mother's ancestors on the one hand, and his father's ancestors on the other, has a choice of exercising effective membership in one of several groups. Commonly, effective membership involves residence with members of the group, exercise of land rights, and fulfilment of obligations imposed on members of the co-resident group. Fortes has suggested that such groups might be called 'kindred groups' (1959, p. 212), but this ignores the ideology of such groups, namely that there is a concept of descent from a real or putative ancestor and that relationships are traced back lineally through males or females, according to circumstances. Unfortunately, we have few detailed studies of such systems apart from those of the Maori, the Gilbert Islanders, and the To'ambaita of Northern Malaita. In New Guinea an early study of such a system was made in 1933 at Möwehaven in New Britain (Todd, 1934); and subsequent studies, mainly in the 1950s, have been carried out among the Mimika and Manikion (Pouwer, 1958), the Huli in the southern Highlands of Papua (Glasse, 1959a, 1959b), and among the Molima of Fergusson Island (Chowning, 1962). Glasse's data show that among the Huli the ambilineage is 'a corporation comprising all the descendants through male and/or female links of a pair of ancestors some four or five generations removed' (1959a, p. 177). It is a political-jural unit in feud, warfare, and compensation, and a land-owning, ritual, and exchange unit. 'It is the fundamental corporate and political-jural unit in Huli Society' (p. 183). The ambilineage is centred on a parish territory; descent linkages are the necessary basis for parish membership, but other qualifications are also required to obtain status within the parish (pp. 177–9). Since parish territories are small, ranging from half to two or three square miles, it is possible for an ambitious man with several wives to be an effective member in several and take an active part in their communal affairs (1959b, pp. 278–82).

The Huli provide us with an example of a system in which optation in affiliation to descent groups is legitimate or institutionalized.

But there are other societies in New Guinea in which there is so much deviation from a rule or ideology of patrilineal descent that some writers have said we are in fact dealing with an 'ambilineal system' (Pouwer, 1960, pp. 114–15); others have said that where conditions are unfavourable, the patrilineal rule cannot be adhered to rigorously, and that what appears to be an ambilineal system, in terms of a quantitative analysis of the composition of localized kin groups, is in fact a broken-down patrilineal descent system or secondary phenomenon of adaptation (van der Leeden, 1960, pp. 127–30); while others again, such as Barnes, would say that some parts of the Highlands are characterized by 'cumulative patrifiliation rather than by agnatic descent' (1962, p. 6).

Pouwer regards the small size of local groups as one factor which influences the pronounced emphasis on bilateral kinship relations in many New Guinea societies. Hogbin and Wedgwood were among the first to stress that throughout much of Melanesia, including New Guinea, the terrain is such that communication is difficult and large concentrations of population are impracticable (except in the Central Highlands). 'Few of the food crops are suitable for storing; and, as they are grown on a system of shifting cultivation, . . . each family needs to have access to considerable areas of agricultural land. . . . It follows from this that Melanesian societies are minute in scale. The same culture and language are often shared by thousands, but the widest social unit possessing a coherent system for the maintenance of internal order consists of the seventy to three hundred persons resident within the boundaries of a clearly defined area seldom more than a few square miles in extent' (Hogbin and Wedgwood, 1953, pp. 241–2). Pouwer deals with this in greater detail and suggests that other factors affecting the size of groups are poor technology, chronic warfare, a high infant mortality due to endemic malaria, pneumonia, dysentery, and inadequate food habits. However, he points out that even where ecological, technological, and demographic factors are relatively favourable, there is a tendency for the Papuan to prefer living and working in small units. In 1957 in the then Netherlands New Guinea (excluding the Central Highlands and semi-controlled areas) the vast majority of villages contained no more than 300 inhabitants, and of these many had fewer than 100 (Pouwer, 1958, pp. 148–50). He suggests that the smallness of the local group and mode of life have important structural consequences. Life in a small group means daily contact with a small number of people, and this circumstance easily leads to a strong emphasis on the nuclear family; strong solidarity among siblings of both sexes is also particularly striking, and these two factors result in a stressing of the bilateral aspects of kinship (p. 151). He cites van der Leeden's statement that among the semi-nomadic Sarmi, who are patrilineal in principle, conditions are so arduous that of all the lineages, the smallest ones are more bilateral, whereas the larger lineages have kept to their patrilineal structure (p. 149). Pouwer also claims that among the Mimika, another semi-nomadic people, conditions are so exacting that 'the Mimika cannot permit himself the luxury of being unilineally organized' (p. 150).

Much of this seems common sense, and one can instance a number of societies in New Guinea where small local groups have to eke out an existence in a harsh environment and where, even if unilineal descent is present, it operates only in a very limited number of situations. There is an extensive utilization of a range of bilateral ties. Dr. Paula Brown also points out: 'Where the clans are small and communities composed of several, permitting local endogamy, the unilineal group may be difficult to discern as an activity group. Co-operation with local kin and affines dilutes the strength of the unilineal group' (1962, p. 68). However, to draw attention to the effect of ecological factors and size of community on the operation of the principle of unilineal descent is not to say that the unilineal principle of descent has some mystical value or virtue such that all stateless societies would adhere rigorously to it if they could.

It is true that, in some African societies which have a segmentary lineage system, 'the unilineal principle is all-pervasive or almost so, and defines the individual's status in the widest sense' (Lewis, 1965, p. 89). But, in comparing the social functions of unilineal descent among the Northern Somali, Cyrenaican Bedouin, Tiv, and Nuer, Lewis found so many variables that he concluded: 'It is in fact extremely difficult to establish that in any overall sense descent in one of a number of lineage societies is "more important" than in others' (p. 98). He also considers the social functions of unilineal descent in some state systems, and in his conclusions to the whole essay he puts forward the view that 'since descent has multiple characteristics in most societies, to say that one society is "strongly" patrilineal or matrilineal, or is more patrilineal or matrilineal than another, has in itself little meaning, except perhaps as an evaluation of native sentiment' (p. 107).

Some of these observations would appear to be highly relevant to the situation in the New Guinea Highlands, where there is considerable density of population, autonomous political groups are, on the whole, much larger than in other parts of New Guinea, and segmentary descent systems exist. As we have seen, Pouwer in his analyses of New Guinea kinship systems has been primarily concerned with the characteristics of small groups. In 1961 he once again stressed the particularly marked flexibility of New Guinea cultures and attributed it to the preponderance of small territorial and genealogical social contexts and the structural consequences derived from these. This preponderance he saw as in part an adaptation to an unfavourable environment and poor technology, but also as representing an independent cultural choice (1961, p. 9). What he does not discuss are the much larger groups, such as the Gahuku-Gama, Kuma, Chimbu, and Kyaka, which had already been studied in the Australian New Guinea Highlands. In many of these there is a marked element of optation in choice of residence and even of clan affiliation, in the sense that a man may not only reside in different parishes before and after marriage, but may also change his clan affiliation.

Barnes, in an interesting article on 'African Models in the New Guinea Highlands', points out that the mistake has sometimes been made of comparing the *de facto* situation in a Highland community, as shown by an ethnographical census, with a non-existent and idealized set of conditions among the Nuer, wrongly inferred from Evans-Pritchard's discussion of the principles of Nuer social structure; he nevertheless thinks there are major differences between a number of African communities on the one hand, and the Chimbu and other communities on the other (1962, p. 5). He admits that in many Highlands societies a majority of adult males in any local community are agnatically related to one another and that most marriages are patri-virilocal, yet he hesitates to call them patrilineal descent groups because in many instances male non-agnates are numerous, and it is often hard to detect any difference in status between them and agnates. An adolescent boy or even an adult man has some choice in deciding whether he will adhere to the local group in which his father is an agnate or to some other group where he can trace a non-agnatic connexion. He lists other characteristics, but these seem to me to be the crucial ones. He considers that the Mae-Enga and some other Highland societies fit into 'an agnatic model', 'but the area as a whole appears to be characterized by cumulative patrifiliation rather than by agnatic descent. . . . In most though not all Highland societies the dogma of descent is absent or is held only weakly; the principle of recruitment to a man's father's group operates, but only concurrently with other principles, and is sanctioned not by an appeal to the notion of descent as such but by reference to the obligations of kinsfolk, differentiated according to relationship and encompassed within a span of only two or three generations. In each generation a substantial majority of men affiliate themselves with their father's group and in this way it acquires some agnatic continuity over generations. It may be similar in demographic appearance and *de facto* kinship ties to a patrilineal group in which accessory segments are continually being assimilated to the authentic core, but its structure and ideology are quite different' (p. 6).

It is presumably on the grounds that the Nuer, according to Evans-Pritchard, have a strong ideology of patrilineal descent that Barnes does not classify their system as one of 'cumulative patrifiliation'. But an analysis of some Nuer communities reveals that they have a number of the characteristics attributed by Barnes to many Highlands societies. Certain clans and lineages have rights in certain tribal areas, and a sufficient number of the dominant groups reside in those areas to act as nuclei of local and political groups. But the composition of some of the communities is very mixed, and in some cases agnates of the dominant lineage may be outnumbered by uterine kin and affines (Evans-Pritchard, 1951, pp. 4–22). What is more, maternal links in some genealogies may be treated as though they were paternal links, and 'cognation becomes regarded for ordinary social purposes within community life as equal to agnation' (p. 16).

Here I would reiterate that while quantitative data must be taken into account in a full analysis, what is crucial is whether there exists an ideology of patrilineal descent. The Nuer possess this; and, with all due respect to him, I think Barnes has underestimated the number of societies in the Highlands which have been described as having an ideology of patrilineal descent and patri-virilocality. Among others, there are the Enga, Chimbu, Kuma, Gahuku-Gama, Kyaka, Mendi, Kamano, Siane, and Bena Bena.

In one of the best articles written to date on this subject, Dr. Paula Brown points out that while the approach of Pouwer and van der Leeden is closer to her own than that held by some other Dutch anthropologists, they have nevertheless been concerned with the variable composition of small groups, and have not taken into account the Highlands societies where population is dense and larger communities are found. For instance, in the Chimbu valley the population density ranges from 250 to 400 per square mile (Brookfield and Brown, 1963, p. 71). In her analysis of Chimbu groups she shows that while membership in them is ordinarily ascribed by birth, it may be achieved and there are optative features in group composition (Brown, 1962, p. 59). Chimbu clans are exogamous, marriage is patri-virilocal, descent group membership and inheritance are patrilineal; clans and their segments are localized (although segment territories are not compact blocks); and the hierarchic and contrapuntal features of segmentary descent groups are present. And she goes on to say that these characteristics are common to most of the New Guinea Highlands societies so far known. Nevertheless, although among the Chimbu 'about 80 per cent of the men, at any time, live on the territory of their natal subclan, garden patrilineally inherited land, and participate in activities organized by leaders of their natal subclan and clan', she found 'very few men who had not at some time in youth or adulthood resided with non-agnatic kin or affines. Every man has several alternative choices of kin and affines whose activities he may join, and where a home can be made for him' (p. 61).[1] As might be expected in this situation, even when a man remains permanently affiliated with his agnatic group, his interests and activities are by no means limited to it. He often visits and helps cognates and affines (p. 61). Nevertheless, 'recruitment into Chimbu clans is not restricted to agnatic descent. . . . Boys who are reared by non-agnates are, in time, fully participating members of their sponsors' group; only some of their agnates may recall their origin and press them to return. Their sons are indistinguishable from the sons of agnatic members of the group' (p. 67). However, she says that such descent groups do not conform to Firth's definition of a 'ramage' or an 'optative' system. 'Chimbu ideology is agnatic; relations between subclans, and between clans in a phratry, are conceived as relations between descendants of brothers' (p. 67).[2]

In explaining an element of optation in filiation, Brown lists both negative and positive factors. On the first count, defeat in war in the past led many people to seek refuge in other groups where they were given residential and gardening land; widows often take their children to become dependants of another man; men may leave their natal group after a serious quarrel or just for a change. On the positive side, it can be said that such individuals are welcome because

1. In an examination of transfers of land in one small agnatic group, it was found that 26 out of 105 were to men outside the clan of the donors and were made in the main to kin, and especially to affines (Brown and Brookfield, 1959, pp. 28 f.).
2. Despite the fact that in day-to-day situations there may be an absence of formalized behaviour between an individual and his maternal kin, nevertheless there are occasions when the particular character of the relationship is given ceremonial expression. When a child begins to walk a gift is made to his matrilateral kin; when a child marries, some share of the marriage payment is handed over to the mother's agnates; and when a man dies, his own agnates make a payment to his mother's agnates (Brown, 1961, pp. 90–91).

ties with non-agnatic kin and affines are interpersonal relations of aid and often close affection (p. 60). These ties permeate nearly all activities and 'are especially prominent in exchange, prestige, wealth and ceremonial; the changes in group composition which occur are a result of some types of mutual aid between kin and affines' (p. 59). What should be stressed is that the gifts and exchanges of food, pigs, and valuables between non-agnates and affines are not an economic necessity, since there is little regional variation in accessibility to goods and other resources, and no seasonal shortage of important foodstuffs. These transactions bring wealth, prestige, and pleasure (p. 62). If one were to follow Pouwer's line of argument, one could say that the environment, resources, and large size of political groups are of a nature which would permit the Chimbu not merely the luxury of being unilineally organized, as indeed they are, but rigorously patrilineal. But, as in many New Guinea societies, prestige depends in part on prowess in war and especially on the accumulation and distribution of wealth, which enables an able and ambitious man not only to meet his own commitments on a lavish scale, but also to assist his own dependants and attract adherents. It is these features—the prevalence of war in the past, the need to maintain the fighting strength of the group, the competition among ambitious men to become big-men, the elaboration of extra-clan ceremonial exchanges—which provide the context for an understanding of an element of optation in clan affiliation in many societies in New Guinea which have an ideology of unilineal descent and patri-virilocal residence. The Kyaka on the northern slopes of the Mount Hagen range are a case in point, and offer some similarities to the Chimbu.

The Kyaka number some 10,000 and have a density of some 140 to the square mile, if forest long uncultivated is excluded. The autonomous political community is smaller than among the Chimbu and is the localized exogamous patriclan. It previously acted as an independent war-making unit; it still co-ordinates the *moka* or ceremonial exchanges carried out by its members, and it collectively performs certain cult and ceremonial activities. As among the Chimbu, there is a segmentary descent system which is *ideologically* patrilineal. Territorial units are associated with named descent groups; but 'genealogical probing reveals that many members are there by virtue of one or more female links, although these make no difference to their status if they have been brought up and have lived the greater part of their lives with the group' (Bulmer, 1960, p. 2).

As among the Chimbu, there is great stress on lateral ties: not only does a marriage involve a sequence of gifts, exchanges, and feasts, but there are subsequently similar transactions between the families of bride and groom, and between their descendants, on such occasions as the birth of children, deaths of the spouses and their children, as well as on other formal occasions (p. 5). In the complex *moka* exchanges of valuables and pigs which bring prestige to participants, *moka* partners are most commonly affines, or mother's brother and sister's son, or cross-cousins, or even maternal parallel cousins. However, Bulmer considers that the most important in terms of frequency and content are those between affines; and if a man has several partners and finds he cannot meet his commitments to all, he is most likely to honour those to his brothers-in-law, most probably to ensure the continuance of his marriage and benefits of matrilateral ties to his children (p. 10). As among the Chimbu and other peoples, individuals achieve positions of influence by accumulating pigs and valuables and using these in loans and ceremonial exchanges. Some of these are able to secure the assistance not merely of distant relatives but even of genealogically unrelatable members of their own or neighbouring settlement groups. Such adherents may be granted garden land, temporarily or permanently, and helped in their marriage payments. In return, they assist their patron in male tasks, such as pig-raising; and, what is especially important, they must 'channel through him such pigs of their own as they are putting into the *moka* exchanges' (pp. 5, 9).

Among the Kuma, who inhabit the area to the west of the Chimbu, the density of population would appear to be lower than among the Kyaka to the west, and much more so than among the Chimbu. However, Reay says that although the government census gives a density of 100 or so persons to the square mile, the area taken into account includes the uninhabited swampy river flats. Hence the actual density is probably twice that figure (1959, p. 3). The localized clan is the autonomous political unit and there is an ideology of patrilineal descent: 'The natives say that every man who is an acknowledged member of any of the named descent groups (phratry, clan, subclan or sub-subclan) is descended in an unbroken line of males from the group ancestor' (p. 33). She states that 'only a minute proportion of clan members leave the parish permanently to settle with others, but other parishes may absorb whole segments of clans that have been routed in warfare or are dying out '(p. 38). A man is not supposed to live permanently in a parish other than his own, and if he does change his residence it is said that he is staying temporarily with kinsfolk or an affine.[1] He has his sponsor in the new community who welcomes him as an addition to his own personal following, since here, as in so many other societies, there is competition among men to become eminent leaders. The newcomer is regarded as an associate member and his sponsor acts as his representative in disputes and clan activities; but his own sons are regarded as full members. One reason for a change of residence is the attraction of being associated with a brother-in-law who has a wide reputation as a renowned leader. Through such a sponsor a man gains some prestige, meets a number of people of other parishes and has 'the sense of belonging to an informed élite' (p. 49). Unfortunately, Reay does not give us any quantitative data on the number of men who leave their parishes permanently, but she states that there are certain clues which suggest that only a relatively small proportion of fully effective clan members have direct agnatic forebears who were not incorporated at some stage from without (p. 51).

In a recent article on the Bena Bena of the Eastern Highlands, Langness shows that there is even greater variation in the composition of local groups than among the Kuma or even the Chimbu. He deals in particular with the political community or tribe called the Korofeigu, which numbers 750 persons and has a density of about 75 to the square mile. It is divided into four exogamous groups ('clans') which, according to native ideology, are patrilineal; these are localized in the sense that members of each reside in a common territory in one or more villages. The groups are segmented into smaller patrilineal groups ('subclans' and 'lineages'). A statistical analysis of one of the localized 'clans' shows that of 110 male residents, 30 per cent are non-agnates; of the 35 adult males, only 20 (57 per cent) have lived their lives in the group territory and constitute its true agnatic core (Langness, 1964, pp. 166–7). Langness also discovered that of 61 known adult male agnates, some 43 per cent were living elsewhere (p. 168). Nevertheless, men living apart from their natal descent groups do not suffer any disabilities and are not even regarded as 'associate members', as they would be among the Kuma. They are addressed by kinship terms and they must observe the rule of exogamy of the group in which they are permanently residing. In other words, while membership of descent groups is determined by birth for a considerable number of males, some achieve it

---

1. It should be noted that here, as among the Chimbu, there is great emphasis on friendship and assistance between brothers-in-law, mother's brother and sister's son, and cross-cousins (pp. 62–4).

by residence. 'The sheer fact of residence in a Bena Bena group can and does determine kinship' (p. 172).

Unfortunately, Langness has not yet published data on the relations between affines or a man and his matrilateral kin, or on the exchanges of pigs and other valuables. But in accounting for the variability in group composition, despite an ideology of patrilineal descent and patrilocal residence, he stresses the endemic warfare which here, as in other parts of New Guinea, led to the incorporation of defeated groups in other political communities. By the same token, group strength had to be maintained at all costs, and hence refugees were a welcome accession to manpower (pp. 173–4). And he also suggests that the antecedent conditions of segmentation, which is so common a feature of descent systems in the Highlands, may be linked with 'the optimum size of groups exploiting land with horticultural techniques, the number of people who can effectively work communally at certain tasks or the optimum number of persons who can organize themselves following relatively informal patterns of leadership. When a group reaches such a size, it splits, with some members following one "big man" and some another' (p. 181).[1]

Meggitt, who has recently published a detailed study of the Mae-Enga, who inhabit an area to the west of the Kyaka, has also concerned himself with the factors affecting the degree of adherence to a principle of patrilineal descent and patri-virilocal residence. The Mae-Enga number some 30,000; their average density of population per square mile is 120, though in places it exceeds 250 (1965, p. 268). Though clans are grouped into subphratries and phratries, the political unit is the clan parish with a population ranging from 100 to 1,000, and a mean population of 350. 'Clan exogamy and patrilineal inheritance of land are explicit social rules. Ideally, therefore, clan parishes should comprise only clansmen, their wives and unmarried daughters. In fact, clansmen may allow a few non-agnatic men to live more or less permanently with them' (p. 9). As in most of the societies we have examined, a parish would give refuge to non-agnates and affines routed in warfare, and this was the more likely to happen when the parish itself was declining in numbers and wished

1. Reay has examined the processes of segmentation among the Kuma, and suggests that large expanding clans, in which segmentation has occurred, decimated one another in continual warfare and surviving segments found refuge in widely scattered groups. Fission might also occur within the clan through severe disagreements (1959, p. 32). A detailed account of processes of segmentation among the Mae-Enga is also given by Meggitt (1965, pp. 49–84).

I

to build up its military strength for defence of clan land. Again, an individual who has no adolescent or adult sons may give his sisters or daughters in marriage to men who are prepared to settle in his parish; or a man with widowed sisters or daughters encourages them to return with their children to his parish. Lastly, an ambitious man of early middle age with very young sons, who wishes to become a prominent leader in the ceremonial exchange cycle and other situations involving the distribution of wealth, may invite one or two agnates of his wives to reside with him and give assistance in the care of gardens and pigs. He helps them in their marriage payments and transactions in the ceremonial exchanges. However, to ensure their continued residence after marriage, he has to obtain for them more or less permanent rights to land, and this can only be done if they can claim an actual or classificatory mother's brother in the parish who is prepared to allot them some gardening land because they are 'children of female agnates' (pp. 27–31). The resident sons of female agnates are distinguished from the agnates of the clan parish, but in the next generation their male offspring are regarded as clan agnates, provided they give full allegiance to the parish. They have full rights in land and receive economic, ritual, and military aid (pp. 32–5).

While almost every clan, however short of land it appears to be, has some non-agnates and affines attached to its parish group, Meggitt stresses that their number depends largely on the amount of available land. In a census of three Mae parishes he found that 86·2 per cent of the adult males lived in their natal patriclan parishes; the corresponding figure for two Laiapu parishes was 92·6 per cent (pp. 268–9). Meggitt had the opportunity to make brief visits to some societies which were peripheral to the Central Enga and had a lower population density, averaging some 30 to the square mile. He gained the impression that the patrilineal descent systems of most of them had little of the rigidity and elaboration of the Central Enga. He made one census of a small Taro parish with 118 residents: of the 32 resident men, only 78 per cent were agnates (pp. 269–70).

On the basis of his research among various groups of Enga, he is of the opinion that land availability is a very important factor in determining the composition of localized kin groups. While he states that the argument for a causal relation between land-availability and stress on agnation is difficult to test at this time because too many variables remain ill-defined, he puts forward the hypothesis that 'where members of a homogeneous society of horticulturalists distinguish in any consistent fashion between agnates and other relatives, the degree to which social groups are structured in terms of agnatic descent and patrilocality varies with the pressure on available agrarian resources' (p. 266).

Now clearly, density of population and fertility of land are important factors which must be taken into account in discussing the composition of localized kin groups. And where a patriclan parish has not in fact got sufficient land to support its own members, it cannot afford to grant any more than very temporary rights of usufruct to non-agnates. The Mae-Enga themselves, as compared with some of the other Highlands peoples on which we have information, lay particular emphasis on what they regard as a situation of chronic land shortage; and one of the main objects of the inter-clan warfare in the past was territorial expansion (p. 268). Meggitt says that even when parishes welcomed immigrants for defence reasons, non-agnates formed at most some 20 to 25 per cent; and the situation was regarded as abnormal and as one to be avoided if possible (p. 29). But in a number of the other Highlands societies, with comparable densities of population, there does not appear to have been an overt emphasis on land shortage. In these we find considerable fluidity in clan affiliation. I refer again to the Kyaka with an effective population density of 140 to the square mile, and to the Chimbu with an even higher density of 250 to 400 per square mile. In both of these, some 20 per cent of the men of parishes were non-agnates. We have no quantitative data from Reay on the composition of Kuma clan parishes, but she states that an effective density of population was twice that of the 100 per square mile given by the government census; and that although there was the dogma of patrilineal descent and inheritance, she believed that in fact only a small proportion of fully effective clan members were directly descended in an unbroken line of males from a group ancestor.

In other words, I do not think that the degree of adherence to a principle of agnatic descent and inheritance can be explained in terms of one factor alone, i.e. effective density of population per square mile. In the study of societies with patrilineal descent, whether they be in New Guinea or in any other part of the world, one must analyse both the ideology and operation of the principle of patrilineal descent within the context of the political, economic, and ritual institutions of the society concerned. To reiterate a point made earlier in this essay, the element of optation in affiliation to descent groups in the Highlands must be examined in the context of the elaboration of extra-clan ceremonial exchanges; ritual collaboration between clans; the competition among ambitious men to be-

come leaders and attract a following not only among their own agnates but also among uterine kin, affines, and even unrelated persons;
the need to maintain the fighting strength of the group when war was
endemic; and, lastly, the value attached in many of these societies to
relationships with non-agnatic kin and affines, not merely in terms of
sentiment but also in terms of mutual co-operation, assistance, and
the exchanges of food, pigs, and valuables.[1]

The type of institutional context which I have outlined for societies
with patrilineal descent and inheritance in the Central Highlands is
not confined to that area, as should be evident from my brief account
of the northern Abelam village of Kalabu presented earlier in this
essay. The Abelam-speaking people, who number some 30,000,
inhabit the Sepik District where both the environment and features
of the economy differ from the Highlands. The autonomous political
unit was the village which consisted of a cluster of named hamlets.
Kalabu itself had a population of about 500 in 1939–40, and its
people were divided into eighteen patriclans. There was an ideology
of patrilineal descent and inheritance, and ideally male agnates
should reside together. Nevertheless, there were strong ties with
uterine kin, and when serious quarrels developed between a man
and the members of his clan, or when he was dissatisfied with its
role in the competitive exchanges of long yams, he might affiliate with
uterine kin. As in many other societies, there was competition among
big-men (who in this society played a prominent role in yam exchanges and initiation ceremonies) for adherents; and when a youth
or adult man for various reasons wished to leave his natal group, he
had no difficulty in changing his place of residence, obtaining rights
to garden land, and entrusting the ritual care of some of his long
yams to the big-man who was his host. It should be stressed that while
in some contexts the agnatic principle was emphasized by informants, in other contexts there was an explicit recognition that in a
range of situations an individual had the right 'to follow the road
of his mother' and ally himself with her clan. The range of factors
which influenced an individual to leave his natal group and those
which were taken into account in making a choice of the group with
which he decided to affiliate himself, either temporarily or per-

1. Forde, in examining the composition of kin groups among the Yakö, also
stresses that any analysis of the functional significance of kin groups 'both cor-
porately in the wider society and for their members, needs to take into account a
number of underlying variables, not only within the field of kinship, but also in the
external factors of economy and demography which may affect the modes of recognition and the application of any general principles or particular rules which
should govern recruitment to such groups' (1963, p. 38).

manently, are discussed in another publication (see Kaberry, 1966). Men who changed their affiliation were not regarded as 'second class citizens', deviants, or capricious persons. What is important is that not merely did the Abelam kinship system display a considerable degree of plasticity, but the Abelam themselves were aware of the complexities of existence, and that if the village, which was the focal point of activities, was to hold together as a corporate unit there must be some fluidity in affiliation. In this they do not differ from many societies which utilize for certain purposes a principle of unilineal descent. Indeed, it is too often the anthropologist who gives to the principle of descent a primacy which, when the full range of principles of association and their values is taken into account, it can be seen in fact not to possess.

The Language of Kachin Kinship: Reflections on a Tikopia Model

EDMUND LEACH

In almost all fields of scientific enquiry the professional practitioners are divided into two camps. There are those who are temperamentally inclined to start off with formal ideal models and work down to the facts of the case, and there are those who prefer to start with the facts and work cautiously upwards to a generalized abstraction. Neither side can see much merit in the work of the other; yet, as a matter of history, it would seem that both have something to contribute; progress in basic understanding often stems quite directly from the polemical dialectic of theorist versus empiricist.

One branch of anthropology in which we can observe this process at work is the study of kinship terminology. This field is often delimited in such a way that the kin terms of a language appear to be the equivalent of a closed set of functionally interconnected algebraic symbols; the theorist can then give his imagination unlimited scope by devising geometrical and componential models which will fit all the members of his symbol set together. For nearly a century this pastime has had an obsessional fascination for a wide assortment of anthropologists. For such 'theorists' the more empirically minded have nothing but scorn, yet I do not think it can be argued that *all* the ingenuity devoted to the study of 'kinship terminology' *per se* has proved wholly futile. Or can it? Raymond Firth's contributions to the study of Tikopia kinship pose this question in a very interesting way.

Apart from a field report published in *Oceania*, Vol. 1, No. 1 (Firth, 1930a), 'Marriage and the Classificatory System of Relationship' (Firth, 1930b) was Firth's first contribution to Tikopia studies, and it may seem odd that this should have been devoted to an analysis of kinship terminology, a topic which functionalist anthropologists of the School of Malinowski have tended to view with disdain. Firth's paper is, in a formal sense, a polemical attack on the 'theorist' stance adopted by W. H. R. Rivers; it sets out to demonstrate in meticulous detail the advantages which accrue from an uncompromising 'empiricism'. It certainly achieved its formal objective; it had the effect of a blockbuster bomb on a mud fort; for the last thirty years it has seemed heresy to suggest that Rivers had said anything in the least sensible about kinship terminology. Yet precisely because Firth's paper was a triumph of destructive polemic, its positive aspects have been very largely neglected. And the positive aspects are important; they have a 'theoretical' as well as 'empirical' interest.

In 1930, Firth's functionalism was of an uncompromising kind. He held that Tikopia kinship terminology could only be understood in its own context; other kinship terminologies could only be understood in their own context, and context meant the whole works:

> What the observer cannot help but perceive as he is actually studying the culture in all its bearings, is the essential practical utility of the classificatory system of counting relationship in its own cultural surroundings. Unlike the rigid travesty of it which is sometimes put forward by theorists for comment and criticism, it reveals itself as a convenient, flexible and commonsense piece of social mechanism (Firth, 1930b, final paragraph).

The logical implication of such an argument is that *any* kind of cross-cultural comparison of kin term systems considered in isolation from their 'cultural surroundings' must be a waste of time. Yet if one reads Firth's paper as a whole, together with the comparable material which appears in various chapters of *We, The Tikopia*, one cannot avoid noticing that Firth himself takes it for granted that 'a kinship terminology' is a self-delimited set of words and that *some* cross-cultural comparison is legitimate, even if the comparison is confined to the zone of Polynesian languages (Firth, 1936a, pp. 277–83). That Firth should have qualified his functionalism in this particular way is illuminating.

Anthropological studies of kinship terminology, from the days of Morgan onwards, share one extraordinary peculiarity. Although a kin term set, however defined, is quite plainly a phenomenon of language, the *linguistic* aspects of kin terms have never been examined at all—phonology is never considered, only meaning. Even in very recent years, when the vogue for the 'componential analysis' of kin term sets has been elaborately developed in the United States by anthropologists trained in the methods of structural linguistics, the enquiry has been narrowly confined to semantic structure, any consideration of phonological factors being rigidly excluded. In the whole vast literature of the subject I am only aware of one short paper which argues explicitly that there are aspects of kin term systems

which call for investigation as problems of phonological linguistics—
and this is by a linguist (Jakobson, 1960) and not an anthropologist.
Yet implicitly it is all there in Firth's paper of 1930.

In 1930, linguistics was still in a very primitive stage of development; it was the 'pre-phonemic' era. Consequently, until someone
makes a phonemic analysis of the Tikopia language there is nothing
much to be learned, linguistically speaking, from the verbatim ver-
nacular texts with which Firth's Tikopia ethnography is so liberally
garnished. But one can get some ideas. Firth understood the obvious
yet repeatedly neglected fact that kin terms must convey meaning as
sound patterns, and that contrasts in meaning are likely to correspond to contrasts in sound pattern. He also seems to have understood, intuitively, another very fundamental principle of modern
linguistics, namely that the phonemic elements which an adult uses
for purposes of communication are established at an early age in the
language of childhood, so that if we are interested in discovering just
what sound contrasts are significant in any language, we shall do
well to pay close attention to the 'errors' embodied in children's
speech.

I would draw the reader's attention to the following features of
Firth's discussions of 'the language of kinship'.

(1) He tolerates cross-cultural comparison, but only within the
    ambit of Polynesian languages; i.e., legitimate comparison is
    linguistic not 'structural-semantic', as it is with Rivers, Rad-
    cliffe-Brown, *et al.*

(2) He draws attention to specific variation of significance cor-
    responding to phonemic shift. Understandably he does not
    press this very far, but he notes the sequence *pu-pa-pe-pae*:

    pu indicates primarily age, sometimes ancestral dignity,
        sometimes a grandfather's position
    pa indicates general married status and is the common title,
        and connotes also fatherhood
    pe indicates essentially a married man of equivalent status
        as the speaker, as a brother, or brother-in-law
    pae . . . a softened form of the housename [*pa*] . . . a polite
        modification (Firth, 1936a, pp. 258, 311).

He also notes that the formal descriptive antithesis between
tamana father and *nana* mother is in practice reduced to *mana/
nana*, a binary opposition which rests on the simplest of all
possible phonemic contrasts.[1]

1. See Jakobson, 1960; also Jakobson and Halle, 1956.

(3) He devotes a whole section to 'the kinship speech of young children' (Firth, 1936a, pp. 272–7), a theme which has been almost entirely neglected by other ethnographers. He does not, it is true, draw linguistic implications from this description, but the report alone is most illuminating. The formal Tikopia terms for 'father's sister' and 'mother's brother' are unmanageable polysyllables, *masikitaŋa* and *tuatina* respectively, and any social theorist who felt that, in the circumstances of Tikopia social structure, these two social statuses *ought* somehow to be opposed as linguistic categories might well despair of ever unravelling the code. But when Firth tells us that children reduce these two words to *titaŋa* and *tatina* respectively the phonemic transformation begins to look quite simple! *Taina* (sibling of same sex; sibling's spouse) seems to belong to the same sub-set of words. In Tonga the equivalent term is a three syllable word *tehina*.

There are many other implications embedded in this early work which were not only missed by the author but are still wholly neglected thirty-six years later. I shall mention only two.

Firstly, although Firth writes as if he knows what a kin term is, i.e., that it can be recognized by inspection, this does not seem to me to be a category which is inherent in his material. One word may be rated as a 'kin term', another as a 'pronoun', another as a 'title', and another as a 'metaphorical usage', but if such distinctions are made they seem to me very arbitrary. Firth thought that the great value of his analysis was that he showed how kin terms are actually employed in their cultural context; what seems to me much more original is that he shows how kin words are used in relation to non-kin words . . . so that the distinction between kinship language and non-kinship language almost disappears.

Secondly, he draws attention to the interesting way in which the Tikopia use the word *tau*, though oddly enough he does not explicitly state that this is a variant of the way they use *tautau*, which he also discusses at length (see especially Firth, 1930b *passim;* Firth, 1936a, pp. 254 f.). A Tikopia may refer to a brother and a sister, who would address one another as *kave*, as *tau kave*, and there are many other analogous uses. Firth describes this word *tau* as 'implying the link or reciprocity between them (the *kave*)' and as 'a relational particle, not altogether of the possessive order, but indicating the existence of a bond between the objects named'. In a bold and unfunctional footnote (Firth, 1936a, p. 254), he even allows himself to point out that such usages are found in parts of Melanesia outside the Western Polynesia language zone! He need not have been so cautious. The Tikopia usage seems to me an example of a rather widespread set of ideas.

Our English twentieth century convention is to use words as if they referred to Aristotelean 'natural kinds'. Our language presumes that objects in the world are naturally discrete and separate, and that if they are to be brought together into some kind of 'system' this can only be done by 'linking them together'. This is a mode of thought that is strictly consistent with the atomism which has been dominant in English philosophy for at least a century. But there is nothing intrinsically 'natural' about this way of perceiving the world; it would correspond more closely to experience if we spoke of objects and entities as becoming separate only when they are torn apart. . . . at the very least this is true of all living creatures; a mother and her child are one before they are two. A great deal may flow from this simple inversion of ideas. It may be, for example, that conventional anthropology is at fault in thinking that the central problem of kinship studies is to show 'how individuals are linked together by relationship', for such a formulation implies that it is conceivable that individuals should *not* be linked together by relationships. Our concern perhaps should not be with how relationships are formed but with how they become weakened.

This is not, of course, how Firth looks at the matter, but such an approach does seem to be implicit in much that he writes. A Tikopia is born into an existing mesh of kin relationships and as life proceeds these relationships do not really change. From the beginning a man's sister is a *kave* and so is his wife, they simply change their quality. The easygoing cluster of relationships (*tautau laui*) and the restrained cluster of relationships (*tautau pariki*) are in existence all the time; only the membership of these categories changes. Ego is never out on his own, an isolated individual; he is always part of a reciprocal group (*tautau laui*), a member of a set of reciprocal pairs (*tau mana* 'father and child'; *tau tuatina*, 'mother's brother and sister's son'; *tau kave*, 'brother and sister'; and so on). Firth shows us all this, but perhaps he does not show it very plain, and his functionalist commitments make him reluctant to formulate any general theory which might be applied to non-Tikopia or even to speakers of non-Polynesian languages.

And I must raise one more point of criticism before I proceed. Firth writes as if 'relationships' could somehow exist independently of the labels by which they are known. The 'classificatory system' is a 'convenient mechanism' for 'counting relationship'. This is an orthodox empiricist-nominalist position; it is not one that I share, but I can see how it might apply to physical objects in our environment. There is clearly a sense in which 'dogs exist' even if we do not choose to operate with a category 'dogs'. But can it be said that 'relationships exist' even if we do not recognize them and classify them with words? I find this a very tricky problem. The notion of order is a human notion and psychologically a most necessary one. In order to use our environment and find our way about in it we must credit it with structure and describe it as an ordered system; indeed, the selector mechanisms at the back of the retina which translate light and shadow into visual perception predispose us to interpret our observations as order rather than chaos. But the word 'relationship' is concerned with the ordering as such, and it entails not human observation but human creation; we do not use words to describe relationships, we create verbal categories which imply relationships, and such verbal categories arise as a consequence of our perceiving the world as an ordered structured system. I fully appreciate that there are complicated existentialist-phenomenologist assumptions at the back of my argument, but on this particular point even such a thorough-going empiricist as Bertrand Russell is in agreement. For Russell the word 'relation' is simply the link term between the concept of structure and the concept of class (Russell, 1948, pp. 270 f.). If we accept this view, then as soon as we recognize that the Tikopia make use of a classificatory set of kin terms, we *must* also recognize that the structure of relations inherent in that matrix of classes has significance both for the Tikopia as users and for us as analysts. The weakness of Firth's analysis is that, in his anxiety to demolish Rivers, he rejects the concept of structure altogether. Kin terms become operational tools for the use of individuals interacting with other individuals, and we lose sight of the fact that the kin term system as a whole must somehow present to the individual a structured paradigm of the society in which he lives.

So I come back to the argument of my opening paragraphs. How can a 'theorist', who is inclined to emphasize the paradigmatic quality of kin term systems considered as a total set, gain advantage from Firth's intensive empirical treatment in which he examines the particular use of particular words by particular individuals in particular situations?

This essay is an attempt to explore some of the possibilities which seem to me latent in Firth's treatment. I shall try to apply his ideas and methods to an entirely different cultural and linguistic context—

that of the Kachin in North Burma. I shall take as 'given' the formal structural analysis of Kachin kinship terminology which I have published previously which purports to demonstrate how the term system is a paradigm of the social structure. Here I shall tackle the same data (or rather parts of the same data) from quite a different point of view. Instead of treating Kachin kin terms as a self-defined closed set of words, I shall examine their context of use in a variety of different dimensions. I shall consider:

(a) Linguistic factors. . . . What sort of sound patterns are involved? How do these sound patterns tie in with other sound patterns in the same language?

(b) Metaphorical factors. . . . A number of the morphemes which Kachins use as kin terms also serve as discriminators of time and space and of parts of the body and as categories of living creatures.

(c) Ideological factors. . . . By this I mean verbal usages which seem to imply a different set of logical assumptions from our own. . . . e.g. the Tikopia *tau* and *tautau* usages described above.

Such complicated information will not of course all fit tidily together into a single matrix. The analysis is unlikely to show anything in particular except that the facts as a whole are pretty messy, but just as there is more to Firth, 1930b than a 'destruction of Rivers', there may be more to what follows than a demonstration of complexity.

As will presently be apparent, the procedures involved in this kind of analysis are very laborious and take up a lot of space. I must make it clear therefore that I am not here attempting a comprehensive analysis of the whole language of Kachin kinship in this modified Firthian style. I am only trying to indicate what might be possible in more spacious circumstances and what kind of conclusions we might expect to derive from such arduous and roundabout procedures. But first a word of caution. I am concerned with problems both of meaning and of linguistic structure. The reader should not forget that some linguists maintain that these two fields of enquiry are best kept well apart. We can distinguish the meaning of utterances only because of contrast and context. CAT differs from SAT because of the contrast between C and S, but whether we should hear 'the cat sat' or 'the cats at' can only be determined by context. Since contexts may vary to an almost indefinite degree, it is surely futile to try to discover just *how* a particular meaning is embedded in a particular pattern of sound? Yet the problem is there. Young children quickly learn to manipulate sound patterns so as to forge a language, and it seems inconceivable that they should be able to do this unless at the child's level of speech there were some rather close consistency between the structure of meanings and the structure of phonology.

It is an assumption of this paper that such structures exist and that they are partly decipherable. I am not suggesting that such structures apply to the whole of a language. Adult vocabulary, grammar, and syntax are all immensely complicated. But, in the beginning, when children first learn to speak, the structure of sounds and meanings must be more or less homologous. If we accept this as a postulate, then kinship words may be expected to show rather special linguistic characteristics.

In every natural language some kinship words must form parts of the basic elements in a child's vocabulary. These need not be 'proper' kinship terms; they are more likely to be a special baby language, but they are likely to conform to a very elementary phonemic code (e.g., the English mama, dada, baba, nana). In a society, such as the Kachin, where personal names are seldom used, and where everyone in sight is categorized as a kinsman of one kind or another, it seems likely that the phonemics of kinship terminology have an even more basic quality.

The Kachins of North Burma speak a language of the Tibeto-Burman group. It is, in the main, monosyllabic, and in some cases tonal distinctions are phonetically significant. However, in most cases distinctions of meaning are achieved *not* by alteration of tone and stress but by the addition of different 'prefixes' (or 'suffixes') to a persisting monosyllabic 'root'. For example, the words *jā* (hard), *ajā* (gold), *gŭmjā* (golden), *kăjā* (good), *lăjā* (difficult), *njā* (darling), *măjā* (obstinate), *shăjā* (persevere) are all variations on the idea conveyed by the root word *jā* (hard, enduring, bright) and, in conversation, where no ambiguity is likely, the root term alone might be used for any of these words. The monosyllabic kinship terms which I discuss in this and in other publications are all 'root' terms in this sense.

Hanson's *Kachin Dictionary* (1906) is lexically impressive but suffers from a variety of defects, e.g.:

(1) Words are arranged alphabetically instead of by 'roots', which leads to a vast amount of redundancy.

(2) Many words which Hanson treats as distinct homonyms are simply the same word applied to different contexts.

(3) Hanson ignores tone and stress so that some words which have the same Hanson spelling are phonologically quite distinct.

(4) Hanson uses grammatical categories drawn from formal Indo-European, which are quite inappropriate.

(5) The letters in Hanson's alphabet do not correspond consistently to phonemic distinctions in the language.

Nevertheless Hanson's spelling is consistent and he had an accurate ear; in most cases he himself draws attention to the phonemic inconsistencies. In what follows I shall write all Kachin words in their Hanson romanization.

Hanson distinguishes the following consonantal sounds:

B, BY, CHY, D, G, GY, J, K, KY, HK, HKR, HKY, L, M, N, NG, NY, P, HP, R, S, SH, T, TS, HT, W, Y, Z, and the

following vowels:

A, Ă, E, Ē, I, U, AI, AU, AW, OI.

The orthography also allows for certain other noises which occur only in interjections and the pronunciation of foreign words, but these do not concern us here.

Of the consonants, G and K are almost always interchangeable, and J and SH very frequently so. The NG is the velar nasal in English 'sing'. The aspiration which distinguishes HK from K, HP from P, and HT from T is always phonemically significant. The semivowel Y by which Hanson separates J from CHY, HK from HKY, and N from NY is audible but not necessarily phonemically significant; e.g., JI and CHYI can mean the same thing. Of the vowels, Ă is an undifferentiated sound, as the 'o' in 'mother'; A is long as in 'ma' at the end of a syllable, but short as in 'man' in the middle of a syllable. A similar long/short distinction applies to Hanson's I (e.g. *mi* as in 'me', but *ming* as in the Chinese dynasty), and U (e.g. *wu* as in 'woo' but *wun* as in 'wool'). E is short as in 'ten'. Of the diphthongs AI is as *y* in 'my'; AU is as *ow* in 'cow'; AW is as 'or'; OI is as *oy* in 'boy'. Hanson rates initial W as a consonant. In some contexts it is not phonemically distinct from U. This is discussed below. The combination which Hanson writes WI overlaps with his OI; thus *dwi* ('sweet') might equally well be *doi*.

Throughout this essay the reader should bear in mind that the grammar of Kachin is quite different from the grammar of English. Almost any Kachin word may serve equally well as a 'noun' or a 'verb', and even when considered as nouns most words have several distinct meanings. Usually (though not always) the different meanings of a word are linked together in some way; in English translation the linkage appears to be one of metaphor, but for a Kachin speaker it is more like a pun—the use of the same idea in different contexts. Here is a relevant example:

> WOI—'grandmother' also 'monkey'
> SHU—'grandchild' also 'frog'.

To call wizened granny a 'monkey' and the crawling infant whom she looks after a 'frog' is a kind of word-play. But used as 'verbs' WOI and SHU have exactly the same meaning, 'to look after a small child':

nang ma woi⎫ nta nga u
⠀⠀⠀⠀⠀⠀shu⎭

you child 'woi'⎫ house be (command)
⠀⠀⠀⠀⠀⠀'shu'⎭

'you stay at home and mind the baby (like a granny)'.

Before I say anything in detail about the language of Kachin kinship I want to say something about the general nature of Kachin verbal categories.

Let us start with the concept of *relationship*, remembering what has been said about the Tikopia concepts of *tau* and *tautau*. Kachins have no equivalent verbalization, but their usage is analogous. They habitually talk as if categories of persons (especially kin) were linked in binary pairs by their intrinsic nature. Thus, in each of the following expressions, the final *ni* is a 'plural affix' which conditions *both* halves of the preceding binary term. The expressions could refer to individuals, but, in all ordinary circumstances, would be taken to refer to groups, as indicated in the gloss on my first example:

(1) *nu-wa ni*—mother-father (plural) . . . the senior males of a lineage plus their wives (only in a special context would the expression be taken to mean one particular pair of parents).

(2) *hpu-nau ni*—elder brother-younger sibling (plural) . . . members of a lineage considered as a whole.

(3) *hpu-wa ni*—elder brother-father (plural). . . the members of a lineage distinguished by generation (see example 10 below).

(4) *măyu-dama ni*—'wife giving lineage'—'wife receiving lineage' (plural) . . . a pair of affinally linked lineages considered as a unity.

(5) *ji-woi ni*—grandfather-grandmother (plural) . . . ancestors.

(6) *kǎshu-kǎsha ni*—grandchild-child (plural) . . . descendants.

(7) *du-sǎlang ni*—chief-elder (plural) . . . the leaders of a community.

When groups are paired in this way they are always mutually exclusive; there is always a factor of similarity and a factor of contrast (e.g., *mǎyu* and *dama* are both affines but contrasted as givers and receivers of women).

Kachins are of course perfectly capable of thinking of each half of such a binary couplet as an entity by itself in the singular, but when they speak in this fashion they use the word *daw*, thus:

(8) *shan hpu-nau daw ai*—they (dual) (as) elder brother-younger sibling 'related' are.

(9) *shanhte mǎyu-dama daw ma ai*—they (plural) (as) affines 'related' are (plural).

(10) *nang hte ngai num hpu-wa daw nga ga ai*—you with me wife elder brother-father 'related' (we) are . . . 'you and I are related as brother and father through our wives' (i.e., because our wives come from the same lineage, we are both *dama* to the same *mǎyu* and should therefore use kinship terms as if we were of the same lineage).

Although I have here translated *daw* as 'related', it is quite clear from other contexts in which this word is used that the notion it conveys is that of something separated—a portion broken off from a larger whole, thus:

(11) *daw mi daw kau e*—'portion' one 'separate' completely . . . 'break off a portion'.

(12) *daw da ai hte mǎren jaw lu na*—'portion' fixed is with same give must . . . 'you must give in accordance with the customary portions'.

(13) *nhtoi daw nna gǎlaw u*—day 'separate' and do it . . . 'fix a day and do it'.

(14) *nang n daw ai mǎjaw hten mat sai*—you not 'separate' because broken was . . . 'because you did not handle it carefully ('separately') it was broken'.

(15) *kǎnu-kǎwa daw yang si ai da, mǎrang daw yang mǎdi ai da*— mother-father 'separate' if die will, rain 'separate' if wet will . . . 'he who leaves his birthplace will die as surely as he who stands in the open in the rain will get wet.'

K

In brief, where we say 'they are *related* (connected) as brother and brother', Kachins say 'they are *distinguishable* as brother and brother'. Apparently Kachins think first of the larger agglomeration and then consider how it can be broken down into its component parts; they do not start with individuals and build them up into collectivities. In terms of the opening paragraph of this essay, they seem to be 'theorists' rather than 'empiricists', and to an anthropologist this may seem a very important distinction.

It follows from this that the metaphors which Kachins employ to represent social links are things which divide rather than things which tie together. I shall return to this point later.

If the ordinary entities of the Kachin world are groups rather than individuals, then it must follow that the concept of 'category' (kind, sort, species) must be very fundamental for a Kachin speaker. How does this idea present itself? How is Nature classified? How does Man differ from not-Man? How do groups of men differ from each other?

The commonest word for a 'kind' is *myu* (also written *amyu*). We meet it in all kinds of contexts; trees, fish, birds, animals, men are all distinguished as *myu*.

> *u ni u zai amyu myu nga ai*
> sacred near sacred wise sort sort are
> 'there are many kinds of tame and wild animal'.[1]

In such a classification pigs (*wa*) are a *myu*, cattle (*nga*) are a *myu*, elephants (*măgwi*) are a *myu*, but there is no single species word which clearly distinguishes human beings as a class from animals as a class. *Myu*, in the context of human beings, means a lineage, and lineages are felt to differ from each other in the same way that animal species differ from each other. Kachin thinking on this point is vaguely 'totemic'; human beings have a kind of affinal relationship with the animal world. Human lineages are associated either as segments of a larger lineage, in which case they are linked as *kăhpu-kănau* (elder brother-younger brother), or as affines *măyu-dama* (wife givers-wife receivers). But the superlineage which embraces all the chiefly lineages

---

1. An explanation of this translation is given below. *U ni u zai* carries the connotation of 'all God's creatures'. *Zai* is the opposite of *hpaji*. *Hpaji* denotes 'wisdom' in the sense of human cunning; *zai* denotes 'wisdom' in the sense of mysterious power. Man has *hpaji* but a tiger (*shăraw*) has *zai*. *Zai* is a quality of creatures of nature and thus means 'wild'. In contrast *ni* means 'near', 'domesticated', 'tame'.

of all clans (*du baw amyu*—'chief head sort') are related as affines (*dama*) to the sky deities (*mu nat*), and the link is through cattle. The affinal tie was first established by the marriage of the first Kachin, Shingra Kumja, to the daughter of the Madai Nat whose name was Madai Jan Hpraw Nga ('Madai Lady White Cow') (see Leach, 1954, p. 269). Analogous to this is the fact that besides meaning pig, the morpheme *WA* can mean (among other things) a human individual and a father. This does not mean that Kachins cannot distinguish between pigs and men or that pigs are the 'totems' of men, but rather that in some contexts both may fall into the same class (they live together under one roof) while in others they may serve as mutual substitutes . . . e.g. when a man sacrifices a pig to the gods, the pig is ritually identified with himself.

A similar ambiguity about the borderline between the human and the non-human is reflected in the category *yam*. This word means domesticated creatures which live in the house but are not members of the house-lineage or their wives. Nowadays it simply means the buffaloes, the cattle, the pigs, and the chickens. Formerly it also included slaves. We should not infer from this that Kachins thought of their slaves as 'beasts'; it is rather that they thought of their beasts as distantly related and somewhat supernatural human beings!

If this category *myu* (kind) is so fundamental, then this category itself must have a beginning, a paradigm. It is easy to see what this is. For a Kachin child the prototype of 'a kind' is a human lineage, but it is not his own lineage which he perceives in this way, for he is inside it. It is the lineage of his mother which appears as a distinct unity—the *măyu ni*. But *măyu* is simply a distorted pronunciation of *myu*, or *vice versa* (Hanson, 1906, p. 15), so the *măyu ni* are the prototype of all species entities. In English etymology there is a comparable relationship between the words 'kind' and 'kin'.

The formal significance of Kachin kin terms can most easily be ascertained by reference to Leach, 1961, ch. 2 or Leach, 1954, Appendix IV. All the terms in question are 'classificatory' and the translations which I use in the present paper are approximations only. All these terms, considered as 'roots', have a variety of non-kinship meanings. When Malinowski observed a similar phenomenon in the case of the Kiriwinan language he evaded serious discussion of the subject by asserting (without proof) that Kiriwinan words which sound alike but have different meanings are really subtly distinguished by tone and stress, or alternatively that the Kiriwinan language is very heavily loaded with true homonyms of the 'pear'-'pair' type.[1]

In the case of the Kachin language I suspect that true homonyms are rather rare. A word takes on new meanings as the context of use is changed, but the meanings are associated, and I do not see why a Kachin speaker should feel that more than one word is involved. When speaking Kachin, one uses the root NU in contexts where the English equivalent would be (a) 'mother', (b) 'home', (c) 'original', (d) 'the soft core of anything'. Such uses are not 'metaphors', they are rather the application of the same idea to different situations. But I think that if we are to understand what the term NU 'really means' *when considered as a kinship term* we need to take these other uses into account.

This is a problem of semantics; but purely linguistic issues are also involved. For example, although the sound distinction which Hanson records as the difference between U and W is plainly audible it does not always correspond to a significant phonemic distinction. This point was clearly understood by Hanson himself. At pp. 42–53 of his *Dictionary* he listed several hundred two-syllable words of which the first syllable is U. He construed this U as:

A general preformative; a shortened form of *nga*—cattle or fish etc. and *wa*—human beings or bamboo; a bird of any kind. The words in U may also be spelled WU.

Correspondingly, under the W entries he lists numerous words in which the first syllable is WA or WU with alternative forms beginning with U. The word WU by itself is stated to mean 'polluted'. What do we make of this? Are we dealing with 'homonyms' or the multiple use of a single concept? So far as these particular words are concerned, Hanson's presentation suggests that WU might equally be written U or UU and WA might be written UA. A hierarchy of categories then appear, as in the diagram at the top of the next page. All these 'kinds' are WU after some fashion, though the discriminations are not logically consistent. Cattle (NGA), Pigs (WA), and Chickens (U) form a class of sacrificial animals in descending order of merit and all are U NI (close or tame U). Comparably, Bamboo, the non-animal natural species most essential to man's domestic and ritual activities, is WA or WU (U).

1. Firth's view of this argument may perhaps be inferred from Firth, 1936a, p. 261: 'I must say that I could not find any differentiation in emotional tone corresponding to difference in propinquity of kinship when the same term was used in varying context, such as Malinowski describes.'

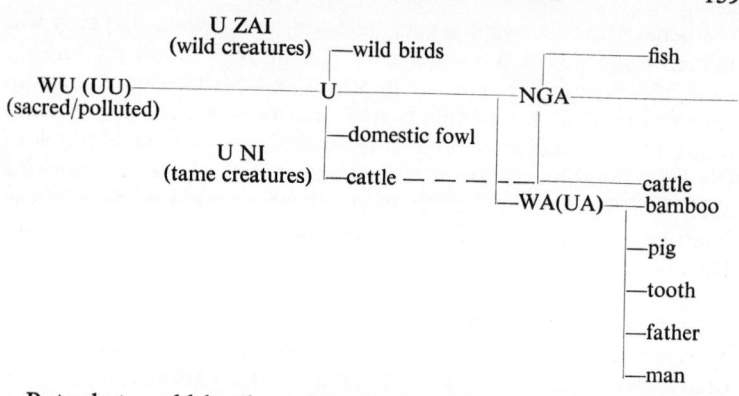

But what could be the point of such an all embracing category? The Kachin creation story throws some light on this:[1]

> *Sumsing lămu ngu na de*
> *Wanang sumwi shawng nga*
> *Ginding aga nga na de*
> *Npan U majan shawng pra.*

'Before the sky (MU) existed, the "WA NANG" mist appeared. Before the earth (GA) existed, the female "NPAN U" appeared.'

As the saga continues, the 'Wa Nang mist' proceeds to copulate with 'Npan U', and the latter gives birth to the earth (GA). 'Wa Nang' seems to mean 'timelessly enduring WA (UA)'. 'Npan U' means 'uncreated U'. The image taken as a whole is of a timeless creative principle U, with male and female components UA and U.

At this level of generality U might be translated as 'God' . . . the ultimate principle of the sacred. The more humdrum use of the same term to denote domestic fowl and domestic animals generally ties in with the fact that these creatures are kept in order that they shall be sacrificed. A man's cattle are the 'sacred part of himself' so that:

> *nanhte a u daw ni*

> your *U* portion (plural)

means 'the cattle of your household'. This expression has an offensive implication since it is intended to remind the hearers that the animals in question will ultimately be sacrificed in connexion with the pending sickness and death of the owners!

1. Text from Hanson, 1906, p. xxii. The translation on p. xxiii is completely misleading.

I believe that such matters are 'relevant' in the sense that they will influence the way that a speaker of Kachin feels about the kinship categories *wa* (father) and *nu* (mother) and perhaps other kinship categories as well. But I admit that the matter is very complicated and that I am not capable of producing an analysis which would look in the least plausible to an unsympathetic reader. In what follows I shall therefore confine myself to relatively simple instances of the interplay between the kinship and non-kinship significances of Kachin sounds.

I have no information which is comparable to Firth's data on the speech errors of Tikopia children, nor do I know how Kachin children's speech differs in lexical range and syntax from Kachin adult speech. But children's speech is linked with children's behaviour. It should therefore be relevant that Kachin children go around naked for several years after birth, mostly in the company of their female elders. In this context they have much to do with the 'domestic' animals—dogs, buffalo, cattle, pigs, chickens. Kachin infants, like other infants, display palpable interest in the facts of sexual difference and in the bodily functions of urination and defecation. In the process of initial category formation these circumstances must all play a prominent part.

One cannot argue *a priori* about what words a child first comes to understand, but it seems likely that in the circumstances of Kachin society most kinship words must be established quite early in a child's vocabulary. I see no reason to suppose that such words are thought of as an exclusive set. Pronouns, words for familiar animals, for simple parts of the human body, words referring to bodily functions, some simple categories of time and space, will all be of at least equal importance with kin words. One might suppose therefore that any 'proto-homonyms' which link categories of this 'elementary' kind with kin terms would have some semantic significance.

In such matters one needs to be cautious and sceptical, but not defeatist. I have already drawn attention to the 'verbal' use of the words for grandmother (*WOI*) and grandchild (*SHU*). Other kin terms have comparable employment. Thus:

SHA—'child'.
    —as verb: 'to eat', 'to sustain oneself'.

nang hpa gălaw sha n ta?
you what do '*sha*' (question)
'What is your occupation? (What do you do for a living?)'

A man who makes his living by cultivating a field is a *yi sha ai wa*
—'field "*sha*"-ing man', but a child who lives to eat rather than eats
to live is simply *sha*!

> *HKAU*—'reciprocal term between male cross-cousins and bro-
> thers-in-law';
> —as verb: 'to be on friendly intimate terms'.

ngai shi hte n hkau ai
I he with not '*hkau*' am
'I am not on speaking terms with him (although he belongs to
the wide category of persons who should be treated as cross-
cousins)'.

> *TSA*—'mother's brother', 'wife's father';
> —as verb: 'to curse'.

dai num a mătsa ga yam ai
This woman's '*tsa*' speech effective is
'this woman's curses come true'.

Incidentally this example shows a 'verbal' use of *yam*. The *yam*
(cattle, slaves) are creatures who have been brought under control
and obey orders. The woman's 'curses' are similarly controlled,
like the genie in Aladdin's lamp.

These particular cases are straightforward, and they certainly reveal
some of the quality which is felt to inhere in the kinship category.
But we need caution. For instance, although Kachin 'mother's
brothers' have the power to curse their nephews and nieces—the
whole of Kachin witchcraft ideology fits in with this—it is not the
case that a 'mother's brother' is invariably felt to be a threatening
figure. On the contrary, he is often the first source of help in times of
domestic trouble at home. Moreover, even if this technique of discovering the basic meaning of a term by pursuing all its associated
ramifications has some justification, it must be recognized that the
procedure quickly becomes exceedingly complicated.

I have already devoted considerable space to showing how the
term *măyu* ('mother's brother's lineage') may be considered the
prototype concept in terms of which the whole Kachin world is
categorized into 'species things', but the word *măyu* has many
other aspects besides this, some of which I have already discussed elsewhere.[1] The different meanings of *măyu* which I there

1. Leach, 1954, p. 80n. At this reference I list as one meaning of *măyu*: (f) 'Green
rice field before it comes to ear'. This needs elaboration. Growing paddy in its
early stages while the ear is still inside the stalk is *matut*, 'bound together'; *măyu*

listed are in fact all associated, but the association is complex:

   YU (Mǎyu). The basic primitive meaning is 'to swallow' with
the noun equivalent, 'the gullet', considered as a greedy demanding entity. In English we can speak of 'downing' (swal-
lowing) a glass of beer. So in Kachin *yu* can mean to 'move
downwards'.

   ngai bum de na yu wa nngai
   I mountain from '*yu*' return am
   'I have come down from the mountain'

Figuratively this can mean 'to lose rank' (cf. Leach, 1954, p. 166
n. 90) and also 'falling' (i.e. nearly ripe) paddy (see p. 141n. above).
   The greed of the gullet makes it the equivalent of 'to want':

   shi sha mǎyu ai—'he eat *mǎyu* is' could mean
   either 'he eats and swallows' *or* 'he wants to eat'.

By analogy with the latter meaning:

   shi galaw mǎyu ai—'he do *mǎyu* is' means 'he wants to do it'.

From the Kachin point of view the pre-eminent quality of the *mǎyu
ni*—the wife-giving affines—is their greediness, their constant demands for gifts and tribute; it is the wife receivers—the *dama ni*—
who always pay.

   mǎyu ni hpu tsun ma ai, dama ni bau gun ma ai
   'the *mǎyu ni* name the price, the *dama ni* carry the gong',

gongs being the prototype of the valuables (*hpǎga*) given as bride-
price.
   The food and wealth which is not devoured by the gullets of human
beings is devoured by rats while still in the possession of the original
owners, and the devastation which rats may cause is mysterious and
invisible. So *YU* means a rat (the animal) and more metaphysically
the destructiveness of witchcraft:

---

is the later stage of growth when it is still green but the 'ear' has broken out of the
stalk sheath and is beginning to bend over. This is a period of maximum food
scarcity and is given a seasonal name, *mǎyu ta*. It is at this period that Kachin
communities hold a large-scale, two- or three-day, ritual, the purpose of which is
to ensure good crops. The name of the ritual is *mǎyu moi* and the period at which
it is held is *mǎyu na*. The form of the ritual which involves all the lineages domi-
ciled in the community is such as to re-emphasize the hierarchy of political
authority and also the associated hierarchy of traditional *mǎyu-dama* relationships. Such a ritual is described in brief outline in Leach, 1954, pp. 173–4, under
the rubric 'an important religious ceremonial held about the beginning of
September'.

nye a nga hpe yu e kǎwa sat kau ya si ai
my cattle (accusative) '*yu*' have bitten and killed
'my cattle have been destroyed by witchcraft';

and no doubt it was the *mǎyu ni* who caused the witchcraft, though one has to be careful about how one says this in public!

Finally we have a usage which makes *mǎyu* mean 'normal', 'ordinary', e.g., *mǎyu si ai*, 'to die a natural death'; *mǎyu ga*, 'ordinary language' (as opposed to poetic language), which seems to tie in with the kinship usage, for, just as the *dama ni* are the 'permanent (*da*) children', so the *mǎyu ni* are the 'ordinary' people, with whom one ordinarily expects to engage in transactions of all kinds. Note, too, how the meaning of *mǎyu* as 'ripening paddy' links in with the meaning of *mǎyu ni* as 'affines' through the ritual of the *mǎyu moi* (see p. 141n. above) and how there is a 'logical' link between *mǎyu* paddy as a source of *mam* (rice) and *mǎyu* people as a source of *nam* (potential brides) and hence to the sustenance of life ('eating'—*sha*), or the perpetuation of life ('children'—*sha*). (See also Leach, 1954, p. 80n.)

The permutations of *dama* are equally complicated. This is a genuinely two-syllable word *da-ma*. *Da*, says Hanson, 'supplies the idea of continuation, constancy or stability', so that *dama* means 'permanent children' and emphasizes the permanence of the relationship and the dependence of the status. I should stress perhaps that this *ma* (child) is not a kinship status but a social status; it can be applied to anyone in a servile dependent position, e.g., the follower of a chief or the servant of a household.

But *da* has other associations. *Dung* is the warp of a loom, and *da* the act of weaving. Hence *dung* and *da* are contrasted as 'length' and 'breadth'. More surprisingly, they are also contrasted as 'North' and 'South'! The explanation of this is that North is viewed as a direction, whereas South is the whole width of the southerly horizon which is traversed daily by the sun (*jan*). The sun (*jan*) moves from East to West across the South (*da*) and the weft thread (*jan*) moves from right to left across the width of the loom (*da*). But *jan*, besides meaning 'sun' and 'weft', also means 'lady' (in a polite sense which is applied alike to wives and sisters) and 'war'. So the *dama* are those with whom we fight and those to whom we give women! (Cf. Leach, 1961, p. 131.)

It seems to me that in these cases the operation of showing how the whole wide spectrum of dictionary meanings fits together gives us a genuinely deeper understanding of the kinship category with which we were initially concerned. But my next example is more difficult. Let us consider *NA*—'elder sister'. There are two other 'primitive' meanings of the same morpheme: (*a*) 'ear', (*b*) 'night'. How can either be connected with 'elder sister'? The verbal aspect of *na*, 'ear', is 'to hear', and in Kachin this sensation is the same as 'to feel' through touch.

> *masha ngai hpe ahtawk ai ngai na nngai*
> man me touch is, I '*na*' am
> 'I feel the man touching me'.

The feeling can be sharp, *lăgat na ai*—'the bee stings'—or soporific, *chyăru na nngai*—'I feel the beer (I am intoxicated)'. *Na* is thus (i) the sensation of experiencing outside influence—'hearing', 'feeling', 'being ill'; (ii) the medium through which the feeling is experienced —'the ear'; (iii) a sign or symptom of such influence—e.g., *ana* (illness), *măna* (madness).

Before we go further we must consider *SIN*. *Sin* is first of all 'the liver' which in Kachin ideology is the most important organ of the body. All forms of sacrifice are accompanied by augury, and it is always the liver which is examined for signs or portents. The liver is 'influence' in a manifest form, and the influence is usually bad. Secondly, *sin* is 'darkness', 'influence' in an unspecific form. Kachins fear the dark as a time of danger; if they go out at night they carry bright flares. Night is the medium through which the influence of darkness is felt, so night is *na* (*na* also means 'black'). Hence *na* is any period of time which is loaded with dangerous influence ... any period of 'tabooed time' during which the members of a village are subject to ritual restrictions—e.g., *măyu na* mentioned above. More generally *na* can refer to any period of time either past or future, because the present is both influenced by the past and predestines the future:

> *măchyi na du mat sai mai yak ai*
> sick period lead finished well difficult is.

This apparently chaotic sequence of words means 'cure is difficult because the illness has prevailed for a long time'. This *na*, which refers to 'the long duration' of a period of time rather than to the period itself, carries much greater tonal stress than the *na* meaning 'night', but seems nevertheless to be 'the same word'.

This is an intricate chain, yet logical, and it seems to me quite plausible that *na* 'ear', *na* 'night', and *na* 'sickness' may all be felt to be aspects of the same idea. But what, if anything, has all this got to do with elder sisters? Clearly the implication is that elder sisters are dangerous persons of evil influence, but why?

'Elder sisters' include of course 'classificatory elder sisters' and they function to some extent as 'nannies' for their younger siblings. For boys, of course, elder sisters are sexually taboo, and since all kinds of sexual misdemeanour evoke supernatural penalties in the form of sickness (*na*), this might be relevant. But the word which means sibling incest is *jaiwawng*. Of greater significance is the fact that the women who look after a young child are placed by that child in four categories:

NU—'mother' including all the wives of father's 'brothers';
NA—'elder sister' including the daughters of father's 'brothers';
NI—primarily 'mother's brother's wife';
WOI—'grandmother'.

Woi has already been discussed; Kachin grannies, like other grannies, tend to spoil their grandchildren (*shu*—'little frogs'). But *nu*, *na*, and *ni* are all in some degree disciplinarians; for the child, their respective roles are evidently distinguished by the three vowel sounds U, A, I. Here we should note that *ni* means 'day' in contrast to *na* 'night' and that *shăni-shăna* ('day-night') is a couplet of the kind discussed previously which is equivalent to *ya* ('a day of twenty-four hours', 'now'). This seems to me the crux.

Children are taught to speak by their female elders, and, in so far as the categories of childhood speech reflect social space, it will tend to be a woman's social space rather than a man's. It must be borne in mind that women ordinarily change their place of residence on marriage, men do not. A married woman classes as 'elder sisters' (*na*) the wives of all men who are in the standing of 'elder brother' (*hpu*) to her husband and these women are ordinarily co-resident with herself.

When a child falls ill, the illness is always attributed to supernatural influence, and although there are various kinds of supernatural influence (which can be distinguished by divination), one constant suspicion is that the cause is witchcraft. Witchcraft is commonly suspected as flowing from the *măyu ni* to the *dama ni*; a child will not be attacked by the evil influences of its own mother's kin but by the evil influences of the 'classificatory mothers', women whom the true mother rates as *na*.[1]

---

1. If Kachins always married their 'mother's brothers' daughters' this situation would not arise since the co-resident wives in any household would all be members of the same lineage. But ordinarily this is not the case. Each household has *măyu-dama* links with a number of different lineages and the mother of a sick child would be suspicious of any co-resident wife who is not of her own lineage.

I have no direct evidence on this point, but I think that the 'typical' relationship between co-resident married 'sisters' must be one of deep distrust. If so, it is understandable that this sinister aspect of 'elder sisters' (*na*) should be instilled into young children from the start.

But *ni* (mother's brother's wife) is a very different matter. Mother (*nu*) and mother's brother's wife (*ni*) are in the reciprocal relationship *ning*. This is the female counterpart to the male relationship *hkau* and stands for friendship and co-operation. From the child's point of view *ni* is the 'friendly aunt'. Appropriately *ni* can also mean 'near' or 'tame' (cf. Leach, 1964, pp. 56–7).

It is true that *moi* (father's sister) is also in *ning* relationship with mother, but *moi*'s standing vis-à-vis the child is quite different from that of *ni*. A mother frequently takes her children to visit members of her own birth lineage. These people are the child's *măyu ni*, and the married women of such households are all *ni* to the child. Visits in the reverse direction are much less likely; a woman has no ordinary cause to visit households which are connected to her only because her husband's sisters have married there. Even on the occasion of a marriage, when a bride is inducted into her new home, the bride's own parents are usually absent from the celebrations which are notoriously occasions which generate ill feeling and recrimination between the parties to the alliance.

From the child's viewpoint *moi* is a visitor, not one whom one visits, and although she is a member of 'our lineage', she belongs to the past rather than to the present.[1] *Moi* in non-kinship contexts means (*a*) 'formerly' and (*b*) 'to offer ritually in return for expected benefits—as in a sacrifice'.[2]

All this is so tortuous that a sceptical reader might reasonably complain that by such arguments one might 'prove' almost anything. Taken by itself this section does *not* demonstrate that a Kachin makes an association between *na* 'elder sister' and *na* 'night', or between *moi* 'father's sister' and *moi* 'formerly', but if we take the

---

1. This is true of *moi*, the visiting aunt. But the category *moi* includes all wives in the senior generation of the *dama ni* and most of these will not be close relatives of Ego at all. For a married girl *moi* includes the mother-in-law, but this is not part of the childish vocabulary. Firth's analysis of the status of the father's sister in Tikopia (Firth, 1936a, pp. 224–5) is very relevant, though it seems to me inconsistent that Firth should claim that the sister's son 'gains' at the expense of the mother's brother. The *măyu-dama* structure implies that among Kachins, as among Tikopia, 'the descendants on the male side [have] an attitude of assistance and protection towards the children of women from their house.'

2. Cf. p. 141n. above on *măyu moi*.

argument 'as a whole' the pattern seems to me to hang together. I want to emphasize two points in particular.

The individual terms we are discussing do not have meaning 'in themselves' but only when considered in relation to other terms. This is true also of the penumbral associated meanings of the same words. It is the *total pattern* which makes a kind of logical sense even when the individual 'metaphors' look like pure chance. Note for example how the time and space meanings of the different kin terms add up to a structured representation of social space. Consider the terms and statuses marked in Fig. 1 and reflect on the fact that, besides their kinship meanings,

NA means night; *NI* means day: *MOI* means formerly;
HKAU means a day's journey: *NING* means a year.

Thus *intervals* of time/space correspond to the *intervals* of social space as expressed by the affinal relationship *măyu/dama*.

Figure 1

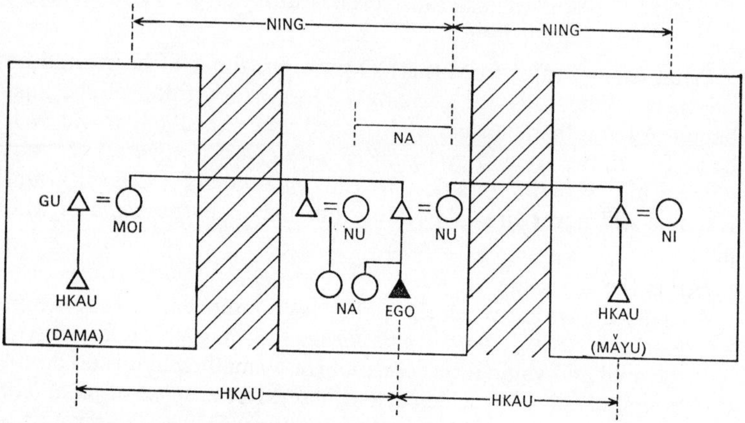

The shaded gaps in the diagram correspond to:

(a) *Intervals of residential space: MOI, NU,* and *NI* always reside in different places.

(b) *Intervals of social space: MĂYU-DAMA* is the basic category distinction on which the 'structure' of the society as a whole is erected.

(c) *Intervals of time space:* NING= 'a year', HKAU= 'a day's journey', MOI= 'formerly'\/'long ago' }, NA= 'night', NI= 'day'\/'near' }.

Perhaps all this is an 'accident'. No doubt in a sense it is, but it is also a rather nice exemplification of Lévi-Strauss's thesis that 'l'univers des primitifs consiste principalement en messages' (Lévi-Strauss, 1962, p. 354).

I want now to consider a structural opposition of a slightly different kind. Over a wide range of cases semantic contrasts in Kachin correspond to a contrast between the unaspirated velar sound which Hanson writes *g* or *k* and the aspirated sound which he writes *hk*. Thus *gu* is the opposite of *hku*, *ga* is the opposite of *hka*.

Let us examine the first of these distinctions, *gu-hku*.

> *gu* is the grain of the rice after it has been *dehusked*. The word thus refers to anything which is *completed* and *ready for use* —e.g. a pregnant woman who has reached her full time. But it also refers to the act of stripping something down to its bare essentials, such as *scaling* a fish, or taking the thatch off a roof; thus it also means *naked*.
>
> *gu* is also a kinship category. For both sexes it is the class of father's sisters' husbands, but for women it is, in addition, the class of potential husbands, 'classificatory father's sisters' sons', and also 'father-in-law'.

What can we infer from this? Does a girl think of her would-be suitors as 'rice ready for cooking'? Does a boy think of the husbands of his father's sisters as 'stripped and naked'? It might well be so for, in the Kachin system, the 'wife givers' (*măyu ni*) are in a strategically superior position to the 'wife takers' (*dama ni*), and Kachins will never tire of pointing out that it is the *dama ni* who pay.

> *hku* is the 'opposite' of *gu* . . . it is an 'empty' grain of rice, the cavity that is left when the *gu* has been removed. Thus it means *famine, a cavity, a hole, a path through the jungle*. It refers also to the anal and vaginal orifices, and for a small child it is no doubt 'holes' of this kind which are primary. In the sense of *path*, *hku* is the 'opposite' of the jungle itself, *nam*. Thus we arrive at a triangle of related but opposed concepts: *gu—hku—nam*:

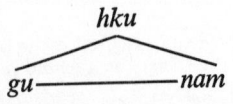

Is it then fortuitous that *nam* like *gu* is a kinship category which is in fact the reciprocal of *gu*, *nam* being the potential wife of a man, just as *gu* is the potential husband of a woman? In Kachin usage *gu-nam* is just one entity, like *hpu-nau*.

Is this all too clever? Is it just a linguistic accident? Perhaps. But what does one mean by a linguistic accident? Let us look at another case.

Consider the *ga-hka* opposition:

ga is *land*, not only in the sense of 'earth' but also in the sense of 'political territory'. Pasi Ga is the name of a village and its adjoining territory. The principal inhabitants of Pasi Ga—the 'owners'—are members of the Pasi lineage. Such a territorial *ga* will always be separated from all adjacent *ga* by a quite definite boundary—a 'partition', *din*. The most common form of such a political partition is a stream, *hka*.

anhte a lăpran e hka din nga ai
'our separation a river the partition is'.

The same form of words may denote separation in terms of social age:

shi hte nye a lăpran e prat lăhkawng din sai
'his with my (our) separation a two generation partition was'.

Hka, as the opposite of *ga*, denotes water as opposed to dry land, but, in the context of territory divided by a stream, the significance of *hka* is the track of the river rather than its wetness. If one is talking of water by itself one uses different words. For example, you do not drink *hka*, you drink *n'tsin* or *hpung*. The point to understand here is that while Kachin rivers are impassable torrents during the wet season, their tracks provide the principal paths through the jungle during the dry season. The only way to move upstream in thick jungle country is to walk along the bed of a stream in dry weather; contrariwise, the easiest way to move downstream is to go down on a raft at the height of the wet season. The contrast between the wet and the dry seasons is very striking. In the dry season the vegetation shrivels, the land dries out and cracks, paths appear in the jungle; in the wet season the cracks disappear, paths are overgrown, the jungle spreads over the rivers which fill with water (*nam*). We have met with *nam* before. Our triangle of opposed meanings is duplicated:

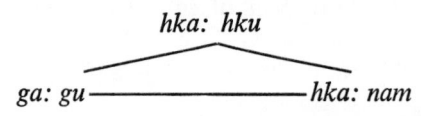

Thus in dry weather a *hka* (stream) is also a *hku* (path through the jungle), while in wet weather a *hka* (stream) is also *nam* (liquid).

Hence the principal Kachin directions are:

up-stream: *hka-hku*

down-stream: *hka-nam*.

It is of the nature of *ga* (dry land) to split of itself. Thus *ga* means dryness and also the act of splitting one thing into two, while *hka*, its opposite, means the 'track' or 'path' or 'imprint' of such a split, the space between two things which have been separated. When traders contract a deal they split a bamboo stick to act as a tally, notching the stick in such a way that the same notch appears on each tally. The act of splitting is *ga*; the notch which records the debt is *hka*; more abstractly, the debt itself is *hka* and the goods which have changed hands to create the debt are *ga*.

Note how as we move across this elaborate spectrum of meanings, *hka* and *ga* remain linked together in antithesis. The structure is the same throughout the whole series of transformations.

The association between *hka* in the sense of a stream dividing two lands, *ga*, and *hka* in the sense of a debt separating (linking) two persons or sets of persons, is not quite so devious as may appear. In the first case the lands, *ga*, are distinguished (*daw*) by a ditch, *hka*. In order to join the divided parts together again it is necessary to fill in the ditch. That which fills in the ditch is itself *ga*, i.e., 'earth' in the case of a ditch, or 'goods' in the case of a debt. The same ap-

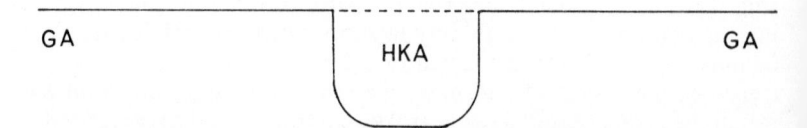

plies to labour. If I hire a labourer I incur a debt which is only re-payable in labour of like kind. So *ga* comes to mean a labourer and his work and *hka* the debt that is owed to a labourer and repay-able by work, *ga*. When *ga* (in the sense of labour) is exchanged on a reciprocal basis, Kachins speak of *ga tsun ai*. They use exactly the same expression to mean 'carry on a conversation'. Evidently *tsun* has here the same range of meanings as English 'exchange', as when we speak of

(*a*) an exchange of words;

(*b*) an exchange of gifts;

(*b*) an exchange of labour.

But the Kachin metaphor rests on a quite material base. *Tsun* is a term employed in fishing in a shallow river. By means of temporary dams the water of the main stream (*hka*), with its fish, is diverted into a narrow arm on one side of the channel. The dam is then switched round so that the water flows into the other half of the channel, leaving the fish high and dry. *Tsun* refers to the whole arrangement of dams and weirs by means of which the water is switched from side to side of the *hka*. The use of *tsun* as a metaphor for reciprocal exchange in a 'debt' (*hka*) situation is thus easily understood. In this case we can show that it is not just a 'verbal accident' that things work out like that. The ordinary way for Kachins to settle a serious feud (*hka*) is to arrange a marriage between the feuding lineages, such that one side (*mǎyu*) give a woman, while the other side (*dama*) give valuables (*ga*) which are partly a bride-price and partly a settlement of the feud debt (*hka*). In the course of the haggling which precedes such an arrangement the potential *mǎyu ni* will lower their price and in doing so they make explicit use of the notion that the *hka* is a kind of ditch which is to be filled in by the payment of the *ga*. The bank of a river is *hka hkin-gau* and the expression *mǎyu hkin-gau shǎnem ai* 'the *mǎyu* lower the bank' refers to the haggle by which the *mǎyu ni* reduce their terms for *ga*.

None of this is easy to follow, but my main point is surely clear. Of the categories we have been examining in this last section, *gu*, *hku*, *ga*, *hka*, and *nam*, only *gu* and *nam* are kinship categories in the ordinary sense. But, in Kachin usage, the whole set of words is intricately tangled up. The kinship relationship *gu-nam* cannot be separated from the rest of the tangle. If we are to understand what the *kinship terms* may mean we must examine the *non-kinship* words as well.

This conclusion may not seem very profound but it has implications for general theory. 'Structuralist' analysis either in linguistics or in social anthropology is commonly thought to entail the slicing of the data of empirical observation into a hierarchy of self-contained and independent levels of analysis. One example of this is the doctrine, which formerly prevailed among Bloomfieldian linguists, that the analysis of phonemic structure should be pursued without regard to phrase structure or semantics; another is the practice among several varieties of anthropologists of treating kinship as 'a thing in itself' (e.g., Murdock, 1949; Lévi-Strauss, 1949; Radcliffe-Brown and Forde, 1950). Firth's 'functionalist' approach,

L

which mixes the levels of anthropological analysis, has commonly been felt to be 'anti-structuralist'—indeed this seems to be the basis of Firth's antipathy to Rivers and his development of the concept of 'social organization' in contrast to the concept of 'social structure'.

But in my present essay I have used an argument based on structural transformation to justify a mixture of levels of analysis, and this fact may turn out to be of some theoretical significance.

As I indicated at the beginning, my essay is incomplete; I have only investigated a part of the Kachin language of kinship[1] and I have certainly not managed to show that 'the [Kachin] classificatory system of counting relationships in its own cultural surroundings . . . reveals itself as a convenient, flexible and commonsense piece of social mechanism.' Nevertheless, I hope that both my conclusions and my methods are things of which my teacher can approve.

1. Certain additional material on the same theme is given in Leach, 1964, pp. 54–62.

Voluntary Associations in Urban Life:
A Case Study of Differential Adaptation

KENNETH LITTLE

In the social life of Freetown, Sierra Leone, an important part is played by voluntary associations known as dancing *compins*.[1] Under urban conditions this kind of organization serves a number of modern and economic objectives. It began, however, as a simple entertainment society which was introduced by the Mandinka tribal ruler after a visit to what was then French Guinea. He brought back with him, in 1930, three *yelibas* (professional musicians) who inspired the performance of dances to a popular Mandinka tune. To give the society a firm basis the members decided to constitute themselves as a benefit club. Later, rival societies were established and were joined by a large number of Temne migrants. The latter, in turn, formed their own associations with branches in different parts of Freetown. By 1953 there were about thirty such *compins* in existence. Branches were also started in the towns up-country (Banton, 1957, pp. 163–83).

The ostensible objective of these dancing *compins* is to perform 'plays' of traditional music and dancing. The dancing which, like the music, shows strong signs of Western influence, is somewhat reminiscent of English country dancing, and a 'play' is generally given in connexion with some important local event. The occasion may be a wedding, to greet a notable visitor, to raise funds for a mosque, or simply an evening's entertainment. It provides an opportunity to collect funds for the association itself, and the money pays for corporate expenses—rent of premises, drums, and other equipment. It is also used for mutual benefit. Members themselves pay a small weekly subscription, and when any member is bereaved a collection is held to which all must contribute. In a typical scheme if a member has lost a father, for example, everyone pays two shillings, or if a sister, one. The cashier hands out £4 or £2 respectively as soon as the death is notified, and then recovers this amount from the collection. A bereaved member must first notify one of the *compin*'s

1. *Compin* is the Krio (Creole) word for company.

153

officials, known as the Reporter, and this sets the machinery in motion. Many *compins* have rules to prevent a member from resigning just after drawing a benefit payment (*ibid.*).

A large number of officials have charge of the various activities and there is a committee. This has the function of maintaining the good name of the *compin*, and of enforcing discipline among the members. For example, all such associations take precautions against the possible seduction of female members, and often have rules to the effect that members found guilty of adultery will be heavily fined and, if unable to pay, will be expelled, along with the woman concerned, from the society. Fines are also levied for failure to attend meetings, unpunctuality, and other minor offences. Most companies assist a member financially if he gets into trouble with the police and is fined for a misdemeanour, such as fighting in the streets. There is a limit, however, to the number of times they will help him in this way, and if he is convicted of a felony he is expelled (*ibid.*).

In Freetown, most members of a dancing *compin* are migrants from rural towns and villages in the provinces. In addition, therefore, to supplying mutual aid and protection, these associations can be seen as a means whereby country-bred people are adjusted to the more impersonal conditions and commercial practices of town life. The association assists this process by introducing the migrant to various economically useful habits, such as thrift, and it assists his social re-orientation by accustoming him to mixing and working with individuals outside his own tribe or lineage. It also sets him new standards of dress and personal hygiene, and it teaches him the urban discipline of punctuality and routine (*ibid.*).

In these and in other respects the functions performed by the Freetown *compins* are very similar to those of other West African voluntary associations, particularly ethnic or tribal unions. The latter are found in most of the larger industrialized towns of Nigeria and Ghana, as well as in the francophone countries, the French term being *associations d'originaires*. They are referred to in this way to distinguish them from associations which also practise mutual aid, but where members are united by other factors, such as age, religion, occupation, and education. In other words, although membership may not be withheld from persons who are not ordinarily affiliated to the particular clan, district, or town concerned, it is generally based upon common origin (Little, 1965, pp. 26–7).

These tribal associations, too, exercise a strict control over their members, including supervision of their public conduct as well as their relations with one another. For example, a member who is reported for quarrelling in the town, or for putting curses on others, may be summarily dealt with. Frequently, it is also decreed that no member shall take legal steps against any other member without first bringing the matter up for the hearing of the meeting (*ibid.*). As in the dancing *compin*, therefore, the sense of solidarity is strong. Members are expected to regard one another as brothers and sisters, to sympathize with one another in time of need or bereavement, visiting one another when sick, and swelling the procession at a funeral. Sociability is also encouraged by the general practice of serving refreshments, including such beverages as tea, palm wine, beer, or stronger drink, at every formal meeting. These aims are explicitly stressed in the constitution of such a society and the desire for unity frequently symbolized in the fairly common custom of wearing a uniform type of dress (*ibid.*).

These features are peculiarly characteristic of voluntary associations formed by migrants, and so the explanation given for the phenomenon usually tends to be on psychological lines. It is pointed out that organizations of this kind represent basically the newly-arrived migrants' response to urban conditions. Belonging, in his rural home, to a compact group of kinsmen and neighbours, he has been used to a highly personal set of relationships. He knows of no other way of community living than this. Consequently, to organize similar practices of mutuality is for him a spontaneous adjustment to his environment (*ibid.*, p. 24).

It is true that in the heterogeneous multi-tribal populations of the newly industrialized towns a good deal of group rivalry and mutual suspicion exists. These are age-old enmities and alliances which divide or unite the various factions. For instance, in Ghana, one of the most obvious is the hostility of the Zabramas and the Gaos to the Hausas, and the friendship between the Moshis and the Zabramas; the Fulani are not popular with any group. These people regard themselves as Muslims, but Islam is not strong enough on its own to override the differences, and so the migrants have only one thing in common: they are foreigners. As such, they are shunned by the indigenous inhabitants for whom any migrant is straightaway associated with the native of the Northern Territories; he is a bushman, a naked barbarian. The migrants retort in similar terms and refer to the people of the Coast as 'sons of slaves' (Rouch, 1954, pp. 59, 62).

Antagonisms of this kind sometimes break out into open warfare, including riots and fights between the younger tribesmen. In order, therefore, to operate more effectively, migrants from the same locality group themselves together. The Ibo, in Nigeria, are an example. On moving into the towns of the West and the North they formed associations to protect themselves from the hostile way in which they were received by the local inhabitants when they took jobs as clerks, policemen, traders, and labourers.

In general terms, therefore, it does seem that one of the main motives for forming tribal and similar associations is the need felt for defence and mutual aid. The difficulty, however, is that not all groups of migrants react to their new environment in the way described. Instead of organizing mutual benefit schemes on modern lines and attempting to acquire urban habits, some tribal groups steadfastly refuse to be 'urbanized'. They take no part in the civic life of the town, hold themselves aloof from fellow tribesmen, and largely retain their own traditional outlook and practices. Fulbe[1] migrants who have moved from Futa Jallon to Lunsar in Sierra Leone illustrate this point. Most of the other adult male inhabitants of this small but relatively industrialized town work for wages in a nearby mine. These men, too, are mainly migrants and they have largely abandoned their traditional family system. The things that they are now interested in are education for their children, up-to-date housing, and other Western symbols of success and achievement. The Fulbe, on the other hand, continue their traditional occupations such as cattle trading. Many of them have rooms or houses in the town, but the Fulbe on the whole do not apply to the mine for work. Being qualified only to perform menial tasks, they would need to accept jobs they regard as degrading. Fulbe young men have a flourishing *compin*, but it is organized on traditional lines. It is solely for amusement and entertainment and has not been adapted to economic purposes (Butcher, 1965).

Basically, the main reason for Fulbe exclusiveness is Islam. Unlike other inhabitants of Lunsar who claim to be Muslims, Fulbe migrants hold strictly to their faith, even to the extent of keeping their children away from Mission schools. In general, they regard co-religionists who do not live up to the same standards as little better than pagans, and they also affect to look down on Africans who are Christians (*ibid.*).

This attitude probably explains why the Fulbe have not tried to bring their traditional institutions up to date. It is less easy, however, to understand why other tribal groups have not followed the example of the Temne in Freetown and organized voluntary associations on similar lines. In particular, there are the Mende who are without

1. Known elsewhere in West Africa as the Fulani or Peulh.

doubt the most Westernized of all the former Protectorate peoples. Through numerous secret societies of their own the Mende have considerable experience of non-kinship forms of association. Moreover, the Mende are, with the exception of the Temne, the most populous tribe in Freetown.

Despite these considerations, although the dancing *compin* has developed rapidly among the Temne, there has been no sign of its appealing to the Mende. The latter inhabitants of Freetown never attempted to form a comparable association; instead, individual Mende occasionally join Temne companies. Furthermore, in the towns of the Mende region up-country, flourishing companies are often to be found, but they are usually under Temne or Mandinka leadership.

Commenting on this apparent paradox, Banton remarks that it is explained

. . . . neither by the different circumstances arising from swamp rice cultivation, nor by influences at work in Freetown, because whereas society labour, *kabɔtɔ*, *kunɛ*, etc., has become very popular on upland farms in the Northern Province, its introduction has been repulsed in Mende country. Young Mende men do sometimes form, on their own initiative, a band known as a *bɛmbɛ*, which hires out its services for hoeing. In some places these bands have developed their own ritual; they require very good food but they will work hard and long. In other places, they have been broken up because of their unruliness—and perhaps because the members' older kinsmen want them to work on the *mawei* farm without remuneration! The *bɛmbɛ* was an institution learnt from the towns; it has never been generally used for any operation other than hoeing and appears now to be declining (Banton, 1957, pp. 194–5).[1]

His suggestion is

. . . . that there is greater scope for private initiative in the traditional social structure of the Temne and more devolution of authority. This may provide an explanation. The Temne chief was in olden times a semi-sacred figure, surrounded by powerful officials, and he did not exercise the personal rule of the Mende chief. Society labour of the *kabɔtɔ* type has a recognized place in the social structure of the Temne and Limba. On the formation of a society the leader pays a fee to the chief to notify him of the event

1. This and other passages from the book are quoted by kind permission of Professor Banton and of the International African Institute.

and he is thereafter held responsible for the society's actions. The bɛmbɛ, on the other hand, is not accorded such a place and consequently its members are apt to behave irresponsibly. The Mende look to the chief to deal with problems which the Temne, thinking them alien to the chief's duties, attempt to solve by their own activities (*ibid.*, p. 195).

Banton directs attention quite rightly to the traditional structure, but he omits to draw together certain important threads, which he himself indicates in analysing the social and political functions of the young men's companies. He shows quite graphically, for example, that in the embryonic social class system of Freetown various tribes were competing for status and that the Temne young men were de-moralized. They had lost pride in their own tribe and there was a danger of complete disintegration.

The Temnes in the City were moving rapidly towards detribal-ization, some becoming Creoles and others Akus and Mandingoes. The first were the educated ones in English and others who were not educated but have come to Freetown to seek jobs. The reason for the exodus from the Temne tribe was the backwardness of the Temnes socially and economically. To be considered favourably was to call yourself a Mandingo, Creole or Aku. This protective measure was adopted in many forms, dress, language, and in joining foreign dances. Consequently every bright looking young Temne is lost to the other tribes and the word Temne is associated with the uncivilized people.[1]

Feeling that their social prestige was low in comparison with other tribes, the Temne young men wanted to show that they could be equally up-to-date, but the older people were uninterested. There being no solution within the indigenous framework of Temne society, some other solution had to be created which would appeal to the younger people, whatever the attitude of the illiterate elders. It was found in the idea of starting their own *compin*. A schoolmaster and a teacher of Arabic gave a lead to this new organization. A number of songs in Temne were composed and a new kind of swing devised. The schoolmaster was an advocate of European education and methods. Since he had already exposed corrupt practices among the tribal elders, he was supported by many of the young men who were dis-satisfied by such lethargy. The society that the schoolmaster and his

1. Quoted by Banton (p. 165) from a brief manuscript history of *Ambas Geda* prepared by the founder for him in 1953.

associates formed was called the *Ambas Geda*. In Temne, *ambas* means 'we have' and *geda* is the Krio (Creole) form of the English 'together'. The name expressed the feeling that, 'We, the Temne have the people and we must bring them in', while its combination of Temne and English words unconsciously typified the blending of tribal elements with items taken from European culture. Some of the *Ambas Geda* songs expressed the conflict between the older and younger generations as well as between it and a rival company:

> Ah, look what is being said,
> Look what is being done!
> How they envy our play.
> Ah, I do believe (in the play)
> As the old folk envy the geda,
> Let them just go on envying!

> I've been done a bad turn, why?
> Though not knowing me, they've
> done me a bad turn; why?
> The old folk have nothing but bad turns
> up their sleeves. Hear me, Allah!

(ibid., pp. 166–7).

About two years after the founding of *Ambas Geda*, one of its best and most popular members was expelled from the association for having seduced a woman on the society's premises. However, the officers gave him every assistance in founding a new society on similar lines. He gave it the name 'Boys London' to make it appear the most civilized of all the companies, and it soon achieved something of the fame of its parent.

From being recreational groups these *compins* then became an important stepping-stone for men with political ambitions. This is shown by the career of one of their leaders. When, during the war, the post of Temne Tribal Headman fell vacant, the young men determined to put up their own candidate. Their choice fell on the schoolmaster who had taken the lead in forming Ambas Geda. He resigned office in the latter organization but intended to keep closely in touch with it and the other companies. The young men supported him because he stood for progressive administration and the elimination of corruption, and their final canvassing won many converts. Since campaign funds did not run to the hire of lorries, his supporters rode in the other candidates' lorries to the polling field. On reaching their destination they unfurled large banners bearing their own

candidate's name, while 4,000 pin-flags were brought out of conceal-
ment and fastened on the clothing of their comrades. The members
of the other companies outside Freetown were also brought in on
chartered lorries. The latter were not entitled to vote, but such was
the effect of the demonstration that the majority of persons present
declared themselves for the young men's candidate (Banton, 1957,
pp. 176–7).

The new Headman[1] entered office with little support among the
elders. Nevertheless, he was able to reinvigorate the Temne Tribal
Administration and he has exercised an authority greater than any of
his predecessors, despite the fact that his legal powers are smaller.
Part of this influence he owes to the fact that the section chiefs in his
administration take care to be on good terms with the companies in
their territories. The dancing companies have also been active in up-
country towns. In several cases they have influenced the election of
paramount chiefs by contributing money to the campaign funds of a
young candidate who was one of their members.

Thus, by founding voluntary associations individual Temne
raised their prestige and rose in the social scale. These organizations
provided new leadership roles for people whose status otherwise was
ascribed to them largely on the basis of the kinship system. By re-
suscitating certain aspects of the traditional culture and adapting it
to urban needs these young men were able to further their modernist
ambitions.[2] This point is significant because organizing and directing
a dancing *compin* provided opportunities of advancement at a time
when the Temne possessed fewer advantages than similar age
groups among the Mende. The latter as a group were more advanced
in education and had a wider contact with the political power structure.

This is shown historically by the fact that missionary education
came to the Mende in the mid-nineteenth century before it came to
other parts of the Protectorate. The first government secondary
school was opened in 1906 at Bo, the principal town in Mende coun-

1. This former Headman now holds office as one of the most senior ministers in
the Sierra Leone government.
2. It is relevant to point out that in many other parts of West Africa tribal associations have served a similar function. Thus, when the major political parties were
constituted in Nigeria, the N.C.N.C., for example, was to a large extent a federation of tribal unions and improvement associations. The Eastern Region House of
Assembly subsequently elected had the most youthful legislature with the median
age between 35 and 39. Many of the representatives concerned were leaders of
tribal unions and similar groups who slipped naturally from these posts into the
legislature (Coleman, 1958, p. 378).

try, and it was not until after the Second World War that a similar school was started in Temneland (Kilson, 1964, p. 103). In respect of primary education, too, although not lavishly provided with schools, Mendeland was much better off than other parts of the Protectorate. As a natural result, by 1953 (the date of Banton's study) a larger proportion of the Mende were either literate or educated than was the case in other Protectorate tribes. Not only were most of the educated paramount chiefs Mende, but most of the posts open in Government service to Protectorate-born individuals went to Mendes. Education was the principal means whereby a person could rise occupationally, and so 'Africanization' of the civil service specially favoured the Mende. Educated Mende men were also to the forefront in organizing political parties. In 1950 the Sierra Leone People's Party was founded under the leadership of Dr. Margai, himself a Mende. In the following year a new constitution was introduced which provided for an elected African majority and party rule. After the election the SLPP emerged as the majority party and the government set up by Dr. Margai included a number of his compatriots as ministers. In the meantime, the Mende have continued to predominate both in party membership and the holding of office. In 1961, for example, five of the SLPP's fourteen native officers, including the Life President and the Parliamentary Leader, were Mende. Also, five of the ministers, including the Prime Minister, and 35 per cent of Sierra Leone legislators were members of this tribe compared with 23 per cent in the case of the Temne (Kilson, 1964, pp. 100–1).

It is possible that this situation helps to explain why the Mende are apparently less interested in voluntary associations. Since they were already politically as well as educationally to the fore, there would be more immediate opportunities of advancement than among the Temne. A Mende young man of ambition had readier means of improving his position occupationally and had not the same need to explore less orthodox channels of social mobility. In short, although individual Mende might feel the urge to engage in associations for purposes of recreation or economic benefit, the desire for personal prestige or positions of leadership could be more easily satisfied elsewhere than among the Temne. This suggestion covers the class of person who has 'Western' aspirations. These are the people—Mission school teachers, junior clerks, sometimes lorry drivers and artisans—who are generally the most active in association affairs.

Also, it must be remembered in this regard that every leader re-requires followers. The person who starts a *compin* may be enterprising, a good talker, and 'progressive' in his ideas—these are essential qualifications; but he has to rely for recruitment mainly upon illiterate men and women. The latter category of migrant may be adjusted to city life but tends to be at the same time highly susceptible to traditional influences, which in Sierra Leone are of a very deep kind.

There is, for example, the Poro which is widespread in Mendeland. The sacred 'spirit' of the society never 'comes out' in Freetown and the other 'cosmopolitan' towns, partly because the Government has power to prevent Poro meetings. This, however, is a comparatively minor restriction because there is nothing to prevent Poro members assembling in secret elsewhere. Indeed, the evidence is that Poro continues to operate both openly and underground. For instance, individual chiefs have been known to enlist the Poro in support of their administration, even for the compulsory initiation of malcontents, and to give permission for the use of Poro initiates in farm work. It is still quite usual to decide succession to the chieftainship by 'swearing' on Poro medicine, and cases are not infrequently settled in the Poro bush rather than open court. Also, in 1955, the compounds of some unpopular chiefs were attacked and they were obliged to flee for their lives. Evidence of the chanting of Poro songs and the consistent pattern of complaint led the subsequent Commission of Inquiry to suggest that these disturbances had been partly facilitated by Poro (*Report*, Sierra Leone, 1956).

In short, despite urbanization the Poro is a powerful force which continues to influence the social life and outlook of traditionally minded people. Its effect is the more significant because the society is adamantly opposed to social change. Initiates entering the bush, for example, are forbidden to take with them anything European in the way of clothes and equipment, and the Poro elders have resolutely refused to allow the initiation schools to be used for modern educational purposes. In addition to rejecting a proposal that up-to-date agricultural information and instruction might be given through the medicine of Poro, they showed active hostility towards an analogous experiment which was tried in Sande, the women's society.[1] The fact that the latter traditional organization has been willing to compromise with modern interests and conditions[2] makes the Poro's atti-

1. In this case, girls undergoing initiation were collected together in camps and instructed in hygiene and mothercraft by former members of the society who had been trained by a Medical Officer (Margai, 1948). This was stigmatized by the Poro leaders as interference in women's business, although the doctor himself kept entirely clear of the actual initiation.
2. At the end of their period of seclusion, the initiated girls make their customary and ceremonial return to ordinary life. They enter the town in procession wearing

tude even more significant. Nearly every adult male Mende individual, irrespective of social class, has been initiated and the society itself is rigidly controlled and organized. There is an 'inner circle' of senior officials whose word is law. Junior members and initiates, having taken the oath, are bound to adhere to Poro rules. They are expected to do what they are told and have no say whatever in society 'policy' (Little, 1965–6).

The Poro also exists among the Temne, but mainly in the southern part of their country. Moreover, unlike the Mende, the Temne are strongly Islamicized. Most of their chiefs are Muslims and Islam itself does not allow its adherents to join secret societies. In addition, a number of other associations, fulfilling some of the same functions as Poro, also claim Temne allegiance. These are the Ragbenle in the east and the Ramena in the central region (Dorjahn, 1959). In other words, the likelihood is that over the Temne as a whole the Poro exercises less control and that fewer Temne than Mende are under Poro supervision.

This, then, could be a further reason why the Mende neither inaugurate dancing *compins* of their own nor join the companies of other tribes in large numbers. Individual Mende young men, observing the personal success achieved by the Temne organizers, might wish to follow suit, but would have less room in which to manoeuvre. 'Progressively-minded' Temne, it appears, had only the conservative outlook and prejudices of the older men to overcome. A Mende, in similar circumstances, would probably be confronted by a whole institution as well as being stigmatized for taking part in 'white man's business'. The Poro elders concerned could not prevent an educated man joining in activities organized by Temne or Mandinka companies. They had no control over these tribes, but they had power over illiterate Mende. The latter could be reminded of their duty as Poro men and, if necessary, threatened with supernatural reprisals. This would be enough to deprive a would-be leader of support. He might succeed in interesting a number of other young men like himself, but ordinary Mende migrants would not flock to his standard. The rank and file members upon whom the dancing *compin* movement depends would not come forward for fear of Poro displeasure.

Conclusion

A number of authors (Banton, 1957; Caprasse, 1959; Clément,

their newest clothes, which are not native style *lappas* and head ties, but European frocks and high-heeled shoes. Every girl who can carries an umbrella (Little, 1951, p. 118).

1956; Wallerstein, 1963) have drawn attention to the function of voluntary associations in the urbanization of developing West African countries. Stress has been laid in particular upon associations organized by younger men of the same ethnic group or tribe. It has been demonstrated that these societies play a major part in the socialization of migrants for purposes of urban life. It has not, however, been explained why this phenomenon is not more general. Admittedly, motives differ and the interest of some groups of migrants is firmly fixed on returning to their tribal homeland. Many others, however, have a widespread desire to assimilate to urban values and standards. Why is it that the latter tribes do not always make the above kind of adaptation?

This article has tried to elucidate the problem by examining the differential response of Mende and Temne migrants. The position of the respective younger male age groups in both the traditional and the modern social structure was analysed and a number of factors came to light. In the case of the Temne there was the low social rating of this tribe in comparison with other tribal inhabitants of Freetown. At the same time, individual young Temne men had a 'modern' outlook and were anxious, despite their relative lack of education, to improve their social status. This situation provided an incentive which was strong enough to overcome the opposition of the older men. The latter had no effective means of controlling the actions of their juniors outside the rural environment. The Mende counterparts of the Temne young men lacked the same incentive to organize themselves associationally. This was partly because on the whole upward social mobility was easier for the Mende than other tribes. Also, a Mende would-be founder of dancing *compins* would have to contend with the vested interests of the secret societies. It is likely that his efforts to recruit a following would be obstructed by still strongly entrenched traditional institutions.

Since Banton's research was conducted in 1953 the Temne have enjoyed wider opportunities of advanced education. Sierra Leone has also moved from colonial rule to self-government. These and other developments make it difficult further to test the differential adaptation described. Nevertheless, if the above analysis is substantially correct some insight may have been gained into the factors which tend, under conditions of rapid social change, to assist or inhibit the emergence of fresh social roles.

Admittedly, it would be difficult to test the latter hypothesis without more complete data. What, however, the present analysis does confirm is that the adaptation of tribally reared people to urban conditions is not a simple process of education. It varies with the social situation and this, in turn, is the product of factors deriving from the traditional structure as well as the urban industrial system. Basically, it is the interplay of these factors that determines the manner in which adaptation is made.

Patrons and Brokers: Rural Leadership in Four Overseas Indian Communities

ADRIAN C. MAYER

ONE of the most important recent political changes in developing societies has been the spread of local self-government. Power in such societies has previously often been held by officials of a colonial or imperial service, and only in recent years has democratic representation at the local level been widely inaugurated. What are the changes in patterns of leadership in these local—usually rural—settlements? Rural leaders under both previous and present conditions are of course concerned with some matters which bear no formal relation to administrative systems, such as the organization of community rites and arbitration councils. In some societies they formerly also had official duties as headmen, etc., being at the same time government agents and mediators between rulers and people. In other societies, the settlements were not officially recognized at all, and no official leadership existed before local government was introduced. The concomitants of this introduction are clearly different in each case. Much has been written about the first kind of situation and this paper will therefore deal with the second.[1]

I take my examples from the overseas Indian communities[2] in Fiji, Trinidad, British Guiana, and Mauritius. My analysis is a consequence of, and a tribute to, the stimulus of Raymond Firth in the study of these communities. For it is due to Firth that research has been carried out in Fiji and Mauritius, and he has actively promoted work in British Guiana. The conference which he convened in February 1957 (Firth, 1957b) to consider factionalism amongst overseas Indians is the only attempt hitherto made to view these communities comparatively. Published material has grown since then, and though

1. I should like to acknowledge the helpful comments made on a draft of this paper by Professor F. G. Bailey, Dr. B. Benedict, and Professor M. Freedman, as well as the Research Scholarship of The Australian National University which first awakened my interest in overseas Indian communities.
2. I use the term 'community' as it is used in these societies, to mean an ethnic section.

the differing emphases of writers make a strict comparison of data difficult, a start should be made to carry on the work he inaugurated.[1]

To simplify my comparison, I have chosen communities with certain important similarities besides that of a lack of local administration. All were formed by people recruited under indenture to produce the sugar which is still their economic mainstay. Immigrants came from the same areas of India, and the same main differences of religion, language, and customs exist. The communities all formed parts of Crown Colonies, and now form roughly the same proportions of the total populations.[2] These factors can be taken as 'equal'. On the other hand, the system of land tenure and the patterns of sugar production differ in each community; these are factors basic to leadership in the period before local government, and form the main non-political variants to be discussed.

I shall consider leadership in the light of two 'ideal types' of leader, the patron and the broker.[3] The patron recruits followers by his power to dispense favours. The broker, on the other hand, is a middleman attracting followers who believe him able to influence the person who controls the favours. Because the four communities I shall compare have had no local administration, there have been few contexts for brokerage. The main contacts with outside agencies have been with estate managements. These managements have delegated power to appointed overseers, and this patronage has been reinforced in some of the communities by wealth and landholding.

The local government systems which are being introduced in these communities call for brokerage rather than patronage, however. In them, the leader is not like a headman or an overseer appointed by an outside agency. The latter may distribute patronage to a small minority and yet keep his position; for his removal depends on the outside agency, and public pressure against him for a biased distribution of favours must coincide with a dereliction in his formal duties if the outside agency is to be persuaded to dismiss him. The leader in a local government system, on the other hand, is constantly

1. This paper was written in the autumn of 1964: a book containing studies of caste in seven overseas Indian communities has since been edited by B. M. Schwartz, and its publication will be a step towards comparative work of the kind advocated here.
2. 49 per cent in Fiji (1960), 47 per cent in British Guiana (1956), 36 per cent in Trinidad (1960), and 67 per cent in Mauritius (1960).
3. The concepts of patron and broker are not new to anthropology, of course. The *praja* ties described by Klass (see below) could, for instance, be compared with Nupe *bara*-ship (Nadel, 1942, pp. 122 f.); and T'ien (1953) provides data about patronage in another immigrant society.

aware of his electorate, for his position depends entirely on its support. As a patron, his favours are inevitably limited, and he may not be able to spread them over the minimum 51 per cent of the electorate which he needs to support him. As a broker, on the other hand, he can make promises to influence outsiders on a widely ranging number of matters, and can blame these outsiders if the favours do not materialize; hence, at least in theory, he can recruit a larger clientele than he can as a patron. I therefore suggest that conditions in these communities have up till now favoured the emergence of patrons, since leaders have been of the appointed variety; but that the new systems of elective local government will be equally if not more favourable to the broker. Indeed, I shall try to show that we can discern a trend of this kind in the data available.

A further difference between patron and broker is that, whereas the client of the former is only interested in his relation with the patron, and does not care about the source of the patron's power, the client of the latter has a relation with the person with whom the broker is in contact, and indeed has called in the broker to influence that relation to his advantage. The implication is that there is more contact with the outside in a brokerage system; and I shall suggest that the links of these overseas Indian communities with other sections of the plural societies in which they exist will therefore increase with the advent of local government.

I now briefly analyse the position in each of the four communities, and then draw the speculative conclusions I have just outlined.

Fiji[1]

Fiji Indians live in settlements measuring something more than one mile square and containing 500–600 people, almost none of whom are members of the non-Indian communities. Over this area are scattered their homesteads, each on the land its owner has leased either from the indigenous Fijians or from the Colonial Sugar Refining Company (CSR).[2] Within this dispersed settlement, wards have grown up which are generally composed of members of the

1. This account is based on my research in three settlements (Mayer, 1961) which together give a picture of the cane growing areas; I have used the term 'Indo-Fijian' in a recent publication (Mayer, 1963a), but here revert to 'Fiji Indian' because 'Indian' is the word currently in use in the other places with which I shall compare Fiji.
2. Most land in Fiji is inalienably owned by Fijians; few Fiji Indians own any of the rare freehold land. The CSR in Fiji became known as the South Pacific Sugar Mills after the completion of my study.

same cultural group, based on religion or region of origin in India, who may also be kin. One-third of the farms are on hillsides where cane cultivation gives way to mixed crops. Here, incomes are smaller, though differences of wealth are comparatively slight and few Indians sub-lease any land or employ more than one labourer. More important is the fact that these mixed farmers are ineligible for positions of leadership reserved for cane farmers. Occasionally, a number of people work in a nearby town; but such men are also part-time farmers and, though they have some different interests, cannot be said to form a separate class.

Settlements are not everywhere physically distinguishable, since farms run down the valleys without any break. This indeterminacy is emphasized by the fact that settlements have no official existence. There is no system of local government among Fiji Indians in settlement or District, although the last twenty years have seen several proposals for its introduction (Mayer, 1963a, pp. 101–3). Fiji Indians are therefore to a large extent free from official contacts. Much of what outside control exists stems not from Government but from the supervision by the CSR of cane cultivation and harvest.

The tenants of CSR land have clauses in their agreements under which a European CSR Field Officer controls their cultivation. For the harvest every cane grower signs an agreement to contribute to a co-operative harvest Gang labour equal to the cost of the Gang's harvest of his own cane. Although the Gang is ultimately controlled by the Field Officer, members elect a head (*sardar*) from amongst themselves who is responsible for its daily operation. The *sardar*'s post is one of the two positions of authority in the settlement. The other exists where there is a school operated by a local committee under the supervision of the Education Department. Here, the Manager and members of the committee are elected by the people of the settlement or settlements with children at the school. The Manager's duties (without which the school would not be officially recognized) include the collection of fees which go towards the teachers' salaries, and the maintenance of buildings and facilities.

The roles of *sardar* and Manager bring with them only minor possibilities for patronage and brokerage. True, a *sardar* can sometimes intercede for a grower with CSR officials (e.g., over the CSR's permission to transfer one of its leases), but this is minimized by the fact that the Field Officer is on the spot and has direct relations with each grower. The *sardar* has power in such daily matters as the allocation of the more favourable parts of fields to be harvested, but this is again under the Field Officer's overall control. Similarly, there appear to be few favours in the hands of a Manager, though he may be able to advance the career of a client's child through his acquaintance with officials, and can sometimes give school repair work to his friends.

Other positions of leadership do not have this semi-statutory authority. There are associations organized to operate a temple or a mosque. In one settlement a so-called Youth Organization claimed to represent the entire population and arrogated to itself duties of arbitration, organization of festivals, and the support of a candidate for the Legislative Council elections. It had proclaimed a boycott of a minority which would not accept its rulings, though homesteads are sufficiently independent for such a boycott not to have seriously inconvenienced its objects (it could not, for instance, extend the boycott to the school or the Gang). In general, social control is effected in informal councils (*panchayat*) or through the courts. The former deal mainly with petty civil disputes; their decisions are at least overtly unanimous, and the arbitrators are often the *sardar* and school Manager. Although the *panchayat*'s decision is openly accepted, covert disagreement may result in a persisting conflict. Where this ends in some sort of fracas, the courts are brought in, the largest category of major cases being assaults. Recourse to the courts is not, however, always to seek solutions to these disputes, but often rather to continue the conflicts in a different context.

None of the settlements studied has formally organized branches of cane growers' unions, though their main supporters are well known, and unions can on occasion mobilize a general following (e.g., when harvest strikes are called). No political parties have existed until recently in Fiji, and there have thus been no party branches in settlements, though here again some men are open supporters of particular Fiji Indian politicians, and the settlement may divide at elections. Besides these outside ties, people may have contacts with members of the administration or Police (often as kin) or with Fiji Indian and European lawyers, or with traders in the town.

There is, however, little advantage to be derived from these ties. The absence of any local government machinery, and the close supervision of the economy by the CSR, means that there are few occasions on which intercession with the administration is needed. The seeking of such intercession is made more difficult by the need to cross community lines, for few Fiji Indians hold high official positions, and there is as yet no full system of ministerial responsibility for Indian Members of the Legislative Council (MLC). Men who stand close to urban lawyers may transact some business for clients;

but, in general, there are few occasions when an aspiring leader can act as broker between a follower and someone who is influential outside the settlement. The only major form of patronage inside the settlements is the provision of credit by storekeepers. Cane farmers, especially, buy on credit and are thereby clients of a storekeeper. Usually, storekeepers try to be neutral in settlement conflicts, but where they aspire to leadership, the provision of credit is an important part of their competition.

In general, then, the physical and institutional nature of the settlement makes it difficult for leaders to emerge. There is a low degree of social articulation, owing to the dispersal of the homesteads and cultural heterogeneity; there are no powerful landlords; the main crop buyer is the CSR; few farmers engage more than one or two labourers and there are no ascribed positions of leadership or dominance. Men who wish to gain power try to capture the few posts of authority in the settlement by becoming *sardar* or Manager. If they are not eligible, they try to have an ally (often a kinsman) elected. Where there is no Gang or school committee, such men may create associations (like the Youth Organization) designed to give them power.

To gain posts for themselves or their friends, men require supporters, for people are elected to these positions, not appointed by some higher authority. Sometimes an aspirant's personality or policy may suffice to gain him adherents; sometimes he can call on the loyalties of kin or cultural group; but often support has to be recruited with more than a domestic *quid pro quo*. We have just seen that there are few such favours to be granted in these settlements. Hence the number of supporters fluctuates widely (save for a small core) and many people manage to remain neutral. Moreover, victory in Gang or school committee brings a power which is restricted by the close control exercised by the CSR and the Education Department. Often, in fact, its main significance appears to be the increase of personal prestige, which can then be used in non-statutory contexts such as the arbitration councils. At present contenders are usually youngish and Fiji-born, educated enough to be able to carry out the clerical duties of *sardar* or Manager. Their links with outside leaders are often tenuous, but must become more important as Fiji moves towards a formal organization of political parties and more self-government at the local and national level.[1]

To sum up, in rural Fiji Indian settlements there is none of that

1. Recent developments have brought to Fiji a new constitution with a considerable degree of self-government as well as a party system.

control over land or jobs or administrative duties which would provide continuing sources of patronage for leaders and enable them to build up relatively unchanging groups of supporters. At the same time, there are few opportunities for such people to act as brokers between settlement residents and the outside, because residents have minimal obligations to the administration, and a paternal CSR takes care of many of their economic needs. Men strive for prestige and power in the few capacities open to them, but their supporters form unstable collectivities in which loyalty to the leader, rather than any sense of identity with other followers, is the predominant feature. Leadership is a matter of personal ambition and ability and, as Firth has noted, 'factional manipulations may serve as substitutes for fully fledged political and social activity' (Firth, 1957b, p. 293).

Trinidad

My analysis of the rural community in Trinidad comes mainly from Klass's work in a village which he calls Amity.[1] This is a nucleated settlement of about 4,000 people, having been formed by a ribbon development along the roads. It contains wards, which can be correlated with economic status—the richer wards contain men with land and responsible jobs, the poorer contain labourers, fishermen, etc. Moreover, the richer people come, on the whole, from higher castes, and caste is a significant factor in social relations.[2]

Nearby cane estates provide some 700 of the 900 adult men with annual or seasonal work. Hence, the drivers (*sardar*) who control recruitment for this work are men of considerable power, especially the chief driver who has a cane harvesting gang of between 100 and 150 Amity men under him. Klass notes that it is customary 'for a father to ask his own "driver" to find a job for his son' (Klass, 1961, p. 69). Apart from this major source of work, there is farming of privately held cane and paddy land. Here, some people own surplus land which they lease to tenants. Klass is thus able to divide Amity's population into two classes. There are the people who control access to jobs or to land, as well as storekeepers who control access to credit; and there are those who seek favours of work or money from these people.

1. Klass, 1961. This village is almost entirely Indian, in contrast to other settlements he mentions, which contain both Indians and Creoles. It may well represent one of several rural patterns, therefore.
2. Almost all Amity people are from the same cultural group. It is impossible to say whether cultural group differences would be more important than caste differences (as they are in Fiji) were there several cultural groups.

This division is reflected in the pattern of social control. Most disputes are contained within the village. Partly, this is because of a belief that the courts dispense 'Creole' rather than 'Indian' justice, and are therefore biased against villagers. But it is also because there exist in the village adequate agents for settling disputes. These are the 'big men' of the landowning, driver, and storekeeper upper class. They derive their position from a relationship known as 'feeling praja'. *Praja* denotes a tie of obligation reciprocally held between an inferior and a superior.[1] A man requests a favour of some kind from another man—a job on the estate, a lease, a credit account; by fulfilling this request, the second man acknowledges him as an inferior, a follower who will provide gifts and moral or even physical support. The superior is no less obligated, however, for he must help his follower when in difficulties and act generously towards him. Some people in the middle range (e.g., small landowners) are inferior to big men and superior to others; but most men are either superior or inferior in all their relationships.

A big man can fairly easily settle a dispute if both disputants feel *praja* to him. A dispute between a big and a small man, on the other hand, is harder to settle because it requires the arbitration of one who is bigger than both of them. Although disputes between men quickly crystallize into conflicts between their immediate kin-groups, the big men can generally step in before this happens, and few factions apparently result. This lack of factions may not only be because quarrels are settled quickly, however, but also because the big men have few reasons for conflict between themselves. Each has his own sphere of pre-eminence. One has the harvest gang, over which he is appointed by the estate instead of being elected in competition with others by his fellow farmers; another has his store, though storekeepers are not in the first rank of big men unless they own land; and a third is master of his farm. Conflict in religious or other associations simply results in secession or an end to the association[2] and, because the village is not an officially recognized entity, there is no statutory (and therefore continuing) village body for whose control the big men might vie. True, there was an attempt to form an unofficial village council[3] in 1955, which failed when the big men on

1. Its normal Hindi meaning is 'progeny; a subject; a tenant' (Lal, 1949), in India finding expression in the relation between ruler (*raja*) and subject (*praja*).
2. E.g., divisions over the 1956 election produced the collapse of an all-village pageant and the splitting of a religious association.
3. 220 such councils were reportedly in existence in Trinidad at the end of 1957 (Community Development Dept., Administrative Report 1957, p. 7).

its committee withdrew after 'losing interest'. Whether this was the real reason or not, big men did not form factions in the council, and their lack of interest may have been due to the fact that there were more satisfactory positions of leadership for them.[1] Even the cricket teams representing different wards never play each other because they are in different leagues. There seem to be few contexts in which disputes develop between groups or between aspirants to village leadership.

Although most people solve their problems inside the village, there are a few people who require the intervention of outsiders. These are mainly taxi drivers, with frequent need of intercession with the police and courts. During Klass's stay, these men felt *praja* to an outsider who was a member of the County Council under whose jurisdiction Amity lay,[2] and also a member of the People's National Movement (PNM). This is one of the two main political parties in Trinidad, the other being the Democratic Labour Party (DLP). As Klass points out, although each party counts both Creoles and Indians among its leaders, the former party is considered by Amity people to be a Creole and the latter an Indian party. The fact that this County Councillor (who was an Indian) stood for the PNM in the 1958 Federal elections did not make it any the less Creole in their eyes. Nevertheless, the events of that election indicate that politicians are viewed not only in party terms but also in the light of ties of personal advantage and obligation. For the Indian voters of Amity did not support the 'Indian' DLP *en masse*, but rather voted for the person to whom they felt the most *praja*. Thus, the taxi drivers supported the PNM candidate because of his brokerage in their favour. The big men voted for the DLP, not so much because of personal obligation as because they felt more *praja* to the DLP for providing schools through the Hindu Mahasabha than they did to the PNM for its candidate's help in improving Amity's streets and lighting through County Council works. The clients of the big men voted as did their patrons. On the other hand, fishermen and other low caste people did not feel *praja* to the big men, and voted for the PNM mainly as a protest against high caste opposition to it. In this way, the ties of personal obligation and village alignment proved

1. This is similar to a village council cited by the Niehoffs, which obtained favours for the village but which functioned without the leading men and was not the centre of any struggle for power (Niehoff and Niehoff, 1960, p. 70).
2. County Councils, with at least nominally executive powers, were started in 1952, having been advisory bodies since 1946. A proposal to form statutory village councils had previously been rejected on the grounds that these would be too small to be socially or economically viable (Rep. Loc. Govt. Cttee 1947, p. 8).

stronger than those of community—the factor supposed by non-Indians to be all-powerful in the Indian community's political behaviour.

The Amity situation, then, suggests a separation of leadership spheres inside and outside the village. No important outside patrons are mentioned, perhaps because of the lack of administrative contact with the village. Again, villagers do not themselves act as brokers with the outside. Moreover, the brokers who act for Amity residents appear only to do so in outside matters and are not used to bring pressure on big men in the village. Villagers are considered 'big' because of criteria existing inside the village, such as land-ownership. They recruit followers by patronage of jobs, tenancies and so forth, and they use their power inside the village rather than in relation to leaders or authorities outside it—for instance, by settling disputes without recourse to the courts. Although the County Council dispenses large sums of money,[1] Amity's big men have apparently no desire to be elected to it. However, leaders in other villages may see it as a step to the Legislative Council,[2] and they and the Amity leaders must realize the political implications of the control of this money. At present, it seems, Amity's big men prefer power inside their village.

British Guiana[3]

In British Guiana, more than one-fifth of the Indian rural population lives on estates (plantations) and about one-half lives in villages.[4] An estate comprises some 8,000 acres; its inhabitants live in barracks or in dwellings which are strung along the roads, being separated into several wards, and it has a central area containing a market place, public buildings, and usually a sugar mill. In the smaller of the two estates described by Jayawardena (population 2,564) almost all people work for the estate; the larger (population 9,272) contains a significant proportion of artisans, storekeepers, white collar workers, and farmers of nearby paddy land who are not estate employees. Over 90 per cent in each estate are Indian.

1. Estimated recurrent and capital grants from Government totalled $8,826,434 (about £1,838,850) for the seven County Councils in 1961 (*Hansard*, 12 April 1961, p. 2304).
2. See e.g. *Hansard*, 29 July 1960, p. 3126.
3. Since its independence the country has been known as Guyana.
4. Data for both types of settlement are provided by a number of articles and books by Jayawardena and Smith (especially Jayawardena, 1963, and Smith, 1962).

The organization of the estate comprises senior management (mainly European) at the top; unskilled and semi-skilled labourers in field and mill at the bottom; and *sardar*, mill foremen, and office staff in the middle. Status, as well as livelihood, is based on this estate hierarchy rather than on any 'horizontal' tie of group or association, for associational activity is minimal. For instance, the work gangs formed are not co-operative bodies as in Fiji, but are simply numbers of individuals employed by the estate. Until recently, only religious associations were allowed; and disputes were settled by a manager's court, and not by councils of residents. Again, the Joint Committees of management and cane union (established in 1949) are closely controlled by management. Religious associations are led by elected chairmen and committees. Electoral campaigns are not among the types of dispute noted by Jayawardena, however, although dissatisfaction with the officers of an association may reinforce other quarrels, and factions may form. It is very difficult, in any case, for a person to become a leader or openly to use what power he has, because of the related concepts of *mati* and 'eye pass'.

Mati ('matey') is the notion that people doing the same work are equal in status and prestige. Any action which can be construed as indicating superiority thereby breaches *mati* and is an 'eye pass'. 'Eye pass' is commonest among unskilled labourers on the same pay rates. Supervisory and clerical staff have fewer *mati* ties and hence fewer 'eye passes', since the orientation of occupation is geared to promotion and differential pay. However, a person who thinks he is superior will consider it an 'eye pass' if a supposedly inferior person acts in such a way as to suggest equality, if not superiority (Skinner, 1960, p. 908).

Mati and 'eye pass' clearly make it hard for a man to become a leader. All who wish to lead in situations involving outsiders (where 'eye pass' does not arise) are seen as equally eligible, whatever their abilities, and are given turns (e.g., on the Joint Committee). This prevents a potential leader from consolidating his position. On the other hand, a man trying to lead inside the group runs up against the danger of 'eye pass' accusations. Hence, not only is any coercive authority absent, but even the few people with influence— the *sardar*, for instance—have to move carefully when trying to reconcile disputants. Too evident an arbitration will bring the accusation of 'playing represente', implying that the arbitrator thinks himself important enough to be able to impose a decision and thereby 'eye pass' his fellows (*mati* here being extended to cover all cane workers or even the whole Indian community). Usually, then, 'eye pass' accusations are made in public quarrels rather than taken before an arbitrator. If there is no apology, public opinion may 'settle' it; a boycott may be tried, though people are too independent for it to be successful for long; or a fight may send the matter to the court. The participants then use the court to decide their quarrel about status. The winner gains prestige, but subsequent defeats will lower his position again. Individual status, rather than leadership, is involved here.

A person who is rising from one status level to another simply severs his *mati* ties by associating with people of higher status. People may accuse him of 'eye passing' them; but they cannot stop him. A boycott is not an effective deterrent because he is already drawing allies from elsewhere; and in any case, even kin cannot be counted upon to support a boycott if their interests do not demand it. Those who try to move up are middle-aged men, active in union or religious association and thereby out of the ordinary run. But such men inevitably leave behind them enemies who feel that they have been 'eye passed', and it seems that factions of loyal followers do not form, but rather that support is recruited on a shifting and *ad hoc* basis. Again, it is individual status, rather than leadership of others, which is involved. Even the people with authority derived from the estate—the *sardar* or the mill foreman—are not leaders with 'real power' (Jayawardena, 1963, p. 137), though they dispense patronage in selecting people for work and are differentiated from others 'by their status in the hierarchy of labour, their badges of office, mannerisms and their ability to realize more fully the ambitions for power and control over persons and resources' (Jayawardena, 1960, pp. 98 f.). We do not know how these men are selected; it is also not clear to what extent either they or the clerical staff act as brokers between labourers and management or outsiders, but the amount of litigation over 'eye pass' suggests that those in close contact with local lawyers may play a significant role as intermediaries. On the whole, however, estate populations have little contact with the outside. The management provides for most economic wants, there is no local government, and the population is less mobile than that living in villages—save for the white-collar element I have mentioned as living in some of the larger estates, which is not dealt with in any detail in the data.

A contrasting situation exists in villages, some mainly Indian and others with Negro majorities. Here, paddy is cultivated on holdings averaging 5–6 acres. However, some men farm more than this, and others lease their surplus to fellow Indians. There are also traders and a white-collar population, especially in villages near George-town, the capital. Hence, there is no single scale of statuses, and the inequalities which exist are changeable since they are based on wealth and a variety of jobs. The rich farmers have little to do socially with the poorer Indians, their relations being 'limited to commercial affairs and to activities that demand ethnic solidarity'.[1] Again, the obligations of patronage may take a rich storekeeper to a client's wedding, but no return invitation need be given. Though the children of rich men may live in the village and lead some of the associations there, they do not 'set the tone of village life' (Smith and Jayawar-dena, 1959, p. 329), and their ambitions lie in Georgetown society. Nevertheless, their existence raises the prestige of the families to which they belong; and, presumably, they can act as brokers for villagers in Georgetown.

The dominant people in such settlements, therefore, are the richer farmers and storekeepers. It is these people who vie with one another, partly over land and trade, partly in the scale of their weddings, and partly over the control of the religious, political, and social associations in the village. There were twenty-four such asso-ciations in a village studied by Smith, with some 300 offices to be filled. No details have been published about the factions which form, but a perpetual conflict of shifting alliances is reported; followers are presumably recruited through the patronage of leases and store credit.

Rivalry is also in theory possible within the Village Councils (VCs) which exist in 78 of the 300 or so coastal settlements. Two-thirds of the VC's nine members are elected[2] on a franchise limited by a property qualification. Their duties are to raise a property tax and spend it on roads and the drainage system of dykes and canals. Development activities are controlled by the Central Govern-ment, and VCs do not therefore have wide powers. Nor are they very active. Indeed, Smith suggests that they could be abolished without much change, for their main work is done by an overseer appointed by the Local Government Board; and Young says that they are of no administrative advantage and, owing to their restricted franchise, have not contributed towards training people for respon-sible government.[3] Nor has the system acted as a spring-board to the

1. Skinner, 1960, p. 907. The remark applies to a Negro-majority village.
2. A Local Government Board nominates the rest, as well as all members where the village is in a Country District.
3. Young, 1958, pp. 214–15. A report published in 1955 recommends that local authorities be made large enough to be economically viable and politically

Legislative Council. In 1953, 8 of the 18 rural constituencies were represented by residents, but none of these had worked their way up through VCs.[1]

Even without local government, however, there are arenas for competition in the villages. Little can be said about the ways in which people recruit followings, but there does appear to be one important difference from the position on the estates. It is that recruitment through patronage by landowners is entirely controlled by them—whereas estate *sardar* dispense patronage which would stop if the estate were to dismiss them. Village leaders are more autonomous in this respect, and their followings may be more stable. But this can only be conjecture until there are full accounts of village leadership.

Mauritius

Of the four countries, Mauritius has the greatest dependence on sugar cane, 40 per cent of its area and 70 per cent of its labour force being devoted to sugar production. At present, about 60 per cent of the sugar is produced by estates, but only some 12 per cent of the rural population live on these and work as permanent employees. The rest is grown by owner-planters, living with other Indians in villages stretching along the roadsides. These consist of distinct neighbourhoods, which sometimes correspond to cultural divisions. The main analysis of rural society has been made by Benedict (1961) from a study of two villages with an 80 per cent Indian population.

Several positions of authority and influence exist. One is that of *sardar*, an estate employee who acts as overseer for both sugar cultivation and harvest. Another is that of job contractor, supplying labour for the estate and taking 10 per cent of the wages as commission. A third is that of crop broker, extending credit to planters in connexion with selling their cane to the mill. People in these positions have direct power over labourers and growers. Their selection by the estate management does not occasion rivalries important enough to be mentioned as factors in village politics.[2] One reason may be that, owing to the large number of *sardar* chosen for dif-

effective, and include the estates. It had been accepted, but not implemented, by 1961.

1. Young, 1958, p. 209. One MLC had sat for one year on a VC.
2. That the estates expect men to be their servants in more than an economic sense is suggested by a cautionary tale about a job contractor whose contract is ended because he fails to produce victory for a political candidate favoured by the estate (Roy, 1960, p. 314).

ferent jobs,[1] there are no disappointed aspirants. Another reason may be that there are now other attractive contexts in which men can seek and exercise power, namely, in the system of statutory local government which has been in existence since 1952.

The main foci of political activity before 1952 were associations founded to promote mutual aid and organize religious observances, called *baitka* by Hindus and *jammat* by Muslims. These tended to be dominated by *sardar*, job contractors, and planters, some of whom had (and still have) considerable amounts of land.[2] Such men were able to provide work for clients and to lend them money. One must suppose that their clientele centred on the *baitka* membership, and that it therefore comprised only a section of the village population—for *baitka* were confined to members of a single cultural group, sometimes in a single ward of the village.

The strength of groups larger than the *baitka* is difficult to assess. Pre-1952 village councils were without statutory basis, and it was reported that at the end of 1946 only three such councils were active.[3] In another sphere, the building of temples and their maintenance called for the co-operation of people in an area larger than a single village. Again, sports clubs covered a larger potential membership than the *baitka*, but it is not clear to what extent these are recent creations. In short, the general picture is of weak and rather unimportant associations, apart from the *baitka*. The main rivalries in villages were between leaders of *baitka*, and just as there were no village associations, so there were no leaders of the village as a whole. One is reminded of the situation in Trinidad.

Major changes in the rural power structure stemmed from the creation of four rural Districts between 1946 and 1955. The countryside was for the first time officially demarcated into villages, and in 1952 (and again in 1955) statutory Village Councils (VCs) were formed of 8 members elected by universal suffrage and 4 officially nominated members, who then elected their officers. The chairman of the 22 to 30 VCs in each District elected from among themselves 7 representatives to sit with nominated members on the District Council (DC). What effects did these changes have on the pattern of leadership?

1. In one village there were at least fifteen (Benedict, 1957, p. 335).
2. E.g., in one village at least one man had over 100 acres of cane land (Benedict, 1961, p. 74).
3. *Mauritius* 1946, p. 26. District Boards existed from 1902 to 1939, but had little effect on villages; some 80 non-statutory village councils were constituted between 1949 and 1952, but were superseded before they could prove themselves.

One new factor is that election to, and control of, the VC became a basis for open rivalry in villages. In only 4 of the 27 VCs of one District were candidates returned without a contest. We do not have comparable figures to tell us how many VC chairmen were elected unanimously, but in any case, unanimous decisions may conceal competition. There was also competition among VC chairmen for the DC places; in one election, 12 chairmen competed for the 7 places, for instance. Was this competition simply concerned with an enhancement of prestige for use in other contexts? Or were there spoils to be gained within the local government system itself?

VCs received Government money through the DC, to which they submitted proposals for expenditure; their power to levy local taxes had not been used up to 1962. The DC, in turn, received most of its income from the Government. In 1961, the 111 VCs had approved estimated expenditures of Rs.478,055—roughly, Re.1 per head,[1] the average VC getting some Rs.4,200.[2] Control of a VC would thus mean the power both to decide on projects and to dispense the resulting money. To what extent could this be used to benefit favoured people or groups? Again, the total expenditure of the four DCs in 1961 was Rs.737,400: if we subtract the amount granted to the VCs, some Rs.250,000 was thus spent directly by these DCs. To what extent did a seat on the DC carry with it the control over these sums of money, as well as the power to decide allocations to VCs? I am not aware of writings which consider such questions; but from the nature of the situation it seems that the exercise of autocratic power was difficult on the VC and impossible on the DC. Opposition was frequent in the former, and a VC chairman would have to attend to the wishes of his allies to maintain his position. In the DC, the 7 elected members were not only sometimes divided among themselves, but were faced by an equal number of nominated colleagues, including the Civil Commissioner of the District and one of its MLCs. It is usual for such an official to resist allocation patterns of too biased a kind; but even without this check, a non-official leader could clearly not afford to favour his own village or those of his allies too blatantly if he wished to continue in office. For he had been elected on the votes of all VC chairmen, and had therefore to favour at least 51 per cent of them. In short, control of money may not be the only or even the main reason for a leader's wishing to be elected to the DC (or the VC).

1. District Admin. Report of 1961.
2. This compares with an estate labourer's income of Rs.900, or the Rs.400 of a bus driver (Benedict, 1961, pp. 70, 72).

Elsewhere (Mayer, 1963b), I have suggested that in a very similar situation in India, the incentive to become a leader in VC and DC stems as much from the role of broker in matters which lead outside the local government system as from the role of patron inside the system. It is clear that powers of patronage are not built into the Mauritian DC and VC roles in the same way as they are into the roles of *sardar* and job contractor. The VC chairman can hire a particular dustman, for instance, but this act is finally subject to judgment by his constituents, some of whom are his rivals. On the other hand, the favours shown by the *sardar* or job contractor are not controlled by the general public but rather by the estate manager who is outside the village system. The tendency in the first case is for leaders to treat people fairly equally: in the second, they can implement their bias within wider limits, so long as it is not of a kind to injure the controlling outsider's own interest; for instance, they can hire particular labourers as long as they maintain the strength of the gang.

The place of patronage on the VC and DC can be contrasted with the ways in which these bodies may be used to increase a leader's sphere of brokerage. A place on the DC means a chance for co-operation and contact with the MLC who is an *ex officio* member. Occasionally, too, the DC is a step towards becoming an MLC.[1] Under the 1948 constitution, voters in each District elected 3 MLCs who could be important as intermediaries with Government and urban circles. Sometimes, of course, their roles as spokesmen for the public and as legislators conflicted; on the DC, for example, the MLC was on the one hand the villager's champion, yet on the other he was a nominated member who had enacted some of the measures against which the villager might protest.[2]

The MLC, whatever his background, had to be well enough educated to cope with Legislative Council and DC business. In this he resembled other brokers, notably teachers, who, Benedict says, form the core of an 'educated' as opposed to a 'traditional' leadership. Teachers and other civil servants are assumed by villagers to be familiar with Government machinery and to be able to manipulate it. *Sardar* and planters, on the other hand, derive their posi-

---

1. E.g. 2 MLCs elected in 1959 had been VC chairman and DC member. That more people did not use the DC as stepping-stone is probably because so many were civil servants and thus ineligible (e.g., 5 out of 7 unofficial members of one DC in 1957 were civil servants).
2. See Benedict, 1961, p. 155. When an MLC was in the DC as a VC chairman his role was even more complex.

N

tion from landowning and their status in the estate system. Officers of the VCs were mainly of the traditional type, probably because they had greater local power to deploy in elections. Nevertheless, there were more educated leaders than in pre-1952 days, partly because the clerical work of the VC demanded them. Mauritius is small enough for people to be able to go to the capital and act as their own brokers without too much loss of time; nevertheless, as the Government extends its operations at the central and local levels, so will brokers with special expertise be required to mediate with the bureaucrat-patrons outside the village. The rivalries of these brokers will tend to occur outside the village, by contrast to the rivalries of traditional leaders which occur over village matters.[1]

Comparison

The five situations I have described differ in many ways. The pattern of settlement, for instance, ranges from the nucleated village of Amity to the scattered homesteads of Fiji. Again, people in Fiji settlements stress differences of religion and region of origin as compared to caste differences in the Trinidad village. Such variations are not of central importance for us, in the sense that they do not contribute directly to the nature of the leader's role, but rather set limits within which it exists.

The system of land tenure, on the other hand, is of direct importance. Where there are large private holdings, as in Trinidad, Mauritius, and the Guianese villages, tenants and labourers will support their rich landlord-patron as individual clients or as members of the association (e.g., the *baitka*) which he controls. This does not happen in Fiji and on the Guianese estates, where there

1. This picture has been somewhat changed by the reorganization of local government in 1962. The DC now has a majority of VC chairmen, and civil servants are no longer allowed to sit on the VC. This means, in particular, that only teachers in schools unaided by Government are eligible. As a result, the focus may shift from the relation between officials and non-officials to the competition between non-officials. The role of the MLC has also recently changed; since 1958 there are no fewer than 40 single-member constituencies, the average number of electors being about 5,500 contained in about 3 VCs. The MLC's area of responsibility is now therefore smaller than that of the DC chairman. Moreover, his influence in a Legislative Council of 40, instead of 19, non-official members is clearly less (unless, as is sometimes the case, parties are evenly matched and every vote is precious). In short, the MLC may become lobby fodder, at the same time as his rural base is diminished. This, added to the exclusion of civil servants from local government, may well diminish the significance of the educated leadership.

are no large landowners; rather, leaders exist in statutory positions of which the most important lie within the systems of sugar production present in each of the four countries. Here, a distinction must be made between the *sardar*, job contractors, etc., appointed by the estate management, and the *sardar* of Fiji who are elected by fellow growers. Appointed *sardar* appear to hold their posts for many years and to build up a basis of patronage thereby, whereas elected *sardar* do not always have time to do this. The former thus come to derive a power from the estate system which is not only lasting but which reflects the importance of the pattern of sugar production as a context of power and prestige—the extreme being in the British Guiana estate, where it is the only such context. The latter are often *sardar* because of power which they have outside the system, and where this is based on shifting alliances, there are constant changes of *sardar*. Hence, land ownership and the kind of estate system have a direct bearing on the kind of leader we meet.

Local government also offers positions of leadership. Here, we pass from Fiji with no statutory local government at all, through British Guiana where a minority of villages (and not the estates) have VCs based on restricted franchise, to Trinidad where elected CCs but not VCs exist, and finally to Mauritius where there are both elected VCs and DCs. As might be expected, the importance of the representative increases with the scope of the system. He is not really significant in British Guiana; in Trinidad, the County Councillor may be a useful intermediary but is by definition usually an outsider; and in Mauritius, VC chairmanship and DC membership are prizes for aspiring local leaders.

Associations exist based on the cultural group—linguistic or sectarian—such as the *baitka* in Mauritius or the temple committee in Trinidad or British Guiana. Again, both Fiji and Trinidad have informal village councils for arbitration and the management of festivals, etc. A major difference between leadership in these bodies and that on the estate or the VC is that no external force upholds them. Hence, quarrels may result in the starting of a rival association. Competition may bedevil the work of the harvest gang or the VC, but it cannot change its membership or stop its statutory operations; whereas in the other associations, the composition and very existence of the body depends ultimately on the relations between leaders. The question of competition between leaders brings in the subject of factions, which underlay the 1957 conference, and on which little new material has since emerged on overseas Indian communities.[1]

1. E.g., Jayawardena mentions factions but does not discuss them; and Benedict

I therefore wish rather to consider the type of relationship which leaders have with their followers. Earlier, I suggested that it is one of patronage and/or brokerage.

In Fiji, there is little opportunity for the patron, either in sugar production or in the few contacts with the administration (e.g., in the school committee). In British Guiana, Trinidad, and Mauritius, the *sardar* have wide powers to hire labour and manage cane production. Except on the Guianese estate, there are also important landowners (often *sardar*) who lease out land and cultivate through labourers. As I have already indicated, all these are powerful patrons. By contrast, brokerage is less well-defined in the data, perhaps because it is often more difficult to identify and involves people outside the local settlement. Nevertheless, brokerage is more emphasized for Trinidad than for the Guianese village or for Fiji, and is stressed for Mauritius. Mauritian civil servants gained VC seats mainly because they could act as brokers with the administration, and even the traditional type of leader was an intermediary when he represented his VC on the DC. I therefore suggest that the broker's role becomes more important as local government spreads.

Local government may bring increased opportunities for brokers; but these are taken by different kinds of broker in different situations in the introduction of local government. An example can be drawn from India, where Bailey has compared two villages in Orissa (Bailey, 1963, pp. 62–7, 99–103). One village 'has a high degree of internal integration and externally is isolated'. Here, ties with the outside of the kind represented by local government are not yet 'legitimized' in the eyes of villagers. Hence, 'real' village leaders such as the hereditary village headmen do not have anything to do with the new local government system; were they to do so, they would come under suspicion and would lose their place as village leaders. Instead, the leaders of the VC and the brokers with outside agencies are other villagers who play a role seen by the inhabitants to be necessary but distasteful. The second village is much less isolated. Many people work in a nearby town and have constant contacts with outside commercial and administrative circles. Here, the local government and the village power systems are intermeshed. Villagers in some cases provide their own contacts with the administration; but where the tasks required are too specialized, they use fellow villagers as brokers, whom they regard as legitimate actual or potential village leaders.

---

notes the existence of twenty-year old factions in one village, but does not give their history.

Let us compare this situation with those in Trinidad and Mauritius. In Amity, we find a village containing a definite pattern of internal power relations but with few links with the administration. Here, leaders (*sardar*, landowners) apparently do not attempt to enter local government through the County Council, and leave brokerage with the administration to other people who are social or even geographical outsiders. The reasons for their non-involvement are not given by Klass, but may include that lack of legitimacy mentioned by Bailey. In Mauritius, on the other hand, the local government system has reached down into the village through the VCs. Leaders are fully involved in local government, for *sardar* and *baitka* heads compete in elections to the VC and DC. Although numbers of people have close direct contacts with the administration, and are often able to act as their own brokers, they also work through others and may well expect their leaders to be their brokers. In fact, the material suggests the same contrast as is shown for the Orissa villages, namely, that when contacts with the administration are external to village politics (and are perhaps not regarded as proper activities for local leaders), brokers will be outsiders; but where local government is part of the village political system, the brokers will include the village leaders.

In one respect the two situations are different. Traditional hereditary positions of village leadership exist in India, but not in the four overseas Indian communities. This gives the introduction of local government an added significance for the latter; for a system which produces village leaders will do much to give local settlements a political and social unity which they have hitherto lacked. Equally important is the implication that this development has for the place of these settlements in the plural societies of which the overseas Indian community forms one section. Hitherto, it seems, the leaders in a settlement were patrons, and operated in a fairly small field which the data indicate was within the community. This is partly because settlements—at least, those studied by anthropologists— usually contained people of a single community, and few patrons had enough favours to be able to build up a following outside it, even had they so desired. Partly, it is doubtless because sentiments of communal solidarity, and a greater ease in doing business with people of one's own community (who may also be linked through kinship etc.) restricted favours to its members. The result is that the patron might be in contact with the outside for the favours he dispensed, but that their distribution was communal. For instance, the *sardar* acquired patronage from the estate management, but used it for fellow Indians who were mainly interested in their relations with him.

The broker, on the other hand, attracts clients who need intercession in their relations with people outside the settlement. But these relations are with people outside the community too, especially in so far as they concern a bureaucracy containing people of all the communities. Hence, the more leaders are brokers rather than patrons —or rather, the more the political system in which settlements exist lends itself to brokerage rather than to patronage—so will leaders develop with broader outside interests and expertise. Such a trend does not necessarily mean a lessening of the plurality of these societies, for it may produce increased rivalry between communities by increasing the competition for favours at the higher, inter-communal level. But it will increase the links between communities, and change the nature of the plurality of these societies.

My account has shown the variations which have grown up over the past century between overseas Indian communities with basically the same origins. It has also shown that, despite the different emphases of the available data, comparisons can be made around a single theme. Whether my conclusions stand the test of further investigation is less important to me than that they may perhaps act as a focus for further research and identification of problems.[1] Unless there is some co-ordination of this kind, the data will continue to be largely incommensurate, and thereby prevent that comparison and formulation of wider propositions about overseas Indian communities for which Firth sought in his pioneering approach to the subject.

1. One might, for example, view political action as an enterprise and the patron-broker as an entrepreneur (Eidheim, 1963).

Shamanism among the Oya Melanau

H. S. MORRIS

The Shaman . . . 'a master of spirits'
Firth (1959)

THE name Melanau is given to a culturally diverse set of peoples in Sarawak who inhabit the lower reaches of the River Rejang and the coastal areas to the north-east as far as Miri. In the Census of 1960 they numbered 44,661, of whom 31,770 were Muslim and approximately 10,000 pagan. Most of these people speak closely related languages, not all of which are mutually intelligible. Traditionally they practised shifting cultivation and had similar types of social organization. Although it is probably legitimate to speak of a Melanau culture and a Melanau type of social structure, it is doubtful how far any one group can thereby be distinguished from another or from related groups in the interior who are not classified as Melanau.

The Melanau of the Oya River numbered 6,852 in 1947 and inhabited some dozen villages on the banks of the river as it flows through the low-lying swamps between the hills and the coast. The upriver villagers mostly grow the sago palm as a cash crop, and those nearer the coast grow rubber and are fishermen. The majority are Muslim, though exactly how many is not known. Most of the pagans live in the upriver villages and it is with them that this paper is mainly concerned.[1]

1. The field work on which this article is based was made possible by grants from the Colonial Social Science Research Council and the Sarawak Government from 1948 to 1950, and from the London School of Economics and Political Science in 1963–64. My thanks are also due to many Government Departments and Administrative Officers in Sarawak. To the Curator of the Sarawak Museum, Mr. Tom Harrisson, and his staff I owe a special debt of gratitude, in particular to Mr. Tuton Kaboy, who worked with me as an assistant in the field. I am also deeply in debt to Professor Firth, Dr. E. R. Leach, and my wife, Barbara E. Ward, who at different times have guided, commented on, and criticized all my work on the Melanau.

THE SOCIAL ORDER

A Melanau village today forms a line of small rectangular wood and thatch houses on piles along both banks of the river. It usually stands on the site of a former longhouse settlement. Villages vary in size from 200 to 1,000 inhabitants and are separated from one another by three or four miles on the river, which is still the only practical route for travel. The swamp jungle on each side of it is dense and often dangerous; and for this reason the people of the different rivers have always tended to be culturally and politically distinct.

The earlier villages consisted of one or at most two longhouses. These were massively built fortresses, often thirty feet above ground, and situated at the confluence of a strategically important tributary stream and the main river. Each house was politically independent within its own territory, and was frequently on terms of active hostility with its Melanau neighbours and the Iban invaders who began to settle on the hills upstream during the nineteenth century. The investment of labour and capital in the longhouses was so great that they were rarely moved or completely rebuilt. When raiding was suppressed under Brooke rule in the latter part of the last century, and the houses became overcrowded, the people simply abandoned them and built separate dwellings on the edge of the river.

Although physically one structure, a longhouse was made up of separately built apartments, each owned and inhabited by one married couple and perhaps one married child. Longhouses were constructed in the form of a row of terrace houses with a common covered verandah like a gallery in front and behind, and they might house two hundred or more people. Much of the village life and ceremonial took place on the front verandah, which was fifteen to twenty feet wide and possibly up to three or four hundred feet long. When the houses were abandoned, no central meeting place replaced the verandah; and much of the culture, especially the performance of communal ceremonies, fell into disuse because the newer houses were small.

In longhouse days the political control of a village was in the hands of a small group of aristocratic elders (*a-nyat*), whose families usually owned the central apartments, and who were the descendants of the village founders. On each side of this core were apartments owned by freemen (*a-bumi*), and at each end of the house were the apartments of freed slaves (*a-dipan*). Most slaves were owned by aristocrats (*a-mantri*). An elaborate set of customary rules (*adat*) regulated the behaviour of the ranks to one another and most other aspects of social life. The *adat*, one of the community's most valued possessions, was in the custody of the aristocratic elders. No single elder was superior to the others, though he might have special knowledge that fitted him for particular tasks. A man with unusual abilities in war would be put in charge of raids, and another with knowledge of rituals might assume leadership on appropriate occasions. But leadership of this kind was not usually formalized as a permanent office, and there were no single political chiefs who ruled villages as of personal right.

Each household was economically independent. The members grew its rice and other crops and were primarily responsible for their own physical and supernatural safety and prosperity. There was generally speaking little specialized division of labour, and a household could normally supply its own needs. Matters which affected other people in the longhouse fell either into the sphere of the *adat* and were therefore regulated by the elders, or, if they were concerned with the supernatural, were in the hands of ritual experts who might or might not be aristocrats.

Traditional Melanau society in the Oya River made use of three overlapping criteria in organizing social life. The first was that of local grouping; the second was that of kinship; and the third was that of hereditary rank. A Melanau thought of himself in each of these social dimensions. He was closely identified with a particular locality, especially with one longhouse whose inhabitants were thought to be, and often were, peculiar and unique in matters of dialect and custom. As an individual, a man or woman was the focal point of a kindred with whom he shared a wide range of social and economic interests regulated by principles of bilateral descent. Lastly, he had by virtue of birth a rank status. In any context the behaviour of one man towards another was largely determined by the fact that the two men were neighbours or strangers, kinsmen or not, of equal or different rank. Within the social order his behaviour was regulated by the *adat*; within the symbolic order similar principles governed his ritual behaviour (Morris, 1953).

THE SYMBOLIC ORDER

The World

For an Oya Melanau the longhouse (*lebo'*), or the modern village (*likou*), and the river on which it stands (*likou*) lie at the centre of the social and symbolic worlds. Beyond the village are the forests, the hills, the sea, and other rivers, whose inhabitants, human, animal, and supernatural, are, or are believed to be, at best indifferent to humans and at worst really dangerous. Every creature in this the middle world (*likou dagan duah*) has his own proper place. Above this world is the overworld (*likou langit* or *likou bah bau*), and below it is the underworld (*likou bah iba'*). The over- and the underworlds each consist of seven superimposed and named worlds, most of which are replicas of the middle world, with rivers, forests, hills, animals, spirits (*tou*), and villages thought to be inhabited by human beings (*tenawan*). When these 'worlds' are thought of as countries like the Oya River they are called *likou*; but when they are discussed as parts of the cosmos they may be called *susun* (layers) or *lapih* (strata) to draw attention to the way in which they are laid one on top of the other. These fifteen 'worlds' constitute the *dunia* or the whole World.

Different informants give different accounts of the *dunia*, but all agree that it is roughly egg-shaped. According to some it is balanced between the horns of a buffalo standing on a long thin fish (*jikan papa*) which swims in an ocean that surrounds everything. Others think that it is held in the hand of a spirit (*tou gerachi*). The sun and the moon revolve around the World, and day in the overworld is night below. Each world (*lapih*) is divided from the others by barriers (*pagar*), though in mythological times, before an impatient woman baking sago biscuits and worried by the close heat of the sun pushed up the sky with a pole, visits to the other worlds by heroes, shamans, and even ordinary people were not uncommon. But even then visits to other worlds often turned out to be dangerous to both the visitors and the visited.

Few people still remember the details of this cosmology. None know any myths of creation: the World and everything in it was created by *Alatala*; and though spirits (*tou*) have powers that are unlike and often greater than those of human beings, they are not thought of as gods, but merely as being different from men. Certain spirits, which are nevertheless still called *tou*, differ from most. Some live in the moon, and their leader, a female called *Biliong*, is especially concerned with the preservation of the proper natural order of things. Any human who disrespects it by mocking or teasing animals, for example, arouses her anger, and she summons thunder and lightning and hail to petrify the offenders (*baliyu*). For most Melanau today *baliyu* is a principle built into the scheme of things by *Alatala*, and they know nothing of *Biliong*. For them the World is the middle world, the sky, the world below, and the land of the dead, which some believe is a part of the underworld and others think is completely elsewhere.

The inhabitants of the World

(i) Human beings

Men and women inhabit the middle world, but they share it with its vegetation, the animals, and the spirits. Each member of these different types of being has its own proper place; and if any being gratuitously or even accidentally interferes with or obtrudes on another, the correct order of things is disturbed and trouble is likely to follow. The proper place of men and women is the village. In it they are relatively safe among friends and kinsmen; it is crowded and companionable (*ramai*); and the risk of meeting hostile humans or of encountering other alien beings is less than anywhere else. At home a man is guided and supported by the social order; only if he flouts the *adat* does he put himself in social or supernatural danger. But a man is everywhere and always in danger from mistakes and malignance.

All human beings are made up of four separate elements: the body (*bieh* or *badan*); the soul (*bedua*), which is thought to be a vaporous replica of the body; the emotions (*nasang*); and a principle of life (*nyawa*). For a man to be alive and healthy these four elements must be joined and undisturbed. The body is subject to accidents and illnesses, most of which can be attributed to breaches of the social *adat* or proper behaviour generally, or to attack by spirits, or even by shamans. At the onset of an attack the *nasang* is upset, and may become so disorganized that the *bedua* begins its journey to the land of the dead, leaving only the *bieh* and *nyawa*. If it does not return, death is inevitable.

The word *bedua* would perhaps be better translated as 'double' (which is its literal meaning) than as 'soul'; but it is convenient to speak of the soul because it is the element which is thought to survive death and make the canoe journey to the land of the dead (*likou a-matai* or *likou pengamou*). At the entrance to this land of the dead, the soul is directed to its appropriate place by a female, *Balou Adat*, who, as there is no other word in the Melanau language to describe her godlike attributes, is called a spirit (*tou*), though with some hesitation. A few souls fail to pass the barrier and haunt the middle world as ghosts (*amou*), where they attempt to steal the souls of the living. To ensure the safe arrival of a dead person at the house of *Balou Adat*, mortuary rites enacting the journey used to be performed. Once the soul is established in the underworld it is not permitted to repass the barrier and gradually relinquishes interest in the living, except to welcome newly arrived kin.

(ii) *Spirits*

No Melanau doubts the existence of spirits, but if asked about them says, 'They are things which cannot be seen; how can we be sure what they are like?' Even so, almost everybody knows of a large number of them and their attributes. Many people who are not experts have sufficient knowledge of their forms and the afflictions they are thought to cause to be able to carve a few of their images for use in curing illness. An expert image maker may have iconographical knowledge of more than a hundred.

The most general classification of spirits is by the region they inhabit; for all, like men, have their proper homes and settings. In the middle world are found air or sky spirits, forest, and river, and sea spirits; the upper and underworlds also have the same types, and all can move from one world to another in a way that humans usually cannot. Spirits are male and female and most are anthropomorphic. Some people think that like the Melanau they are hierarchically ranked within their categories, each of which has its own leader, who has authority over all his kind, whatever world he inhabits. According to one shaman:

> Spirits do not worry humans if their lives are comfortable. If they are poor and cannot find enough to eat, they become dangerous and eat men. A strong *tou*, such as is useful to a shaman, is rich; and can if he wishes keep the poor ones in order. Some of the worst spirits are slaves.

Although people tell stories of marriages between humans and spirits and of men becoming spirits, others deny that this is possible. But all agree that animals, plants, humans, and spirits are distinct orders of beings who happen to share the same environment—a fact which entails ordered rules of behaviour. A Muslim, who had been a pagan as a child, explained the matter thus:

> A powerful man once met an angel (*melaikat*) and asked for immortality.[1] The angel called a meeting of all trees, animals, and other living things. The trees spoke first. If men did not die, they said, all the trees would be felled to make farms. The animals spoke next and said that if men did not die and all the trees were felled, there would be no shelter from the sun and the hunters, and all the animals would be killed. The animals therefore asked the angel to bring 160 types of illness to kill men, and the trees asked for 112 kinds of remedy for the illnesses. Everybody except

1. *Melaikat*: a Malay word rarely used by pagans in the Oya River.

the man agreed to this. He asked that he and his wife should be turned into rainbows, and his wish was granted. Since then men have had to know what spirits cause illness and what herbs or other remedies will cure them.

The Melanaus' technical equipment gave them little control over the natural forces of their environment, and by personifying these forces and placing them in a system of relationships, stated in much the same terms as they used in handling the social order, and backed by the same kinds of moral sanction, they were helped to comprehend the environment and live in it with a greater sense of security.

Relations among the inhabitants of the World

The ideal of behaviour implicit in the myth set out in the last section does not imply that the quality of all relationships ought to be the same. Within a village, relations, however formal, were expected to be basically friendly; whereas those between neighbouring longhouses or with foreign peoples, such as the Iban or the Kayan, were thought to be potentially always hostile and at times actively dangerous unless treated with caution. Similarly, relations between humans and spirits were those of co-existence rather than of friendly co-operation. Unguarded behaviour always carried the risk of misfortune or deprivation on one side or the other.

In one story a man found a woman and her daughter stealing fish from his traps in the forest. He seized them, and even though they were spirits, insisted on being taken to their longhouse, access to which was by a ladder that to human eyes appeared to be a large tree. He married the daughter, and after a child was born took them both to his own longhouse. Their arrival caused much trouble and the ultimate destruction of the village and scattering of its inhabitants.

This myth is placed in historical times, but another refers to the days before barriers were erected between the different 'layers' of the World. A fisherman caught his hook on a snag and dived in to free it. He found it in the roof of a longhouse built in a country just like his own. The leader of the house, who was the ruler of that 'world' (*likou yang*) allowed him to stay. He was given rice to eat—a food which no human had then seen. He lived there the best part of a year and helped cultivate the farms and harvest the crops. Eventually he was permitted to return to his family on condition that he took no rice seed with him; but when he went he concealed five grains in his foreskin. He planted them on the river bank by his own house, and from them comes all the rice in this 'world'. When the people of the underworld saw the roots, their ruler was so angry that he closed his kingdom; and no humans, except shamans, have ever again been able to visit it.

Most people believe that although human beings may become ghosts they cannot become spirits. In certain myths, however, they do, usually in consequence of disregarding the rules of proper behaviour. A hunter wounded a pig in a forest, and when he caught up with it found that a hunting spirit (*tou gerachi*) was holding it up and drinking the blood. Instead of wisely going away, even though the spirit was at fault in taking another's pig, the hunter foolishly demanded some of the blood and refused to leave until he had some to drink as well. Eventually the spirit gave him some and he was at once transformed into a hunting spirit. When he returned home his wife sent him back to his proper place in the forest.

The lesson in these and similar stories is usually the same. Generally it is the human who suffers the more seriously for overstepping the boundaries of correct behaviour, but sometimes it is an animal or spirit. The suffering may be regarded as a punishment, or it may be looked on as a warning that an offence has been committed and that expiation is required to restore the proper order of things. According to the shaman quoted in the last section, spirits do not transgress the moral order and attack men unless hunger or poor control of their nature drives them. If they do, they can be brought to order by their fellows and rulers. To help men there are techniques for avoiding danger, and experts who know how to restore the balance when it has been upset, how to cure the harm caused by wrong or mistaken behaviour.

Mediation and mediators

(1) Adat, vows, dreams, and augury

The safest way of keeping out of trouble is to observe the *adat*, both in its social sense and in the extended meaning of proper behaviour towards the symbolic order. But there are additional safeguards. A man about to embark on a risky project may make a vow (*niat*) to give a feast of thanksgiving if he accomplishes it safely; or he may, particularly if he is old, promise to give the most important of the shamanistic ceremonies (*aiyun*) for the enjoyment of the spirits in return for good health in the coming year.

Impending disaster or foolish behaviour may also be averted by a warning dream (*nupei*); for dreams are one of the most important

links between men and the symbolic order, and the correct understanding and interpretation of them is a serious matter. They may be
conventional warnings whose meaning everybody knows (for
example, to dream of a loose tooth in the right jaw foretells the
probable death of somebody in the household), or they may be
addressed personally to the dreamer, when they usually take the
form of a benevolent old man or woman who gives warning or confers a favour. Nobody is quite sure who these persons are: they are
not ancestors and everybody hesitates to call them spirits (*tou*), unless the dreamer is a shaman or a potential shaman and the spirit is
instructing him. Similarly, the flight of birds and the behaviour of
certain animals carry warnings of danger. Auguries (*baya'*) are
thought to be messages to prevent foolish behaviour; but from whom
or exactly why they are sent is no longer known, though few dis-
believe their efficacy.

If, in spite of the guidance of the *adat* and common sense combined
with other warnings, a man does get into trouble and is not immediately killed, he is likely to suffer an illness of greater or lesser
severity. He will then resort to mediators who are expert in diagnos-
ing the cause of the trouble and prescribing the correct expiation or
remedy for restoring the balance of nature and right relations among
the different orders of being.

(2) *Image makers and herbalist magicians*

A man who has met with an accident or incurred an illness may
first go to a herbalist magician (*dukun*) in the hope that his trouble is
not serious; but he will soon, if not at the same time, also consult a
carver of sickness images. From the symptoms of the illness the
image maker decides what spirit may be attacking the soul (*bedua*)
of the man. He then carves a likeness (*bilum*) of the spirit and spits
betel nut juice at it, commanding the spirit to enter it. He holds the
image over the sick person and pours water over it on to him, after
which the image is taken to its appropriate place, that is, the dwelling place of the spirit in the forest or elsewhere. If the diagnosis is
correct, the spirit is compelled to enter its image for three days and
refrain from attacking the sick person. Both men and women may
become *dukun* or *bilum* makers. These experts are not likely to be
shamans, but if they are, they will not normally prescribe medicines
or carve images if they are active shamans.

(3) *Shamans*

A man does not usually go to shamans (*a-bayoh*) for guidance in correct behaviour until misfortune has overtaken him, because the shaman's principal task is to repair damage caused by spirits, not avert it. A shaman is a man or woman who is 'a master of spirits'. Normally himself a spirit-medium, the shaman is thought to control spirits by ritual techniques (Firth, 1959, p. 141).[1] Because of his familiarity with spirits and their habits, a shaman's advice about avoiding their attentions carries weight, but is seldom sought until it is needed for diagnosis and cure. At the same time he is potentially as dangerous as the spirits which possess him, and he must therefore be treated with circumspection.[2]

1. The term *a-bayoh* denotes both spirit-medium and shaman, but the distinction made by Firth is well understood by the Melanau. '*Spirit possession* is a form of trance in which actions of a person are interpreted as evidence of a control of his behaviour by a spirit normally external to him. *Spirit-mediumship* is normally a form of possession in which the person is conceived as serving as an intermediary between spirits and men. The accent here is on communication; the actions and words of the medium must be translatable, which differentiates them from the behaviour in mere spirit possession or madness' (Firth, 1959, p. 141).

2. No Oya Melanau myth explicitly tells of the origin of shamans; but the following is a summary of an episode in the *Mueh Rejang*, a series of versified stories formerly sung on ceremonial occasions.

A man, *Bunga Lawan*, lived in a house on the bank of the very wide river, *Ngam Pusan*. On an island in it was a large tree, at the top of which *Balou Belian* and her sister *Urip Raman* lived in a house. A rattan (*sega'wai*) ladder led to the ground. One day *Bunga Lawan* fell from the ladder and lay seriously injured at the foot of the tree. His four friends, *Juga, Sedawa, Panglima,* and *Ntala,* found him and did not know what to do for they could not see the ladder. They therefore fetched four threads—*Juga,* a white one, *Sedawa* black, *Panglima* red, and *Ntala* yellow. All tried to throw their threads up and round the floor posts of the house, but only *Ntala*'s yellow one reached. He then climbed up to the house, followed by *Juga* and *Sedawa. Panglima* remained on the ground. All this took one month.

Balou Belian enquired the reason for the visit and *Ntala* told of *Bunga Lawan*'s accident and death while they were trying to ascend the tree. He asked her to restore *Bunga Lawan* to life. The three men and the two women descended by way of the yellow thread, and *Balou Belian* picked up the bones of *Bunga Lawan*—all that remained of him—and wrapped them in a rich red cloth. They then crossed the river to *Bunga Lawan*'s house. *Balou Belian* asked the men to make preparations for an *aiyun* ceremony (see p. 204), and to hang up a swing or cradle of *wai sega'* rattan. She placed the bundle of bones wrapped in the cloth on it and began to rock the swing backwards and forwards. After six nights the bones again became flesh; but it was not until the seventh night that *Bunga Lawan* was able to speak. He at once asked *Balou Belian* to bathe him in coconut milk, after which he was completely restored to life and sense.

For her services *Bunga Lawan* gave her seven beads, one spearhead, one brass bowl, and one piece of gold. He escorted her and her sister home and later married *Balou Belian*. (Note continued on p. 199.)

Unlike the herbalist magician and image maker, a shaman does not determine the causes of misfortune or illness by reference to symptoms, using his own judgment and experience; but he speaks in trance as the vehicle of his familiar spirit who makes the diagnosis. Because the shaman is, so to speak, the meeting place of men and spirits, he is a man set apart in some respects from other men; and because, too, of his special position, his relationships with spirits and men alike require care in their handling. His 'public' relations with spirits occur mainly in curative ceremonies and mortuary rites; but if his moral nature is not upright, or if he lacks the strength to control the ill-nature of his familiars, he may, it is thought, prey on other men in private and act as a witch.

(4) *Shamanistic ceremonies*

A shaman is able to approach the symbolic world with safety only if he can rely on spirit friends who have chosen him and taught him their names and the correct modes of calling them to him. A spirit, in the words of one shaman, may not be casually summoned: 'He is not just called; if his name is not known he will not come: it is like making unintelligible noises at people.' When the spirit arrives it uses the shaman's body, surrounding it, most people think, like a garment.

The incantation to the spirit is accompanied by beating a rhythm, peculiar to shamans, on the drum which the shaman acquired on becoming a full practitioner. He covers his head with a cloth, and when the spirit arrives he hisses loudly and shakes his head violently from side to side, so that in a female shaman her long, unbound hair swings round and round. One man described the taking of possession in these words:

It is like being hit on the head; you fall sideways. You have to shake your head from side to side and hiss. The eyes are hot as when you smell an onion. [Another shaman described the approach of the spirit as being swallowed in a ball of fire, so that she was burned up in the heat.] The nature of a spirit is like a mad-

---

In modern Melanau *balou* means widow, but *belian* has no significance. Cf. Wilkinson, 1959, Part 1:

Belian. I. Shaman, sorcerer, sorceress in touch with the spirit world. . . . The word . . . is in use in Java, Bali, Borneo and Halmahera and is (etym.) the true word for shaman . . . .

Most of the elements of this myth can be paralleled in shamanistic cults elsewhere. Cf. Eliade, 1964, pp. 145–214.

O

man, and when a spirit is in me my nature is fierce and my talk angry. Spirits are all bad, and if the shaman is bad he will eat humans.

In addition to his drum and headcloth, a shaman must also have iron, usually in the shape of a spearhead, to bite for strength whenever he summons spirits. It is also needed for the patient and any assistant who may come into close proximity with the shaman and his familiars. Finally he will need water and certain kinds of foliage for washing and brushing the sickness out of the patient. These elements are the minimum essential equipment needed in any of the shamanistic curative ceremonies, which, because many of the spirits called up live in the underworld where night is day, are always held after dark.

(A) Curative ceremonies

In marked contrast with the proper distance that ought to be maintained between the different orders of being, the shaman's relationship with his familiar spirits is one of friendship; but in some senses it is always improper and attended by risk. He therefore does not call on them frivolously. Like human beings, spirits are busy creatures and resent unnecessary interruptions to their daily affairs. Like humans, too, they enjoy entertainment, good food, sweet scents, music, dancing, and good talk; so that if anybody through a shaman wishes to invite them to help him, he must provide a suitable reception, as he would were he to invite his friends and relatives to help him at a work party. For this reason shamanistic curing ceremonies are regarded as a series of entertainments, as it were, which ranges from a private domestic séance, where the shaman calls up a few of his more reliable spirits (like close friends visiting the family) to help in a household crisis, to the important and prolonged *aiyun* ceremony, which, though sponsored by one household, invites most of the village to attend (as at a wedding or mourning) and a large concourse of spirits as well. The equipment and ceremonial are consequently more elaborate.

(i) Caring for the sick (Mingat a-pedih)

This is the simplest routine ceremony to diagnose and cure illness, and usually lasts one evening only. The shaman and his equipment must be fetched by a member of the household while the patient is made ready by a spouse or a parent. He is placed with his head to the east on a sleeping mat, visible to but apart from visitors. When all is prepared, the shaman and the patient bite a spearhead, and the shaman pours water or possibly coconut juice over the patient, who is now ready for treatment. He has been put into a ritual condition which separates him and also the assistant (spouse or parent) from the rest of the household, who, unless it is absolutely necessary, do not approach them until the ceremony is completed.

After the preparation the patient is taken back to his sleeping mat, and the shaman covers his own head and face in a cloth and begins an incantation to one of his familiars. On the spirit's arrival the shaman removes his headcloth, and the spirit asks why he has been summoned. The assistant shows him the patient, whom the shaman then examines. He may hold up his drum, which is open at one end, and place a lighted candle between the skin on the other end and the patient, and look through it into the patient's body to discover the cause of the illness. If the inspection is successful, the spirit through the shaman tells the assistant and the audience what is wrong; and they ask him to help. If he refuses he immediately departs, and the shaman hisses violently and shakes his head until the spirit has gone. The shaman then yawns several times and asks the assistant what happened. After discussing the matter, he summons up another familiar.

But if the first spirit does diagnose the cause of the illness, he will usually help cure it, though he may temporarily have to leave the shaman, still in trance, to fetch another spirit, who may not be a familiar, to assist him. When diagnosis and treatment are both agreed on, the shaman holds up his right hand and sings, asking for *pijer* from the sky spirits. *Pijer* are minute transparent stones and flowers from the overworld. At the end of the chant he shuts his hand, catching the gift, and rubs both palms together. He then presses the *pijer* into the crown of the patient's head. More are asked for and are pressed into the base of the throat, the belly, the back, and other places that are sore. The *pijer* are to strengthen the patient and help drive out the sickness.

The next step is to clean out the sickness and repair the damage it has done, so that the soul, if it has departed, may return in safety. First the shaman puts his lips on the places where the *pijer* were inserted and sucks out the sickness, at the same time silently bidding it depart. He then takes a bunch of leaves (*daun tebawan: Premna foetida* Reinw.) and sweeps the patient from head to foot, sometimes singing aloud, but always bidding the sickness to go.

The treatment of the patient by this spirit is now complete, but before going he may stop to gossip and perhaps examine and treat other people. He may also advise further treatment of the patient by other spirits; for the cause of the illness may not be simple or single, and any one familiar's powers are limited. Moreover, if the 'attack' has come from a spirit who has ill-will towards the patient, or who, on the contrary, has taken a liking for him and wishes to establish a permanent relationship of friendship, then the condition can be cured only by fetching the spirit concerned. The shaman's familiar may not be able to do this because he is not on good terms with the attacking spirit, or because the attacker intends the patient to undergo further ceremonies which will allow him to make his wishes known, and which may lead to the patient's full initiation as a spirit-medium and practising shaman. But whether further treatment is advised or not, the shaman always summons other familiars, sometimes as many as fifteen to twenty in an evening.

The Melanau do not believe that all illnesses and deaths are caused by spirit attack. A common cold or other small ailment may be attributed to 'wind' (*angin* or *pangai*)—an evil influence which floats in the air and affects human beings. Some animals, notably crocodiles, have the power to seize a man's soul, and if it is not released by a shaman, the man will eventually be eaten by the animal. A very old person is thought to die naturally, but if he first suffers a long or sudden illness he is usually thought to be the victim of spirit attack. A man's soul may begin the journey to the land of the dead for many reasons, and if a herbalist or image maker cannot bring it back and restore a healthy balance, then the shaman and his familiars take over. It is the familiars who can find out whether the soul is being attacked by a witch, an animal, or another spirit. If the attack is by a hostile spirit, the man's recovery depends upon his making correct expiation; but if the illness is caused by a spirit's wanting the man's friendship, then the man must accept the fact, however unwelcome; for if he does not the spirit may kill him. He may resist for a time and continue in poor health, hoping that the spirit will desist; for the man's death will defeat the object of the attack, which is to establish a relationship with a human in this and in no other world. It is this wish on the part of spirits to have friends in this world which makes it quite uncertain that a shaman will continue to be one in the land of the dead. It is thought that shamans undoubtedly exist there, but that they do not visit this world in order to make contact with human beings.

When the ceremony of caring for the sick is over and the last spirit has gone, the patient may be de-sanctified by a further washing. This is not always thought necessary, but restrictions on the food he may eat and on undertaking ordinary work away from the house are usual. Sometimes the shaman and the assistant may also de-sanctify themselves by taking a special bath, though that is not often considered essential after a simple 'caring for the sick'.

In some respects caring for the sick is an informal ceremony, but the means it uses and the relationships it establishes between the social and the symbolic orders are not regarded casually. The space occupied by the shaman and his patient is sacred. It is a sanctuary in which men and spirits meet; it is also a small model of the World (*dunia*). In it the forces of good and evil are, so to say, more concentrated than in the ordinary world; and to enter it without rites of purification and strengthening is dangerous. Leaving it is also danger-ous and requires further rites to adjust the humans to their normal life. The subsequent ceremonies of curing, which are also parts of the initiation of a shaman,'attract a greater number of human and spirit guests, and therefore need a larger sanctuary, which is more fully furnished, and which, because of the greater number of beings present, is so to speak more concentratedly sacred and must be treated with more formality.

(ii) Escorting the spirits (*Menurun tou*) and Beguda[1]

(a) Menurun tou

When it becomes clear that the patient is not cured, or the illness recurs, he may decide to hold the *menurun tou* ceremony to ask the shaman's familiars to fetch the spirit who is causing the trouble, in the hope that the patient will be possessed by that spirit who will thus make his wishes known.

In this ceremony, which takes place on three successive evenings, the sacred area set aside for and the equipment used by the shaman, the assistant, the patient, and the spirits, are more carefully demar-cated and more elaborate. There may be offerings of food; sweet-scented flowers are soaked in the water used for lustration; and in-stead of brushing the patient with leaves the shaman uses an un-opened inflorescence of the pinang palm (*Areca catechu*), which must be taken from the eastern side of the tree. A larger number of spirits is summoned, and a lay drummer is employed so that the invited spirits may dance and sing on taking possession of the shaman or patient. In all other respects, however, the procedure is the same as in 'caring for the sick'.

1. Wilkinson, 1959, Part 1:
   Guda; *Goda*: Inciting; tempting; bringing pressure to bear; to rack. Etym., even of forcible pressure, but usually of seduction or temptation.

(b) Beguda

A more elaborate form of the ceremony is *beguda*. It too lasts three evenings and has the same purpose as *menurun tou*, but is distinguished from it by the use of two pinang palm inflorescences and of woven decorations in the sanctuary. One inflorescence is wrapped in red cloth and hung from the roof (known as the sky) in the middle of a circlet of rattan (*sega' wai: Calamus* sp.). The other inflorescence is used for brushing the patient.

The importance of this ceremony is that it is a necessary preliminary to the *aiyun*, and in it the 'attacking' spirit is *expected* to take possession of the patient, who in turn is now expected to accept the perhaps unwelcome fact that he must enter a permanent and possibly dangerous association with a spirit. Exactly what the relationship will entail is slowly revealed by the spirit in dreams of instruction during the following months. Instead of waiting, however, the spirit may order the patient to undertake an immediate *aiyun* ceremony to confirm the friendship and complete his initiation as a spirit-medium in order to begin practice as a shaman with the least possible delay.

(iii) The Aiyun ceremony[1]

The *aiyun* is the greatest of the shamanistic ceremonies, and the Melanau describe it as the 'end of our remedies'. A man who has agreed to *paiyun* knows that unless his ceremony appeases the spirit which is afflicting him, so that it takes possession of him, makes its wishes known, and allows him to recover his health, there is no more he can do except perform another *aiyun*. The purpose of the ceremony, then, is threefold: first, to cure the patient; second, to restore the balance between the social and symbolic orders; and third, to complete the patient's formal period of training as a shaman.

An *aiyun* may last five, seven, or even nine nights. Except for the annual ritual cleansing of the village (*kaul*) which is not a shamanistic ceremony, the *aiyun* is the most crowded and festive (*ramai*) occasion on which human beings and spirits meet. The preparations for it must be suitable and sumptuous. The material and ritual elements are basically those of the caring for the sick ceremony; but the sanctuary is larger, more carefully marked out, and more richly furnished. It is a large rectangle occupying as much as a third of the house's

1. Wilkinson, 1959, Part 1: '*Ayun*. Swaying, swinging . . .' In Melanau *aiyun* is either a baby's cradle or the rattan swing on which the shaman and patients sit and rock backwards and forwards waiting for the spirits to take possession. The Sarawak Malay verb *beraiyun* (Melanau *paiyun*) is the term most commonly used for the ceremony in the literature.

floor space, and is explicitly a model of the World. A white cloth is spread above the area to represent the sky, and a model house (*abun*) for the reception of the overworld spirits is placed on a rafter at the upstream end of the enclosure, close to one point of attachment of a rattan swing (*wai sega*) which is suspended right across the area. This swing is also called the *aiyun*, and it ought to be hung so that those who sit on it can swing east and west. It belongs to the officiating shaman and is the bridge that all spirits use to enter the sanctuary. Beside the *abun* is the end of a woven ladder (*taga yang*) which passes out of the building to a model boat (*rabong*) below—the place of reception for water and underworld spirits. From the centre of the 'sky' hangs one pinang inflorescence wrapped in red cloth, and in the sanctuary, below the *abun* and *taga yang*, is a bunch of bananas and a coconut. Food offerings are placed in the *abun*, the *rabong*, and on the floor of the sanctuary along with the rest of the essential equipment; the second pinang inflorescence for brushing the patients, a spearhead, a lighted candle, rice to feed the spirits, braziers and benzoin, and the shaman's drum. Outside the enclosure is a set of drums, brass gongs, Malay drums and tambourines, and even a violin, so that the orchestra may provide music appropriate to each spirit as it arrives.

The officiating shaman is known as the 'father' or 'mother' of the *aiyun*, and in addressing his or her familiars the shaman calls himself or herself their 'grandfather' or 'grandmother'.[1] The shaman must have one lay assistant (*seladai*) even though other shamans may be helping. Assistant shamans are reluctant to participate fully because of the five days' confinement to the house and the prohibitions on bathing, foods, and intercourse with spouses. The patient is known as the pupil (*murip*), and ever after remains in a kind of child relationship with the father or mother of his *aiyun*.

For the first three nights only the shaman, his assistants, and the

1. The use of these kinship terms in the context of the sanctuary indicates that the shaman is for the time being indeed a master of spirits and men. The model of the World in which he is operating is of his construction and under his control. The terms indicate, too, that he is more than a mere intermediary; he is also a man of high position and power, the host of a varied collection of guests whose comfort and safety are in his keeping. In one aspect of his role he is a diplomat, so to speak, standing between the human and the non-human orders; but he is at the same time more than that, since he exercises power over the beings in 'his World'. It sometimes happens that on arrival a spirit is confused and alarmed, and he is reassured by the shaman himself or his lay assistant. The following words spoken at one *aiyun* by a lay assistant are typical: 'Do not be afraid. You are invited by your grandfather. It is he who is in charge of this crowded and friendly (*ramai*) occasion.'

patient may participate in the ceremony. Before entering the sanctuary they are purified; *pijer* are pressed into the swing; the spirits are fed with rice; and the patient is treated by all the shamans present. At this stage these are the only people who may mount the swing in order to receive spirit visitors. During the third evening the shaman, holding his spearhead, leads the patient, followed by the assistant and participant shamans, to the edge of the river, where they scoop out water with their hands and catch fish and other water beasts, which are, however, visible only to the shamans. If the patient, catches one that is dangerous or spiny, it is a sign that he will become a powerful and venomous (*bisa'*) shaman. The procession then returns to the sanctuary, and anybody who needs treatment may mount the swing. These are people who are ill and wishing to be cured, or who already have familiar spirits and wish to be possessed by them or by new familiars in order to learn their wishes.

At dawn, after the last evening's performance, three canoes in the river are lashed together and planks are laid across them to make a platform. Some of the decorations from the sanctuary are placed at each corner. The model boat (*rabong*) from below the house is put in the middle, and the shaman, the assistants, the patient, the orchestra, and paddlers go aboard. The three joined canoes are then paddled upstream to the head of the village and downstream again to a point on the bank well below it. The shaman stands at the prow calling spirits and casting rice for them to eat, and the orchestra plays. Other canoes, crowded with visitors, are lashed behind the three leading canoes, and the procession moves slowly through the village, gathering the spirits to it as it goes. At the chosen point on the river bank the model boat is raised on to a trestle and the decorations and offerings are placed in and around it. The patient and any others who wish, crouch beneath the trestle and the shaman and the helpers throw water over them. After much splashing and laughter, the procession returns to the house, where the sanctuary is dismantled under the supervision of the shaman. The participants in the ceremony are already partly de-sanctified by washing under the *rabong*, but the shaman, the lay assistant, the patient, and other helpers may sit on the swing once more; they are not, however, possessed by spirits, who are now supposed to have returned to their proper places after the purification below the village. The participants, unless they have received treatment which imposes taboos, are now free to return to normal life; but the return of the shaman and the patient from the sacred world of the sanctuary and the release of the patient from the special condition into which he entered when he began the series of *rites de passage*, beginning with the initial ceremony of caring for the sick and ending with the *aiyun*, are slower. Both shaman and patient are bound by restrictions on food, work, and movement for at least three days and sometimes until the next new moon.

If the *aiyun* has been successful, the patient's formal initiation as a spirit-medium is now complete and he should regain his health. But he may still have to undergo a prolonged period of instruction in dreams before his new status is firmly established; and he is in some senses still in a transitional state. Before he ventures to practise as a shaman, even though invited to do so by other villagers, he must be secure in his relationship with his familiar; and he usually waits for more spirits to approach him in friendship, either in dreams or at *aiyun* ceremonies. This final training may be as difficult for the shaman and his household as any of the earlier stages when he was ill and emotionally unstable. The symptoms are still much the same as before, but the problem is now seen as a struggle between a human and spirits to set up an acceptable, though necessarily anomalous, relationship. With the help of his familiars, the shaman's soul at this time may visit different regions of the over- and underworlds; for to be effective he needs experience, powerful spirit friends, and a knowledge of their habits. It is, however, just such beings who are most dangerous. Failure to gain moral control over his familiars may cause him to become a witch and even to be executed by his fellow-villagers.

(B) *Mortuary ceremonies*

Traditionally a dead person is mourned for three, five, or seven nights. His body is then either buried in the ground or, if a first-born infant son, or formerly if a person of rank and importance, is placed on a platform to await interment. During the wake, ceremonies are performed to see the soul safely on its journey to the underworld; but, except in one or two minor rites in which spirits are consulted to mark the progress of the journey, the services of a shaman are not needed. When the soul arrives at the house of *Balou Adat* at the entrance to the land of the dead, a shaman is sent to take gifts and to bring back the souls of any living people who have accompanied the dead person. This task the shaman fulfils during the *platu* ceremony.[1]

1. The Melanau verb *pla* means to paddle a canoe. See also Buck, 1933, and Jamuh, 1951.

A white mat known as the canoe is spread on the floor. Beside it is a woman's paddle and on it are three woven images of the spirits that guide a soul to the land of the dead, and also a pillow, a piece of gold, a spearhead, and the shaman's drum. Before beginning, the shaman tests one or two assistants who are to accompany him on the journey. These people have fasted all day, and in the test the shaman presses the carotid artery to render them temporarily unconscious and thus free their souls.

The shaman then sits on the mat and calls up a familiar to help him on his way. When it arrives, and if it agrees to go, he picks up the paddle, sits in the posture of a woman, and with the help of his paddlers sets off. On arrival he takes the gifts, some of which are for the relatives of the recently dead person who will come to *Balou Adat*'s house to take him to his new home. Holding the gold and the spearhead, he steps off the mat and acts and talks as if he were going up into the house and were throwing food to the guardian dogs. The shaman and his assistants may go further into the land of the dead, if those he is sent to visit are no longer at the house. After he meets them, the living people at the ceremony, whose souls have made the journey with the dead person, are brought to him, and he presses *pijer* into their heads so that their souls may easily return. Sometimes the shaman himself brings them back; at other times he entrusts them to a fowl, which first has a few drops of blood taken from under the wing and is then thrown high over the heads of the assembly. His task completed, the shaman now returns home as fast as possible and in some apprehension because he and his assistants have tried to 'steal' goods from the underworld.

The *platu* represents a journey and, unlike other shamanistic ceremonies, is not thought of as a festive meeting of men and spirits. Consequently music and elaborate preparations and decorations are not required; nevertheless, the 'canoe' is a sanctuary, both sacred and dangerous.

Shamanism and witchcraft

The dangers of being a shaman are reiterated in most conversations on the subject, and stories are told of men and women who, under the influence of familiar spirits, have turned rogue. Such stories are always set in the past. At night, it is said, such a shaman takes off his head and it flies to the sleeping place of its victim, where, according to some, it drinks his blood, or, according to others, eats his soul. In any event illness and death are believed to follow.

There are many stories and some official records of the killing of such witches, though by no means all known witches died violently. One woman, whose husband had died not long before, reported in 1950 that she had divorced him many years earlier because he was a witch. She discovered the fact, she said, when she woke one night and found his headless body beside her. She was afraid to remain married to him, because the nature of such a man is completely under the control of his familiars; and he is therefore extremely dangerous. He takes offence at the slightest rebuff and does not spare the lives of even his own children. In another story the execution of a female witch did not end the matter, for her head continued to prey on the villagers from the grave, and was not stopped until the head was disinterred and reburied at a greater distance from the body and the village.

The Melanau term *a-bayoh* refers principally to practising shamans. It also applies to a spirit-medium who possesses familiars but who does not practise as a shaman. Witches are always known as *a-bayoh bisa'* (venomous *bayoh*), but so also is a powerful and effective shaman. The only difference is that a witch has not mastered his familiars, and instead of acting as an intermediary preys on human beings. The victim is usually warned of this kind of attack by a dream of heads floating over his sleeping place. Sometimes another member of the household is warned in this way and not the victim himself. Illness or fatigue confirms the suspicion. It is said that a man in such circumstances first consults another shaman whose familiars attempt to dissuade the witch's spirits from continuing the attack; and that only if that fails does the victim or somebody else attack the witch physically. It is also believed that any human who has allowed his familiars to dominate him so completely is probably unable ever to control them again, though certain witches are said to have achieved this.

SHAMANISM AND THE SOCIAL ORDER

At any time the number of practising shamans in the Oya River has always been small, and between 1948 and 1965 probably never exceeded a dozen. A man or woman needed to be seriously inconvenienced by prolonged ailments before undertaking the whole series of initiatory ceremonies. Moreover the illness had to be of a kind that did not leave him altogether unfit for an active life. All successful shamans have had histories of emotional disturbances and physical illness that go back several years, often to adolescence; most, too, are men and women of some imagination and intelligence. In addition to the practising shamans there is also a much larger number of

men and women who are spirit-mediums, in that they have performed an *aiyun* and are fully possessed by familiars, but who are not
compelled by them to practise as shamans, for the time being at any
rate.

A shaman may be either a man or woman, but men, even more
than women, are reluctant to assume the role. Correct Melanau
etiquette, as prescribed by custom (*adat*), is contravened by the
unseemly behaviour of people under possession; and though illness
may force a man into spirit-mediumship, most men strongly resist the
further step of becoming an active shaman. A slave who attempted
to practise might be thought presumptuous and unlikely to achieve
an equal and satisfactory relationship with high ranking and therefore powerful spirits. Moreover, the role of a shaman is in many
respects androgynous. There are stories of male shamans who lived
as transvestites and of women who were unbecomingly masculine
in the role; the possibility of such behaviour is still today an element
in the reluctance to become a full practitioner. Male shamans are
seldom regarded with favour by the aristocrats and elders, who are
the custodians of the social *adat*, and who fear that a shaman may
use his knowledge of the symbolic *adat* to claim unwarranted authority. An aristocratic man in this position could be intolerable; and
though it might be easier to resist a shaman of lower rank, there is
always the fear of other-wordly retaliation. Such threats to entrenched rank are less from women, and most of the practising shamans are in fact women. Of the men who take up practice most
come from middle-ranking families. The male witches who are remembered from the past appear usually to have been men who were
unduly ambitious, and who for one reason or another were unable
to achieve secular honours, or who, like most of the women witches,
had uncertain tempers and were unable to get on with their neighbours.

A method of resolving some of these difficulties would have been
to confine shamanship to certain middle-ranking lines of descent,
and if the ideal of endogamous marriage within the ranks had been
observed, the threat to aristocratic interests would have been averted.
A solution of this kind was in fact attempted, for it is said, 'The
spirits follow the blood', meaning that when a shaman dies his familiars are likely to establish an association with a close relative. But in
a bilateral system of succession and inheritance, combined, as it is
among the Oya Melanau, with a system of ranking in which an individual may use his pedigree in almost any way that is useful to
claim position, and in which the ideal of rank endogamy is not
strictly observed, a man can in fact aspire to almost any position

in the society. To achieve high rank without the qualifications of birth he needs to be rich. He may, however, find his attempt resisted by the elders; consequently, an ambitious man who finds his opportunities for gaining power and prestige limited or blocked may, particularly if there is a history of spirit-mediumship in his family, try to realize his aims by becoming a shaman. But it is, and apparently always was, one of the last lines of endeavour.[1]

1. The following brief histories of two shamans indicate some of the reasons that led them to take up practice.

In 1964 N. was a man of 50 to 60 years. He was a man of middle rank (*bangsa bumi*), who for nearly thirty years had had a high reputation as a shaman in the Oya River. His grandmother and other relatives had also been shamans, and the friends and relatives among whom he had lived most of his life were ritual experts of various kinds, but none were of the highest rank. When he was adolescent he was seriously ill and remained for many months covered with a painful skin eruption. Eventually he retired to a solitary hut in the forest where a spirit who was both a snake and a woman instructed him in dreams how to cure himself by bathing in mud. He returned home and married a woman of the same rank as himself who came from the same section of the village. They had little sago land and were forced to work for other people. Neither was physically strong and both were often ill. Several children died. In time he performed an *aiyun* and was possessed by a well-known familiar of his grandmother. His wife and the neighbours refused to allow him not to practise, but at first he did so unobtrusively and reluctantly. He was afraid, he said, that his familiar would turn on him if he refused. After a time he became guardian of the *blisieng* of Medong, the ritual object housing spirits used in the annual cleansing of the village ceremony. This office, which did not require its holder to be a shaman, also came to him from his mother's line and brought him into close contact with the elders, who were unwilling, however, to accept him as a member of their circle in the administration of the *adat*. On several occasions he quarrelled with the headman and other elders over the arrangement of village ceremonies. He gradually extended his practice to other villages and gained a great reputation, but was pointedly excluded from the company of the elders. In the 1950s when the price of sago slumped, he and his wife were compelled to retire to the River Igan to cultivate rubber gardens in some isolation; but he was still constantly pressed to return for shamanistic ceremonies. As the economic rewards were little, he tended to refuse, but often accepted if he was asked to act as an elder at a wedding. In 1964 he had almost established a position as an elder in the river, but not that of one whose word carried much weight in secular matters.

In 1964 S. was a widow living with her son-in-law and grandchildren. She too was middle rank (*bumi*). Although none of her immediate forebears had been shamans, her family—her brother—had been guardians of the *blisieng*. In 1950 she was a spirit-medium, and had, she said, always been delicate from adolescence. She did not practise as a shaman, except domestically. In 1954 she and her husband were seriously ill and her husband died. The news was kept from her as long as possible, and her recovery was slow. She performed an *aiyun* to help. and began to practise curing in a small way. Being a modest and diffident woman, she did so reluctantly, and has never acquired a great reputation; but in 1964 was one of the three shamans (all female) who regularly practised in the village.

The social position which a man, or a woman, can hope to achieve as a shaman depends on a number of factors. The economic rewards are small and consist mainly of ritual gifts—spears, small amounts of gold, food, fowls, clothes, and a little money. Shamans therefore need other forms of economic support and practise part-time only. They do not participate in the administration of the *adat* or even act as leaders in the major communal rituals, unless they also have the proper secular qualifications and the confidence of the elders. Some reported witches seem to have exacted economic toll for a time, but the enterprise always was insecure and usually ended in failure.

Although the shaman's role as a mediator provokes ambivalent feelings, it is nonetheless recognized as a necessary service to the community. Some of his familiars are publicly known because they have consorted with his predecessors; but most are private, and their names and attributes remain unknown until he chooses to reveal them. His familiars are also appropriate in some ways to his position in life and his experience: a man who is widely travelled, for example, is likely to have Kayan and other foreign spirits for familiars. This fact adds to his reputation, so that Malays and even Chinese traders may send for him from distant places. Today women and the younger male mediums are more likely to be possessed by Malay (i.e., Muslim) spirits than by the older 'traditional' type of spirit. Everybody now has some knowledge of the Malay language, and Malay customs are increasingly widespread. The orthodox Muslim ban on all relations with any spirits is, however, either unknown or disregarded. To the shaman it makes little difference whether his spirits' attributes are publicly well-known or not, whether they are good or evil, so long as they are thought to be powerful and he is believed to be in control of them.

The ostensible reason for a shamanistic ceremony is the private need of one individual, but it may have other functions. Matters concerning the village as a whole are often raised by the spirits at a séance; and controversial subjects can then be discussed openly or indirectly in ways not always possible elsewhere. The opinions of a spirit may carry weight because his sources of knowledge are thought to be greater than those of the villagers; but they can be ignored, too, either because the information is judged to be irrelevant, or because people are sceptical about that particular shaman and his familiars, or about the reality of his possession on that special occasion. For the Oya Melanau, however, shamanistic ceremonies do have a considerable significance: they are certainly more than merely minor mechanisms in helping to form public opinion. An *aiyun*, for example, involves a large part of the neighbourhood and draws together many people in social and religious activity. Whatever opinions people may hold of the principal shaman, the occasion is sacred, permeated by a sense of danger, awe, and mystery, and is one of the greatest affirmations of pagan beliefs.

The Relationship Between the Social and the Symbolic Orders

The relationship between a system of religious beliefs and a social system has in the past been viewed in a number of different ways.[1] Since Durkheim's work on the subject at the beginning of the century many anthropologists have considered religious beliefs to be collective representations corresponding closely, if not always exactly, with the system of social groups in the society holding the beliefs. Melanau beliefs and practices, for example, may be regarded as 'one way of describing certain types of human behaviour; the anthropologist's jargon and his use of structural models are other devices for describing the same types of human behaviour' (Leach, 1954, p. 14). Each 'layer' of the Melanau World is thought to be constructed on principles that are the same everywhere, and the inhabitants are held to be related to one another in the same general ways. The behaviour of a man of a particular locality and rank in this the middle world necessarily reveals his position in it; but the rules which govern his behaviour to other Melanau are different from those which apply to foreigners, whether Iban, Kayan, or entities of a completely different kind, such as animals or spirits.

1. In this paper I am principally concerned to examine Melanau beliefs about shamanism as a functional part of the social system which validates norms of behaviour, and I am not concerned to study their meaning as part of the Melanau system of classification and symbolism. In my opinion the two types of investigation are quite distinct and equally valid. The former approach, though derived from Durkheim, owes its development in England largely to Malinowski and his students.

> Myth fulfils in primitive culture an indispensable function: it expresses, enhances, and codifies belief; it safeguards and enforces morality; it vouches for the efficiency of ritual and contains practical rules for the guidance of man . . . it is . . . a pragmatic charter of primitive faith and moral wisdom (Malinowski, 1948, p. 79).

Firth takes essentially the same view when he writes: 'Religious belief helps to provide organizing principles for human existence. In its content, its form, and its expression it is related to the attempts of people to give coherence to their universe of relations, physical as well as social' (Firth, 1951, p. 225).

Iban *adat*, for instance, is known to be different from Melanau *adat*, and it is assumed that other creatures also have their own peculiar *adat*; but whatever the customs of 'foreign' beings may be, it is necessary for a Melanau to have rules for dealing with them. These rules *may* be simpler and fewer than those governing a man's own village, but to be ignorant of or to ignore them can only cause trouble. A Melanau undertaking an *aiyun* or the ceremony of giving his daughter in marriage can do so with safety and satisfaction to himself and others only if he has knowledge of the appropriate *adat*; and in doing so he can be thought of as 'saying things about social status' (Leach, 1954, p. 279). He does it in a language, as it were, which he shares with other Oya Melanau; and in it he indicates aspects not only of his rank, wealth, age, sex, and religious affiliations, but he also tells of his relationship with the spirit world. As in all language, too, the full implications of such statements can be properly understood only in the actual context.

The Melanau, then, look on spirits and other non-human beings as members of foreign societies, so to speak, all of which make up the World or cosmos. Every creature has its appropriate place and mode of life; so that every creature and each part of the World is governed by its own particular *adat*. Ideally the whole is permeated and regulated by a principle of order—a principle of *Adat*, in contrast with particular and local *adat*.[1] Like Melanau or Iban people, the various members of the non-human order are governed by their own *adat*, and nobody supposes that these must closely resemble one another, but it is believed that every creature everywhere is subject to *Adat* in general and to an *adat* in particular. It is as if the Melanau thought that the World and the different beings in it formed a kind of loose composite or 'international' society knit together by a commonly held idea of a 'rule of law' (*Adat*), and by

1. This interpretation of Melanau statements was formulated in the field, and when put to informants was agreed to by them. Accounts of views held by other peoples in Borneo were found at a later stage to be in substantial agreement with Melanau ideas. Cf. Schärer, 1963, p. 75. 'It is not only humanity that possesses *hadat*, but also every creature or thing (animal, plant, river, etc.), every phenomenon (e.g. celestial phenomena), every period and every action, for the entire cosmos is ordered by the total godhead and every member and every part of the cosmos possesses its own place in this order, allocated by the total godhead, and has to live and act according to this ordained place.' Of the Iban in Sarawak, A. J. N. Richards writes: 'By the proper conduct of ritual, from the major and minor "festivals" (*gawai*) to the provision of offerings, the exercise of "magic" and utterance of words of power, the people and their possessions must be kept in a satisfactory state of balance among themselves and in relation to the "unseen powers" ' (Richards, 1963, p. 1).

certain practical arrangements for avoiding or resolving conflicts that arise between beings subject to different *adat*.

The shaman is, as it were, a kind of diplomat who is on good terms with members of various non-human societies. His spirit friends instruct him in the appropriate *adat* in each case and protect him from the dangers of offending influential personalities. Because of his special relationship with them, they are willing to help him to manipulate circumstances for the benefit of his human principals. Nevertheless, the occupation, in spite of all safeguards, is hazardous. By definition the role of shaman places a human in a marginal position which is indicated by his ambiguous behaviour under possession and by the transvestite characteristics displayed in certain circumstances and less often, by some shamans permanently. The marginal nature of the role is reinforced, too, by the belief that he must possess unusual moral qualities if he is to control his familiars successfully and use his special knowledge in mediating between humans and non-humans.

A meeting between potentially hostile beings of any kind is necessarily dangerous; and when it occurs in a 'charged' area such as a sanctuary, then the dangers are likely to be redoubled. The efficacy of the sanctuary and the truce observed in it derive in part from the belief that it is both a model of the larger World and in some sense a reproduction of an earlier stage of history when there were no barriers and all beings were able to mingle freely and safely. At the same time this 're-creation' exists in the present World where matters are differently ordered; moreover, the powers of all beings mingling in it are concentrated, so to say, in a small compass, and are consequently even more dangerous. Any human who enters it is in a greater or lesser degree contaminated by its 'holiness'; and for his own sake and other people's safety he must be carefully prepared before submitting to such an ordeal. He also needs ritual purification and a period of isolated 'decontamination' after being subjected to such dangers. The initiation of a shaman and every encounter with spirits under his guidance are therefore *rites de passage*, which subject him and other participants in them to all the conditions and limitations of such rituals.

Although many shamans and experts believe that spirits and other non-human beings have a 'social' order that in some respects corresponds with that of the Melanau (for they speak of invisible longhouses, spirit rajas, and high and low ranking spirits), nevertheless nobody is dogmatic about it. These are 'things not seen; how can we know?' Besides, the matter is not very important; nobody expects

P

foreign villages and their *adat* to be replicas of Melanau villages. On the other hand, everybody does expect that the basic rules which govern a Melanau in his behaviour to alien beings, whether human or not, shall be approximately of the same kind throughout the World. In this, and only in this sense can the social and the symbolic orders be said to correspond.

Any collectively held view of the symbolic order is, of course, among other things, normative in purpose. There is therefore always likely to be a tendency for the social and symbolic orders to correspond. The Melanau of Sarawak live, and apparently always have lived, in a highly diversified social environment in which many cultural and linguistic groups are interspersed with and closely related to one another. In so far as this environment forms a system it is a composite or plural one. The model of the World which the Melanau use for thinking about themselves indicates this state of affairs. Furthermore, the view that all human and non-human societies constitute a field of diplomatic relations, so to speak, is one that they share with many of the other peoples of Borneo, and it may also be that it is an outlook more generally characteristic of multi-cultural situations of this kind, in which the constituent parts, though in the main politically and economically independent of one another, do nevertheless form one kind of loose composite or plural society.

Reflections on Durkheim and Aboriginal Religion

W. E. H. STANNER

ONE of the first reviewers of *The Elementary Forms of the Religious Life* described it as the work of 'a veteran in Australian ethnology' (Goldenweiser, 1915, p. 719). He might better have said 'veteran at a distance'. Durkheim of course had never visited Australia, but apparently he had read every significant work about its ethnography; Lowie's observation (1937, p. 211) that he was 'saturated' with the technical literature was not an over-statement. It has been said that he 'could have chosen to write [the work] without more than passing reference to Australian or any other primitive peoples' (Seger, 1957, p. 20). In that case it would have made as little mark comparatively as, say, his posthumous *L'éducation morale*. The imperious quality of *The Elementary Forms* came from the junction of revolutionary theses and apparent factual support at a particular time in the history of anthropology. A comment which Durkheim himself made on the French socialists—that 'the research was undertaken to establish the doctrine . . . far from the doctrine resulting from the research' (Peyre, 1960, p. vii)—could justifiably be made concerning *The Elementary Forms*, but it would not detract from the masterly ethnographic feat, even though a detailed analysis would certainly show much wrestling and contrivance to make the facts fit the doctrine. In this paper I do not undertake to make a thorough assessment of this 'brilliant but unconvincing treatise on religion' (Goldenweiser, 1914, p. 288) against the findings of modern Australian anthropology. To do so would be a very formidable task, and whether the work should be so assessed is perhaps itself a question. I wish, rather, to reflect on some particular questions that arose in my own fieldwork, which was much affected by Durkheim's approach. Was the Australian ethnographic material merely illustrative (Seger, 1957, p. 69) for Durkheim? Had it only an accidental role in the development of his ideas on religion to the point which they reached in *The Elementary Forms*? Is it the case, as Talcott Parsons seems to argue (1937, p. 410n), that no empirical fault is to be found with the contentions of fact involved in Durkheim's 'sacred' and 'profane' classes, and in the conception of sacred things as things of symbolic significance? To what extent did Durkheim succeed in his main purpose—'to go underneath the symbol to the reality which it represents and which gives it its meaning'?

Under Durkheim's editorship *L'Année Sociologique* from the first showed a lively and critical interest in aboriginal society. He himself contributed original articles largely concerned with aboriginal culture—on the prohibition and origins of incest (Vol. I), totemism (Vol. V), and marriage systems (Vol. VIII). He also wrote, with Mauss, on primitive forms of classification, one-third of the study having to do with aboriginal data (Vol. VI). There is little to suggest that he thought personal unfamiliarity with aboriginal life a disadvantage. At more than a dozen places in *The Elementary Forms* he looked back approvingly at the early papers without evident wish to make significant changes in their approach or argument.

The studies mentioned fell within what Talcott Parsons (1937, p. 304) has called Durkheim's 'transitional' period following on the breakdown of the theoretical synthesis exemplified by *The Rules of Sociological Method* (1895) and *Suicide* (1897). It is more to my purpose to mention that they overlapped some primary contributions to the ethnography of Australia. The more important were R. H. Mathews's papers from 1894 on; the report of *The Horn Scientific Expedition to Central Australia* (1896); Roth's *Ethnological Studies among the North-West-Central Queensland Aborigines* (1897); two major works by Spencer and Gillen: *The Native Tribes of Central Australia* (1899) and *The Northern Tribes of Central Australia* (1904); and Howitt's *The Native Tribes of South-east Australia* (1904). These were the product of the first more or less systematic researches. To some extent all were guided by theoretical ideas. We have now lost a full sense of the impact they made. Nothing since the explorers' journals had attracted such intellectual attention to Australia. According to one judgment of the day, armchair anthropologists capitalized the accounts 'with the daring, but not always with the success, of a Cortes or a Pizarro', so much so that 'the quiet noncombatant student is astonished to find himself in the theatre of war, and hardly knows where to seek a bomb-proof burrow that he may hide his head from the shells of their polemics' (Hartland, 1900, pp. 57–8).

Spencer and Gillen's work especially 'fascinated the anthropological world' (Elkin, 1964, p. 241). Frazer said that it had earned the gratitude of all future generations. He identified the central Australians as 'humanity in the chrysalis stage'; he assumed that this was one and the same as 'the totem stage'; and (though later he recanted) he pronounced the *intichiuma* ceremonies to be 'the actual observance of that totem sacrament which Robertson Smith, with the intuition of genius, divined years ago, but of which positive examples have hitherto been wanting' (Frazer, 1899, p. 838). Durkheim, feeling his way towards a new synthesis, was also clearly captivated by what seemed an extraordinary primitivity.

In the decade during which he developed the substance of *The Elementary Forms*, anthropology was still largely a prisoner of the cults of social evolution and historicism. Two assumptions in particular were yet scarcely questioned. One was that the nature of anything is entirely comprehended in its development, the other that the proper way to interpret the facts of human social life is by historical explanation. At this previsionary level, on which so much depends, there was not much to choose between any of the anthropologists writing around the turn of the century. For all their other differences, Frazer and Durkheim, to choose two natural opposites, were at one in accepting that the field of study was mankind at all times and in all places; that enquiry must begin with the most primitive and simple institutional forms; that the method must be the historical analysis of development; and that the data of aboriginal society were splendidly adapted to the purpose. Durkheim, in spite of his already well-developed sociology of co-existent functions, did not break radically with the genetic-historic viewpoint. In the first sentence of the first article in the first volume of *L'Année* we find him saying: 'In order to understand a practice or an institution, a judicial or moral rule, it is necessary to trace it as nearly as possible to its origin; for between the form it now takes and what it has been, there is a rigorous relationship.' He tried to avoid the crudities of historicism, the 'tumultuous and summary comparisons' of the loose comparative method, and the 'cartesian' or dialectical approach to theory, but in what I have called the previsionary aspect he remained very much of his time. For example, in order to deal with 'origins' in 'a wholly relative sense', he substituted the idea of 'ever-present causes' for 'absolute beginnings', but went on to speak almost in the same breath, and without very clear discriminations, of 'genesis', 'prototypes', and 'stages', so that much of the effect of the caution was lost. The loose comparative method may have many guises, and to one of them he fell victim. His conceptions of totemism (Pater Schmidt's appellation 'pantotemism' was fully justified) and the clan-totem relation were essentially 'cartesian'—'a logical concept, a pure possibility, constructed simply by force of thought' (Durkheim, 1915, p. 4), although he believed them to be based concretely. The effect of the 'model' was to wrench varied facts from many particular contexts. It has sometimes been argued that, as with the thesis and the proof, the framework and the content of Durkheim's thought can and should be separated, and it may readily be agreed that it would be absurd to judge the worth, say, of his theory of social functions as essentially connected with his dogma of origins and causes. At the same time, to separate them in a study of *The Elementary Forms* requires something like an act of violence. It is this fact of organic connexion which impels one to wonder if one is justified in reducing the Australian material to a merely illustrative place in the development of his thought.

A main proposition of *The Elementary Forms*—that 'religion is something eminently social'—was first formulated in *The Division of Labour* (1893). It may be found in the criticism of Fustel de Coulanges for having supposed the primitive family to be constituted on a religious basis, or, as Durkheim said, for having deduced 'social arrangements' from 'the religious idea'. Durkheim argued that 'on the contrary it is [the social arrangements] that explain the power and nature of the religious idea' (Durkheim, 1947, p. 179). He had apparently read Frazer's first study of totemism (1887) while *The Division of Labour* was in a late stage of preparation as a doctoral dissertation (Alpert, 1939, p. 37), but had not yet conceived of totemism either as part of the social arrangements leading to religion or as the source of all religions. That inspiration evidently did not come until 1895 in circumstances that remain somewhat unclear. Certainly, it owed nothing to Frazer, who had had no theory of totemism at that time, though he was moving towards the first of three theories, and still regarded it simply as a two-sided phenomenon, religious and social. It may have drawn, but only in a very general way, on the thought of Spencer, Lubbock, Tylor, Caird, Jevons, and other English writers on the history of religion. But Durkheim was critical of all of them, and it is clear that his main dependence was on McLennan's pupil, Robertson Smith, to whose studies he appears to have turned when lecturing on religion at Bordeaux University in 1894–5 (Parsons, 1937, p. 409n; Alpert, 1939, p. 215). But, somewhat oddly, this dependence was not avowed—and then only under challenge—until twelve years after the event. In 1907 he wrote: 'it was only in 1895 that I had a clear understanding of the capital role played by religion in social life. It was in that year that, for the first time, I found the means of approaching the study of religion sociologically. It was a revelation to me. The course of 1895 marks a line of demarcation in the development of my thought; so much so that all previous researches had to be taken up again with renewed efforts in order to be placed in harmony with these new views' (quoted by Alpert, 1939, pp. 67, 215).

It may be doubted if the 'new views' were yet wholly of one piece. Some observations made nearer the time of the 'revelation' suggest that he may not yet have cast the die for the primacy of society over religion. In 1897, when criticizing a materialist view of history, he wrote: 'sociologists and historians tend more and more to agree on this common affirmation: that religion is the most primitive of all social phenomena. It is out of it that there have come, by successive transformations, all the other manifestations of collective activity, law, morality, art, science, political forms, etc. In the beginning, all is religious' (*ibid.*, p. 54). In *Suicide*, published in the same year, the general thought of *The Elementary Forms* is adumbrated quite clearly. He may be read in several places (Durkheim, 1952, pp. 170, 254, 312) to say that religious conceptions are the products of the social milieu (e.g. religion is the system of symbols by means of which a society becomes conscious of itself). Yet in others he seems to make religion the determining element (pp. 334, 374–5). This ambiguity never disappeared entirely. It is heavily concentrated in the propositions stated in *The Elementary Forms* that 'nearly all the great social institutions have been born in religion' (economic activity being tentatively excluded) and that 'society is the soul of religion'. In a simple sense the matter might be said to turn on a question of whether conceptual or chronological primacy is being asserted. But such a distinction would seem to strike at the heart of the Durkheimian thesis. If there is 'a rigorous relationship' between primordial and developed forms—'a continuous series of intermediaries'—as between pristine exogamy and contemporary codes of marriage, then the distinction cannot apply. Evidently one must reformulate the thesis as the price of a possible acceptance. Alpert has said (p. 55), it seems to me correctly, that what Durkheim was really stating was 'the *identity* of religious thought and of social thought and consequently the social character of thought in general' (my italics). Identity, not being a relation, does not require either primacies or causalities to be asserted. Fundamentally, it was the failure to break with historicism that prevented the proposition from emerging clearly as one of identity. In this connexion it is interesting to note Parsons's suggestion (1937, p. 427) that the signi-

ficant way of putting Durkheim's proposition is not 'religion is a
social phenomenon' so much as 'society is a religious phenomenon'.
But the conversion is not possible logically. The original proposition
was not symmetrical—all R is S, but not all S is R, at least, on Durkheim's reasoning. At all events, it would seem that, up to 1897, in
spite of the 'revelation', Durkheim had no systematic or final answer
to three questions: the intimate but elusive relations between religion
and social order; the place of religion in a sociological schema;
and the status of religion as determined or determining.

Two things may be noted about the post-1897 period, during which
Durkheim took up the sociology of religion in earnest. It was also
the period of the great Australian ethnographic publications and, as
well, the period in which his general sociology came under sharpest
attack. Two of the more severe criticisms will serve as examples.
I will take them from a single critic (Tosti, 1898, pp. 464–78).
The central postulate, that society is a reality *sui generis,* had led the
nominalist Tarde to accuse Durkheim, in Tosti's words, of 'reproducing in the field of sociology the ontological delusion of mediaeval
realism, by conceiving society as an essence or a transcendental unity'.
Tosti, from much the same position, said that 'Durkheim completely
overlooks the fact that a compound is explained both by the character of its elements and by the law of their interaction. He tries to
explain the "product" by the "product" itself, thus overthrowing the
scientific conception of cause. It is a startling error of logic, the more
surprising in a logician of Durkheim's subtility.' Durkheim replied
that both critics had misunderstood him, and that surely was so.
The statement 'a society is a reality *sui generis*' is equivalent to the
statement 'there is such a thing as a social system'. The idea of a
social system as a *relational* system, as Durkheim developed it,
will not sustain the philosophical interpretation that Tarde (who
incidentally was described by some of *his* critics as an ontologist)
put upon it. His charge of 'social realism' (for that is what it amoun-
ted to) can readily be rebutted from Durkheim's writings. Nevertheless, there was some excuse for the criticism. On occasions, in trying
to force an idea to precision, or to destroy a rival conception, Durkheim used an unfortunately realist language. There was less ground
for Tosti's criticism. He did not do justice to Durkheim's conceptions
of society and of causation. Durkheim sought to find causes *and*
conditions (this, incidentally, was the title of Book II of *The Division
of Labour*); he accepted the fact of multiple causes; he sought to
extract causes from the intensive analysis of correlations; and he
dealt with causes, conditions, and correlations within many-variable

systems of functional interdependences. Tosti's charge of 'explaining the product by the product', if pressed radically, would make any study of the connexions between social variables quite impossible. It would seem to require psychological and sociological study to be complete and simultaneous.

It was probably with these criticisms in mind that Durkheim wrote his next paper, 'Individual and Collective Representations', published in the *Revue de Métaphysique et de Morale* in May 1898. This was extremely important from the viewpoint of *The Elementary Forms*. It made a sustained attack on attempts to reduce sociology to a corollary of individual psychology, and to treat society as an epiphenomenon of individual life. In *The Division of Labour* and *Suicide*, Durkheim had proclaimed society as something external to the individual, endowed with a power of constraint on him and, therefore, not deriving from him. Now, dangerously, he introduced the idea of the social as the 'hyperspiritual', a distinct reality obeying laws of its own. 'Despite its metaphysical appearance,' he said, 'this word designates nothing more than a body of natural facts which are explained by natural causes. It does, however, warn us that the new world thus opened to science surpasses all others in complexity; it is not merely a lower field of study conceived in more ambitious terms, but one in which the laws may not be discovered by the methods of interior analysis alone.' There was one passage which is particularly interesting for its suggestion of something relatively *un*determined and potentially *beyond* institutional control in the cognitive and moral orders. While maintaining the social nature of religion, he admitted that many religious phenomena—e.g. myths, legends, theogonic systems, and popular cosmogonies—that grow out of religious thought are not directly related to particular features of social structure. They are 'social products of the second degree', or 'partially autonomous realities with their own way of life' which are 'relatively free of their matrix'. He compared these phenomena with images and conceptions, as distinct from sense-impressions, forming in the individual psyche, and said that 'a special branch of sociology, which does not yet exist, should be devoted to research into the laws of collective ideation'. He was referring to the derivatives rather than the concomitants of synthesis (Peristiany, 1953, p. xxiv). A hint to the same effect, not followed up as far as I am aware, was contained in *The Elementary Forms* in the apparent query whether religious beliefs depend on necessities as universal and permanent as do religious rites (p. 428). There were many such tantalizing asides.

The ethnographic papers followed. In the same year as 'Individual and Collective Representations' he wrote on incest (Vol. I of *L'Année*). This paper, now much neglected, could be described as a first cast, rough but nevertheless recognizable, of the foundations of *The Elementary Forms*. Many of the leading conceptions are stated clearly—among them the diametric opposition of 'the sacred' and 'the profane', totemism as religious principle, the duality of religious ideas, the religious origin of exogamy, and the primordial connexion of clan and totem. In Vol. II he took up the question of the definition of religion—unsatisfactorily, according to a reference in *The Elementary Forms* (pp. 23n., 47n.)—the definition coming to seem to him too formal and too neglectful of the content of religious ideas. Its real weakness seems rather to have been that in defining religion by the obligatoriness of beliefs it did not provide any means of discriminating between beliefs of religion, morals, and science. It also had elements of circularity (Webb, 1916, p. 60n.).

Now, in the same year (1899), Frazer's second article on, and first theory of, totemism appeared in the *Fortnightly Review*. In its way it could have served as another 'line of demarcation' for Durkheim. Something may be said for a view that, in relation to his developing second synthesis, Frazer had begun to assume for Durkheim the role that Spencer had played in relation to the first synthesis. Spencer's individualism, utilitarianism, and nominalism were not more opposed to Durkheim's views of 1893 than were Frazer's views of religion, magic, and totemism to Durkheim's views of 1897–1904. Frazer had now begun to discount, and would soon pooh-pooh, the religious character and significance of totemism. By 1905 he would see in it only 'a few rudimentary germs of theology'; for the rest, magic; and under his guidance, Baldwin Spencer, who had come to be Durkheim's main factual authority, was now sailing with the same wind. Durkheim's paper on totemism, 1902, and his study, with Mauss, of primitive classification, 1903, reveal him as almost diametrically opposed to Frazer. The rather crude statement in the paper on incest that 'the totem is a god and totemism a cult' deepens. 'A totem, in short,' he says, 'is not a mere name but before all and above all . . . a religious principle . . . one and consubstantial with the person in whom it has its dwelling place; it forms part of his personality' (*L'Année*, Vol. V, pp. 110–11). He saw it also of course as essentially social, but in a vastly different sense from Frazer's 'social'. His definition of religion was now also centrally in terms of sacredness, a concept which Frazer had used in a characteristically unanalysed way. (The papers, incidentally, make clear too that Durk-

heim had begun seriously to misunderstand Australian social organization, by making false distinctions between 'the totemic clan' and
the local group or clan, and by depending too heavily on the central
Australian material. 'The clan,' he says, 'is an amorphous group, a
floating mass, with no very defined individuality; its contours
especially have made no material marks on the soil.') As to the essay
on classification, it remains one of the cardinal documents for an
understanding of the second subject of *The Elementary Forms*: an
enquiry into the most fundamental categories of human thought. A
single extract will sufficiently indicate its content and argument.
'Society was not simply a model which classificatory thought followed,' Durkheim and Mauss wrote, 'it was its own divisions which
served as divisions for the system of classification. The first logical
categories were social categories; the first classes of things were
classes of men, into which these things were integrated. It was because
men were grouped, and thought of themselves in the form of groups,
that in their ideas they grouped other things, and in the beginning the
two modes of grouping were merged to the point of being indistinct.
Moieties were the first genera; clans, the first species. Things were
thought to be integral parts of society, and it was their place in
society which determined their place in nature' (Durkheim and
Mauss, 1963, pp. 82f.). It is interesting to note that this essay was
explicitly contra-Frazer: 'Far from it being the case, as Frazer seems
to think, that the social relations of men are based on logical relations
between things, in reality it is the former which have provided the
prototype for the latter' (*ibid.*, p. 82).

One other paper should be referred to: *La détermination du fait
moral* (1907). It was published at or about the time Durkheim was
giving his second course on religion, this time at the Sorbonne.
Presumably it reflected the ideas explored in those lectures and further developed for *The Elementary Forms*. It sketched the main structure of concepts and argument of that book. The dichotomy of 'the
sacred' and 'the profane' was set out clearly. So were the ideas that
morality begins with the membership of groups; that all moral systems are thus functions of social organizations and vary with the
social structures of those who practise them; that each society has, in
the main, the morality that suits it; that society is not only the source
but also the end of all morality, since its end is the realization of
society's ideal of itself; that there must be moral elements in religion
and religious elements in morality; that morality would no longer be
morality if it had no element of religion; that moral values necessarily
take on sacredness; and that this is why no ethic has ever existed

which did not have a religious character. Society, Durkheim now has it, commands us because it is exterior and superior to us; because the moral distance between it and us makes it an authority before which our will defers; and because, in deferring, we defer to a hyperspiritual reality from which flows everything that matters to us. In these terms he essayed to meet his chief theoretical problems: how to explain the essence of morality, and how to 'place' religion in society, that reality which transcends man while being immanent in him. 'In the world of experience,' he wrote, 'I know of only one being that possesses a richer and more complex moral reality than our own, and that is the collective being. I am mistaken; there is another being which could play the same part, and that is the Divinity. Between God and society lies the choice. I shall not examine here the reasons that may be advanced in favour of either solution, both of which are coherent. I can only add that I myself am quite indifferent to this choice, since I see in the Divinity only society transfigured and symbolically expressed.'

It will be apparent from this notional sketch that by 1907 Durkheim had overcome, in principle, the schematic and conceptual difficulties standing in the way of his religious sociology. The essential instrument had been the rounding out of his theory of social control: the theory that in society people are constrained by a sense of an imperative duty, arising from the axiology of life, to obey rules which are necessarily objectified in religious and quasi-religious symbols. This approach allowed him to rectify one shortcoming—too formal a stress on pure obligation—which he had found in his first definition of religion. There remained the second shortcoming: a certain neglect of the content of religious ideas. In this respect the Australian material was so apt to his needs that on this ground alone one might well ask if it was more than the vehicle of his purpose. His general propositions were of such range that only history and ethnography could provide a persuasive content. He was entirely satisfied that aboriginal Australia would do so if studied with strict regard for scientific method. That given, there was 'no reason for not extending the most general results of our research to other religions'. But there was another difficulty—that of proof. A crucial experiment was the central ideal of his conception of positive science. It was here that the new Australian ethnography came into its own. The reports made possible, for the first time, something like a continental view of a whole people, an exhaustive account of the simplest known instance. 'We have not dreamed for a moment,' he wrote, 'of ignoring the fact that an extended verification may add to the authority of a theory, but it is equally true that when a law has been proved by one well-made experiment, this proof is valid universally.' *The Elementary Forms* was the 'well-made experiment'.

One need not oppose a contention that Durkheim's main impulse was to complete a theoretical system. The book itself, with its thirty or more references to all the preceding works, presses that conclusion on one. Nevertheless, the mating of the theoretical problems to Australian answers—let us not press the opposite possibility— was something more than a happy conjunction. To argue that without the aboriginal material the book could not have been written would be to go too far. Indeed, as I have tried to show, it had already been written in more general terms in the decade 1898–1907. It could not, however, have been the book that for all its faults remains indispensable to the philosophical, sociological, and—let us not fail to say—the ethnographic education of any anthropologist.

Durkheim at first intended to publish under the title *Elementary Forms of Thought and Religious Life*. In 1909 three parts appeared as articles with titles consonant with that intention. The introduction, plus a part omitted from the book, was printed in the *Revue de Métaphysique et de Morale* as 'Sociologie religieuse et théorie de la connaissance', and versions of the second and third chapters in the *Revue Philosophique* as 'Examen critique des systèmes classiques sur les origines de la pensée religieuse'. I have not seen any explanation of the change of title, but the effect was to obscure the second though in no way secondary object of study: an attempt to 'renovate the theory of knowledge' by a new examination of the categories. This was unfortunate because the book's longer perspective went far beyond religion. It looked in the direction of a grander sociology based on what might be called a natural positivist epistemology— 'natural' in the sense of being grounded on social reality, which to Durkheim's positivist mentality was the highest reality observable in the moral and intellectual orders. It was by means of this episte-mology that in his view religion, morals, and science could be conci-liated. The sociology of religion only mediated that longer vision. *The Elementary Forms of the Religious Life* was not the consumma-tion of his thought: it was but antepenultimate.

Another curious change of title, again unexplained, was made in the English translation (1915) by Joseph Swain, and in the later re-printing (1926). The sub-title of the original French edition, *Le système totémique en Australie*, was dropped. It may be presumed that the author consented, but if so it is hard to suggest a motive.

Was it from deference to the trend of opinion among anthropologists?
(I have in mind Pater Schmidt's question—1935, pp. 115–16: how
was it possible for Durkheim not merely to defend the religious
character of totemism but to exalt it to the position of the source of
all religion at a time when 'all other researchers were more and more
definitely denying any connexion between totemism and religion
whatsoever'?) It seems unlikely. There had been a large deflation
of totemism, not only of its religious significance, since Tylor's sceptical statement (1898, pp. 138–48) even though speculation still bal-
looned (Hartland, 1900, *loc. cit.*). But not to air his convictions would
have been very unlike Durkheim. He took no great part (but see
Folklore, June 1904, and Lang, 1905, pp. 91–110) in the violent controversy which went on, in books and learned and literary journals,
about and round totemism, culminating in the *Anthropos* collo-
quium of 1914–17; but an explanation is not hard to give. As
Frazer had done after the criticisms of the first edition of *The
Golden Bough*, he let the controversy for the most part pass him by
while preparing a definitive answer. The language he then used shows
how irked he had been by the spate of new theories following on
those of the classical writers. Tylor, he said, had begged the question;
Jevons's hypothesis left the problems inexplicable; Frazer's changing
theories were inconceivable; Lang's explained nothing; Schmidt's
did not interest him; and so on. Deference in the title would indeed
have been odd when there was so little in the book.

It might be argued rather more convincingly that the change of
title blazoned Durkheim's thesis that 'religion has a meaning and a
reasonableness that the most intransigent rationalist cannot misunderstand'. The scepticism about totemism disturbed him less than
the 'bleakly hostile' attitude to religion which had dominated anthropology and sociology (Evans-Pritchard, 1962, p. 29). There was
no doubt whatever in this mind about the religious significance of
totemism. 'We cannot repeat too frequently that the importance we
attach to totemism is absolutely independent of whether it was
universal or not.' If universal, all to the good; if not, no matter.
What he sought to prove was the proposition that the believer is not
deceived, that 'when the Australian is carried outside himself and
feels a new life flowing within him whose intensity surprises him, he
is not the dupe of an illusion. . . .' Totemism was but the vehicle or
material of proof. The sharpest barbs in all his writings—'lying fic-
tions', 'extraordinary dupery', 'vain fantasy', 'presupposition of a
thoroughgoing idiocy'—were shot at the entailments of the illusion-
ist theories.

A third aspect of the title invites comment. It lures a reader into reading the book in a deceptive light. The work substantially is a study of the sociology of totemism and of the social determination of categories. Whether totemism is the sort of entity Durkheim imagined it to be, and whether it can be identified with primitive religion or religion at all, are important questions, but they are not central if the view stated earlier—that the fundamental object was to establish the identity of religious and social thought and therefore the social character of all, including scientific, thought—is correct. From such a viewpoint there may come, for some at least, an impulse to turn back and to study again and again this inexhaustibly interesting scholar. There is a widespread view that everything of value which he wrote has long since been incorporated into the theory and practice of social anthropology. This does not seem to me true. On the other hand, two of his leading conceptions have notably helped the other influences (Horton, 1960, pp. 201–26) which have restricted the social anthropologist's approach to religion. I refer to the categorial use of 'the sacred' and 'the profane' and to the insistence on giving religious symbols an empirical reference only.

Historians of ideas will no doubt wish to say much about Durkheim's inclination to dichotomism and dualism. The sacred-profane division is one of the most pre-emptive. After 1899 it had a leading place in his thought. The static or timeless character of the conception contrasts with the dynamic character of his theory of value, on which it really depends.

One doubts if many anthropologists subscribe literally to the thesis of a 'bipartite division of the whole universe, known and knowable, into two classes which embrace all that exists, but which radically exclude each other'. Such was its established force, however, that in studying aboriginal religion I blamed myself for incompetence when the facts would not fit it. I might have saved myself much trouble by following up more quickly a hint given by van Gennep in *The Rites of Passage* (1960, p. 1), that an intermediate stage between sacred and profane is necessary. I will not concern myself with the many criticisms that have been made of the concept of 'the sacred'. I will argue not only that 'the profane' is the weaker of the two categories, but that the dichotomy itself is unusable except at the cost of undue interference with the facts of observation.

My criticism of the schema as such arose in the first place from the difficulty of finding a conceptual home for facts which, excluded from the first category, should have fallen within the second, but would not do so. I came to two conclusions: that even if we accept the categories as given, a third—which I shall call the mundane—is necessary, and Durkheim himself tacitly admitted the necessity; secondly, that there is an important class of facts, so far inadequately explained, which bring the worth of the schema, whether double- or triple-barrelled, into question.

Anyone may observe that the Australian aborigines in their religious rites use objects which in that context are not in any degree or sense sacred. They include natural objects (water, fire, earth, food) and manufactured objects (cosmetics, tools, weapons, musical instruments). All have utility and common value and some, in particular contexts, may have symbolic value. They are brought into direct association, even into physical contact, with sacred objects and persons without taking on sacredness and without having deleterious effect. Neither in the general sense of having to be kept *pro fanum*, nor in the more restrictive sense of having to be used guardedly because of some property or postulated quality inimical to sacred things or persons, can they be described as 'profane'. They are simply ordinary, common, or mundane things that happen to be useful. The matter is simple but not trivial.

Durkheim implicitly admitted a third category in referring, as he did frequently, to 'ordinary things', 'things of common use', 'the ordinary plane of life', 'reasons of temporal utility', and so on, but he suppressed it on the schematic plane in the interest of the dichotomy. His two classes can 'embrace all that exists' only at the cost of an ambiguous second class. Perhaps one may infer from his comment on the terms *sacré* and *profane*—that the two classes are only 'well enough translated' by them—that he sensed some difficulty. But one may doubt if he appreciated the act of suppression.

The aboriginal universe of 'all that exists' is not divided in fact, and therefore should not be divided in theory, into two classes. To use the dichotomy is to disregard what is the case. One may say so confidently in spite of the commonness of dual organizations in aboriginal society and dualistic tendencies in the intellectual culture. Not even the facts of these orders support Durkheim's thesis. The two moieties of a segmented tribe or group of tribes might be said to 'embrace all that exists' in that, between them, they include all persons in that universe. It might also be said that they 'radically exclude each other' in that no one person belongs to both. But the moieties do not exhibit 'absolute heterogeneity'; they are not 'profoundly differentiated'; they are not 'radically opposed' (1915,

p. 38). They are interdependent. Groups which, say, paint each other but not themselves in order to celebrate joint religious rites do not form 'two worlds between which there is nothing in common' (p. 39). Again, the schedule of totems in some tribes may be said virtually to 'embrace all that exists' in making symbols from all significant things in the environment and in apportioning the symbols between groups which, within limits, 'radically exclude each other' in the sense stated. Sometimes a principle signifying opposition—as between light and dark, or land and sea—may be found to categorize each such group. But *all* the totems have meaning for *all* the groups as a condition of joint social and religious life. It is far from being the case that they 'cannot even approach each other and keep their own nature at the same time' (p. 40). The fact is that they intermix by system while preserving their identities. Similarly, Durkheim's dual categories have a different character from the dualism exhibited in aboriginal thought. The first is that of intractable hostility between unlike things that can never meet. The second is that of perennial struggle between couplets or complementary opposites, e.g. left hand and right hand. One could not say of these facts that 'in all the history of human thought there exists no other example of two categories of things so profoundly differentiated or so radically opposed to one another' (p. 38). How did we ever give credence to such an image of aboriginal life? Two domains of *life* that 'cannot even approach each other and keep their own nature at the same time': *both* domains being lived in by the *same* persons? Two categories of *thought* between which there is 'nothing in common': not even the practice of interdependence? Two classes of things and actions so 'absolutely heterogeneous' that there is between them a 'break of continuity' (p. 39) amounting to 'logical chasm' (p. 40): so that beliefs and practices could not have had *any* significance for the same persons in ordinary life? The approach simply will not do. It makes too many difficulties of classification and analysis, and the heuristic value is illusory. It appears to be due to following a false lead from divisions of the *noa-tabu* kind. From another point of view it is a typical congestion resulting from Durkheim's love of dualism and of realist or substantialist terms, a combination which did repeated disservice to his true theoretical outlook. The conception of a society as 'a system of active forces' is beyond question a relational theory. The criticism one would make of the way in which he developed it is that he hovered between an unrigorous statics and a covert dynamics. This remains an essential criticism of the functional-structural anthropology which he influenced.

Q

When *The Elementary Forms* was published there was immediate criticism of, among much else, the concept of 'the sacred'. I am not aware that there was as much, or as continuous, examination of 'the profane'. In Durkheim's usage it connoted one or all of the following: commonness (work is 'an eminent form of profane activity'); minor sacredness (the less sacred is 'profane' in relation to the more sacred); non-sacredness (the two classes have 'nothing in common'); and anti-sacredness (profane things can 'destroy' sacredness). Things so disparate cannot form a class unless a class can be marked by a property, its absence, and its contrary. To retain the categorial usage is unjustifiable.

If we subtract from 'all that exists' *both* the sacred and the mundane, what is left is still too complex for simple appellation. On religious occasions the aborigines keep a number of things *pro fanum* for distinct reasons. Certain songs and dances would simply have no place in a liturgical formulary, but there is nothing 'ritually dangerous' about them. Much the same is the case with levity and quarrels. Their tone would be alien; they might possibly imply disrespect; but they would not be sacrilegious. Certain foods, on the other hand, are ruled out because it is supposed that they would endanger the lives or well-being of neophytes if eaten in other than a given order or from any but the hands of an elder. The danger is of impersonal, magical causation, though the food in itself is good. The same magical danger would arise from contact with female possessions or exuviae. On the other hand, the presence of a stranger or a woman at a sanctified place might be a provocative desecration without any necessary magical element. That is too great a load of distinct meanings even for a remaindered 'all that exists'. It is a fact that the aborigines take great care to protect sacred things, persons, occasions, and situations from anything—ritually dangerous things and acts, breaches of secrecy, disrespect—that may derogate from them. My own impression is that the care is exercised more against persons than against impure or dangerous things, and that malignant or careless human actions cause more upsets than magical effects. Human acts (trespass on the ritual ground, breach of secrecy) 'profane' the sacra but not in the same sense as magical effects. There is little point in trying to couple them under a single notion.

It seems then that although Durkheim's system requires, and implicity admits, a third category, not even three categories could suffice to represent the facts adequately in a dynamic analysis. The conceptual, to say nothing of the logical, difficulties of the system are too many to mention, but a few points may be noted in connexion with the empirical difficulties. The dual categories, it will be remembered, were in the first place classes of things and, by extension, became classes of persons, ideas, situations, values, and other components of action. The theory of two 'worlds' or 'domains' was a further extension. It will be remembered too that Durkheim thought the 'incompatibility' between the 'propitiously sacred' and the 'unpropitiously sacred' just as 'all-exclusive as that between the sacred and the profane'. In a tantalizing aside he remarked that the incompatibility (ambiguity, bipolarity) 'is not peculiar to the idea of sacredness alone' (p. 414). Did he imply that 'the profane', like 'the sacred', also 'gravitate[s] about two contrary poles between which there is the same opposition as between the pure and the impure, the saint and the sacrilegious, the divine and the diabolic'? So that there would be a purifying and a defiling sacred, and an ennobling and a vulgarizing profane? What he actually wrote probably cannot be pressed that far, but some of the problems of the dichotomy would be easier to unravel if that had been his meaning. For example, it would then almost be possible to rephrase them in terms of two continua, one of positive and negative sacred values, and one of positive and negative secular values. But a problem would still remain: the insistence that the opposition between the categories is unlike any other in human thought, such that compared with it 'the traditional opposition of good and bad is nothing'. That appears to rule out a conversion of the categories to schedules of values in a scale along a continuum such that there is a positive stretch, a point of transition, and a negative stretch. That this evidently cannot be done is curious, because Durkheim insists that sacredness is not an intrinsic property of things. It is a quality attributed to or 'superposed' on them; a quality which, therefore, can change over time, be acquired and lost. If there are, as he says, 'eminent' values then there must be lesser values of the same order on the same scale. Negative values are also implied. Logically, the antithetical notions should also refer to qualities, not properties, and should respond to conceptualization in value-terms.

The difficulties may be expressed figuratively. Let a rectangle be the supposititious 'whole universe' divided into two 'domains' which 'exclude each other' and together exhaust 'all that exists'. S contains all that is sacred, P all that is profane. The uniformity of S does not properly convey the 'ambiguity' and 'polarity' of 'the sacred', and the shared boundary between S and P does not properly convey the 'sort of logical chasm' and 'break of continuity' asserted to lie between the two domains. We need another system of divisions, such

that a cross-division is made within S to show S̄ as the 'polar opposite' of S, with a domain O interposing between S–S̄ and P. This is
the only condition on which S–S̄ and P can have 'nothing in common'
except co-existence within the 'whole universe' of the rectangle. But
what then of O? A 'dichotomous' universe of three necessary parts?
A universe 'exhausted' by two parts but requiring a third in order to
be possible? One part containing its own antithesis, the other(s) uniform? The complex part susceptible of being destroyed only from
that part with which contact is 'impossible'? I can see no way of
dealing with these and other such questions in the terms Durkheim
used. On the other hand, the problems are at least eased if the implicit third category is made explicit. Then O becomes the domain of
mundane things. The construction may be ready to say: sacred things
may readily lose their sacredness and become commonplace, which
is in line with empirical experience and would not contravene Durkheim's idea of sacredness. (Even in the aboriginal tradition the
sacred bullroarer had a secular valuation as well, and when the tradition collapsed the secular value succeeded the sacred value.) But
the construction also seems to say: sacred values must become commonplace before they can become profane, which does not sound
Durkheimian, and is difficult to translate into empirical terms.
The trouble obviously arises from the static categorial forms. While
these are retained a trichotomy has no advantage over a dichotomy.
The schema, plainly, is empirically inadequate while at the same time
being caught up with conceptual and logical difficulties. It requires a
conversion from the categorial plane to the plane of human interactions or, as I would prefer to say, operations and transactions about
things of value. Actually, there are excellent bases in Durkheim's
thought for so doing. His general theory of society as 'a system of active forces', his conception of symbolic relations, and his axiology
(the theory of the ideals and values by which social persons direct
their behaviour), would probably allow the conversion to be made.

It was in part in this sense that I remarked earlier that *The Elementary Forms* was but antepenultimate in the development of his
thought. His untimely death left a large potential undeveloped. But
as far as *The Elementary Forms* is concerned, the utility of one
bequest—the strained, static categories—has long been used up.

The conclusion of *The Elementary Forms* rings with a conviction
that, inexplicable and disconcerting as aboriginal religious symbols
might seem at first, 'the mystery which appears to surround them is
wholly superficial and disappears before a more painstaking obser-

vation' (p. 429). Durkheim was confident that he had demonstrated the referent of the symbols to be concrete and unmysterious. What in fact he had done was to use novel material, in an extraordinarily vivid way, to vindicate a postulate which permanently invested his thought: that there *cannot* be 'an aspect of reality which evades ordinary knowledge as well as science'. His was not the ordinary positivist dogma— that it is meaningless to set up a transempirical reality—but rather a profession of faith in the destiny of science to discover and identify the empirical reality which, since there could be no other, *must* be behind the distorting veil of mythological imagination. To keep his promise (p. 1) to proceed 'with all the exactness and fidelity that an ethnographer or an historian' could bring to the task, required at least an open mind towards the opaque symbols, in which aboriginal religion abounds, which no amount of 'painstaking observation' can interpret, and towards the multitude of others which, more transparent, appear to point to 'aspects of "reality" significant to human life and experience, yet outside the range of scientific observation and analysis' (Parsons, 1937, p. 421).

Part of the difficulty seems to have been due to a flaw in his analysis of symbolism. Parsons has suggested that it was a failure to appreciate the 'double incidence' of non-empirical symbols, and I consider the criticism a basic one. Take the word 'rainbow' in an aboriginal totemic universe. The 'double incidence' is (1) word⟶ event and (2) event⟶ totemic ancestor. In both cases the cognitive structures and functions are similar, but the organized sense-perceptions of the first are replaced in the second by ideas, only more or less organized, which refer to an imagined object. If the ideas constituting the symbolic relation (2) are to be intelligible there must be some sort of conceptualization of the object. Men, being the makers as well as the interpreters of symbols, must as makers produce operable symbols if as interpreters they are to make use of them. It may be for this reason that the conceptual imagery of religious symbol-making is drawn largely but by no means wholly from familiar situations of social life. The supposed properties of objects, it seems, are transposed to the symbols in terms that are *already* meaningful. But neither the imagery, nor the situations from which it is drawn, are themselves the referents: on the view here put forward, they are, or provide, only an idiom in which the referents are conceptualized. Durkheim did not make this particular error, but he short-circuited the analysis of the symbolizing process in another way, by imposing the philosophical postulate that non-empirical symbolic referents *must* be distorted representations of empirical reality. This led to two substantial errors. He assumed—to a modern student unjustifiably —that the aborigines were incapable (in part because of his belief that they had an 'insufficient aptitude for abstracting and generalizing') of objectifying in symbols a deeper view of life. He thus did not enquire seriously into the dimension of 'ultimate concern' exemplified, strongly if darkly, in their symbolism. Secondly, he did not perceive that there is a 'multiple' as well as a 'double incidence' in the symbols. By this is meant that there are cognitive aspects of the feelings, valuations, and aspirations which as well as the conceptualizations go with the symbols. Durkheim, as positivist, did not follow the analysis through to the realm which, as sociologist, he was magnificently equipped to study.

When *The Elementary Forms* was in preparation less was known than at present of the aboriginal myths, that great repository of religious cognition, but enough was known to make a modern reader wonder why it was that Durkheim did not see that his thesis was very depreciatory of man. It did not presuppose a 'thoroughgoing idiocy' as bad as that which he had found unacceptable in Frazer's account of the origin of totemism, but it did not credit primitive man with any capacity to form judgments of experience, to objectify in symbols determinants of social life more ultimate than any which arise from human association as such, or from an idealization of it. One cannot criticize Durkheim for pressing the view that the task of science is to go 'behind' the symbolisms. What cannot be accepted is the posture that he demonstrated the concrete collectivity to be the only possible referent.

If anything can be said with certainty of the belief-systems which have been studied it is that they do *not* symbolize the clan, or any other concrete social entity, or even idealizations of them, although these elements may colour or mediate what is symbolized. On the other hand, it seems incontestable that in a broad sense they *do* symbolize 'aspects of reality significant to human life and experience': we are not constrained to uphold Parsons's further contention that such aspects are 'outside the range of scientific observation and analysis'. In my recent monograph *On Aboriginal Religion* I have tried to show that in fact some very perceptive truths about human experience, and about the condition of man's life, are expressed in aboriginal myths and rites. The expression is in a metaphorical idiom and it makes use of many vehicles of dramatic imagination. Here and there the reflective imagination breaks through to the plane of explicit statement. In a few places in *The Elementary Forms* one may sense that Durkheim was not unmindful of this aspect of aboriginal religious thought. It must of course remain an open question whether somewhat better information on the rites and beliefs would have led him to see that his philosophical presuppositions were preventing the facts from telling an essential part of their story. On the whole, however, he was rather too imbued with the notion of the primitivism of the aborigines to let us suppose that he would have thought it a fruitful field of further inquiry, and indeed the question scarcely came within the possibilities of his study. One of the things which distinguishes his from the present period is the extent to which the whole stance of anthropology, with its emphasis on the historical-hierarchical viewpoint, forced on enquiry a more or less systematic misrepresentation of the experiential aspect of institutions, in particular of religion.

It would be unjust to include Durkheim among the scholars who at the least were not displeased to see religion and science at each other's throats (Evans-Pritchard, 1962). He inveighed against 'subtle theologies', against 'theological and confessional prejudice', and against the 'hegemony of faith' over religious thought, but he did not deny religion, as he said, 'in principle'. How could he, since he saw it as a necessary and thus eternal part of man's life and thought? He denied only its right to dogmatize upon the nature of things and its claim of special competence to know man and the world. It might —indeed, by its nature must—essay to go beyond science. In this way he seemed to leave open to it, rather surprisingly, a legitimate field of metaphysical speculation. The only boundaries he set were that it must not claim or deny things for which it had no scientific authority. In this aspect his positivism was scarcely Comtean. The tone of conscious superiority to illusion which had characterized so many anthropological writers on religion cannot be found in his work. He stood apart in other respects as well: for example, in his dislike of historical materialism, and in the zeal with which he sought to correct what he called the 'moral mediocrity' of his time. He was not alone in considering all religions of equal value and dignity, but as far as I am aware, no other scholar of such eminence was prepared at the time to treat the cognitive elements of primitive religion, including 'the crude cults of the Australian tribes', with such seriousness. Here indeed was a change from his predecessors. It was at once the penalty and tragedy of his approach that for systematic reasons he could not accommodate the postulational and experiential elements of aboriginal religion.

It has been said with much truth that *petitio principii* was a besetting scholarly vice of Durkheim (Needham, in Durkheim and Mauss, 1963, p. xiv n.). Is it not strange that this was so ? He had the sharpest of eyes for question-begging. Note as an early illustration how he had dismissed—as a 'refusal of explanation', a posing rather than a resolution of a question—any attempt to account for exogamy and the prohibition of incest by 'an instinctive repulsion that man feels for consanguineous marriage'. This, as he pointed out, says only that man condemns incest because it appears condemnable to him. Yet from the very sentences (see the paper on incest) in which he made the objection he went on to state propositions, afterwards made into the anatomy of *The Elementary Forms*, which then and later were as much in need of proof as the vast conclusions drawn from them— the primordiality of clan and totem, the indissoluble link between them, totemism as religious principle. There is something like the hyperbole of question-begging in the whole suite of now familiar statements: the clan is the *fons et origo* of totemism; clan and totem mutually imply each other; the clan presupposes a totem; a totem has meaning only in and through the clan; to take away the totem makes the clan no longer representable; the group is possible only on the totem as condition. A single doubt—on the 'ism' of totemism, or that a non-totemic clan may not be 'an amorphous group, a floating mass, with no very defined individuality; its contours especially, have made no material marks on the soil'—if entertained, however briefly, might have toppled the edifice. Goldenweiser's incisive criticisms (1910) came too late, but why was it that Durkheim paid no attention whatever to the cautions of Tylor, 'whose lightest word carries with it all the weight that justly attaches to any utterance of one whom we all regard as the most eminent of anthropologists' (Jevons, 1901)? One has to look deeper than a mere nodding over matters of logic. Perhaps the explanation may be found in an absolute dedication to a single central vision. His sociocentric fixation was all-consuming. In this respect he was, in Sir Isaiah Berlin's terms, the arch-hedgehog.[1] The insistence that *all* relations run *from* the social order *to* the social order was a sort of theodicy justifying the worship of sociological science. There could be but one mould for everything: beliefs, rites, sentiments, social forms, categories of thought, schemes of classification, scientific concepts. It is this vision which explains the quality, a pervasive atmosphere of inevitability, that every reader

1. The reference is to a line from the Greek poet Archilochus: 'the fox knows many things but the hedgehog knows one big thing'. See Isaiah Berlin's *The Hedgehog and the Fox*. The description of Tolstoy—'by nature a fox, by belief a hedgehog'—in many ways fits Durkheim equally well.

of *The Elementary Forms* must have noticed. It produces a sense, which grows always stronger, that the earnest stress on scientific method, the painstaking empiricism, the textual care, the dazzling erudition, the sinewy argument are supererogatory, which is not in any way to say unauthentic, but merely that in the beginning was the end.

Durkheim's thought does not lend itself to apt summary or to an easy scrutiny of sequences. It courses like a vine covered with a profusion of laterals and spurs. The totality eludes an ordinary span of mind. *The Elementary Forms* is particularly difficult. How does one reach a unitary critical view of a work with two profound objects and half a dozen major theses? The difficulties, whether of focus or estimate, can in part be overcome by an ethnographic and theoretical annotation[1] of that third of the book (pp. 87–239) which shapes much of the Australian material for the culminating analysis.

One must resist the disposition of some commentators (e.g. Talcott Parsons, 1937, p. 411) to suggest that the ethnographic details are incidental to the general theoretical enquiry into the structure and principles of religion. I should be inclined to argue that to make the separation is a mistake with respect to any subject of the book. In the matter of aboriginal religion, the concern of this paper, the details are the very stuff of the 'crucial experiment'. Durkheim himself saw them as such. The experiment is crucial *to* the general theory. For this reason the theory stands or falls by those details until a test is made of some other set of materials. The critical literature reveals other dangers that flow from separation. At one extreme the student is offered what may be called 'sublimated Durkheim', e.g. Ginsberg's epitomization that the essence of the viewpoint is that 'religious ideas are collective ideas which represent collective realities' (1956, p. 231). At the other extreme the offer may be 'potted Durkheim', e.g. an impression that the function of religion is simply to be there, to support the structure and process of society as and when needed. From the first all that is provocative has gone; the second transforms a theory of transcended selves into a theory of public conveniences.

There is a chain of reasoning in six lines on p. 88 which shows, as well as any passage can, why it is essential to criticize *The Elementary Forms* ethnographically. Three propositions are stated: there should be a cult more fundamental and primitive than animism and naturism; there is such a cult; and that cult is totemism. One could say without logic-chopping that all the modes of *petitio principii* are

1. Which I have prepared in part but here omitted.

there exemplified. The contentions were abstractly determined but not, I would say, established by the preceding pages, but pp. 87–239 transfer the inadequate certainties to what follows. The whole course of Durkheim's reasoning on religion required him to find empirical instances of fundamental and primitive social groups whose members were united, not by blood or common habitat, but solely by having the same name and emblem and by participating in the same cult. Sure enough, he found what he sought. A freakish, passing state of affairs in Australian ethnography gave some of the central Australian material the appearance of satisfying the requirement. In this respect the very merit of his approach—'concentration upon one clearly determined type'—was a prime cause of his undoing. He subdued a whole class of symbolized relations to the factitious importance of a sub-class which, as we now know, had been described inadequately.

The insistence on making religion—at least at the end of its historical course of 'rigorous relationships' with primordial causes—dependent on society inevitably put Durkheim at the mercy of his grasp of the society chosen for the crucial experiment. His insight from afar was in many ways brilliantly penetrating. He had a good sense of the factual shortcomings of the standing accounts and remarked on particular weaknesses, e.g. the poor studies of initiation rites. But, as I remarked earlier, nothing in the book suggests a feeling of being greatly handicapped. On the contrary, the tone was one of supreme confidence that enough was known to test and prove the thesis. The 'society' on which the argument turned was largely a figment to which, as Ginsberg has correctly said, Durkheim attributed 'powers and qualities as mysterious and baffling as any assigned to the gods by the religions of the world' (1956, p. 242).

Economic Concentration and Malay Peasant Society

M. G. SWIFT

IN this paper[1] I want to make a *prima facie* case for a generalization about recent trends in Malay peasant economy. The generalization has far-reaching consequences for the development of Malay society, and, indirectly, for the social and political development of the whole Malaysian nation.

I maintain that every important field of peasant economic activity shows a change from a fairly equal distribution of wealth to one where a small number of peasants are set off from their fellow villagers by substantially greater income and possessions. A secondary feature of this process, more removed from the usual anthropological concern with village studies, is a related tendency for ownership of village assets to pass from the peasants to other groups in society. I am not asserting a clear nation-wide polarization of Malay society between a land-owning, exploiting class, and mass of tenants and labourers. This may well be the long-term outcome of the concentration process I hypothesize, but such a prediction would rely too much on the assumption that Malay peasant society will not be affected by other far-reaching influences for change from the wider plural society of which it is but a part. Even the more short-run limited analysis attempted here relies on the *ceteris paribus* assumption, but I do not think this robs the generalization of value in understanding contemporary Malay society, nor does it preclude *limited* predictions about its future development.

Apart from the possibility of its being falsified by *extraneous* events (extraneous to its frame of reference), the generalization is further weakened by its narrow empirical foundations. There are a number of anthropological analyses of Malay peasantry, and other studies, by both economists and geographers, provide information

1. Many people have assisted in the preparation of this article, by providing information, discussing difficult points with me, criticizing drafts, or doing all of these things. I am particularly grateful for the help of Dr. M. R. Allen, Dr. E. K. Fisk, Syed Husin Ali, Dr. Chandra Jayawardena, Mr. A. R. Mokhzani, Dr. J. Purcall, Dr. W. Roff, and Che Zainab H. Kassim.

relevant to the problem. Unfortunately most studies lack the historical depth necessary for an analysis of trends, and the areas studied are neither numerous enough nor so selected as to form a random sample of Malay villages.

Readers familiar with the work of writers on Malayan agricultural economics, especially Dr. E. K. Fisk and Professor U. A. Aziz, will find much that is familiar in the argument which follows; I am not claiming a new discovery, but rather attempting to develop the sociological consequences of the concentration process, and at the same time arguing to social anthropologists that macro-changes in the economic foundations of Malay society should have a central place in their micro-analyses of Malay villages.

Most Malay peasants live from the cultivation of rice and rubber. Differences in the nature of these two crops make it useful to discuss them separately. Many other Malays, of similar cultural and economic level to the peasant agriculturalist, live by fishing. Under some definitions fishermen are not peasants, but it is more useful here to treat them with the peasantry, and also to regard as members of peasant society tenants and landless members of Malay villages (Firth, 1946, p. 22; 1964b, pp. 17–18).[1]

Rice cultivation

T. B. Wilson, in the most extensive discussion of Malay *padi* economics yet published (1958), clearly shows the existence of a 'high degree of concentration of ownership' in the sense of a 'great variation in the area of land per landowner'. This information, picturing the situation at the time the survey was made, cannot reveal whether the degree of concentration is changing, and some of Wilson's remarks imply that the degree of concentration is explained by the conditions under which the land was first brought into cultivation, especially by the strength of former 'feudal' control. Such influences are of obvious importance in understanding contemporary conditions, but they can merely explain a 'given' difference between areas in their degree of concentration deriving from their early history of settlement.

The point at issue here is rather different. Granted historical differences in the degree of concentration between areas, are all of them, nevertheless, subject to an increase in its extent? I believe this will be found to be so whether the area investigated is one where large

1. Students of Malay society will more fully understand my usage of the term peasant if I explain that it is intended as a translation of *orang kampong* with all the connotations that expression has in Malay.

landholdings date from the era of independent Malay administration or a newly developed Government settlement scheme, where all holdings are initially equal and regulations should preclude both fragmentation and the concentration of land ownership. Direct support for this belief comes from the investigations of A. R. Mokhzani. Working in Perlis he found both a marked tendency for poorer peasants to lose their land and for this land to pass to a small class of rich peasants rather than to previously landless villagers (Mokhzani, 1963). Even more significant information comes from his recent study of the Tanjong Karang irrigation area, undertaken as a sociologist working with a research team from the Department of Economics of the University of Malaya. Tanjong Karang was developed by Government, so that landholding was not determined by 'feudal' factors, but it has been cultivated long enough for sale and inheritance to affect ownership. In Tanjong Karang all holdings were initially of equal size, and ownership is ostensibly governed by regulations designed both to prevent the fragmentation of individual lots and the accumulation of multiple lots in individual hands. Despite these rules, Mokhzani found both the sale and accumulation of half units, and people owning three or more units (of three acres each). These transfers are not, and cannot be, registered; the land is therefore not held under legally registered title, but the economic and social pressures making for fragmentation and concentration have proved too strong for mere regulation.[1]

1. Unregistered transfers of property are common throughout Malay society, affecting boats (Firth, 1946, p. 135) as well as land. There are many reasons for this. Many States have a large administrative backlog in registration. Moreover, to the peasant socially effective ownership in the village is normally adequate without official countenancing. Peasants commonly shrink from contact with officialdom. It is an unfamiliar world where they are ill at ease, and where even the simplest transaction can waste much time. Transfers also involve some expense, but peasants would still fail to register them even if there were no fee. On inheritance the undivided title symbolizes the unity of the heirs. To the peasant legally registered division of a dead parent's property is tantamount to severing the ties which united the family through the deceased. When the division of the estate satisfies all heirs, and relations between them are good, the undivided title symbolizes these good relations. Even when the heirs cannot agree on an equitable division of the estate, they can avoid the issue by a rough-and-ready division which is not registered; this course provides an acceptable temporary compromise without prejudicing the claims of the dissatisfied heirs. I have noticed a tendency for legal division to take place in the second generation, when grandchildren endeavour to sort things out, complicated as they are by further division of the initial shares. The grandchildren do not feel as close as their parents, and are not bound by the *wasiat* (will, or death-bed wish, which Malays are very loth to flout) of their grandparent, the registered owner, who probably asked his children to stay together and not quarrel over property.

Recent work by Dr. J. Purcall (1964) in Province Wellesley provides further evidence for the concentration hypothesis. Purcall's synchronic study shows extensive tenantry and a high degree of concentration of ownership. His judgment (personal communication) that these features are becoming more pronounced derives indirect statistical support from a comparison of the four villages he studied, for it appears that the village of most recent settlement has a lower level of tenancy than the others; the argument being that the longer an area has been cultivated, the further advanced is the process of concentration.

If we may assume at least the probability of a country-wide tendency towards land concentration, how is it to be explained? Ultimately the explanation must be sought in the increase of the Malay rural population[1] which has outstripped any increase in rice production. Although Government has over the years carried out several extensive schemes to provide new *padi* land, and is currently engaged in much rural development work through FLDA and other schemes, while at the same time endeavouring to raise the productivity of land already under cultivation by irrigation works and technical advice and assistance, such developments cannot keep pace with the increasing numbers dependent on *padi* planting for their main income.[2]

In simplified form the argument may be presented as an arithmetical average the numerator of which is the number of souls expecting support from rice planting, and the denominator the area of land available to provide that support multiplied by 'y', the state of technique.

$$\frac{\text{Souls entitled to support}}{\text{'y'} \times \text{cultivated area}}$$

If the natural rate of population increase outstrips the increase in the denominator the peasantry face impoverishment unless employment off the land can absorb a significant number of the increase in population, or they can find additional sources of income within the village economy, so that the average does not represent their total income position.

1. Caldwell (1963) calculated the increase in Malay rural population during the decade 1947–57 at 17 per cent.
2. Two articles by Dr. Fisk (Fisk, 1963a and 1963b) demonstrate clearly the extent of the problems which confront the Malaysian Government in its attempts to improve the Malay peasant economy, and justify my pessimistic view on the likelihood of any radical improvement in this sector.

In general neither of these mitigating influences has been strong enough. Duck-rearing, or fish from the *padi* fields, may provide additional income, but do not suffice to change the picture of almost complete dependence on rice cultivation. Against this must be set the decline in rural handicrafts in the face of industrial competition. Nor is there enough outside (urban) employment for surplus villagers. Malaya as a whole is faced with a gigantic problem in finding employment for her rapidly increasing young population, and it would require enormous investment simply to provide work for all the young people who enter the labour market each year (Wheelwright, 1965, pp. 62–70). What is more, the special place of the Malays in the Malayan plural society places them at a great disadvantage in competing for what work is available. During the Emergency (1948–60) enrolment in the Security Forces was a very important source of employment for village Malays, but this avenue of escape from the village closed as the Emergency ended.[1]

In Malaya the large alluvial valleys best suited for rice cultivation are already under intense cultivation. But, as the famous terracing feats of some Asian peoples show, with enough hard work even the most difficult terrain can be made to yield a crop. Throughout Malaya there are areas which could be made into rice fields with little technical difficulty. The problem is rather one of cost. If the Malay population were increasing only slowly then it is conceivable that the area of rice land might be increased in step with the growth of rural population, even, perhaps, from the resources of the village economy itself; but to provide new *padi* land at the same rate as population has recently increased would require a rate of capital accumulation far beyond the resources of the peasantry, and even beyond the resources of the nation, even if there were not so much more attractive alternative opportunities for investment.

Population pressure on resources provides the background for the analysis which follows. The next task is to explain why the process leads to concentration rather than general impoverishment, and at the same time to introduce any more sociological variables which may be relevant to our understanding of this broad demographic and economic process.

The typical Malay peasant maintains a precarious balance between income and consumption. There are no national statistics on aver-

1. Mobilization to counter Indonesian *Konfrontasi* may serve to create employment opportunities for village youths in the same way as the Emergency, and if so might serve to bring about a welcome reallocation of the Malaysian national income towards the Malay, although hardly on the same scale as the Emergency.

age incomes, but collecting data from a number of sources, Fisk (1963a, p. 167) finds a range of incomes per household of between $(Mal.)60·00 to $120·00 per month. Obviously people with such low incomes have a low standard of living and cannot save much. This would be so whatever the ethnic or social group in question, but I think there are also certain special Malay characteristics which will tend to maintain consumption at the level of current income. I have discussed the Malay economic personality elsewhere (Swift, 1962) and shall merely repeat my view that it is marked by fatalism and a short-run economic orientation. These characteristics are emphasized by a combination of extreme Malay concern with shame (*malu*) and the absence of clearly defined status groups *within* the peasantry. These make the peasant strive for a level of consumption rather higher than he can afford.

Of course there are status differences among peasants, but these are generally differences in acquired status, expressed through a style of life which primarily reflects income level. In the village, prestige is potentially open to anyone who is successful economically. The Malay peasant does not believe that he is inherently inferior to any other peasant, and so, given the powerful driving force of *malu* and the fact that status is largely expressed through durable consumer goods, he will strive to possess whatever his neighbour owns. This striving could theoretically give rise to long-term plans for economic accumulation, but because of the other facets of the peasant's economic personality it is rather seen in the allocation of his current income.

Malay family organization intensifies the situation. Divorce is very frequent, and the durability of a marriage is very closely related to continued successful performance of marital roles.[1] The Malay husband role emphasizes provision for the financial needs of the family, and so the husband is under pressure to buy for his wife and children whatever his neighbours buy for theirs. At the same time the high divorce rate, and the wife's consequent insecurity, make her reluctant to accept present abstinence in the long-run interests of the family as a collectivity.

Even the parent-child relation in the Malay family works for a high rate of consumption. One form of the frequently remarked indulgence by Malay parents of their young children is meeting their demands for things which have to be bought: cakes, sweets, ice-

1. In terms of current theories which define social structure by mutuality of role expectations, this statement is a truism. The matter is not one of fulfilment and non-fulfilment, but of degree, of a tolerable level of non-fulfilment; tolerance must be lower in a society where divorce is normal and readily obtained.

cream, and toys. Trivial as these items may be, they can add up to a large amount for a peasant with a large family and a low income.

I now want to call upon the well-known 'demonstration effect'. There may be parts of Asia where the peasantry do not continually see the products of modern industry, or where, if they see them, their view of their proper place in society prevents them feeling a desire for them or a right to hope for them.[1] This is certainly not the case in Malaya. For the Malay villager both direct observation of town life and mass media, such as radio, films, and the press, present as both normal and desirable a standard of life higher than the average peasant can afford, but which, nevertheless, he wants and feels he should be able to afford. The effect of this is that the socially normal standards against which the peasant has to match his stable, or even declining, income, are continually rising.

I certainly do not consider the Malay peasant profligate. For most peasants even survival on their low incomes requires great care and skill in the day-to-day management of their affairs. The question is rather one of the motives and attitudes which partly determine economic behaviour than a simple matter of careful foresight. Social features other than poverty inhibit the peasantry from making adequate provision for the future. Some test of this can be made if we consider peasant reactions to a sudden rise in real income. Despite increases in the cost of living, the high rubber prices of the Korean War boom produced substantial increases in real income for rubber-growing smallholders.[2] All accounts indicate that they reacted by raising their consumption standards, so that the collapse of the boom found them possessing consumer durables, many of which were subsequently pawned or repossessed, but with no improvement in their long-run income earning capacity or in reserves. In a similar, if less dramatic, fashion, my own field work (in Negri Sembilan) was carried out during a time of good rubber prices, and I was able to observe, over two years, how increased income was taken up by gradual improvements in day-to-day consumption or the acquisition of goods such as furniture and wireless sets. It is true that these illustrations refer to rubber growers, but they serve to docu-

1. This would seem to be the view of Burmese peasants as described by Nash (1965) where the emphasis is on cutting wants to meet income. While the Malay peasant may not be entrepreneurial in his attempts to meet his wants, he leaves the observer little doubt that he feels them, even if he appears to do little practical about meeting them.
2. Although not especially concerned with the peasant economy, Meek's (in Silcock, 1961) study of the Korean War boom gives an indication of its effects on peasant incomes.

R

ment common peasant economic attitudes (and similar windfall increases in income are not readily illustrated from rice cultivation).

The peasant, then, consumes nearly all his income. For the rice-grower the position is made worse by the seasonal nature of his crop. Until a few years ago most Malay *padi* farmers harvested a single crop, and even with the increasing practice of double-cropping the peasant will receive money in significant amounts only twice a year. Typically he needs credit to buy consumption goods until the harvest. This has proved a fertile source of exploitation by the rice-dealer/storekeeper who can tie the cultivator to him through debt, or alternatively by the rich Malay who has the resources to buy grain in the fields before it is ready for harvesting at prices substantially lower than he will eventually receive.[1] Recently Government credit agencies, and close control of the licensing of rice-dealers and millers, mitigated this form of exploitation, but however successful these reforms may be, they can only ensure that the peasant receives a larger proportion of the value of his crop, or the tenant of his share; they cannot reverse the long-term pressures of population on living standards.

I do not believe that land changes hands frequently through such seasonal debt. It might. One hears occasionally of peasants becoming more and more indebted with each season until they are forced to part with their land. I see such exploitation, where it occurs, as a further obstacle to peasant saving, although further data from the impoverished North-west may force me to revise this impression.

Land sale occurs primarily as a response to 'extraordinary expenditures'—non-recurrent financial obligations too large to meet from current income, while the peasant possesses no adequate savings.

Ceremonials are a prime occasion for such extraordinary expenditures.[2] Marriages are the most expensive ceremonies, a daughter's wedding normally costing more than a son's. Even with a son's wedding the widespread practice of giving marriage expenses (*belanja kahwin*) to the bride's family, and the status significance of these expenses to both families, make it a costly event. A man who cannot afford a proper wedding for his child will postpone the ceremony, but he cannot do this indefinitely. Malay society places great emphasis on the early marriage of girls, and the fear of *malu* makes village gossip, or its likelihood, a powerful sanction against undue postponement (Swift, 1965, p. 114). If waiting does not produce a

1. By this *jual janji* arrangement the rich Malay avoids the sin of usury (*riba*).
2. The rituals are simple and inexpensive; it is the associated feasting which is costly.

windfall, what can the peasant parent do but sell or mortgage his land? He will probably prefer to mortgage, for he can then cling to the hope that he will eventually be able to redeem the land; but it can only be a faint hope—if he could not save before, how can he do so now that his income is even lower? I know, and my observations are supported by Mokhzani (personal communication), that mortgage is frequently followed at some later date by outright sale.

Ceremonial expenses are the most common extraordinary expenditures, and the example which would occur most readily to peasants, but there are many others. Sickness, for example, can cause great economic difficulty. Obviously, if sickness should prevent the peasant working, it will cause direct loss of income, but apart from this, seeking cures can be very expensive. If a member of his family is sick, the peasant will first seek the help of the local curers (*bomoh, dukun*). These people will not be very expensive, but neither is the peasant inclined to put great faith in them. When the local *dukun* are ineffective, he will look farther afield for prestigious curers, and is quite likely to incur heavy expenses to meet the curers' charges and travelling expenses, so that he is forced to sell or mortgage land.

Serious involvement with the law can also mean economic disaster for the family and near kin of the accused, since Malays will sell or pawn land to raise money for legal expenses, or to pay fines and damages, on behalf of close kin. People will even eat into their capital to visit children who are living some distance away. Perhaps a mother will become worried that her daughter, living with her wage-earning husband away from the village, is not being properly treated; or she may become *rindu* (pining for the absent) for her grandchildren. I suspect that women are especially liable to be seized by such feelings when other women in the village have recently been to visit their children or grandchildren. When in the grip of such feelings a woman will find no peace, and give her husband no peace, until he has raised the money for her to travel.

In some parts of Malaya the pilgrimage to Mecca provides a powerful incentive for elderly peasants to sell their property. Nowadays Government control of the pilgrimage endeavours to restrain people from making the journey if they will be destitute on their return, but it is said to have been common in the past for people to use everything they possessed to get to Mecca, hoping that they would die there. Ideological pressures are also working to lessen the harmful effects of the pilgrimage on the peasantry. The *haj* is one of the Five Pillars of Islam, but it is only obligatory on those who can afford it. Responsible religious teaching emphasizes the conditional nature of the obligation and points out that, so far from gaining merit (*pahala*) from the pilgrimage, the person who ruins himself and his family to make the journey is doing wrong. Even so, the pilgrimage still remains a powerful incentive for pious peasants to sell land.

All these occasions for extraordinary expenditure will not have the same importance for every individual. A childless couple might escape all of them. Also the list could easily be extended, for it is merely intended to illustrate the concept of extraordinary expenditures with only a few examples amongst those I have known.

Extraordinary expenditures derive their great significance from those features of peasant society which prevent people saving, so that to meet them land must frequently change hands.

In this context we must also consider another feature of peasant economy and society, their commercialization. This appears in the growing tendency for peasants to concentrate on the production of a cash crop while using money for all their other needs, and in the decline of traditional co-operative obligations in favour of paid services. At the same time as population pressure threatens the peasant's income standard, and the socially acceptable level of average consumption is rising, more and more of the peasant's needs and obligations are expressed through the cash nexus. Where once a man would have prepared for his child's wedding by accumulating village products, and would have expected substantial contributions from his kin and neighbours, he now has to buy goods. Where once he would have furbished his house for the occasion by the co-operative labour of these kin and neighbours, he will now probably need to hire a carpenter, and to buy timber rather than collect it from the jungle.

Extraordinary expenditures represent calls on income which is already allocated to day-to-day consumption. Logically complementary would be a failure to receive expected income—for this too might force a peasant to sell land so that his family might survive. Agricultural production is in constant danger of natural calamity, and even if physical production is maintained, price fluctuations may reduce the monetary return below the level at which the peasant can meet his cash commitments. Although any of these factors might cause hardship to Malay peasants, I do not think they would prove major causes of land transfer. Natural disaster is likely to be only temporary; floods and droughts are not likely to be prolonged, and the Malayan climate will normally allow planting out of season if the main crop is lost. Hit by a temporary setback of this kind, the peasant will probably struggle along until the next harvest rather than sell land to maintain consumption. He is helped in this by the low level of fixed cash obligations. In Malaya land taxes are low, and the normal methods of cultivation do not entail great outlay of working capital. On the other hand, Government control limits the fluctuations in the price of rice. The peasant may not get the full Government guaranteed price,[1] but at least he is not confronted by the great price fluctuations typical of so many tropical export crops.

The peasant can also manage without most purchased consumption goods for a while, if he must. Various subsistence techniques, such as collecting wild vegetables and catching fish, can be used for short periods, while expenditure on items such as clothes and school books is simply postponed. Moreover, as long as the disaster is not general, the peasant will normally be able to supplement his income by wage work until he receives his new crop. Another possibility is that there will be a subsidiary local industry to which the temporarily distressed cultivator may turn; making sago leaf thatch is an example.

My argument is that selling land to maintain consumption income is not a major cause of land transfer, not that it never occurs. Old people, who cannot work their own land while it will not support them as rentiers, may sell some of it when they need money, and so might a divorcee with children to support.

Once the peasant has sold his land he has little hope of acquiring more except by purchase, for in the main areas of rice cultivation there is no longer free land awaiting clearance. Also, because few of them have savings, most peasants are not in a position to buy land when it becomes available. Most small independent proprietors just manage to survive; some of them, confronted by extraordinary expenditures which force them to sell land, fall from the ranks of independent producers with little hope of restoring their position. The land they sell is bought by those few rich peasants with a savable surplus above their (socially defined) consumption needs, or by outsiders with savings. New land adds to their surplus, permitting further accumulation.

If most people cannot save, how then are some people able to buy property when others are forced to sell? Now we are considering the position of a small minority, and if we wish to know why, in any particular village, two or three people are richer than their fellows, we could well ask the other villagers. They will probably mention one or both of two factors: meanness and a fortunate inheritance.

1. Allegations of middle-man exploitation are frequent in the Malay press; cf. e.g. *Berita Minggu*, 14 March 1965, pp. 4–5.

The meanness will probably seem merely normal care and foresight to a Westerner. I have been struck by the way economically successful peasants are judged mildly deviant by village standards. They will carefully save when others would spend, and work when others rest. Such activity is accompanied by a chorus of direct or indirect comment disparaging the effort. 'Do you want to own everything? . . . What is the good of all that wealth if you won't allow your children to taste it? . . . Just look at him, he's the richest man in the village and is still not satisfied. . . . Come now, we are not strangers (are related). Lend me—[although because we are not strangers there isn't much hope that I'll repay you].' The rich peasant meets many social pressures which call for unusual insensitivity to *malu* and the opinions of others if they are to be resisted. But if they are not withstood the richer man will quickly fall to the level of his fellows—hence my reference to the richer peasant as mildly deviant.

Fortunate inheritance simply means that if a wealthy man has only one or two children they will inherit much property and be favourably placed to continue accumulating land. If, on the other hand, he has many heirs, individual shares will probably be too small to permit further saving. Both Muslim law and village custom (which generally gives equal shares to all children) favour land fragmentation, and each devolution sees the land divided into smaller and smaller parcels, frequently too tiny for economic use.[1]

Malu has already been used in this argument as an explanation of some of the pressure which keeps the consumption of the average peasant at about the level of his current income. It may also be used as a supplementary factor explaining the ability of the richer man to save. *Malu* makes the ordinary peasant endeavour to maintain the consumption level of his fellows. Once he is obviously trying to surpass them he lays himself open to *malu* in another way, for, unless he is very skilful in asserting his status, his fellow villagers will mock his pretensions. This will be especially so if he appears to be trying to 'crash the class barrier', modelling his life on that of the westernized upper class rather than on village standards.

Peasant values constrain the behaviour of rich villagers in another relevant way. All peasants value highly the acquisition of land; to own enough land to live in comfort without working is the most generally cherished goal. To most peasants this remains a lottery phantasy, but to the peasant with a savable surplus it provides a

1. Investigations of land fragmentation tend to concentrate on legal ownership. There is need for further study of fragmentation in use, for this certainly does not completely reflect the multiple small titles.

powerful stimulus to direct his savings into land accumulation, especially as social restraints limit his expenditure in direct consumption.

Given the assumptions of considerable population increase far outstripping any increase in the resources available for its support, and of some initial income differentiation, the argument of transfer from poor to richer peasants is logical and simple. Land concentration is interesting enough as an intra-village process, but it becomes more significant when Malay peasant society is seen in the context of the national society.

Malaysia is a plural society. A common feature of such societies is the way commercial development and population pressure lead to the transfer of land from the original inhabitants to migrants. The ethnic dimension makes this process into much more than a simple matter of economic concentration.

In Malaya too the Malays typically lose their land to encroachments from migrants, especially the Chinese, but also through usury to Chetties and Sikhs. For most Malay peasants this ethnic transfer has historical rather than contemporary importance, because, in the major areas of Malay settlement, the land has been made into Malay Reservation. Within a reservation only a Malay may acquire land, so that a Malay owning reservation land can only sell it to another Malay, and cannot use it as pledge to get money from a usurer.[1] As we are now discussing rice land it should also be mentioned that in Malaya few people other than Malays practise rice cultivation. Thus, while the reservation policy obstructs any desire on the part of other races to own rice land, the attractions of other forms of investment make it doubtful whether any such desire is strongly felt.

To digress: with lands other than ricefields, and outside Malay reservations, the process of transfer of Malay land to other, wealthier groups continues. Thus, as Malayan towns grow they encroach on, and sometimes surround, Malay villages. When this occurs, slowly perhaps but surely, the Malays will sell out and move to remoter areas. Any reader who has the opportunity to drive around either Singapore or Penang looking at areas where Chinese live in Malay houses, which they would not build, or occupy land well covered with fruit trees, which they would not plant, or who sees the numbers of Chinese living in what the guide books will still

---

1. To most Malays taking interest is a serious sin; pledging land to a moneylender would therefore normally mean pledging it to a non-Malay. Both Javanese and Arab Muslim usurers flourished in Java, so one cannot assume that Islam will preclude absolutely the growth of usury among Malays.

assure him are Malay areas, can soon convince himself of the extent of this process.

There is thus continual migrant pressure on Malay land, but this is contained in most agricultural areas by the policy of Malay reservations. However, there are other sources of extra-village money for the purchase of peasant land. The most important of them is salaried employment, above all Government employment. Every village has people, still regarded as members, who work and live outside the village, or who have done so. Most of them hold quite poorly paid positions which will not allow much saving for land acquisition, but white-collar workers can and do save to buy land. Civil servants frequently use their savings for the purchase of village property, especially in an area where they have kinship connexions. Until recently it seemed the major goal of most Malay civil servants to acquire enough land while in the service to permit a comfortable retirement to their village of origin. The policy of Malay reservations, restricting the demand for Malay land and therefore restricting the price, must be a valuable aid to them in their pursuit of this goal.

A number of recent developments have, I think, worked to lessen the attractiveness of land purchase. As Malaya becomes more urbanized, the town-dwelling civil servant becomes more socially and culturally differentiated from the village Malay and closer to other non-Malay town bourgeois of similar occupation and style of life. Many civil servants now appreciate the amenities of town life and do not relish the idiocy of rural life on retirement. Accordingly, they make the purchase of a town house their first saving goal; quite apart from its eventual use after retirement, a town house is frequently quite a profitable investment in the meantime. Independence has also seen much growth of secondary and tertiary industry in Malaya, bringing increased opportunities for investment in stocks and shares. Nevertheless, even with additional outlets for investment, land buying still continues. Government regulations are so framed as severely to restrict a serving officer's opportunities to acquire property, but they are widely evaded, for example by the registration of land purchases in the name of some complaisant relative.

Land concentration is therefore not simply a matter of differentiation in the village, but also includes the transfer of peasant land to an upper, official class.

Rubber growing

Much of the preceding discussion can be applied directly to peasant rubber growing. But some contrasts should also be noted. First, there is the much greater attractiveness of rubber land as an invest-ment, which means that the demand is not confined solely to Malays. But, as with rice fields, most Malay rubber is protected by the reser-vation policy, so that the effects of concentration are largely con-fined to the Malay section of the plural society. Another way in which the reservation policy aids the Malay rentier should also be noted. Reservation restricts ownership, but it does not impose restrictions on the people to whom the land may be let on a profit-sharing basis or who may be employed to work it; a 'Malay' holding may there-fore be benefiting a Malay landlord and a Chinese contractor and labourers (Fisk, 1964, pp. 50 ff.).[1]

Secondly, the continuous receipt of income rules out the need for consumer credit. The tapper receives his income every few days, and can even use the proceeds of a morning's tapping to buy his evening meal. Finally, for much of Malaya the shortage of rubber land is not an ecological or a cost 'given', but a consequence of official policy. When rubber became known as a smallholder crop it was adopted enthusiastically by the Malay peasant. Unfortunately, only a few years after the new crop became popular, Government began to restrict output, and forbade (to all intents and purposes) new planting (Bauer, 1948). With some slight modifications the prohibition of new planting was maintained until Independence. Nowadays many FLDA settlement schemes include quite generous allotments of land for rubber planting, but this cannot provide for all the peasants who would like to clear jungle and plant rubber (so turning their labour into capital), simply extending cultivation into the jungle reserves surrounding their village, without any of the expensive accessories of a full-blown development scheme and with-out any need for migration. Fringe Alienation schemes improve the position slightly in this respect, but as with rice-planting, any likely increase in acreage can hardly cope with expected population in-creases, let alone make any significant impact on existing land hunger.

In rice cultivation it is the land, albeit much improved by irrigation works, which is the valuable asset. With rubber it is the trees which give value to the land. This raises the possibility that even if the acreage is fixed, the trees planted on the land might be improved, especially now that much superior planting material is available,

---

1. I would normally expect Malay landlords who were living in a village to feel obliged to employ Malays if they wanted work, otherwise much hostility would follow their refusal to *tolong bangsa* (help one's race), a nationalist slogan which was widely heard when I lived in Malaya and which certainly reflected popular feeling.

while much peasant rubber is old, damaged, or diseased. The Malaysian Government will make a grant of $(Mal.)750·00 for every acre satisfactorily replanted. The peasants complain (as peasants will) that this is not enough, but it would certainly go much of the way towards replanting costs if the peasant used as much as possible of his own labour. But few smallholders will replant. Many of them know that by replanting with superior stock they will acquire a much more valuable asset and make a long-term profit, but few of them, especially owner-tappers who can just manage with the output of their one small lot, are prepared to destroy their source of income for from five to seven years. During two years of field work, in an atmosphere of constant propaganda for replanting, I met only one owner of a single smallholding (c. 3 acres) who had done this.

The owner of several holdings (and most of the larger owners hold their land in this way, since they were acquired either by piecemeal development or the purchase of scattered lots as they came on the market) can fairly readily take out one or more lots from tapping and replant, while living on the income from his other plots. Indeed, if the owner is an absentee still receiving an official salary, he may well be more interested in improving the income potential of his property than in current return. In this way the replanting and subsidy scheme work to subsidize a further improvement in the position of those landowners already better off than most, so further accentuating the effects of the concentration process.

This ability of the larger village landowner to replant is an important economy of scale. It has also been suggested that recent technical improvements have increased the importance of economies of scale. It seems to me that economies of scale can almost as readily be obtained for the smallholder through co-operative or specialized private agencies, and this appears to be happening with latex collection as an alternative to the production of sheet rubber. But even if we grant the competitive advantage which new economies of scale give to estates, this advantage cannot be used to explain the concentration of peasant holdings.

The statistical division between estates and smallholdings is usually placed at 100 acres. But 100 acres would be an unusually large village holding, and concentration as it occurs in the village is usually within the statistical category of smallholdings. It therefore does not amount to the creation of estates out of smallholdings (in a manner analogous to the Enclosures of the Agrarian Revolution).

Theoretically, the proprietor of several small village holdings may be in a position to integrate their operation so as to derive some economies, but I did not see it happen, except perhaps for a man taking one or more plots out of operation to replant, and not many peasant proprietors wish to do even this. Far from observing economies of scale, I have been impressed by a very important diseconomy involved in operating several scattered holdings: the difficulty of controlling labour. Rubber holdings can be badly damaged by careless work; they also yield a daily return. By occasional visits the owner can inspect the standard of tapping and general care, but to check the yield he must be present when the worker is preparing sheet from the latex, and even then he may be cheated over the proportion of scrap to sheet rubber.[1] An alternative to share-tapping is to let the holding to someone who pays a fixed rent and then retains all the yield. This is dangerous. When the agreement is negotiated the tapper will give all manner of assurances on the care with which he will treat the trees, but, once he starts work, he is naturally more likely to tap to maximize his returns without regard for the state of the holding.

The owner who employs several tappers cannot keep a daily check on them all; he cannot rely on the workers' sense of obligation; nor does he wield any sanctions beyond terminating the tapping agreement (sacking the tapper), leaving the tapper with whatever he has stolen from the owner, while he has to find another tapper who will probably be no more reliable than the other.

If kinsmen and affines are employed they will be more trustworthy, but their use raises control problems of another kind. As kin they have a legitimate expectation that the conditions of the share agreement will not be rigidly applied to them. They will not cheat the owner, but they will ask for favours which he is obliged to grant. At least in my personal observation, village owners of multiple holdings found the control of share-tappers a continual harassment.

The absentee owner is in an even worse position, for he cannot be continually checking his tappers' performance. One reason for the willingness of absentee owners to replant, beyond their lesser need for current income, may be that the labour problem makes it so difficult for them to secure an adequate current return, so that replanting represents little sacrifice.

---

1. Scrap is the latex which drips into the cup after the main supply has been collected, or which adheres to the channel the tapper makes in the bark. The tapper may neglect to empty all the cups, later taking the contents of those he left as scrap, or he may collect the latex early, while the sap is still flowing freely, again increasing the scrap. Scrap belongs to the tapper, and is as valuable to him as sheet rubber since he does not have to share it with the owner of the holding.

In summary, we may say that, as with rice, the combination of population growth and a stock of capital resources increasing at a much slower rate brings most of the peasantry down to the socially defined minimum consumption level; even peasants who have satisfactorily adjusted incomings and outgoings at this level are unlikely to make adequate provision for extraordinary expenditures, and so when they arise, are likely to have to sell or mortgage their assets. These then pass into the hands of richer peasants or the salariat. This salariat, while they may be of village origin or acknowledge village connexions, now have many characteristics of a separate urbanized class.

My main sources for this discussion of smallholder rubber growing are the work of Syed Husin Ali in Johore and my own research in Negri Sembilan (see S. Husin Ali, 1964, and Swift, 1962, 1964, 1965).

The fishing industry

Concentration of ownership and income differentiation are also to be seen in the Malay fishing industry, but arise there from radically different causes. For information on this industry we rely mainly on Firth's classic monograph (1946), but reference to a later study of Malay fishermen in Southern Thailand (Fraser, 1960) permits an interesting comparison.

This concentration on the east coast, although dictated by the availability of material, represents a major gap in the discussion. The Malay fishermen of the west coast have their own problems, or perhaps it would be better to say their own version of common problems, as can be seen in the controversy over *belat pok* fish traps which ranged the small boat fishermen against the wealthier fish trap owners, and in the newer issue of *pukat harimau*, purse seines worked from trawlers, which has even given rise to serious violence.[1]

Firth's analysis shows that, just as with other peasants, fishing communities are differentiated in income and ownership of productive assets. But, in major contrast to rice and rubber cultivation, fishing seems characterized by greater divisibility in both technique and economic organization. A variety of techniques allow even small amounts of capital to be put to productive use, while, with major capital items such as boats and nets, shared ownership seems common even when the item is not technically divisible. In such circumstances

1. Cf. *Straits Times*, 2 November 1965. A sea battle took place off Tjg. Piandang, Kuala Kurau, between inshore fishermen and trawlermen from Pangkor in which one man was killed and several injured. I am told that this struggle largely ranges Chinese against Malays.

a poor man, with industry and luck, may accumulate a small amount of capital and gradually build it into a boat, a section of a large net, or a share of one of these. Clearly not everyone in the society will be successfully mobile in this way, but at least the chances are greater than those of a landless labourer acquiring his own rice or rubber holding, because of the much greater initial investment the latter must make to acquire a worthwhile piece of land.

To what extent do these conditions still obtain? A complete answer to this question must await the publication of Professor Firth's restudy of Kelantan, but I am fortunately able to anticipate this information to some extent.[1] The major change is towards more capital-intensive production methods. One figure will serve to illustrate this point: Firth estimates the value of a contemporary boat group at $(Mal.)40,000. Even then the Malay industry remains confined in its operations and is distressed by trawler competition.

Capitalization at this level must reduce the chances of upward mobility. More than this, Firth reports that the control of fishing is tending to pass from the master fishermen to middleman dealers because of the difficulty of mobilizing the large amounts of capital now required.

If we contrast this position with that of the Rusembilan fishing community in Patani (Fraser, 1960), the main difference which emerges is the relative economic backwardness of Thailand, as if these border regions were now catching up with earlier developments in Malaya. This shows in two important ways. The people of Rusembilan are developing rubber holdings, apparently little hindered by administrative regulations. We also read how men, who do not themselves possess much capital, can develop holdings for others, retaining some property for themselves, or may even struggle with the development alone. The avenue for the conversion of one's labour directly into capital is therefore not closed in Thailand (Fraser, 1960, pp. 67–9). Secondly, the fishing techniques now being introduced in Rusembilan merely involve buying motors, a matter of hundreds of dollars rather than the thousands now required in Kelantan.

Rusembilan, therefore, while having differences of wealth within the community, does not show the same hindrances to peasant econo-

1. I was privileged to attend the Research Seminar in Kuala Lumpur of the London-Cornell Project at which Professor Firth discussed his new material, and he has kindly answered further written queries. Errors in the use of this material are my own. (Detailed data have now been made available in the 2nd edition of *Malay Fishermen*, 1966.)

mic mobility I have discussed for Malaya, nor the same pressures to economic concentration. Nor, given the disadvantaged position of the Malays in Thailand, does society contain the same Malay élites as have emerged with the modernization and Independence of Malaya.

The social implications of the concentration process

Traditional (pre-British) Malay society was evidently not equalitarian. Classical literature and historical sources (which can still include first- or second-hand memories), point to a markedly superior status position for an aristocracy comprising people of royal descent and others of distinguished but non-royal family, especially members of families with hereditary right to court office or district chieftainships (Gullick, 1958). Within the upper class highest status went to holders of political power and those most closely related to them. Little is known about the internal differentiation of the lower class comprising the mass of the people (*rayat*) beyond accounts of the nature and extent of debt-slavery during the disturbed times which preceded British control.

Whatever the traditional facts, the former social organization no longer exists, and the implications of economic change must be worked out for a different model. A basic element in building a model of contemporary Malay social organization is the stratification of society into two broad social classes, a Westernized upper class and the peasantry. The upper class is primarily composed of Western educated administrators and their families, but also includes those vestiges of the traditional aristocracy who have had their economic position secured by receipt of political pensions and other opportunities, a few business men, and, since Independence, some political leaders. Within this group traditional status is highly prized by those who possess it, but cannot be regarded as a primary determinant of class position.

Within the peasantry claims to traditional status have little meaning. British control meant the 'decapitation' of Malay society (Fallers, 1961, p. 109; Redfield, 1956, p. 78). Administration has taken away the powers of locally based traditional political leadership and created a new administrative hierarchy outside peasant society. I have found Malay peasant society fundamentally equalitarian internally, while externally accepting a two-class conception of Malay society in which the peasants occupy the lower position.

In the village, judgments of people's worth are continually made;

these operate to put pressure on both social extremes; on the unsuccessful to achieve average standards, but also on the successful not to flout and endanger these standards. Pressures of mockery, criticism, and thinly veiled hostility can work effectively in a village because of Malay sensitivity to the opinion of others.

Families with claims to traditional rank may still feel their superiority. *Raja* families are proud, and endeavour to maintain rank endogamy as long as this does not conflict too much with social reality. (An educated commoner with a good job will probably be an acceptable son-in-law if there is no equivalent *raja* available.) This special position of *raja* can be marked in areas where they form a large proportion of the population, say in a former royal settlement, but their ability to feel superior among themselves is not the same as securing general acceptance of their own estimation of their worth. *Syed* too may feel proud; diehards among them still maintain that according to religious law a *Sharifah* may not marry any other than a *Syed*, and it is only a few years since the newspapers were reporting the efforts of a *Syed* family in Johore to get their daughter's marriage set aside on just this ground. But in general, if their pride shows in the slightest arrogance it will be resented rather than accepted by ordinary folk. If anything, people with traditional status pretensions must be especially careful not to give their neighbours the impression that they are *sombong* (proud or stuck up) for otherwise *raja* will be mocked, sometimes openly, as *raja bangsat* (poverty-stricken prince) while the *Syed* will be called an Arab beggar or *penjual ayat* (charm-seller).

Wealth, an acquired characteristic, entitles a man to respect, and is a necessary qualification for effective village leadership. In general, most Malay village wealth is new wealth, since it derives from economic expansion during the British occupation, especially the creation of a smallholding rubber industry. So wealth is not only in principle an acquired characteristic but in fact one. The respect accorded to wealth properly used takes the form of individual respect for the man who by his own skill, character, or luck has become richer than his fellows.

A special position for the wealthy is hard to combine with the ideology of equality which is given institutional expression in patterns of village co-operation and mutual assistance between neighbours. On the one hand, the rich man is worthy of respect and entitled to exercise leadership; on the other hand he is merely a fellow villager, neighbour or kinsman, and should not feel that the fate which has brought him wealth entitles him to behave differently from anyone else. The social ambiguity is combined with a marked psychological ambivalence, so that at times the rich man is regarded with intense jealousy and hostility by his neighbours.

Not only is this current differentiation by wealth alone within the village quite a new phenomenon, it is also an unstable one in the early phase of the concentration process. By instability I mean that most wealthy peasants do not possess sufficient property to pass on large enough inheritance shares to make their heirs wealthy men in their turn. Unless the shares are large enough to give the heirs the crucial surplus for accumulation, one devolution will bring the family livelihood down to the ordinary level where an unfortunate exposure to the need for extraordinary expenditures can only be met by selling property. Although I have written elsewhere of classes within the peasantry (Swift, 1965) the great likelihood of downward generational mobility for the children of wealthy peasants now makes me incline towards reserving the term class for those situations where concentration has progressed so far that there is a good chance that children of wealthy peasants will be wealthy in their turn. This would provide a terminological recognition of the social transformation involved at this vague but nonetheless crucial stage in the development of the concentration process.

If there is an increasing trend towards concentration of landownership within the village there will be correspondingly marked changes in the social status organization. As the few wealthy peasants become increasingly differentiated in their income from their fellows, we may also expect their special social position to become more marked, and their increasing exclusion from patterns of equalitarian village solidarity.

Accelerated accumulation will also permit the wealthy to pass their position on to their children. There are a number of ways in which this might be done. The most obvious is simply to give the child enough land to make him wealthy too. Secondly, a parent's wealth might be used to give the child education and a place in the official class. Thirdly, wealth might be used to finance other business activities. At present there is little sign of the second and third alternatives taking place. As for education, class ideas inhibit the aspirations of even wealthy peasants for their children's future. Although some village parents may send their child to an English school for a year or two they are generally half-hearted about it, and the many problems which face a child from a Malay village adjusting to such a novel environment offer little encouragement to either child or parent. Even parents whose income matches that of a minor official are limited in their perceptions of what their child might become.

They desire that he be wealthy and influential in village society, but seem to give little consideration to the possibility of crashing the class barrier into the official class. With new business ventures too there is little peasant activity. This is a major problem in its own right, and here I can only mention the great obstacles which confront all Malay economic ventures, stemming from the plural society and the dominance by other ethnic groups of most of the Malayan economy.

While the position of the wealthy becomes more pronounced, the rest of the population will sink from independent landholding into either tenantry or labouring. At present the status position of the tenant is not very different from that of the small landholder, so long as he receives a comparable income. In village society there is no clear distinction between the man who works only his own land, the man who owns some land and rents some, and the man who rents all the land he works. But the same population pressure which reduces the size of average holdings will also worsen the position of the tenant and labourer. From Perlis, a rice area, Mokhzani reports that rents are rising; newspapers write of the various devices now used to exploit tenants, e.g. the exaction of 'tea-money' before allowing occupancy; and also from Perlis there is an account of a campaign in 1965 to exclude outside labour (from Kelantan and Thailand) from the work of rice harvesting, in the interests of local workers needing employment. My own work indicated a labour shortage, but that was almost a decade ago during a time when many young men were still serving with the security forces, and every year brings more youths seeking employment from the same limited capital stock.

If we may assume the development of pronounced economic differentiation within the village, then we may also predict corresponding changes in village social organization adjusting to the presence of élite families in village society. But the limited statistical evidence available does not exclude the possibility that what seems a trend towards the concentration of wealth will be offset by the effects of division on inheritance, and here it must be borne in mind that Malay families are much larger than they were even a generation ago. If this be so, then population pressure will lead to a general impoverishment of the peasantry, in which the emergence of some individuals as relatively wealthy is only a temporary phase.

Apart from concentration of land within the village, there is another aspect of the process, the passing of village land into the hands of an upper class who invest their savings in land. To this upper class agriculture is not their sole, or even their main, source

S

of wealth. Inheritance therefore cannot have the same effects in halting the concentration process. The death of a retired civil servant may well see the property which provided him with a comfortable retirement dispersed so that none of his heirs can live from this source alone. But they are most unlikely to need to do so; the children of officials will almost certainly, in good time, themselves take up salaried employment. The rich peasant remains an agriculturalist; neither he nor his family will be very different from other villagers. The absentee landowner, in contrast, is distinguished from the peasantry by much more than economic criteria. His ability to transmit class position to his children depends not on his ability to transmit land but on his ability to secure the correct employment qualifications for his children; an ability not hindered by the operation of inheritance rules.

The first generation of Malay Government servants in Malaya were naturally mainly of village origin. The second and third generations, in turn, while they might not have been born of village parents, at least maintained substantial ties with peasant kin, and probably retired to live among their relatives. In the village they were accorded a superior status that was little tainted by perception of class conflict. In general the peasantry accept the superiority of the official class, and would probably expect and welcome leadership from any member of that class living among them. There was, moreover, little foundation for economic conflict, for much of the official's income would derive from his salary or pension, and even when derived from the ownership of land it would not jar in a society where most people were independent proprietors themselves having the goal of one day owning enough land not to have to work.

Changes outside peasant society have led to the growth and differentiation of the administration and of a Westernized urban bourgeoisie generally. The development of this class in an independent Malaya is a very important social phenomenon which awaits detailed investigation; for example, the ability of the shared interests and culture of this class, although still limited by ethnic divisions, to counterbalance the communal feelings of the lower classes in each ethnic community, could be an important source of stability for Malayan society.

Discussion of this class must be largely hypothetical at this stage of Malaysian sociological development. Nevertheless an important feature of its growth is clearly relevant to our argument here, that is, the greater barriers between the two main classes of Malay society thus raised. An obvious example is the way in which independence has opened senior posts to Malays. Such changes have widened the gap between officials and peasantry now that the Malay official is not confined to junior positions in constant contact with the villagers.[1]

If national developments continually widen the gap between official and peasant, while economic processes increasingly place control of peasant land in absentee hands and the economic position of the peasantry generally deteriorates, we may expect the incipient but rarely expressed peasant opposition to the upper class to become more pronounced, especially if other sectors of the economy continue to prosper.

Such a development will have enormous political implications for Malaysia since the present political organization is largely founded on the willingness of the Malay peasantry to give their support to the United Malay Nationalist Organization, and through it to the Alliance Party. Contemporary Malayan policies are marked by the diversion of large amounts of government revenue to rural improvements. Such measures are a political necessity, given the potential power of the Malay peasantry and their poverty. But these ameliorative policies can only have a limited effect; the provision of roads, bridges, and schools may seem of great value to a population comprising mainly small independent landowners, but it does little to relieve the distress of the impoverished tenant or labourer, or indeed of the peasant who still owns land but too little of it. Land development schemes are more relevant, but even here, despite the great efforts being made, only a small number of those needing help may expect to benefit from them.[2]

Sophisticated ideological controversy is rare in Malaysian politics, and this gave particular interest to a recent (1965) debate between the Prime Minister of Singapore and the Federal Minister of Information (part of the general polemic which developed before the expulsion of Singapore from the Malaysian Federation). The point at issue was the relative importance of race and class in Malayan politics. One side points to the poverty of the Malays, as an ethnic group, compared with the Chinese, and maintains that the correction of this imbalance must be the primary political goal. The other side, pointing to the existence of some wealthy Malays and many poor

1. Mokhzani, 1964, provides useful insights into this, as well as other stratification issues.
2. The role of these schemes and others in providing politically effective symbolic reassurance should not be overlooked; I confess that I have tended to judge them by their adequacy to achieve their ostensible instrumental goals. (Edelman, 1964, especially chapter 2.)

Chinese, replies that this is the real situation needing correction, by a social democratic solution of the problems of poverty among all races of Malaysian citizens, that is to say, political action organized for class rather than ethnic goals.

In the consideration of this question much depends on the definition of class employed; if, as for the polemical Marx, class simply means an emotive division into the oppressed and the oppressors, class can provide ideological support for an anti-communal socialist programme, albeit one that will find little echo in the consciousness of the oppressed, who respond much more readily to racist slogans. But if, as for the analytic Marx, class refers to the place a social group occupies in the system of production, it is clear that in the ethnic specialization of Malayan plural society race and class largely coincide. In Malaya knowledge of an individual's race permits a fairly accurate prediction of his occupation or economic function, and vice versa. This is not to say that the Malays are a class and the Chinese a class, but rather that each ethnic group comprises a collection of classes with little overlap.

If the processes I have hypothesized, the creation of a multi-racial Westernized bourgeoisie, impoverishment of the peasantry, and urban unemployment (swelled by Malays who can find neither land nor employment in the village), become increasingly pronounced, they will obviously have far-reaching consequences for the structure of Malaysian society as a whole. A simplicist (vulgar) Marxist interpretation would be to predict an emerging lower class consciousness and class struggle transcending ethnic barriers. This might well be the outcome, but dissatisfaction can be channelled in other directions. Racial hostility is always a likely outcome even of *intra*-ethnic group tensions, for ethnic dislikes are firmly ingrained in the cultures of the various Malayan communities.

While we cannot predict confidently what form they will take, it is obvious that economic concentration must imply many short-run changes in Malay and therefore Malayan social organization. In the long run population pressure produces some sort of Malthusian breakdown, but obviously other things will cease to be equal long before that point is reached.

In this final section of my paper I have endeavoured to indicate the sort of social consequences which might follow from a process of economic concentration in Malay peasant society, and to suggest that this process with its consequences should be seen in the framework of other forces affecting Malayan society. To this end I have emphasized some aspects of contemporary social organization rather than attempt to give a rounded picture of the way village life now is. It is possible for a field observer, with his limited period of contact with his subject, not to be aware of concentration as a trend at all. It will probably merely seem that some individuals in the village have built up a measure of economic superiority which receives some status recognition, a degree of economic differentiation quite consistent with the persistence of the existing social organization, or even required by it, since it makes possible limited leadership. This was my initial view; my village contained three richer families, and from informants' accounts it seemed that there had been roughly the same number a generation ago; one man had maintained his father's position, another had declined but still held a better than average position, while the most aggressive accumulator had started from nothing and was still increasing his holdings. It seemed to me then that this merely represented another Asian version of the story of from clogs to clogs in three generations. Families within the village improved their position or declined owing to partition on inheritance, misfortune, or mismanagement, but the structure remained the same. When, however, I began to take a longer view it became apparent that land was now much scarcer; there was little opportunity for the man who did not already own land to acquire any, as he might have done in earlier times. Families were much larger, and it was apparent that small pieces of rice and rubber land which might now, with difficulty, support a family could not possibly support all the families which would grow in a few years from that family. As my investigations progressed I also began to learn of pieces of land within the general vicinity of the village which were not owned by peasants at all but had been bought, when their former peasant owner was forced to sell, by people still seen as vaguely connected with the village but who were now pursuing upper-class careers and no longer formed active parts of village society. This led me to the conclusion, which I now wish to generalize for all Malaya, that there are two aspects of changes in landholding to be observed. There is still a process of circulation among the peasant economic élites; fathers do build positions which their descendants cannot maintain; but this process must not obscure the trend of structural change represented by the concentration process.

I think that my argument is made conceptually clearer if the two aspects of changes in landholding are related to Lockwood's distinction between social integration and system integration, and to his focus on 'the propensity to social change arising from the functional incompatibility between an institutional order and its material base.'

Land concentration is a question of system integration, and much of my argument is concerned to direct attention to the consequences of this for the integration of social roles (Lockwood, 1964).

The position taken in the essay calls for both special research and a reorientation of conventional community study projects. First, it needs to be established by properly collected economic statistics whether or not concentration is a nation-wide process, and how far it has proceeded. Has it, for example, passed the point at which it might be reversed by the effects of inheritance division? The same type of general information is needed on the economic position of the peasantry. For example, are average incomes declining, are the incomes of owners, tenants (sharers), and labourers moving in the same direction? It is also important to establish, assuming that extensive concentration is found to be taking place, what type of person is acquiring the land, the rich peasant or the official—or indeed some other type of person, perhaps a new business class called forth by the Government's cosseting of some forms of Malay enterprise. These questions share the characteristic of being more usually the province of the economist rather than the anthropologist, although any properly conducted fieldwork would consider them for the small unit of observation. They also call for the survey techniques of the economic statistician rather than the subtle skills of the participant observer.

Secondly, to provide a firm basis for an analysis of the social implications of the concentration process we need a much more precise knowledge of Malay social organization and of the structure of the national society of which the Malay is only a part. Beginnings in this direction can be seen, but valuable as recent and current sociological investigations in Malaya have been, they are still much too scanty, and too marked by the anthropological bias which finds a niche in the countryside and endeavours to understand the society from that vantage point.

It is a generally accepted truism today that the main feature distinguishing peasantry from tribesmen is their involvement in a dominating and exploiting wider society. Whether authors prefer to emphasize the political dominance, the economic exploitation, or cultural hegemony of the non-peasant élite, there is general agreement that peasants are subjected to occasionally decisive and always important external social constraints. Above all in this paper I have been arguing by implication that these external constraints, this all-important social and cultural setting within which the small social sub-systems called villages function, be given explicit attention in their own right, and not merely studied as the anthropologist sees them directly influencing his people and their village. A corollary of this position is an argument for the loosening of the traditional boundaries separating the specialized social sciences so that they may be brought to bear in unison in interpreting the changing patterns of Malay (and Malaysian) society.

Chinese Fishermen in Hong Kong: Their Post-Peasant Economy

BARBARA E. WARD

KAU SAI is a village situated on the shores of a narrow strait between two small islands in the Port Shelter area of the waters of the British Crown Colony of Hong Kong (see McCoy, 1965; Ward, 1954, 1965, and 1966). In 1952 its total population was about 390, made up of 17 Hakka and 45 Cantonese speaking families. The Hakka all lived in small grey stone houses built parallel to the water front. Most of their men were away from home, earning wages in a variety of employments in the cities of Victoria and Kowloon; the women added to the family income by rearing pigs, for whose fodder they cultivated groundnuts and sweet potatoes on patches cleared by themselves on the hillsides, and cutting firewood and grass, which they sold to the fishermen for fuel. One Hakka man ran a small shop. All but two of the Cantonese men gained their livelihood from fishing and dwelt with their entire families on board their fishing boats. They owned no house property on land. Their boats (on average about 30 feet long and 10 feet in the beam) were moored in regular lines at permanent moorings, each man's boat in its accustomed place, which was usually said to have been occupied by his forebears for several generations. Two ex-fishing families lived ashore: one running the main shop (cf. King, 1954), the other, a very old man, paid a small wage to act as caretaker for the village temple.

In that year, 1952, Kau Sai had a village school of a kind. Its one all-age class, which met in a section of the temple, had to be dismissed on rainy days because the dogma of temple architecture decreed the existence of a large rectangular opening in the unceiled roof. Its one teacher was barely qualified. Most of the eighteen or so pupils were children of Hakka speaking landsmen. Only four fishermen's children went to school at all, all of them intermittently, and all of them boys.

In 1953 all the Hakka families were moved, at the government's initiative and expense, to a newly constructed village on the mainland. Their subsequent history does not concern us here. The schoolmaster went with them. All teaching stopped.

By 1962 Kau Sai boasted a purpose-built school house with three separate, well-equipped, and entirely waterproof classrooms, a concrete basket-ball pitch, and a magnificent latrine; there were three well-qualified schoolmasters, two of them fluent in English; there were 118 pupils, most of them attending regularly and all of them fishermen's children—including all the fishermen's school-age daughters (even three who were upwards of sixteen years old). The total population of the village was now 404. This was divided into 59 families, all but one being Cantonese speaking. The single Hakka family was that of the temple caretaker newly employed by the fishermen to take the place of the old man who had died. Three of the Cantonese families were those of ex-fishermen now running small shops and living ashore. The remaining 55 Cantonese families all gained their livelihood from fishing, but at least eight of them owned house property on land, and lived in it. More were planning to follow their example.

Contrasts between the fishermen's standards of living at the beginning and the end of the ten years 1952–62 could be multiplied almost indefinitely. Speaking generally, food was better, clothing more, hygiene and health had greatly improved. Most families were in fact richer, but a few were poorer—or appeared to be so, perhaps because they had not shared the improvement in the lot of the majority. There were other changes too. Despite the removal of the Hakka, the population was larger. This was partly because Kau Sai, like most other fishing settlements in Hong Kong at the time, had received an influx of fishing families from China, but as the number of immigrant fishing families just about balanced the number of land families who had been moved away, the net increase in the population is to be explained in terms of a reduction in infant and child mortality. By 1962 most Kau Sai babies were being born in a government sponsored clinic at the nearest market town and not on board the fishing boats, and most of them now lived. Whereas in 1952 there were about 70 children under the age of 16, in 1962 there were between 170 and 180—and their heads were not covered with the suppurating boils upon which a fieldworker had felt obliged to expend so much of her limited knowledge of first aid only ten years before.

These were all measurable changes. 1962 showed organizational and structural changes in Kau Sai as well: the village now had a regularly elected Representative—a fisherman.[1] Two co-operative

1. Village Representatives are the officially recognized spokesmen of their communities. They act as channels of communication with the administration,

societies had been formed. Several marriages were described as having been made by free choice—an impossible example of immorality
by 1952 standards. Several young men had left fishing to take up
shore jobs in the big cities or the nearest market town. Several girls
had married non-fishermen and gone to live ashore. Already those
few fishing families with their own houses on land had adapted themselves to a new organization and division of labour. Even among
those who still lived on board their boats there were noticeable
alterations in the relationships between parents and children.

Most striking of all, however, and obvious even to the most
casual observer, was the one outstanding change which the people of
Kau Sai themselves would certainly have placed first: namely, that
whereas in 1952 all but one of their boats had been wind-driven,
by mid-1963 only one was not mechanized. In other words, what
had been going on was a technological revolution in microcosm,
and most of the above changes (which continue in full swing at the
time of writing) were closely connected with it.

Fish has always been Hong Kong's most important primary product. By 1950 the industry provided a livelihood for about 60,000
people (men, women, and children), almost all of whom lived their
whole lives aboard the fishing boats, which numbered at that time
about 6,000 in all. This was probably the largest fishing fleet in the
whole of the then British Commonwealth and Empire. It is the more
remarkable that this production was almost entirely in the hands of
local men, owning and operating their own craft with the help of
family labour and in many cases hired hands. By 1950, thanks in
part to the strenuous efforts of the Colony's administration which
had set up a satisfactory method of marketing fish, and in part to the
hard work and natural resilience of the fishermen, the Hong Kong
fishing industry was well on the way to total recovery from the start-
lingly low condition to which it had sunk during the Japanese occupation. In that year the marketing of more than 30,000 tons of fish
was recorded, representing a wholesale value of more than $H.K.
38,000,000. This is not small-scale business.[1]

---

and can be called upon to advise. The methods by which they are selected
are not uniform, but it is the administration's intention that they should be as
'representative' as their title in English implies. Like most Hong Kong boat
people, the Kau Sai fishermen had previously had to be content to be 'represented' by a landsman in whose appointment they had taken no part.

1. *Hong Kong Annual Report* 1950, p. 41. These figures include both fresh and
salt marine fish. Ten years later the fishing fleet numbered over 10,400 and the
fishing population about 86,000. The quantity of 'fisheries products' sold through
the wholesale markets in 1960 was 47,229 tons with a total value of

Nevertheless, the general attitude of the non-fishing public in Hong Kong, when it thought about the fishermen at all, was that they were an economically depressed section of the population, and largely deservedly so because of the feckless ways which were considered inherent in their 'gypsy-like' boat-dwelling mode of existence and their consequent lack of education. The fishermen, for their part, though hotly contesting these landsmen's views when expressed by landsmen, yet largely shared them—or rather that section of them which described their own general poverty and conservatism. That same year 1950, which followed immediately on the final success of the People's Government in China, saw the first beginnings of large-scale industrial development in Hong Kong. It is probably true to say that no one would have predicted that the fishermen would take part in it.

It is well known that the rapid industrial development in Hong Kong which has occurred since the Second World War was largely a by-product of political change in China. It would be possible to argue that this was also conducive to at least an increased overall income for Hong Kong's fishermen, for the swollen population and (despite the quite genuine and much advertised poverty) its rising standard of living necessarily entailed a bigger demand for their products. However, the immediate closing of Chinese markets for all Hong Kong's salt fish—up to that time the major export product —meant that in fact the first effect of the 1949 revolution in China was deeply depressing to the Hong Kong fishing industry.

Nevertheless, at the beginning of 1950 there were already as many as fifty-five mechanized fishing vessels in operation. Ten years later the figure had jumped to 3,329. Today (1965) it stands at between 6,000 and 7,000—more than 60 per cent of the present-day total number of fishing craft.

There are obviously a great many questions that one could ask about so profound and rapid a change. Those with which this paper is concerned fall broadly under two headings: first, how was it that in this free enterprise economy, without coercion of any kind, these so long believed to be ultra-conservative peasants were so eager to adopt such a revolutionary technological innovation; and second, what are likely to be its economic and social consequences?

Let us first consider the somewhat contentious term that has just been used: peasants. It was, of course, Professor Raymond Firth

---

$H.K.53,904,468 (*Hong Kong Annual Report* 1960, p. 381). Since the Second World War the exchange value of the Hong Kong dollar has varied very closely around $H.K.16 to £1 sterling.

who first proposed including certain kinds of fishing community along with certain kinds of agricultural community in one broad 'peasant' category. His criteria for such a category were essentially economic and structural (Firth, 1946, especially pp. 22–27). They included: primary production, with usually some self-subsistence; limited specialization; a limited dependence upon markets external to the community itself, which are usually not fully integrated into the world market; a considerable amount of home production of capital equipment; a general lack of wage labour, and dependence upon family labour; a common dependence upon credit, but not usually upon a specialist class of moneylenders. These broad economic criteria are undoubtedly as applicable to the mixed farming and fishing communities of the east coast of Malaya, with which Firth was primarily concerned, as they are (with variations of degree and emphasis) to many entirely land-based agricultural communities in the Orient and elsewhere. It does not follow, however, that all Oriental primary producers except those engaged in plantation agriculture must be similarly classified. On the contrary, the very insight which can be gained from studying Firth's brilliant recognition of the similarities between fishing and agricultural communities in Malaya leads us to remark the numerous dissimilarities between fishermen and traditional peasant farmers in Hong Kong.

It is true that the Hong Kong fishermen are, in effect, and have long been, producers of a cash crop, part of which goes to provide for their own subsistence. But although fish is their most frequently consumed protein, and essential for their nutrition, only a very small portion of their diet is fish. And everything else has to be purchased. So does almost every other item of consumption—clothing, personal equipment of all kinds, even fuel. The experience of the Japanese occupation showed how quickly these fishermen could be reduced to starvation when they could no longer market their fish. Theirs is much more than a partial dependence upon the market.

Moreover, even long before mechanization, the level of their technology was such that the necessary capital equipment had become highly specialized. Different types of fish require different methods, different gear, and different boats, and most Hong Kong fishermen specialize not simply as fishermen (none of them owns land or performs any agricultural work) but as, say, trawlermen, long-liners, seine-netters, gill-netters, and so on. Such a degree of specialization and technical sophistication is inevitably expensive. With the exception of sails, which are now rapidly going out of use, some (nowadays very few) nets, and fish traps, virtually all capital equipment is acquired by purchase from specialist craftsmen or stores in the market towns. By peasant standards (which are seldom capital intensive) the amount of capital required in relation to annual income is particularly large. In 1960, for example, a new medium-sized junk used for inshore purse-seining cost about $H.K.6,000, and an appropriate marine diesel engine to go with it about $H.K.10,000 more. The gross income of the most successful purse-seiner pair in Kau Sai that year was between $H.K.25,000 and $H.K.30,000, of the least successful around $H.K.7,000. It is obvious that one result of this situation is that loans have to be obtained. Apart from a few fairly small sums, these are nearly all negotiated outside the fishing communities themselves. The traditional source of loans was the fish-dealer; and the overwhelming majority of fish-dealers were, and are, specialists in their own turn, living on land in the market towns and often belonging to a different language group from the fishermen who are their clients.

Thus these southern Chinese fishermen have long been almost completely dependent not only upon a market that is external to their communities, and one which (it must be added) has for more than a century been linked with the world market, but also upon a specialist class of similarly external moneylender-middlemen. When to these facts is added the further point that on the larger fishing craft (trawlers and deep-sea long-liners) wage labour is the traditional, universal, and essential supplement to family labour, and that even on the smaller inshore craft it has long been far from uncommon,[1] the usefulness of placing these fishermen in a general 'peasant' economic category of the kind put forward by Firth becomes increasingly doubtful. Nevertheless, until mechanization has taken place and brought with it full modernization in at least some of the ways discussed below, they remain both structurally and culturally distinct enough from the local traders and other 'non-peasants' to make it useful to class them in a separate category, for which the term 'post-peasant' will serve our present purposes well enough.[2]

1. Deep-sea trawlers, which stay at sea for sometimes as many as ten days or more, employ an average of about thirty wage earning fishermen; a long-liner sometimes employs as many as fifty. Both types of deep-sea craft often carry women employees as well as men. By no means all the inshore owner-operators achieve their ambition of managing with family labour alone. Many carry one, two, or even as many as four or more hired men—and this on boats which double as family homes and have an overall length of about thirty to thirty-five feet.
2. Since I wrote this paper my attention has been drawn to an article by Ernestine Friedl (Friedl, 1964), in which, quoting Foster (Foster, George M., *Traditional Cultures and the Impact of Technological Change*, New York, 1962) and Geertz

The value of distinguishing such an intermediate category, between, for example, the traditional peasant rice farmers, on the one hand, and the local traders and others, on the other hand, becomes clear when we turn to comparison. We have seen that these post-peasant fishermen have long been fully enmeshed in a money economy. They have also long been familiar with such calculations as are necessary for planned saving towards capital investment, giving and raising credit, and so on. They are far indeed from being economically unsophisticated subsistence producers, and it is reasonable to suppose that their relative economic 'know-how' is one of the significant factors explaining the readiness with which they are modernizing their technology. Yet the Kau Sai fishermen regard their own economic sophistication as being considerably less than that of other Chinese. They deplore this state of affairs, and frequently mention it in explanation of their (in their own eyes) relative poverty, saying that they can easily be cheated because landsmen are more knowledgeable. There is some truth in their complaint, but it should be noted that the landsmen of whom they complain are not peasants but traders and middlemen. The fact that fishermen have less economic expertise than these should surprise no one; they could still be better equipped in this respect than local peasant agriculturalists. Whether or not they are so, I am not in a position to say, but certainly it is a fact that the indigenous rice farmers of Hong Kong have been much slower to accept change than the fishermen.

Closely connected with economic 'know-how' is the prevailing set of values, which gives the highest esteem to the man who makes good in the economic sense. This is a widespread attitude among present-day Chinese in Hong Kong and overseas. The fishermen are by no means the only Chinese of whom it can be said that no one really expects behaviour other than that directed towards the rational pursuit of self-interest, and it would be very difficult to contrast them with others on this count. On the other hand, it might be arguable that the fishermen are especially likely to manifest this particular facet of Chinese values because—like their thrusting compatriots overseas—they are relatively free of the restraints which might have been imposed by certain other Chinese values which were embedded in what is usually known as 'the gentry tradition'. As a rule, southern Chinese fishing villages contained no gentry. Moreover,

---

(Geertz, Clifford, 'Studies in Peasant Life: Community and Society', in *Biennial Review of Anthropology*, B. J. Siegel ed., Stanford, 1962), she postulates a similar intermediate (transitional) post-peasant category.

Chinese fishermen, unlike many even very poor landsmen, had no ties with gentry kinsmen or affines, nor did they have much, if any, opportunity of ever rising to the ranks of the gentry through the examination system. Their ideas of gentry values—which undoubtedly, if they were asked, they would describe as 'best' and 'truly Chinese'—were in fact culled largely from the Cantonese operas they saw several times a year: dramatic tales which are much loved and usually known by heart, but which are little more directly relevant to their own daily life than are the tales of traditional pantomime to ours in England. If there is anything in the argument that the vigorous business methods of, say, the overseas Chinese may partly be ascribed to their freedom from both external and internalized gentry controls, it could equally apply to the fishermen of Hong Kong—but not, presumably, to the same extent to many Chinese peasants.

There is another feature which the south Chinese fishermen and the Chinese overseas have in common. Both are relatively free of clan and lineage obligations. For reasons probably mainly connected with their potential spatial mobility and the lack of land, these fishermen do not have a developed lineage system, nor any real concept of one. This is not the place to enter into the argument whether or not lineage ties and the claims of poorer members upon richer ones may act as a deterrent to economic enterprise, but if they sometimes do have a restraining influence, then these fishermen were in this respect also less restricted than most of the land-based peasants of south China. Their kinship structure has in fact far more in common with that of Chinese townsmen in, say, Hong Kong or Singapore (and overseas Chinese in general).

Their economic groupings reflect this situation, as, no doubt, they also contribute towards its development. In Kau Sai the labour units are all family units with or without the addition of one or two (sometimes more) hired men. Each family (man, wife—occasionally wives—children, including often married sons and daughters-in-law and grandchildren, but excluding married daughters and their offspring) lives on board a fishing boat and engages as a unit in both production and consumption. The boats are all owned by their operators, and licensed in the name of the family head who is also captain, so to speak, of the crew. In day-to-day matters, each boat-household (or, for those engaging in operations requiring two boats, each pair of boat-households) is an independent unit with full freedom to take decisions on its own account.

The fishermen are free in other senses too. They pay no rent, the resources they tap are theoretically unlimited, and with their sea-worthy floating homes they are potentially more physically mobile than almost any other human group. In all these ways their situation appears to contrast favourably with that of most other primary producers, certainly with that of any ordinary land-based Chinese peasants.

Everything put forward so far would apply with equal force to the sea fishermen of the rest of the south China coast and to the fishermen of Hong Kong—and would have applied also for at least the last century, probably much longer. One might ask, therefore, why it was that, the socio-economic circumstances being apparently so similar and so favourable, rapid technological change did not occur among these fishermen before 1949, and even after 1949 did not occur with the same rapidity outside Hong Kong.

There is one very simple answer which is glaringly obvious: it is that suitable engines for mechanization were not available anywhere in the Far East much before 1949. Nevertheless, obvious, and indeed crucial, though this fact is, it does not supply the whole answer. As so often, the truth is not necessarily the whole truth, and if we rest content with the obvious we may fail to take account of other equally significant factors. For one thing, mechanization is not the only technological change that has occurred; for another thing, even when engines were becoming available they were not adopted immediately everywhere at the same rate.

One of the other technological changes was connected with the night-time bright-light fishing which is practised by the (pair) purse-seine fishermen. The lamps in use today are almost exclusively kerosene pressure lamps, with incandescent mantles inside specially made glass globes. These have been standard since the early thirties. Before the War of 1914 flaring torches of burning pine wood were used, and had a long history. During that war the carbide lamps which were then in use on most road vehicles first appeared in Hong Kong. They were not readily available until after 1918, but as soon as they were, the bright-light fishermen seem to have snapped them up. In about two years, so my informants told me, flaring pine tor-ches had disappeared from the local scene entirely. They reappeared for a time during the Japanese occupation. The early thirties, so I was assured, showed a similar rapid change-over to kerosene lamps.

But carbide and kerosene lamps, and another technical innova-tion that was taken up almost overnight in the mid-fifties—nylon nets and lines—have qualities which engines large enough to power Chinese fishing junks do not. They require little or no special techni-

T

cal skill, they are cheap, and their introduction brings with it no significant technical or organizational changes. Marine engines, assuming them to be available, require of their operators a certain standard of education and of their owners a considerable outlay of capital, and inevitably entail either a change in methods of fishing or in methods of organizing the fishing enterprise, or both.

Before about 1930 virtually no fisherman in either Hong Kong or south China received any education at all. In Kau Sai in 1950 one could assume that most of the men over fifty were illiterate, many of those over thirty were just literate, and many of the younger ones rather more so; no women could read or write. Under Hong Kong law sea-going vessels fitted with mechanical propulsion must carry a licensed coxswain and a licensed engineer. To obtain the licences it is necessary to pass special written examinations and, of course, receive the necessary preliminary instruction. Unless a fisherman owning and operating his own craft is willing to employ an already qualified man (and because of the expense few are so willing; moreover few qualified men are available), it is necessary to have at least one family member educated enough to take the courses and pass the examinations. From about 1940 onwards this would probably not have been beyond the bounds of possibility for at least a fair number of fishing families in Hong Kong. Evidence from China is not complete, but there is reason to believe that the situation there was rather worse (at least up to 1949). But at that time, in any case, there were no engines on the market, and from 1941 of course nearly all children ceased to attend school for a few years. There is thus a real sense in which mechanization could not have 'caught on' much before 1950, even if the market had been overflowing with cheap engines, because of the educational block.

Furthermore, the educational difficulty having been at least partially met, the economic difficulty remained. I listed earlier several social factors which appeared theoretically to make it possible for these sea fishermen to be economically more enterprising than other Chinese peasants. But in fact they were not in a position to exploit their theoretical advantages in practice. It was implied above that fishermen were more fortunate than farmers because the resources they tapped were theoretically unlimited. This is true in the sense that sea fishing grounds off these coasts are open to all without legal or customary restrictions. But at least four sets of circumstance limit their actual exploitation: natural fluctuations in the fish populations and their movements, which can only very partially be predicted; hazards of weather, especially in the typhoon season which lasts from May to October inclusive; technical limitations of boats and gear and methods of fishing, including the distances that can be travelled in a given time and the positioning of markets—because fish, even now when ice is available, is a highly perishable commodity and the south China waters are tropical; and, finally, limitations in the skill and knowledge of the fishermen. The former two considerations, being limitations inherent in the nature of the product and the local climate, lie outside our present sphere of enquiry, but the latter two concern us directly.

As far as technical and technological matters are concerned, it is clear that, while they were still using wind-driven craft, the geographical limits within which all but the largest deep-sea going vessels could work were narrow, and even the deep-sea fishermen— who could go much further afield—were closely limited as to the seasons they could operate in, for fear of bad weather. Mechanization was a prerequisite to the fuller exploitation of the theoretically unlimited resources. This particular economic advantage in being a fisherman (and not a farmer) therefore did not apply before the moment of technological change, and so must be discounted in any comparison with land-based peasants.

The skill and knowledge of the fishermen are likewise limited to certain types of fishing and certain localities. At least for the inshore fishermen, such as those of Kau Sai, skill depends upon the fairly slow building up of knowledge about the fishing grounds, knowledge of this kind coming only from personal experience. Only one thing limits its scope: the opportunity to learn about new areas. But opportunity is hard to come by. Some time at the height of the inshore long-lining season in 1952, Ma Yao-Foon and three other Kau Sai long-linermen decided to try their luck on a different stretch of the coast. They were away about six weeks. When the four little boats came sailing in to Kau Sai again everybody wanted to know how they had fared. The answer was a dismal one: they had come back to Kau Sai because it was the only place they could make a living. No, there had been no objection from the local fishermen up the coast, and the fishing grounds were probably good, but they had not been able to spend enough time there to discover their full potentialities. Once their savings had been used up they had had to return. In other words, they had had to give up their exploration of new fishing grounds because they were unable to tide themselves over the initial period of trial and error. Their savings were insufficient, and no shopkeeper in the strange district would give them credit.

Here we arrive at the economic crux of the matter. We argued earlier that these fishermen are potentially completely mobile; in fact they are anchored. We stated also that they paid no rent, and implied by this that they enjoyed an economic and legal freedom very different from the situation of most ordinary land peasants in south China. But in fact the fishermen too are tied. Like so many producers of cash crops, they are involved in most cases much less in a cash nexus than in a credit nexus. Very few of them ever have much cash in hand; instead they stand in a more or less complicated series of credit relationships, taking loans for capital expenditure on the one hand and running up credit accounts at a shop or shops, for everyday current expenditure, on the other. Almost any capital outlay requires a loan, and, as we have seen, loans have traditionally been obtained from the middlemen-dealers in the wholesale trading of fish. The result has been the setting up of long-term personal creditor-debtor relationships between dealers and fishermen, which have frequently been held to be the source of all the fishermen's one-time poverty. Today, at least, few Kau Sai fishermen are willing to agree that 'their' middlemen are the wicked parasites they are sometimes declared to be, but there is no doubt that in the past the opportunities for cheating the fishermen were many and that by no means all middlemen resisted temptation.

Immediately after the Japanese war the government of Hong Kong stepped in for the first time. A government controlled wholesale marketing organization was set up, and it was made illegal to sell or buy marine fish wholesale anywhere else than in an authorized market. In this way fishermen were assured of fair weights, public auctions, and published prices, and if they wished they could themselves handle their own fish on to the auction floor. At the same time the Fish Marketing Organization launched the first of a number of loan schemes which were to ensure a fixed rate of interest and open accounting. By 1950 the advantages of mechanization were patent for all to see and suitable diesel engines were beginning to be available. Accordingly, the loan schemes were increased, partly from an allocation from the Colonial Development and Welfare Fund, and a revolving fund instituted specifically for the purpose of helping mechanization.

A Kau Sai man was one of the first two inshore fishermen to take advantage of this scheme. That was in 1950. Since then several thousand other fishermen have followed suit, and several thousand more have mechanized their craft with the aid of loans taken in the traditional way from middlemen, and in some cases other outsiders. The middlemen-dealers, whatever their position in the past, are now in competition with the official loan schemes with their fixed rates of interest, and, as they no longer themselves control the wholesaling of fish, their potential stranglehold on the industry has been broken. The Hong Kong Government claims that without its intervention the rapid mechanization of the fishing fleets would have been impossible; it may well be right.

The argument so far, then, is that this rapid technological change was possible because the economic attitudes of the fishermen and the social structure of the fishing communities were already so favourable that when the opportunity to adopt useful technical change was offered it was likely to be seized upon, unless blocked by something else. By 1950 the opportunity to mechanize did appear—engines were available. By then, too, the possible educational block had been partly removed, and governmental action in freeing the market, injecting money, and providing training courses and encouragement was all that was required to set a revolution in process.

What of the consequences of this rapid mechanization? Most of the more obvious social changes have already been listed: better education, improved standard of living, greater self-respect for a hitherto despised group, and so on. Figures of actual *per capita* income range up to, and in some cases beyond, twice the pre-mechanization income in money terms. Certainly there is clear ocular evidence of greater affluence. There is also evidence of the beginning of certain predictable economic and further technical changes which in their turn will inevitably have social concomitants.

The industry as a whole may be roughly divided into (*a*) deep-sea fishing, and (*b*) inshore fishing. The former requires a much greater capital outlay than the latter, and a much larger labour force. The capital requirements are already beginning to go beyond the limits possible for a single owner operator, even with official (i.e. Fish Marketing Organization) assistance, or even, probably, in co-operative organization. It is predictable that this section of the fishing industry of Hong Kong will show a fairly rapid change-over to land-based capitalist ownership, employing hired crews at all levels on the fishing craft. A few Japanese owned and British owned trawler companies have been operating from Hong Kong for some years, using more or less modern fishing craft; the local type boats are likely to fall under similar capitalist—but Chinese—organization very soon. This will inevitably result in the full proletarianization of the deep-sea fishing industry, though a few existing owner-operators who have been exceptionally fortunate in recent years will set up as capitalists themselves. Women and children will very soon be absent from these capitalist owned boats, and will live ashore. This in itself will give the opportunity to change the design of these craft to more definitely functional lines (from the point of view of both mechanization and propulsion) and make possible the introduction of further technological advances in fishing methods—echo-sounders, mechanical winches, refrigeration plants, for example. The present long-liners are already going out of business, largely because of over-capitalization on the one hand and labour troubles on the other. In five years from now there may well be none left, and in another five years there will be hardly any owner-operated trawlers either. Fewer fishing firms, with a much smaller and more highly specialized labour force, will be at work. The displaced fishermen will have to find other employment. Probably very few will remain at sea at all. When it is remembered that almost every one of these fishermen has been a water-dweller all his life, and most of them descend from generations of water people, it becomes clear that this will be a revolution indeed.

(It has already begun. Quite a number of the waiters who work in the new Chinese restaurants which have sprung up all over the British Isles in the last dozen years, and are now spreading on to the Continent as well, are ex-fishermen from Hong Kong.)

Even the present-day long-liner and trawler owners (particularly the former, who have been the virtual aristocrats of the local fishermen) will mostly become wage-earners, probably as officers on the boats if they stay on the boats at all. A few will, as we have said, become capitalist employers. A third section, also few in number, is likely to set up in retail business, dealing in fishery goods of all kinds, as ship-chandlers and so on, and probably engaging in money-lending too. This type of business already exists, of course, though few ex-fishermen have managed to break into it. The larger-scale business firms of this kind are likely gradually to acquire their own deep-sea fishing boats. In other words, they are likely to supply the major part of the shore-based capitalist ownership predicted above. This is already happening.

The following story of one particularly successful fishing family illustrates one possible set of processes. Lau Kam-Ch'ing of Cheung Chau is the eldest of several brothers who in 1950 owned and operated a pair of wind driven deep-sea trawlers. A series of good seasons gave them the chance to consider mechanization, and with the help of a loan from the Fish Marketing Organization they duly installed engines and refitted their junks. Lau Kam-Ch'ing himself seldom went fishing. It was believed in the family that he brought bad luck, and after consulting a suitable oracle, in the form of the god at his local temple, he decided to move ashore to live. He was well able to afford to do so. Thereafter he acted as the shore-based manager of the trawling business. His brothers operated the junks, and all profits were pooled and shared. Lau Kam-Ch'ing then decided to educate his son to prepare him for his future role as business manager. The boy was intelligent and hard-working and ultimately was sent to one of the fishery colleges in Japan—the first Hong Kong fisherman's child ever known to have received higher education. On his return his father set up as a ship's supplier, the boy's Japanese contacts proving very useful for this business. Lau Kam-Ch'ing and his brothers with the now grown-up second generation still work as a family business, owning between them three pairs of mechanized trawlers, with which they are currently experimenting with more modern techniques, as well as the shop. They are also known to be ready to lend money to fishermen who require it. Few of the deep-sea men will succeed to this extent; most will become hired men or give up fishing and look for employment ashore. A few will maintain their independence at the cost of becoming smaller-scale fishermen in the inshore branch of the industry.

There it is unlikely that change will be quite so rapid or radical. There will probably remain for quite a long time a fairly large number (possibly some thousands) of medium-sized craft, fishing the inshore and nearer waters, owned and operated by independent men, employing still their own family's labour with perhaps one or two hired hands. As things are at present, it seems likely that these independent owner-operators will survive and flourish at least for some time, provided only that the waters are not overfished (there is a real and mounting danger of this) and that the demand for their products remains high (there seems to be no foreseeable danger of it decreasing, rather the reverse). The period of their survival as what might be called independent 'yeoman' fishermen may be quite long, but the ultimately necessary adoption of new techniques, which will certainly prove expensive, will probably force them out in time. Individuals have already shown the course which the forcing out process is likely to take—through over-capitalization to subsequent failure. Chung Fuk-Shun, of Kau Sai, for example, already saw the writing on the wall in 1963. Three years earlier he had invested in a new boat with a more powerful engine. His only son operated the boat with the help of the son's wife, a brother, and his wife and two hired men. The venture prospered so well that by the end of 1961 he was determined to repeat the process and build an even bigger boat with a still more powerful engine. This done, he found he now had to employ at least six hired men, and although fuel bills were almost twice as heavy as before, catches remained much the same. Half way through 1963 he realized that he was only just breaking even, and that his chance of fully paying off the loans he had had to raise for the capital expenditure was slight. He is still in business but only just.[1]

Although this class of independent fishermen, depending still mainly on family labour, is likely to continue to exist for some time, it does not follow that the traditional customs and social structure of the fishing communities will also survive. Women, or some of them, and children are already beginning to move ashore to live. Increased affluence has made this possible; increased comfort and safety and above all the insatiable demand for schooling, make it desirable. No fisherman now fails to see the need for education. Coxswains' and engineers' certificates, successful marketing, coping with government regulations, all depend on it. Educated daughters are at a premium as wives, too, and the fact that one by-product of educating a daughter is that she may marry out of the water communities is often seen as an advantage rather than the opposite. So, for the nearish future, say thirty to fifty years, one can foresee this middle class of fishermen remaining economically independent, becoming gradually smaller, and beginning socially to merge more and more with the land population with which it will have increasing cultural and structural links.

What of the present-day poor fishermen, the smallest independent owner-operators and those who are already hired labourers, whose wives usually run small ferrying or hawking businesses on sampans? These men will either go out of the industry altogether, or become hired men on other boats; the women and children will remain as now on their sampans, but will do all they can to move ashore. This may not be too difficult if their husbands can get any sort of shore employment. In any case, the wives of hired men, living on their own sampans, do not usually move far afield and their children as a result have often been better educated than the sons and daughters of their husbands' employers.

1. The following extract from a letter received from Chung Fuk-Shun in July 1966 shows that even this is no longer true. It was written in English for him. '... my family life is not so well. In the last few month I have been sale my fishing boat. ... Would you please to make the voucher for my son Kam Ho. Do you remember him? He like to go over to England to work. If you can make the voucher for him please don't worry the job, because I had a Chinese friend in England, he had a Chinese restaurant. ... '

So much for the emergence of a clear three-class stratification which I predict will be the immediate and direct effect of the current technological revolution which is sweeping the Hong Kong fishing fleet. Two points seem to require a little further notice: the movement to land dwelling and the changing position of women. The evidence on both these matters is already perfectly clear, as also is the connexion between them. Chung's daughter, for example, married a non-fisherman in 1958 and moved to live with him in an apartment in a large new tenement block on Hong Kong island. It was a free choice marriage. The girl had her third baby a few months ago, and for a time had to give up her job in a factory which makes electric torches. She is the envy of every woman in Kau Sai, and nothing that she has done would have been possible even ten years ago. Going ashore is particularly liked by the women. Not only does it indicate a sheer gain in prestige which is applicable to both sexes, for water-dwelling has so long been despised, but for women it also spells far less drudgery, less discomfort in pregnancy, and much less actual physical danger for themselves and their young children (it is a remarkable fact that virtually no fisherwomen can swim). It also gives an opportunity for a woman to earn a small but independent income, either by working in a factory, where this is possible, or in petty trade, or, most frequently today, in some form of out-work, especially the making of plastic flowers which has become extremely popular since about 1960. But above all, the major attraction of living ashore is that the children can attend school regularly. This is the point that the water people themselves mention first and most frequently, men and women alike.

In the long run, the cumulative effect of all these developments will be to integrate the one-time boat people completely into the rest of the Chinese population. In fact Chinese in language, social structure, personality, and almost all aspects of culture, as I have demonstrated elsewhere, the water-people have continued to be regarded as but little removed from their supposed barbarian origins and they are well aware of their low status. The land-people have a number of myths about them, their believed-in physical peculiarities and immoral and un-Chinese activities. Among the myths is the belief that boat people were traditionally 'always' forbidden to take the imperial examinations, to marry land people, or even to live ashore. Whatever the truth of this vexed question in the past (see Ch'en Hsü-ching, n.d.; Ch'ü T'ung-tsu, 1961, pp. 130–2; Ho Ko-en, 1959–60), it is certain that there are no prohibitions at the present time. It is also highly probable that it has long been quite easy for an aspiring boatman to 'pass' into the land population, just as it has been relatively common for unsuccessful landsmen to become boat people. The immediate future is likely to see a rapid speeding up of this process of assimilation in the landwards direction.

References

Alpert, H., 1939. *Emile Durkheim and his Sociology*, New York.
Bailey, F. G., 1963. *Politics and Social Change: Orissa in 1959*, Berkeley.
Bakić, V., 1962. *Porodično pravo*, Savremena Administracija, Belgrade.
Banton, M., 1957. *West African City: A Study of Tribal Life in Freetown*, London.
Barnes, J. A., 1961. 'Physical and Social Kinship', *Philosophy of Science*, vol. 28.
Barnes, J. A., 1962. 'African Models in the New Guinea Highlands', *Man*, vol. 62, art. 2.
Barnes, J. A., 1964. 'Discussion: Physical and Social Facts in Anthropology', *Philosophy of Science*, vol. 31.
Bauer, P. T., 1948. *Report on a Visit to the Rubber Growing Small-Holdings of Malaya*, H.M.S.O., London.
Beardsley, R. K., 1965. 'Cultural Anthropology: Prehistoric and Contemporary Aspects', in Hall, J. W. and Beardsley, R. K., *Twelve Doors to Japan*, New York.
Beattie, J., 1964. *Other Cultures: Aims, Methods and Achievements in Social Anthropology*, London.
Beidelman, T. O., 1963. 'Terms of Address as Clues to Social Relationships', in Gouldner, A. W. and Gouldner, H. P., eds., *Modern Sociology*, London and New York.
Belshaw, C. S., 1965. *Traditional Exchange and Modern Markets*, Englewood Cliffs, N.J.
Benedict, B., 1957. 'Factionalism in Mauritian Villages', *British Journal of Sociology*, vol. 8, No. 4.
Benedict, B., 1961. *Indians in a Plural Society*, H.M.S.O., London.
Benedict, B., 1963. 'Dependency and Development in the Seychelles', *Social Service Quarterly*, Summer.
Benedict, B., 1966. *People of the Seychelles*, H.M.S.O., London.
Bičanić, R., 1956. 'Occupational Heterogeneity of Peasant Families in the Period of Accelerated Industrialization', *Transactions of the Third World Congress of Sociology*, vol. 4, London.
Blau, P. M., 1964. *Exchange and Power in Social Life*, New York.
Bott, E., 1957. *Family and Social Network*, London.
Brookfield, H. C. and Brown, P., 1963. *Struggle for Land: Agriculture and Group Territories among the Chimbu of the New Guinea Highlands*, Melbourne.
Brown, P., 1961. 'Chimbu Death Payments', *Journal of the Royal Anthropological Institute*, vol. 91.

Brown, P., 1962. 'Non-agnates among the Patrilineal Chimbu', *Journal of the Polynesian Society*, vol. 71.

Brown, P. and Brookfield, H. C., 1959. 'Chimbu Land and Society', *Oceania*, vol. 30, No. 1.

Buck, W. S. B., 1933. 'Notes on the Oya Milanos', *Sarawak Museum Journal*.

Bulmer, R., 1960. 'Political Aspects of the Moka Ceremonial Exchange System among the Kyaka People of the Western Highlands of New Guinea', *Oceania*, vol. 31, No. 1.

Butcher, D., 1965. *The Role of the Fulbe in the Urban Life and Economy of Lunsar, Sierra Leone*, unpublished Ph.D. thesis, Edinburgh University.

Caldwell, J. C., 1963. 'The Demographic Background', in Silcock, T. H. and Fisk, E. K., eds., *The Political Economy of Independent Malaya*, Canberra.

Caprasse, P., 1959. 'Leaders africains en milieu urbain', *Centre d'Etudes des Problèmes Sociaux Indigènes, Collection de Mémoires*, vol. 5.

Ch'en Hsü-ching, n.d. [1936?] *Tanka Researches*, Canton (in Chinese).

Chowning, A., 1962. 'Cognatic Kin Groups among the Molima of Fergusson Island', *Ethnology*, vol. 1.

Ch'ü T'ung-tsu, 1961. *Law and Society in Traditional China*, Paris.

Clément, P., 1956. 'Social Effects of Urbanization in Stanleyville, Belgian Congo', in *Social Implications of Industrialization and Urbanization in Africa South of the Sahara*, Unesco, Paris.

Coleman, J. S., 1958. *Nigeria: Background to Nationalism*, London, Berkeley, and Los Angeles.

Cook, S., 1966. 'The Obsolete "Anti-Market" Mentality: A Critique of the Substantive Approach to Economic Anthropology', *American Anthropologist*, vol. 68, No. 2.

Dedijer, V., 1961. *The Beloved Land*, London.

De Groot, J. J. M., 1886. *Les fêtes annuellement célébrées à Emoui (Amoy)*, trans. Chavannes, C. G., *Annales du Musée Guimet*, vol. 11, Paris.

De Groot, J. J. M., 1907. *The Religious System of China*, vol. 5, Leiden.

De Groot, J. J. M., 1910. *The Religious System of China*, vol. 6, Leiden.

Dore, R. P., 1958. *City Life in Japan, A Study of a Tokyo Ward*, London.

Dorjahn, V. R., 1959. 'The Organization and Functions of the Ragbenle Society of the Temne', *Africa*, vol. 29, No. 2.

Durkheim, E., 1915. *The Elementary Forms of the Religious Life*, trans. Swain, J. W., London.

Durkheim, E., 1947. *The Division of Labor in Society*, trans. Simpson, G., Glencoe, Ill.

Durkheim, E., 1952. *Suicide*, trans. Spaulding, J. A. and Simpson, G., ed. Simpson, G., London.

Durkheim, E. and Mauss, M., 1963. *Primitive Classification*, trans. and ed. Needham, R., London.

Edelman, M., 1964. *The Symbolic Uses of Politics*, Urbana, Ill.

Eidheim, H., 1963. 'Entrepreneurship in Politics', in Barth, F., ed., *The Role of the Entrepreneur in Social Change in Northern Norway*, Årbok for Universitetet i Bergen: Humanistisk Serie, No. 3, Bergen and Oslo.

Eliade, M., 1964. *Shamanism*, trans. Trask, W. R., London.

Elkin, A. P., 1964. 'A Landmark in Australian Aboriginal Anthropology: A Review' (of Stanner, W. E. H. and Sheils, H., *Australian Aboriginal Studies: A Symposium of Papers Presented at the* 1961 *Research Conference*), Oceania, vol. 34, No. 4.

Elliott, A. J. A., 1955. *Chinese Spirit-Medium Cults in Singapore*, L. S. E. Monographs on Social Anthropology, No. 14, London.

Erlich, V. S., 1964. *Porodica u transformaciji*, Zagreb.

Evans-Pritchard, E. E., 1951. *Kinship and Marriage among the Nuer*, Oxford.

Evans-Pritchard, E. E., 1962. *Essays in Social Anthropology*, London.

Evans-Pritchard, E. E., 1965. *The Position of Women in Primitive Societies and Other Essays in Social Anthropology*, London.

Fabre, A., 1935. 'Avril au pays des aïeux', *Collectanea Commissionis Synodalis*, vol. 8, Catholic Church in China, Peking.

Fabre, A., 1937. *Film de la vie chinoise, Proverbes et locutions*, Hong Kong.

Fallers, L. A., 1961. 'Are African Cultivators to be called "Peasants"?', *Current Anthropology*, vol. 3, No. 2, April.

Firth, R., 1925. 'The Maori Carver', *Journal of the Polynesian Society*, vol. 34.

Firth, R., 1929. *Primitive Economics of the New Zealand Maori*, London.

Firth, R., 1930a. 'Report on Research in Tikopia', *Oceania*, vol. 1, No. 1.

Firth, R., 1930b. 'Marriage and the Classificatory System of Relationship', *Journal of the Royal Anthropological Institute*, vol. 60.

Firth, R., 1936a. *We, The Tikopia, A Sociological Study of Kinship in Primitive Polynesia*, London.

Firth, R., 1936b. *Art and Life in New Guinea*, London.

Firth, R., 1939. *Primitive Polynesian Economy*, London.

Firth, R., 1946. *Malay Fishermen, Their Peasant Economy*, London (second edn. 1966).

Firth, R., 1951. *Elements of Social Organization*, London.

Firth, R., 1955. *The Fate of the Soul, An Interpretation of Some Primitive Concepts* (Frazer Lecture, 1955), Cambridge.

Firth, R., ed., 1956. *Two Studies of Kinship in London*, L.S.E. Monographs on Social Anthropology, No. 15, London.

Firth, R., 1957a. 'A Note on Descent Groups in Polynesia', *Man*, vol. 57, art. 2.

Firth, R., 1957b. 'Introduction: Factions in Indian and Overseas Indian Societies', *British Journal of Sociology*, vol. 8, No. 4.

Firth, R., 1959. 'Problem and Assumption in an Anthropological Study of Religion', *Journal of the Royal Anthropological Institute*, vol. 89, pt. 2.

Firth, R., 1963. 'Bilateral Descent Groups: An Operational Viewpoint', in Schapera, I., ed., *Studies in Kinship and Marriage, Dedicated to Brenda Z. Seligman on her 80th Birthday*, Royal Anthropological Institute, Occasional Paper No. 16, London.

Firth, R., 1964a. 'Family and Kinship in Industrial Society', in *The Development of Industrial Societies*, The Sociological Review, Monograph No. 8, Keele.

Firth, R., 1964b. 'Capital, Saving and Credit in Peasant Societies: A Viewpoint from Economic Anthropology', in Firth R. and Yamey, B. S., eds., *Capital, Saving and Credit in Peasant Societies*, London.

Fisk, E. K., 1963a. 'Features of the Rural Economy', in Silcock, T. H. and Fisk, E. K., eds., *The Political Economy of Independent Malaya*, Canberra.

Fisk, E. K., 1963b. 'Rural Development Policy', in Silcock, T. H. and Fisk, E. K., eds., *The Political Economy of Independent Malaya*, Canberra.

Fisk, E. K., 1964. *Studies in the Rural Economy of South-East Asia*, Singapore.

Forde, D., 1963. 'Unilineal Fact or Fiction: An Analysis of the Composition of Kin-Groups among the Yakö', in Schapera, I., ed., *Studies in Kinship and Marriage, Dedicated to Brenda Z. Seligman on her 80th Birthday*, Royal Anthropological Institute, Occasional Paper No. 16, London.

Forge, A., 1962. 'Paint—A Magical Substance', *Palette*, No. 9, Basle.

Forge, A., 1966. 'Art and Environment in the Sepik', *Proceedings of the Royal Anthropological Institute, 1965*, London.

Fortes, M., 1959. 'Descent, Filiation and Affinity: A Rejoinder to Dr. Leach', *Man*, vol. 59, arts. 309, 331.

Fortes, M., 1962. 'Introduction' to Goody, J., ed., *The Developmental Cycle in Domestic Groups*, Cambridge Papers in Social Anthropology, No. 1, Cambridge.

Fortes, M., 1965. 'Some Reflections on Ancestor Worship in Africa', in Fortes, M. and Dieterlen, G., eds., *African Systems of Thought*, London.

Francis, R. G. and Stone, R. C., 1956. *Service and Procedure in Bureaucracy*, Minneapolis.

Fraser, T. M., 1960. *Rusembilan: A Malay Fishing Village in Southern Thailand*, Ithaca, N.Y.

Frazer, J. G., 1899. 'The Origin of Totemism', *The Fortnightly Review*, April-May.

Freedman, M., 1957. *Chinese Family and Marriage in Singapore*, H.M.S.O., London.

Freedman, M., 1958. *Lineage Organization in Southeastern China*, L.S.E. Monographs on Social Anthropology, No. 18, London.

Freedman, M., 1966. *Chinese Lineage and Society: Fukien and Kwangtung*, L.S.E. Monographs on Social Anthropology, No. 33, London.

Fried, M., 1957. 'The Classification of Corporate Unilineal Descent Groups', *Journal of the Royal Anthropological Institute*, vol. 87, pt. 1.

Friedl, E., 1964. 'Lagging Emulation in Post-Peasant Society', *American Anthropologist*, vol. 66, No. 3, pt. 1.

Gallin, B., 1966. *Hsin Hsing, Taiwan: A Chinese Village in Change*, Berkeley and Los Angeles.

Geertz, C., 1963. *Peddlers and Princes*, Chicago.

Gennep, A. van, 1960. *The Rites of Passage*, trans. Vizedom, M. B. and Caffee, G. L., Chicago, Ill.

Giles, H. A., 1879. 'Mesmerism, Planchette, and Spiritualism in China', *Fraser's Magazine*, n.s. vol. 19, Feb.

Ginsberg, M., 1956. *On the Diversity of Morals (Essays in Sociology and Social Philosophy*, vol. 1), London.

Glasse, R. M., 1959a. 'The Huli Descent System: A Preliminary Account', *Oceania*, vol. 29, No. 3.

Glasse, R. M., 1959b. 'Revenge and Distress among the Huli', *Mankind*, vol. 5.

Gluckman, M., 1965. *Politics, Law and Ritual in Tribal Society*, Oxford.

Goldenweiser, A. A., 1910. 'Totemism, An Analytical Study', *Journal of American Folklore*, vol. 23.

Goldenweiser, A. A., 1914. In W. Schmidt, 'Introduction' to 'Das Problem des Totemismus', *Anthropos*, vol. 9.

Goldenweiser, A. A., 1915. Review of Durkheim, 'Les formes élémentaires de la vie religieuse', *American Anthropologist*, vol. 17.

Goode, W. J., 1964. *The Family*, Englewood Cliffs, N.J.

Goodenough, W. H., 1955. 'A Problem in Malayo-Polynesian Social Organization', *American Anthropologist*, vol. 57.

Granet, M., 1951. *La religion des Chinois*, 2nd edn., Paris.

Gullick, J. M., 1958. *Indigenous Political Systems of Western Malaya*, L.S.E. Monographs on Social Anthropology, No. 17, London.

Halpern, J., 1958. *A Serbian Village*, New York.

Halpern, J., 1965. 'Peasant Culture and Urbanization in Yugoslavia', *Human Organization*, vol. 24.

Hanson, O., 1906. *A Dictionary of the Kachin Language*, Rangoon.

Hartland, E. S., 1900. 'Totemism and Some Recent Discoveries' (Presidential Address), *Folklore*, vol. 11.

Herskovits, M. J., 1952. *Economic Anthropology*, New York.

Hickey, G. C., 1964. *Village in Vietnam*, New Haven and London.

Ho Ko-en, 1959–60. 'A Study of the Boat People', *Journal of Oriental Studies*, vol. 5, Nos. 1 and 2, Hong Kong.

Hogbin, H. I. and Wedgwood, C. H., 1953. 'Local Groupings in Melanesia', *Oceania*, vol. 23, No. 4.

Homans, G., 1960. 'Social Behavior as Exchange', in Homans, G. *Sentiments and Activities*, Glencoe, Ill.

Horton, R., 1960. 'A Definition of Religion and its Uses', *Journal of the Royal Anthropological Institute*, vol. 90, pt. 2.

Howitt, A. W., 1904. *The Native Tribes of South-east Australia*, London.

Hsu, F. L. K., 1949. *Under the Ancestors' Shadow: Chinese Culture and Personality*, London.

Husin Ali, S., 1964. *Social Stratification in Kampong Bagan*, Monographs of the Malaysian Branch of the Royal Asiatic Society, No. 1, Singapore.

Jakobson, R., 1960. 'Why "Mama" and "Papa"?', in Kaplan, B. and Wapner, S., eds., *Perspectives in Psychological Theory*, New York.

Jakobson, R. and Halle, M., 1956. *Fundamentals of Language*, The Hague.

Jamuh, G., 1951. 'Some Melanau Pastimes', *Sarawak Museum Journal*.

Jayawardena, C., 1960. 'Marital Stability in Two Guianese Sugar Estate Communities', *Social and Economic Studies*, vol. 9, No. 1.

Jayawardena, C., 1963. *Conflict and Solidarity in a Guianese Plantation*, L.S.E. Monographs on Social Anthropology, No. 25, London.

Jevons, F. B., 1901. 'The Place of Totemism in the Evolution of Religion', *Folklore*, vol. 10.

Kaberry, P. M., 1941. 'The Abelam Tribe, Sepik District, New Guinea', *Oceania*, vol. 11, Nos. 3, 4.

Kaberry, P. M., 1941–2. 'Law and Political Organization in the Abelam Tribe, New Guinea', *Oceania*, vol. 12, Nos. 1, 3, 4.

Kaberry, P. M., 1966. 'Political Organization among the Northern Abelam', *Anthropological Forum*, vol. 1, Nos. 3, 4.

Kilson, M., 1964. 'The Pragmatic-Pluralistic Pattern: Sierra Leone', in Coleman, J. S. and Rosberg, C. G., eds., *Political Parties and National Integration in Tropical Africa*, Berkeley, Calif.

King, H. F. F., 1954. 'Duopoly in a Hong Kong Fishing Village', *Journal of Oriental Studies*, vol. 1, No. 1, Hong Kong.

Klass, M., 1961. *East Indians in Trinidad*, New York and London.

Krige, J. D. and Krige, E. J., 1954. 'The Lovedu of the Transvaal', in Forde, D., ed., *African Worlds, Studies in the Cosmological Ideas and Social Values of African Peoples*, London.

Kulp, D. H., 1925. *Country Life in South China, The Sociology of Familism*, New York.

Lal, Ram Narain, 1949. *The Student's Practical Dictionary*, Allahabad.

Lancaster, L., 1958. 'Kinship in Anglo-Saxon Society', *British Journal of Sociology*, vol. 9, Nos. 3, 4.

Lancaster, L., 1961. 'Some Conceptual Problems in the Study of Family and Kin Ties in the British Isles', *British Journal of Sociology*, vol. 12, No. 4.

Lane, Sir C., 1953. *The Laws of Seychelles in Force on the 30th June, 1952*, 4 vols. London.

Lang, A., 1905. *The Secret of the Totem*, London.

Langness, L. L., 1964. 'Some Problems in the Conceptualization of Highlands Social Structure', in Watson, J. B., ed., *New Guinea, The Central Highlands*, Special Publication, *American Anthropologist*, vol. 66, No. 4, pt. 2.

Lazarsfeld, P. F. and Merton, R. K., 1954. 'Friendship as Social Process: A Substantive and Methodological Analysis', in Berger, M., Abel, T., and Page, C. H., eds., *Freedom and Control in Modern Society*, New York.

Leach, E. R., 1954. *Political Systems of Highland Burma*, London.

Leach, E. R., 1958. 'Concerning Trobriand Clans and the Kinship Category *Tabu*', in Goody, J., ed., *The Developmental Cycle in Domestic Groups*, Cambridge Papers in Social Anthropology, No. 1, Cambridge.

Leach, E. R., 1961. *Rethinking Anthropology*, L.S.E. Monographs on Social Anthropology, No. 22, London.

Leach, E. R., 1962. 'On Certain Unconsidered Aspects of Double Descent Systems', *Man*, vol. 62, art. 214.

Leach, E. R., 1964. 'Anthropological Aspects of Language: Animal Categories and Verbal Abuse', in Lenneberg, E. D., ed., *New Directions in the Study of Language*, Cambridge, Mass.

Leeden, A. C. van der, 1960. 'Social Structure in New Guinea', *Bijdragen tot de Taal-, Land- en Volkenkunde*, vol. 116.

Lévi-Strauss, C., 1949. *Les structures élémentaires de la parenté*, Paris.

Lévi-Strauss, C., 1962. *La pensée sauvage*, Paris.

Levy, M. J., 1952. *The Structure of Society*, Princeton, N.J.

Lewis, I. M., 1965. 'Problems in the Comparative Study of Unilineal Descent', in *The Relevance of Models for Social Anthropology*, A.S.A. Monographs, no. 1 (ed. M. Banton), London.

Linton, R., 1936. *The Study of Man*, New York.

Little, K., 1951. *The Mende of Sierra Leone*, London.

Little, K., 1965. *West African Urbanization: A Study of Voluntary Associations in Social Change*, Cambridge.

Little, K., 1965-6. 'The Political Function of the Poro', *Africa*, vol. 35, No. 4, vol. 36, No. 1.

Lockwood, D., 1964. 'Social Integration and System Integration', in Zollschan, G. K. and Hirsch, W., eds., *Explorations in Social Change*, London.

Lowie, R. H., 1937. *The History of Ethnological Theory*, New York.

McCoy, J., 1965. 'The Dialects of the Hong Kong Boat People: Kau Sai', *Journal of the Hong Kong Branch of the Royal Asiatic Society*, vol. 5.

Mair, L., 1963. *New Nations*, London.

Malinowski, B., 1921. 'The Primitive Economics of the Trobriand Islanders', *The Economic Journal*, vol. 31.

Malinowski, B., 1922. *Argonauts of the Western Pacific*, London.

Malinowski, B., 1948. 'Myth in Primitive Psychology', in Malinowski, B., *Magic, Science and Religion and Other Essays*, Boston.

Margai, M. A. S., 1948. 'Welfare Work in a Secret Society', *African Affairs*, March.

Marris, P., 1958. *Widows and their Families*, London.

Mauss, M., 1923-4. 'Essai sur le don, Forme et raison de l'échange dans les sociétés archaïques,' *Année Sociologique*, 2nd series, vol. 1.

U

Mayer, A. C., 1961. *Peasants in the Pacific*, London and Berkeley.

Mayer, A. C., 1963a. *Indians in Fiji*, Oxford.

Mayer, A. C., 1963b. 'Some Political Implications of Community Development in India', *European Journal of Sociology*, vol, 4, No. 1.

Mayer, A. C., 1965. 'The Significance of Quasi-Groups in the Study of Complex Societies', in *The Social Anthropology of Complex Societies*, A.S.A. Monographs, no. 4 (ed. M. Banton), London.

Mead, M., 1947. *The Mountain Arapesh, III. The Socio-Economic Life*, Anthropological Papers, American Museum of Natural History, vol. 40, pt. 3, New York.

Meek, P., 1961. 'Malaya: A Study of Governmental Response to the Korean War Boom', in Silcock, T. H., ed., *Readings in Malayan Economics*, Singapore.

Meggitt, M. J., 1965. *The Lineage System of the Mae-Enga of New Guinea*, Edinburgh and London.

Merton, R. K., 1957. *Social Theory and Social Structure*, rev. edn. London.

Meyer, A., 1910. *Die bäuerliche Hauskommunion (Zadruga) in der Königreichen Kroatien und Slavonien*, Heidelberg.

Middleton, J., 1960. *Lugbara Religion, Ritual and Authority among an East African People*, London.

Mintz, S. W., 1964. 'The Employment of Capital by Market Women in Haiti', in Firth, R. and Yamey, B. S., eds., *Capital, Saving and Credit in Peasant Societies*, London.

Mokhzani, A. R., 1963. *The Economy of a Perlis Village, Malaya, with special reference to the problems of capital accumulation*, unpublished M.A. thesis, University of London.

Mokhzani, A. R., 1964. *The Study of Social Stratification and Social Mobility in Malaya*, mimeo.

Morris H. S., 1953. *Report on a Melanau Sago Producing Community in Sarawak*, H.M.S.O., London

Murdock, G. P., 1949. *Social Structure*, New Haven.

Nadel, S. F., 1942. *A Black Byzantium*, Oxford.

Nakane Chie, 1967. *Kinship and Economic Organization in Rural Japan*, L.S.E. Monographs on Social Anthropology, No. 32, London.

Nash, M., 1958. *Machine Age Maya*, American Anthropological Association, Memoir No. 87, Menasha, Wis.

Nash, M., 1965. *The Golden Road to Modernity*, New York.

Niehoff, A. and Niehoff, J., 1960. *East Indians in the West Indies*, Milwaukee Public Museum, Publications in Anthropology, No. 6, Milwaukee.

Notes and Queries on Anthropology, 1951. 6th edn. (Royal Anthropological Institute), London.

Osgood, C., 1951. *The Koreans and their Culture*, New York.

Osgood, C., 1963. *Village Life in Old China, A Community Study of Kao Yao, Yünnan*, New York.

Parsons, T., 1937. *The Structure of Social Action*, New York.

Parsons, T. and Smelser, N., 1956. *Economy and Society*, London.

Peristiany, J. G., 1953. Introduction to Durkheim, E., *Sociology and Philosophy*, trans. Pocock, D. F., London.

Peyre, H., 1960. Foreword to Durkheim, E., *Montesquieu and Rousseau, Forerunners of Sociology*, Ann Arbor, Michigan.

Plath, D. W., 1964. 'Where the Family of God is the Family: The Role of the Dead in Japanese Households', *American Anthropologist*, vol. 66, No. 2.

Polanyi, K. *et al.*, 1957. *Trade and Market in the Early Empires*, Glencoe, Ill.

Polya, G., 1957. *How to Solve it: A New Aspect of Mathematical Method*, 2nd edn., New York.

Pouwer, J., 1958. 'Anthropological Research in Netherlands New Guinea since 1950' (Prepared by the Bureau for Native Affairs, Hollandia, Netherlands New Guinea), *Oceania*, vol. 29, No. 2.

Pouwer, J., 1960. ' "Loosely structured societies" in Netherlands New Guinea', *Bijdragen tot de Taal-, Land- en Volkenkunde*, vol. 116.

Pouwer, J., 1961. 'New Guinea as a Field for Ethnological Study: A Preliminary Analysis', *Bijdragen tot de Taal-, Land- en Volkenkunde*, vol. 117.

Purcall, J., 1964. *Marketing of Padi from Four Villages in Province Wellesley*, MS.

Radcliffe-Brown, A. R. 1952. *Structure and Function in Primitive Society*, London.

Radcliffe-Brown, A. R. and Forde, D., eds., 1950. *African Systems of Kinship and Marriage*, London.

Rayner, L., 1957. *Women in a Village*, London.

Reay, M., 1959. *The Kuma: Freedom and Conformity in the New Guinea Highlands*, Melbourne.

Redfield, R., 1956. *Peasant Society and Culture*, Chicago.

Rehfisch, F., 1960. 'The Dynamics of Multilineality on the Mambila Plateau', *Africa*, vol. 30.

Report on Commission of Inquiry into Disturbances in the Protectorate, 1956. Sierra Leone.

Report on the 1947 Population Census (Sarawak and Brunei), *A*, 1950. Kuching.

Report on the Census of the Population Taken on 15th June 1960, 1962. Kuching.

Richards, A. J. N., 1963. *Dayak Adat Law in the Second Division*, Kuching.

Rosser, C. and Harris, C., 1965. *The Family and Social Change, A Study of Family and Kinship in a South Wales Town*, London.

Roth, W. E., 1897. *Ethnological Studies among the North-West-Central Queensland Aborigines*, Government Printer, Brisbane.

Rouch, J., 1954. *Migration in the Gold Coast*, Accra.

Roy, J. N., 1960. *Mauritius in Transition*, Port Louis.

Russell, B., 1948. *Human Knowledge*, London.

Sahlins, M. and Service, E., 1960. *Evolution and Culture*, Ann Arbor, Michigan.

Salisbury, R. F., 1962. *From Stone to Steel*, Melbourne.

Savezni Zavod za Statistiku, F. N. R. J., 1962. *Stanovništvo i domaćinstva: osnovne strukture prema popisu 1961* (Census 1961), Belgrade.

Schärer, H., 1963. *Ngaju Religion*, trans. Needham, R., The Hague.

Schmidt, W., 1935. *The Origin and Growth of Religion*, London.

Scott, R., 1961. *Limuria, the Lesser Dependencies of Mauritius*, London.

Seger, I., 1957. *Durkheim and his Critics on the Sociology of Religion*, Bureau of Applied Social Research, Columbia University, New York.

Seychelles: Report for the Years 1961 and 1962, 1963. H.M.S.O., London.

Silcock, T. H., ed., 1961. *Readings in Malayan Economics*, Singapore.

Skinner, E. P., 1960. 'Group Dynamics in British Guiana', in Rubin, V., ed., *Social and Cultural Pluralism in the Caribbean* (*Annals of the New York Academy of Sciences*, vol. 183, No. 5), New York.

Smith, R. T., 1956. *The Negro Family in British Guiana*, London.

Smith, R. T., 1962. *British Guiana*, Oxford.

Smith, R. T., 1963. 'Culture and Social Structure in the Caribbean: Some Recent Work on Family and Kinship Studies', *Comparative Studies in Society and History*, vol. 6, No. 1.

Smith, R. T. and Jayawardena, C., 1959. 'Family and Marriage amongst East Indians in British Guiana', *Social and Economic Studies*, vol. 8, No. 4.

Spencer, B., ed., 1896. *Report on the Work of the Horn Scientific Expedition to Central Australia*, London and Melbourne.

Spencer, B. and Gillen, F. J., 1899. *The Native Tribes of Central Australia*, London.

Spencer, B. and Gillen, F. J., 1904. *The Northern Tribes of Central Australia*, London.

Spiro, M. E., 1964. 'Religion and the Irrational', *Proceedings of the 1964 Annual Spring Meeting of the American Ethnological Society*, Seattle.

Srinivas, M. N. and Béteille, A., 1964. 'Networks in Indian Social Structure', *Man*, vol. 64, art. 212.

Statistički Godišnjak F.N.R.J., 1962. Savezni Zavod za Statistiku, Belgrade.

Steward, J., 1955. *Theory of Culture Change*, Urbana, Ill.

Swift, M. G., 1962. 'Malay Peasants', in Lambert, R. D. and Hoselitz, B. F., eds., *The Role of Savings and Wealth in Southern Asia and the West*, Unesco, Paris.

Swift, M. G., 1964. 'Capital, Saving and Credit in a Malay Peasant Economy', in Firth, R. and Yamey, B. S., eds., *Capital, Saving and Credit in Peasant Societies*, London.

Swift, M. G., 1965. *Malay Peasant Society in Jelebu*, L.S.E. Monographs on Social Anthropology, No. 29, London.

Tax, S., 1953. *Penny Capitalism*, Smithsonian Institution, Institute of Social Anthropology, Publication No. 16, Washington, D.C.

T'ien Ju-k'ang, 1953. *The Chinese of Sarawak, A Study of Social Structure*, L.S.E. Monographs on Social Anthropology, No. 12, London.

Tjan Tjoe Som, 1949. *Po Hu T"ung, The Comprehensive Discussions in the White Tiger Hall*, vol. 1, Leiden.

Todd, J. A., 1934. 'Report on Research Work in South-West New Britain, Territory of New Guinea', *Oceania*, vol. 5, Nos. 1, 2.

Tončić, D., ed., 1902. *Zakon od 9. Svibnja 1889. o zadrugama i zakon od 30. Travnja 1902. o promjeni odnosno nadopunjenju nekih ustanova zak. od 9 Svibnja 1889 o zadr.*, Zagreb.

Tosti, G., 1898. 'Suicide in the Light of Recent Studies', *American Journal of Sociology*, vol. 3.

Townsend, P., 1957. *The Family Life of Old People*, London.

Townsend, P., 1964. ' "Family and Kinship in Industrial Society", A Comment', in *The Development of Industrial Societies*, The Sociological Review, Monograph No. 8, Keele.

Tylor, E. B., 1898. 'Remarks on Totemism, with Especial Reference to Some Modern Theories concerning it', *Journal of the Royal Anthropological Institute*, vol. 28 (n.s. vol. 1).

Vukosavljević, S., 1962. *Pisma sa sela*, Sociološka Biblioteka, Savremena Škola, Belgrade.

Wallerstein, I., 1960. 'Ethnicity and National Integration in West Africa', *Cahiers d'Etudes Africaines*, No. 3.

Wallerstein, I., 1963. 'The Political Role of Voluntary Associations in Middle Africa', in Coleman, J. S. and Rosberg, C., eds., *Political Groups in Middle Africa*, Berkeley, Calif.

Ward, B. E., 1954. 'A Hong Kong Fishing Village', *Journal of Oriental Studies*, vol. 1, No. 1, Hong Kong.

Ward, B. E., 1965. 'Varieties of the Conscious Model: The Fishermen of South China', in *The Relevance of Models for Social Anthropology*, A.S.A. Monographs, No. 1 (ed. M. Banton), London.

Ward, B. E., 1966. 'Sociological Self-Awareness: Some Uses of the Conscious Model', *Man*, n.s. vol. 1, No. 2.

Webb, A. W. T., 1960a. *Agricultural Census of the Seychelles Colony: Report and Tables for 1960*, Seychelles.

Webb, A. W. T., 1960b. *Population Census of the Seychelles Colony: Report and Tables for 1960*, Seychelles.

Webb, C. C. J., 1916. *Group Theories of Religion and the Individual*, London.

Weber, M., 1946. 'Class, Status, Party', in Gerth, H. H. and Mills, C. W., *From Max Weber: Essays in Sociology*, New York.

Wheelwright, E. L., 1965. *Industrialization in Malaya*, Melbourne.

White, L., 1959. *The Evolution of Culture*, New York.

Whyte, W. J., 1956. *The Organization Man*, New York.

Wilkinson, R. J., 1959. *A Malay-English Dictionary (Romanised)*, London.

Willmott, P. and Young, M., 1960. *Family and Class in a London Suburb*, London.

Wilson, T. R., 1958. *The Economics of Padi Production in North Malaya, Part I*, Kuala Lumpur.

Wolf, E., 1966. 'Kinship, Friendship and Patron-Client Relations', in *The Social Anthropology of Complex Societies*, A.S.A. Monographs, No. 4 (ed. M. Banton), London.

Young, A., 1958. *The Approaches to Local Self-Government in British Guiana*, London.

Young, M., 1954. 'The Role of the Extended Family in Disaster', *Human Relations*, vol. 7, No. 3.

Young, M. and Willmott, P., 1957. *Family and Kinship in East London*, London.